Heisey's Lead Blown  Glassware

Factory of A. H. HEISEY & CO., NEWARK, OHIO, U. S. A.

All Plates Are Taken
From Original Heisey Catalogs
#75, #109, #212, #17

1993 Printing
© Copyright 1991

L-W Book Sales
Box 69
Gas City, IN 46933

GENERAL INDEX

ITEM	PLATE NUMBERS
HURRICANE LAMP	462–465
ICE BUCKETS & TUBS	166, 223, 232, 362, 367, 414, 417, 427, 435
ICE CREAM TRAYS	123
ICE TEA TUMBLERS, Footed	40, 391
ICE TEA TUMBLERS, Misc.	8, 391
JARS, Misc.	188, 199, 202, 230, 234, 244, 426
JELLIES	235, 415, 420, 425, 430, 434
MUSHROOM COVER	198
MUSTARD JARS	121, 427, 435
NAPPIES	80, 84, 130, 140, 150, 151, 155, 156, 173, 184, 191, 205, 207, 208, 214, 224, 228, 245, 247, 251, 252, 331
OIL BOTTLES	80, 84, 130, 140, 150, 151, 155, 156, 173, 184, 191, 205, 207, 208, 214, 224, 228, 245, 247, 251, 252, 331
PICKLE JARS	122, 152, 169
PITCHERS	133, 143, 151, 175, 179, 186, 194, 209, 218, 219, 225, 229, 239, 246, 248, 253, 333, 347, 374, 414, 427, 435, 478, 495, 496
PLATES, Misc.	79, 81–85, 215, 233, 251, 253, 318–324, 349, 372, 402, 410, 418, 421, 428, 432, 436, 438, 441, 442
PUNCH BOWLS, Misc.	91–101, 132, 142, 164, 174, 176, 217, 227, 237, 336, 365, 356, 395, 399, 406
SALTS & PEPPERS, Misc.	111–114, 137, 146, 154, 168, 182, 222, 226, 230, 243, 248, 325, 326, 339, 343, 396, 397, 407, 427, 431, 435, 443, 498
SHERBETS, Misc.	58–66, 72, 314
SODAS, Footed & Handled	311, 391, 428
SODAS, Misc.	12–21, 211, 212, 242, 310, 311, 390
STEMWARE LINES	23–67
STEMWARE, Misc.	23, 27–29, 167, 489, 490
STRAW JARS & TRAYS	192, 244, 368
SUNDAES	72
SYRUPS, Sanitary	119, 120, 146, 196, 204, 206
TANKARDS	165, 166, 240
TOOTHPICKS & SHOT GLASSES	152, 226, 243
TUMBLERS, Bar	9, 10, 16, 220, 309, 353, 369, 389
TUMBLERS, Footed	42, 428
TUMBLERS, Hotel and Table	1–6, 8, 11, 12–21, 136, 145, 209, 220, 306–308, 353, 375, 388, 478
VASES	189, 190, 200, 255–271, 405, 407, 408, 413, 431, 437, 473, 493, 494
WATER BOTTLES	108, 134, 138, 154, 165, 368
WATER SETS	87–89, 171
WINES	33, 34, 36
WINE & WHISKEY SETS	86, 183

PATTERN INDEX

STEMWARE LINES INDEX

PATTERN NO.	PLATE NO.	PATTERN NO.	PLATE NO.
#150	135	#1405	375, 404
#300	43, 144	#1425	405
#337	44, 45, 312	#1469	409
#341	46, 167, 393	#1486	416
#347	47	#1506	428
#348	48	#3304	467
#349	49	#3333	468
#351	50, 180, 181	#3350	469
#359	51, 52, 313	#3368	470
#363	54, 312	#3389	471
#369	53, 210	#3390	472
#393	55, 221	#3404	474
#393½	55	#3408	475
#411	337	#3411	476
#412	398, 340	#4004	477
#413	341	#4055	479
#433	56, 241	#4085	480
#438	57	#4090	481
#451	343	#4091	482
#1055	24	#4092	483
#1056	25	#5003	484
#1170	347	#5009	485
#1184	353, 400	#5010	486
#1252	363	#5011	487
#1404	401	#5013	488

AIRDALE

RABBIT

MALLARD
Wings Half-Way

MALLARD
Wings Up

MALLARD
Wings Down

RABBIT P.W.

PIG

ELEPHANT, Large

ELEPHANT, AMBER,
Small

ELEPHANT, Small

CLYDSDALE

FLYING MARE

SHOW HORSE

GIRAFFE
Head Turned

DONKEY

FISH BOWL

FISH BOOKENDS

ASIATIC PHEASANT

STANDING
PONY

KICKING
PONY

REARING
PONY

PLUG
HORSE

SCOTTIE DOG

SITTING
DUCKLING

FLOATING
DUCKLING

SPARROW

GIRL

VICTORIAN
BELLE

PIGLET
STANDING

CYGNET

BUNNY

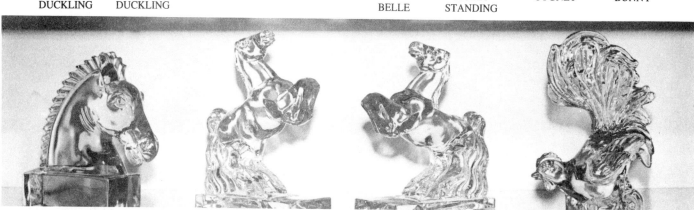

HORSEHEAD
BOOKENDS

REARING HORSE
BOOKEND

FIGHTING ROOSTER

GOOSE WINGS
Half-Way

RAM'S HEAD

CHERUB
CANDLESTICK

TROPICAL
FISH

HORSEHEAD,
Large

RINGNECK
PHEASANT

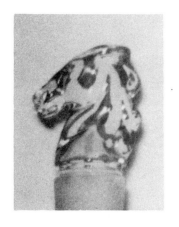

HORSEHEAD
STOPPER

POUTER
PIGEON

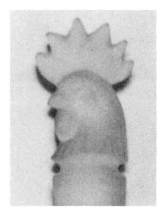

ROOSTER
STOPPER

ROOSTER VASE

FISH
BOOKEND

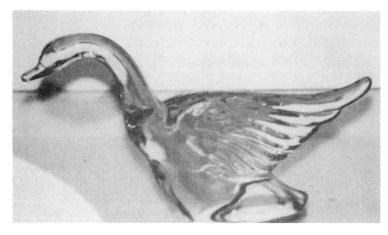

GOOSE WINGS
Half-Way

FILLY HORSE

A. H. HEISEY & CO., NEWARK, OHIO.

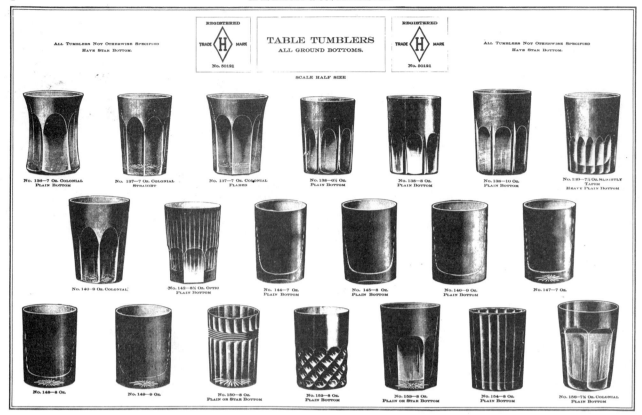

ALL TUMBLERS NOT OTHERWISE SPECIFIED
HAVE STAR BOTTOM.

REGISTERED
TRADE H MARK
No. 50121

TABLE TUMBLERS
ALL GROUND BOTTOMS.

REGISTERED
TRADE H MARK
No. 50121

ALL TUMBLERS NOT OTHERWISE SPECIFIED
HAVE STAR BOTTOM.

SCALE HALF SIZE

No. 136—7 Oz. Colonial
Plain Bottom

No. 137—7 Oz. Colonial
Straight

No. 137—7 Oz. Colonial
Flared

No. 138—6½ Oz.
Plain Bottom

No. 138—8 Oz.
Plain Bottom

No. 138—10 Oz.
Plain Bottom

No. 139—7½ Oz. Slightly
Taper
Heavy Plain Bottom

No. 140—9 Oz. Colonial

No. 142—8½ Oz. Optic
Plain Bottom

No. 144—7 Oz.
Plain Bottom

No. 145—8 Oz.
Plain Bottom

No. 146—9 Oz.
Plain Bottom

No. 147—7 Oz.

No. 148—8 Oz.

No. 149—9 Oz.

No. 150—8 Oz.
Plain or Star Bottom

No. 152—8 Oz.
Plain Bottom

No. 153—8 Oz.
Plain or Star Bottom

No. 154—8 Oz.
Plain Bottom

No. 156—7½ Oz. Colonial
Plain Bottom

A. H. HEISEY & CO., NEWARK, OHIO.

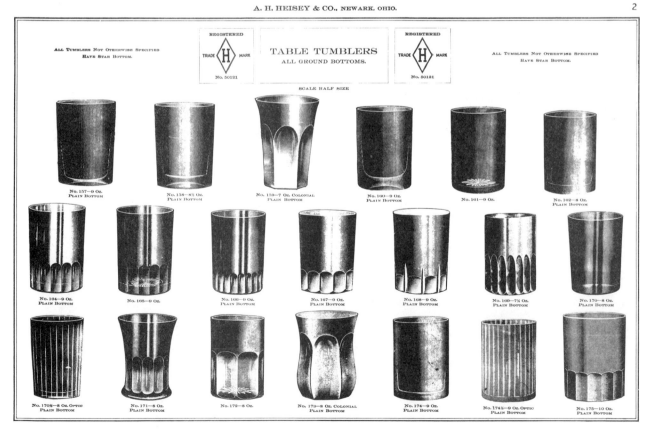

ALL TUMBLERS NOT OTHERWISE SPECIFIED
HAVE STAR BOTTOM.

REGISTERED
TRADE H MARK
No. 50121

TABLE TUMBLERS
ALL GROUND BOTTOMS.

REGISTERED
TRADE H MARK
No. 50121

ALL TUMBLERS NOT OTHERWISE SPECIFIED
HAVE STAR BOTTOM.

SCALE HALF SIZE

No. 157—9 Oz.
Plain Bottom

No. 158—8½ Oz.
Plain Bottom

No. 159—7 Oz. Colonial
Plain Bottom

No. 160—9 Oz.
Plain Bottom

No. 161—9 Oz.

No. 162—8 Oz.
Plain Bottom

No. 164—9 Oz.
Plain Bottom

No. 165—9 Oz.

No. 166—9 Oz.
Plain Bottom

No. 167—9 Oz.
Plain Bottom

No. 168—9 Oz.
Plain Bottom

No. 169—7½ Oz.
Plain Bottom

No. 170—8 Oz.
Plain Bottom

No. 170½—8 Oz. Optic
Plain Bottom

No. 171—8 Oz.
Plain Bottom

No. 172—8 Oz.

No. 173—8 Oz. Colonial
Plain Bottom

No. 174—9 Oz.
Plain Bottom

No. 174½—9 Oz. Optic
Plain Bottom

No. 175—10 Oz.
Plain Bottom

ALL TUMBLERS NOT OTHERWISE SPECIFIED
HAVE STAR BOTTOM.

TABLE TUMBLERS
ALL GROUND BOTTOMS.

ALL TUMBLERS NOT OTHERWISE SPECIFIED
HAVE STAR BOTTOM.

SCALE HALF SIZE

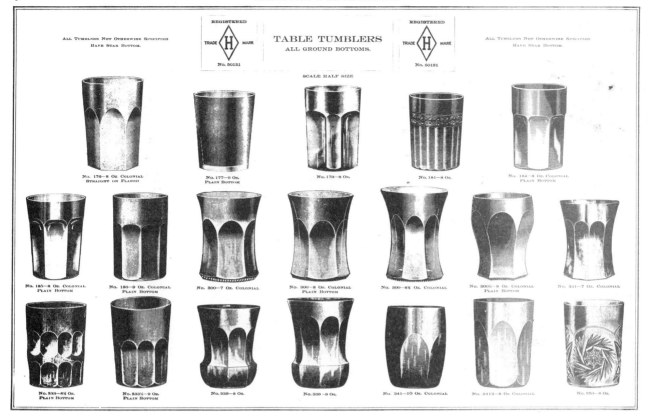

No. 176—8 Oz. Colonial
Straight or Flared

No. 177—9 Oz.
Plain Bottom

No. 179—8 Oz.

No. 181—8 Oz.

No. 184—8 Oz. Colonial
Plain Bottom

No. 185—8 Oz. Colonial
Plain Bottom

No. 186—9 Oz. Colonial
Plain Bottom

No. 300—7 Oz. Colonial

No. 300—8 Oz. Colonial
Plain Bottom

No. 300—8½ Oz. Colonial

No. 300½—8 Oz. Colonial
Plain Bottom

No. 331—7 Oz. Colonial

No. 333—8½ Oz.
Plain Bottom

No. 333½—9 Oz.
Plain Bottom

No. 339—8 Oz.

No. 339—9 Oz.

No. 341—10 Oz. Colonial

No. 341½—8 Oz. Colonial

No. 350—8 Oz.

ALL TUMBLERS NOT OTHERWISE SPECIFIED
HAVE STAR BOTTOM.

TABLE TUMBLERS
ALL GROUND BOTTOMS.

ALL TUMBLERS NOT OTHERWISE SPECIFIED
HAVE STAR BOTTOM.

SCALE HALF SIZE

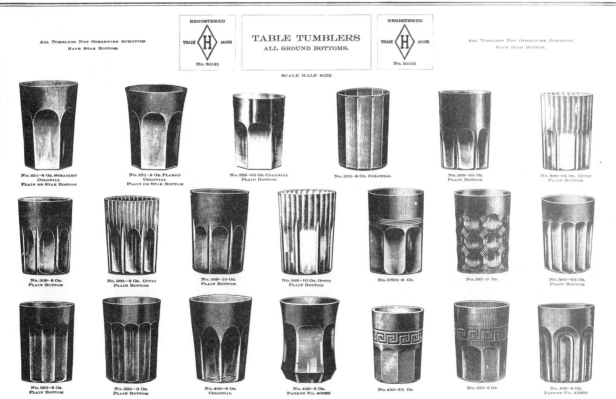

No. 351—8 Oz. Straight
Colonial
Plain or Star Bottom

No. 351—8 Oz. Flared
Colonial
Plain or Star Bottom

No. 352—6½ Oz. Colonial
Plain Bottom

No. 353—8 Oz. Colonial

No. 369—6½ Oz.
Plain Bottom

No. 369—6½ Oz. Optic
Plain Bottom

No. 369—8 Oz.
Plain Bottom

No. 369—8 Oz. Optic
Plain Bottom

No. 369—10 Oz.
Plain Bottom

No. 369—10 Oz. Optic
Plain Bottom

No. 379½—8 Oz.

No. 385—9 Oz.

No. 393—6½ Oz.
Plain Bottom

No. 393—8 Oz.
Plain Bottom

No. 393—9 Oz.
Plain Bottom

No. 400—9 Oz.
Colonial

No. 429—8 Oz.
Patent No. 40686

No. 433—5½ Oz.

No. 433—8 Oz.

No. 439—8 Oz.
Patent No. 42260

ALL TUMBLERS NOT OTHERWISE SPECIFIED
HAVE STAR BOTTOM.

REGISTERED
TRADE H MARK
No. 50121

HOTEL NON-NESTING
TUMBLERS
ALL GROUND BOTTOMS.

REGISTERED
TRADE H MARK
No. 50121

ALL TUMBLERS NOT OTHERWISE SPECIFIED
HAVE STAR BOTTOM.

SCALE HALF SIZE

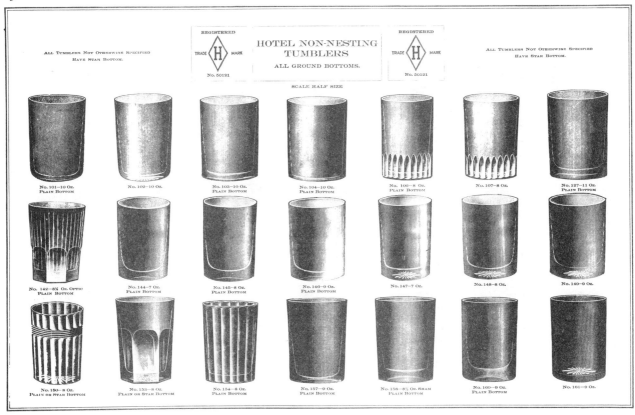

No. 101—10 Oz.
PLAIN BOTTOM

No. 102—10 Oz.

No. 103—10 Oz.
PLAIN BOTTOM

No. 104—10 Oz.
PLAIN BOTTOM

No. 106—8 Oz.
PLAIN BOTTOM

No. 107—8 Oz.

No. 127—11 Oz.
PLAIN BOTTOM

No. 142—8½ Oz. OPTIC
PLAIN BOTTOM

No. 144—7 Oz.
PLAIN BOTTOM

No. 145—8 Oz.
PLAIN BOTTOM

No. 146—9 Oz.
PLAIN BOTTOM

No. 147—7 Oz.

No. 148—8 Oz.

No. 149—9 Oz.

No. 150—8 Oz.
PLAIN OR STAR BOTTOM

No. 153—8 Oz.
PLAIN OR STAR BOTTOM

No. 154—8 Oz.
PLAIN BOTTOM

No. 157—9 Oz.
PLAIN BOTTOM

No. 158—8½ Oz. SHAM
PLAIN BOTTOM

No. 160—9 Oz.
PLAIN BOTTOM

No. 161—9 Oz.

ALL TUMBLERS NOT OTHERWISE SPECIFIED
HAVE STAR BOTTOM.

REGISTERED
TRADE H MARK
No. 50121

HOTEL NON-NESTING
TUMBLERS
ALL GROUND BOTTOMS.

REGISTERED
TRADE H MARK
No. 50121

ALL TUMBLERS NOT OTHERWISE SPECIFIED
HAVE STAR BOTTOM.

SCALE HALF SIZE

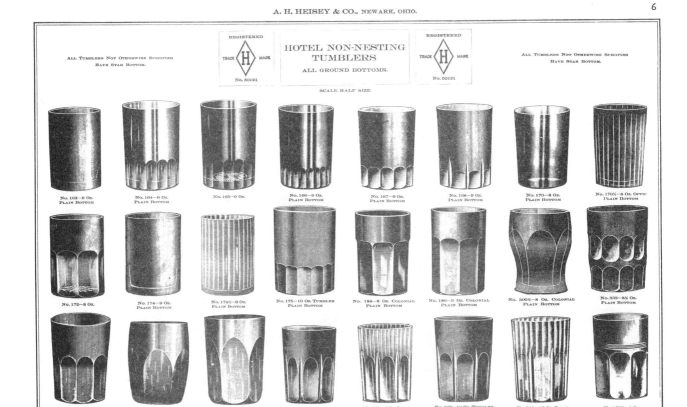

No. 162—9 Oz.
PLAIN BOTTOM

No. 164—9 Oz.
PLAIN BOTTOM

No. 165—9 Oz.

No. 166—9 Oz.
PLAIN BOTTOM

No. 167—9 Oz.
PLAIN BOTTOM

No. 168—9 Oz.
PLAIN BOTTOM

No. 170—8 Oz.
PLAIN BOTTOM

No. 170½—8 Oz. OPTIC
PLAIN BOTTOM

No. 172—8 Oz.

No. 174—9 Oz.
PLAIN BOTTOM

No. 174½—9 Oz.
PLAIN BOTTOM

No. 175—10 Oz. TUMBLER
PLAIN BOTTOM

No. 184—8 Oz. COLONIAL
PLAIN BOTTOM

No. 186—9 Oz. COLONIAL
PLAIN BOTTOM

No. 300½—8 Oz. COLONIAL
PLAIN BOTTOM

No. 333—8½ Oz.
PLAIN BOTTOM

No. 333½—9 Oz.
PLAIN BOTTOM

No. 341—10 Oz. COLONIAL

No. 341½—8 Oz. COLONIAL

No. 369—8 Oz.
PLAIN BOTTOM

No. 369—8 Oz. OPTIC
PLAIN BOTTOM

No. 369—10 Oz. TUMBLER
PLAIN BOTTOM GROUND

No. 369—10 Oz. OPTIC
PLAIN BOTTOM

No. 370½—8 Oz.

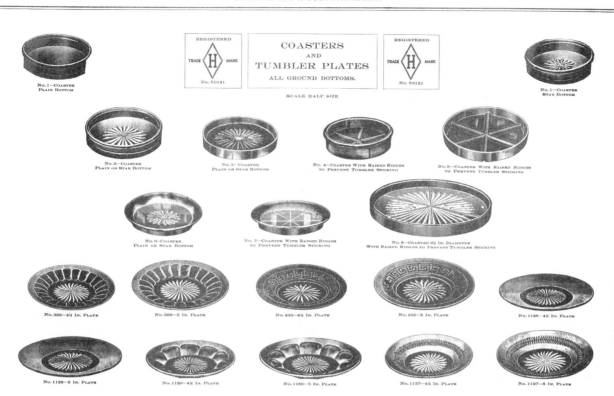

REGISTERED
TRADE H MARK
No. 50121

COASTERS
AND
TUMBLER PLATES
ALL GROUND BOTTOMS.

REGISTERED
TRADE H MARK
No. 50121

SCALE HALF SIZE

No. 1—COASTER
PLAIN BOTTOM

No. 1—COASTER
STAR BOTTOM

No. 2—COASTER
PLAIN OR STAR BOTTOM

No. 3—COASTER
PLAIN OR STAR BOTTOM

No. 4—COASTER WITH RAISED RIDGES
TO PREVENT TUMBLER STICKING

No. 5—COASTER WITH RAISED RIDGES
TO PREVENT TUMBLER STICKING

No. 6—COASTER
PLAIN OR STAR BOTTOM

No. 7—COASTER WITH RAISED RIDGES
TO PREVENT TUMBLER STICKING

No. 8—COASTER 6½ IN. DIAMETER
WITH RAISED RIDGES TO PREVENT TUMBLER STICKING

No. 393—4½ IN. PLATE

No. 393—5 IN. PLATE

No. 433—4½ IN. PLATE

No. 433—5 IN. PLATE

No. 1125—4½ IN. PLATE

No. 1125—5 IN. PLATE

No. 1150—4½ IN. PLATE

No. 1150—5 IN. PLATE

No. 1127—4½ IN. PLATE

No. 1127—5 IN. PLATE

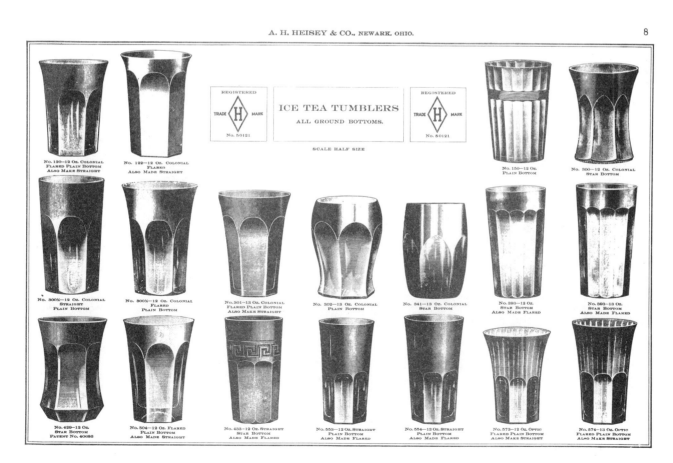

REGISTERED
TRADE H MARK
No. 50121

ICE TEA TUMBLERS
ALL GROUND BOTTOMS.

REGISTERED
TRADE H MARK
No. 50121

SCALE HALF SIZE

No. 120—12 OZ. COLONIAL
FLARED PLAIN BOTTOM
ALSO MADE STRAIGHT

No. 122—12 OZ. COLONIAL
FLARED
ALSO MADE STRAIGHT

No. 150—12 OZ.
PLAIN BOTTOM

No. 300—12 OZ. COLONIAL
STAR BOTTOM

No. 300½—12 OZ. COLONIAL
FLARED PLAIN BOTTOM
STRAIGHT
PLAIN BOTTOM

No. 300½—12 OZ. COLONIAL
FLARED
PLAIN BOTTOM

No. 301—13 OZ. COLONIAL
FLARED PLAIN BOTTOM
ALSO MADE STRAIGHT

No. 302—13 OZ. COLONIAL
STAR BOTTOM

No. 341—13 OZ. COLONIAL
PLAIN BOTTOM

No. 393—12 OZ.
STAR BOTTOM
ALSO MADE FLARED

No. 393—13 OZ.
STAR BOTTOM
ALSO MADE FLARED

No. 429—12 OZ.
STAR BOTTOM
PATENT No. 40686

No. 504—12 OZ. FLARED
PLAIN BOTTOM
ALSO MADE STRAIGHT

No. 453—12 OZ. STRAIGHT
STAR BOTTOM
ALSO MADE FLARED

No. 553—12 OZ. STRAIGHT
PLAIN BOTTOM
ALSO MADE FLARED

No. 554—13 OZ. STRAIGHT
PLAIN BOTTOM
ALSO MADE FLARED

No. 573—12 OZ. OPTIC
FLARED PLAIN BOTTOM
ALSO MADE STRAIGHT

No. 574—13 OZ. OPTIC
FLARED PLAIN BOTTOM
ALSO MADE STRAIGHT

A. H. HEISEY & CO., NEWARK, OHIO.

BAR TUMBLERS
ALL GROUND BOTTOMS.

SCALE HALF SIZE

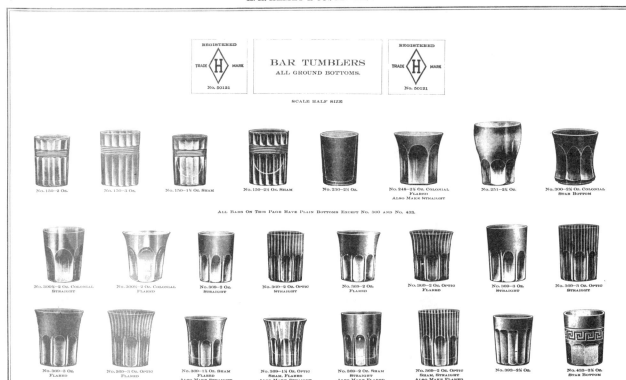

No. 150—2 Oz. No. 150—3 Oz. No. 150—1½ Oz. Sham No. 150—2½ Oz. Sham No. 236—2½ Oz. No. 248—2½ Oz. Colonial Flared Also Make Straight No. 251—2½ Oz. No. 300—2½ Oz. Colonial Star Bottom

ALL BARS ON THIS PAGE HAVE PLAIN BOTTOMS EXCEPT NO. 300 AND NO. 433.

No. 300½—2 Oz. Colonial Straight No. 300½—2 Oz. Colonial Flared No. 369—2 Oz. Straight No. 369—2 Oz. Optic Straight No. 369—2 Oz. Flared No. 369—2 Oz. Optic Flared No. 369—3 Oz. Straight No. 369—3 Oz. Optic Straight

No. 369—3 Oz. Flared No. 369—3 Oz. Optic Flared No. 369—1½ Oz. Sham Flared Also Make Straight No. 369—1½ Oz. Optic Sham, Flared Also Make Straight No. 369—2 Oz. Sham Straight Also Make Flared No. 369—2 Oz. Optic Sham, Straight Also Make Flared No. 393—2½ Oz. No. 433—2½ Oz. Star Bottom

---

A. H. HEISEY & CO., NEWARK, OHIO.

ALES AND
WATER BARS
ALL GROUND BOTTOMS.

SCALE HALF SIZE

ALL ITEMS ON THIS PAGE HAVE PLAIN BOTTOMS UNLESS OTHERWISE SPECIFIED

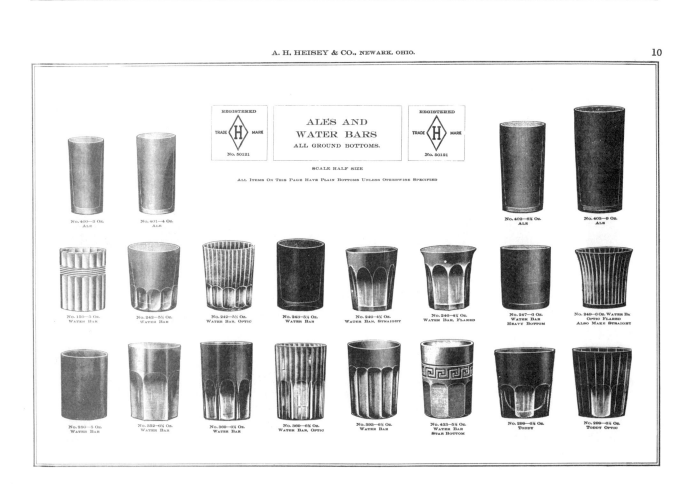

No. 400—3 Oz. Ale No. 401—4 Oz. Ale No. 402—6½ Oz. Ale No. 403—9 Oz. Ale

No. 150—3 Oz. Water Bar No. 242—5½ Oz. Water Bar No. 242—5½ Oz. Water Bar, Optic No. 243—5½ Oz. Water Bar No. 246—4½ Oz. Water Bar, Straight No. 246—4½ Oz. Water Bar, Flared No. 247—6 Oz. Water Bar Heavy Bottom No. 249—6 Oz. Water Bar Optic Flared Also Makes Straight

No. 250—5 Oz. Water Bar No. 352—6½ Oz. Water Bar No. 369—6½ Oz. Water Bar No. 369—6½ Oz. Water Bar, Optic No. 393—6½ Oz. Water Bar No. 433—5½ Oz. Water Bar Star Bottom No. 299—6½ Oz. Toddy No. 299—6½ Oz. Toddy Optic

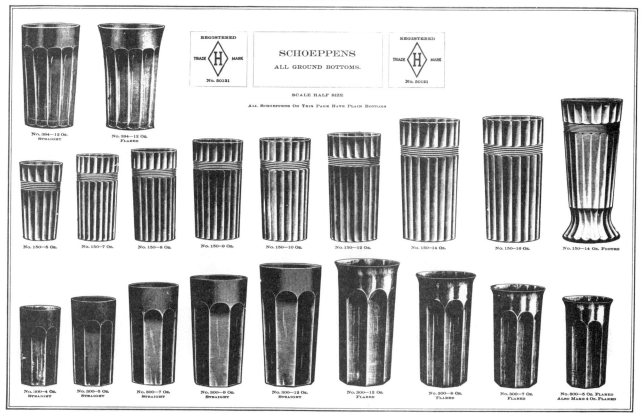

REGISTERED TRADE H MARK No. 50121

SCHOEPPENS
ALL GROUND BOTTOMS.

REGISTERED TRADE H MARK No. 50121

SCALE HALF SIZE

ALL SCHOEPPENS ON THIS PAGE HAVE PLAIN BOTTOMS

No. 394—12 Oz. STRAIGHT   No. 394—12 Oz. FLARED

No. 150—5 Oz.   No. 150—7 Oz.   No. 150—8 Oz.   No. 150—9 Oz.   No. 150—10 Oz.   No. 150—12 Oz.   No. 150—14 Oz.   No. 150—16 Oz.   No. 150—14 Oz. FOOTED

No. 300—4 Oz. STRAIGHT   No. 300—5 Oz. STRAIGHT   No. 300—7 Oz. STRAIGHT   No. 300—9 Oz. STRAIGHT   No. 300—12 Oz. STRAIGHT   No. 300—12 Oz. FLARED   No. 300—9 Oz. FLARED   No. 300—7 Oz. FLARED   No. 300—5 Oz. FLARED ALSO MAKE 4 Oz. FLARED

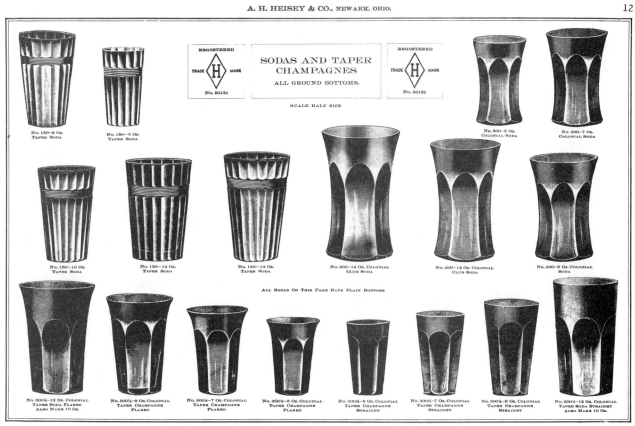

REGISTERED TRADE H MARK No. 50121

SODAS AND TAPER
CHAMPAGNES
ALL GROUND BOTTOMS.

REGISTERED TRADE H MARK No. 50121

SCALE HALF SIZE

No. 150—8 Oz. TAPER SODA   No. 150—5 Oz. TAPER SODA   No. 300—5 Oz. COLONIAL SODA   No. 300—7 Oz. COLONIAL SODA

No. 150—10 Oz. TAPER SODA   No. 150—12 Oz. TAPER SODA   No. 150—14 Oz. TAPER SODA   No. 300—14 Oz. COLONIAL CLUB SODA   No. 300—12 Oz. COLONIAL CLUB SODA   No. 300—9 Oz. COLONIAL SODA

ALL SODAS ON THIS PAGE HAVE PLAIN BOTTOMS

No. 300½—12 Oz. COLONIAL TAPER SODA FLARED ALSO MAKE 10 Oz.   No. 300½—9 Oz. COLONIAL TAPER CHAMPAGNE FLARED   No. 300½—7 Oz. COLONIAL TAPER CHAMPAGNE FLARED   No. 300½—5 Oz. COLONIAL TAPER CHAMPAGNE FLARED   No. 300½—5 Oz. COLONIAL TAPER CHAMPAGNE STRAIGHT   No. 300½—7 Oz. COLONIAL TAPER CHAMPAGNE STRAIGHT   No. 300½—9 Oz. COLONIAL TAPER CHAMPAGNE STRAIGHT   No. 300½—12 Oz. COLONIAL TAPER SODA STRAIGHT ALSO MAKE 10 Oz.

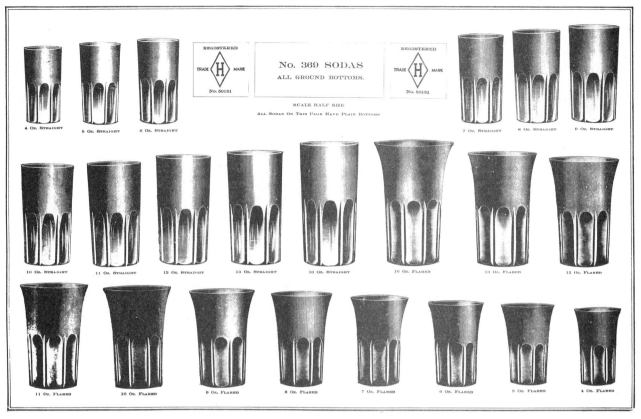

REGISTERED TRADE H MARK No. 50121

No. 369 SODAS
ALL GROUND BOTTOMS.

REGISTERED TRADE H MARK No. 50121

SCALE HALF SIZE
ALL SODAS ON THIS PAGE HAVE PLAIN BOTTOMS

4 Oz. STRAIGHT   5 Oz. STRAIGHT   6 Oz. STRAIGHT   7 Oz. STRAIGHT   8 Oz. STRAIGHT   9 Oz. STRAIGHT

10 Oz. STRAIGHT   11 Oz. STRAIGHT   12 Oz. STRAIGHT   13 Oz. STRAIGHT   16 Oz. STRAIGHT   16 Oz. FLARED   13 Oz. FLARED   12 Oz. FLARED

11 Oz. FLARED   10 Oz. FLARED   9 Oz. FLARED   8 Oz. FLARED   7 Oz. FLARED   6 Oz. FLARED   5 Oz. FLARED   4 Oz. FLARED

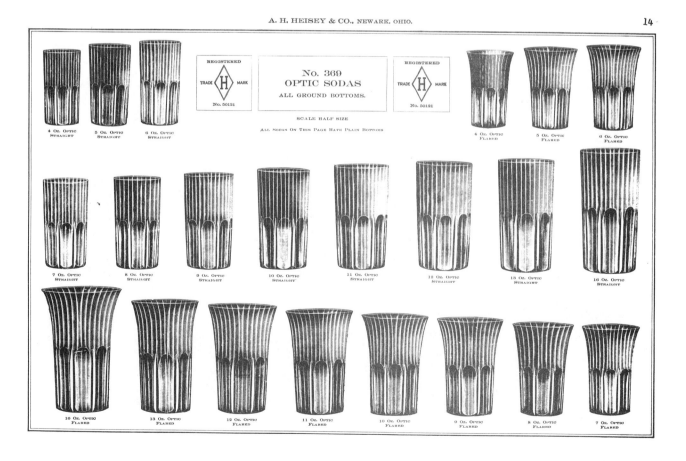

REGISTERED TRADE H MARK No. 50121

**No. 369
OPTIC SODAS**
ALL GROUND BOTTOMS.

REGISTERED TRADE H MARK No. 50121

SCALE HALF SIZE
ALL SODAS ON THIS PAGE HAVE PLAIN BOTTOMS

4 Oz. OPTIC STRAIGHT   5 Oz. OPTIC STRAIGHT   6 Oz. OPTIC STRAIGHT   4 Oz. OPTIC FLARED   5 Oz. OPTIC FLARED   6 Oz. OPTIC FLARED

7 Oz. OPTIC STRAIGHT   8 Oz. OPTIC STRAIGHT   9 Oz. OPTIC STRAIGHT   10 Oz. OPTIC STRAIGHT   11 Oz. OPTIC STRAIGHT   12 Oz. OPTIC STRAIGHT   13 Oz. OPTIC STRAIGHT   16 Oz. OPTIC STRAIGHT

16 Oz. OPTIC FLARED   13 Oz. OPTIC FLARED   12 Oz. OPTIC FLARED   11 Oz. OPTIC FLARED   10 Oz. OPTIC FLARED   9 Oz. OPTIC FLARED   8 Oz. OPTIC FLARED   7 Oz. OPTIC FLARED

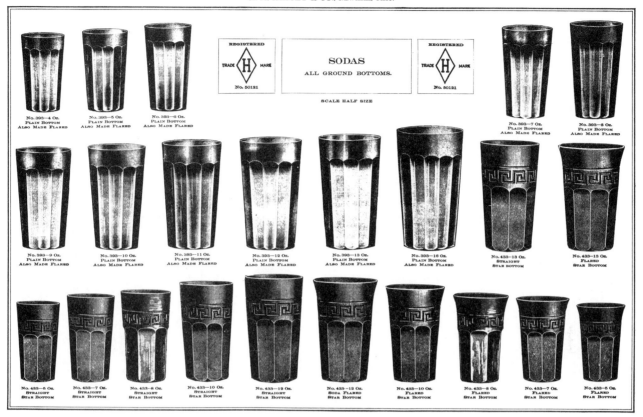

SODAS
ALL GROUND BOTTOMS.

REGISTERED
TRADE H MARK
No. 50121

REGISTERED
TRADE H MARK
No. 50121

SCALE HALF SIZE

No. 393—4 Oz.
PLAIN BOTTOM
ALSO MADE FLARED

No. 393—5 Oz.
PLAIN BOTTOM
ALSO MADE FLARED

No. 393—6 Oz.
PLAIN BOTTOM
ALSO MADE FLARED

No. 393—7 Oz.
PLAIN BOTTOM
ALSO MADE FLARED

No. 393—8 Oz.
PLAIN BOTTOM
ALSO MADE FLARED

No. 393—9 Oz.
PLAIN BOTTOM
ALSO MADE FLARED

No. 393—10 Oz.
PLAIN BOTTOM
ALSO MADE FLARED

No. 393—11 Oz.
PLAIN BOTTOM
ALSO MADE FLARED

No. 393—12 Oz.
PLAIN BOTTOM
ALSO MADE FLARED

No. 393—13 Oz.
PLAIN BOTTOM
ALSO MADE FLARED

No. 393—16 Oz.
PLAIN BOTTOM
ALSO MADE FLARED

No. 433—13 Oz.
STRAIGHT
STAR BOTTOM

No. 433—13 Oz.
FLARED
STAR BOTTOM

No. 433—5 Oz.
STRAIGHT
STAR BOTTOM

No. 433—7 Oz.
STRAIGHT
STAR BOTTOM

No. 433—8 Oz.
STRAIGHT
STAR BOTTOM

No. 433—10 Oz.
STRAIGHT
STAR BOTTOM

No. 433—12 Oz.
STRAIGHT
STAR BOTTOM

No. 433—12 Oz.
SODA FLARED
STAR BOTTOM

No. 433—10 Oz.
FLARED
STAR BOTTOM

No. 433—8 Oz.
FLARED
STAR BOTTOM

No. 433—7 Oz.
FLARED
STAR BOTTOM

No. 433—5 Oz.
FLARED
STAR BOTTOM

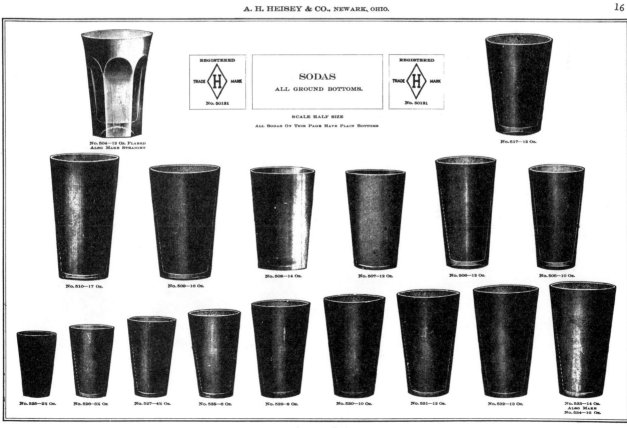

SODAS
ALL GROUND BOTTOMS.

REGISTERED
TRADE H MARK
No. 50121

REGISTERED
TRADE H MARK
No. 50121

SCALE HALF SIZE
ALL SODAS ON THIS PAGE HAVE PLAIN BOTTOMS

No. 504—12 Oz. FLARED
ALSO MAKE STRAIGHT

No. 517—12 Oz.

No. 510—17 Oz.

No. 509—16 Oz.

No. 508—14 Oz.

No. 507—12 Oz.

No. 506—12 Oz.

No. 505—10 Oz.

No. 525—2½ Oz.

No. 526—3½ Oz.

No. 527—4½ Oz.

No. 528—6 Oz.

No. 529—8 Oz.

No. 530—10 Oz.

No. 531—12 Oz.

No. 532—13 Oz.

No. 533—14 Oz.
ALSO MAKE
No. 534—16 Oz.

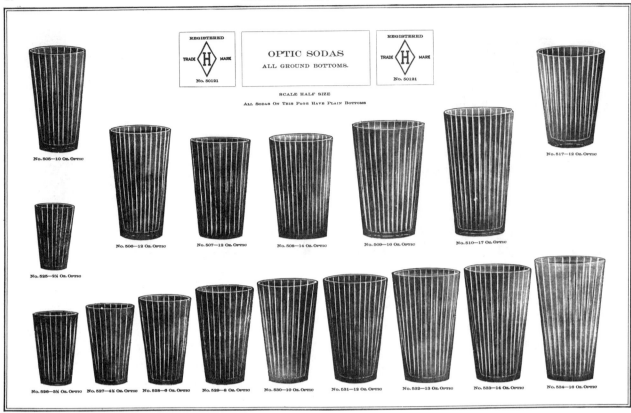

REGISTERED TRADE H MARK No. 50121

OPTIC SODAS
ALL GROUND BOTTOMS.

REGISTERED TRADE H MARK No. 50121

SCALE HALF SIZE

ALL SODAS ON THIS PAGE HAVE PLAIN BOTTOMS

No. 505—10 Oz. Optic

No. 517—12 Oz. Optic

No. 525—2½ Oz. Optic

No. 506—12 Oz. Optic
No. 507—12 Oz. Optic
No. 508—14 Oz. Optic
No. 509—16 Oz. Optic
No. 510—17 Oz. Optic

No. 526—3½ Oz. Optic
No. 527—4½ Oz. Optic
No. 528—6 Oz. Optic
No. 529—8 Oz. Optic
No. 530—10 Oz. Optic
No. 531—12 Oz. Optic
No. 532—13 Oz. Optic
No. 533—14 Oz. Optic
No. 534—16 Oz. Optic

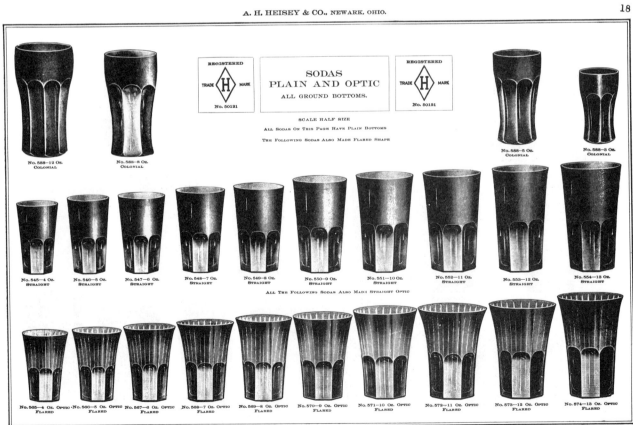

REGISTERED TRADE H MARK No. 50121

SODAS
PLAIN AND OPTIC
ALL GROUND BOTTOMS.

REGISTERED TRADE H MARK No. 50121

SCALE HALF SIZE

ALL SODAS ON THIS PAGE HAVE PLAIN BOTTOMS

THE FOLLOWING SODAS ALSO MADE FLARED SHAPE

No. 588—12 Oz. COLONIAL

No. 588—8 Oz. COLONIAL

No. 588—5 Oz. COLONIAL

No. 588—3 Oz. COLONIAL

No. 545—4 Oz. STRAIGHT
No. 546—5 Oz. STRAIGHT
No. 547—6 Oz. STRAIGHT
No. 548—7 Oz. STRAIGHT
No. 549—8 Oz. STRAIGHT
No. 550—9 Oz. STRAIGHT
No. 551—10 Oz. STRAIGHT
No. 552—11 Oz. STRAIGHT
No. 553—12 Oz. STRAIGHT
No. 554—13 Oz. STRAIGHT

ALL THE FOLLOWING SODAS ALSO MADE STRAIGHT OPTIC

No. 565—4 Oz. OPTIC FLARED
No. 566—5 Oz. OPTIC FLARED
No. 567—6 Oz. OPTIC FLARED
No. 568—7 Oz. OPTIC FLARED
No. 569—8 Oz. OPTIC FLARED
No. 570—9 Oz. OPTIC FLARED
No. 571—10 Oz. OPTIC FLARED
No. 572—11 Oz. OPTIC FLARED
No. 573—12 Oz. OPTIC FLARED
No. 574—13 Oz. OPTIC FLARED

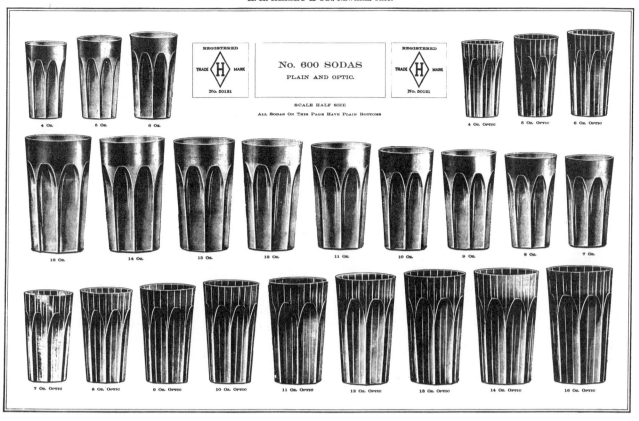

REGISTERED TRADE H MARK No. 50121

No. 600 SODAS

PLAIN AND OPTIC.

REGISTERED TRADE H MARK No. 50121

SCALE HALF SIZE

ALL SODAS ON THIS PAGE HAVE PLAIN BOTTOMS

4 Oz.   5 Oz.   6 Oz.   4 Oz. Optic   5 Oz. Optic   6 Oz. Optic

16 Oz.   14 Oz.   13 Oz.   12 Oz.   11 Oz.   10 Oz.   9 Oz.   8 Oz.   7 Oz.

7 Oz. Optic   8 Oz. Optic   9 Oz. Optic   10 Oz. Optic   11 Oz. Optic   12 Oz. Optic   13 Oz. Optic   14 Oz. Optic   16 Oz. Optic

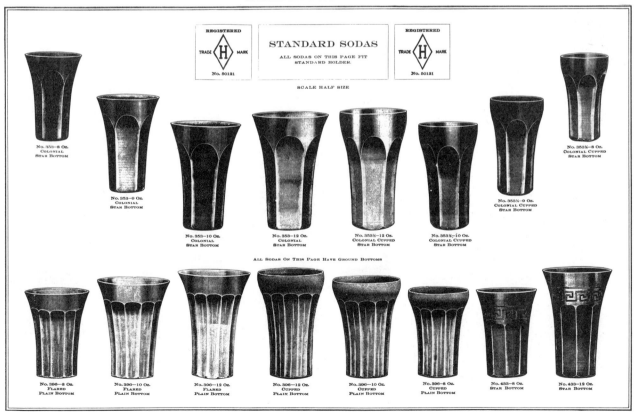

REGISTERED TRADE H MARK No. 50121

STANDARD SODAS

ALL SODAS ON THIS PAGE FIT STANDARD HOLDER.

REGISTERED TRADE H MARK No. 50121

SCALE HALF SIZE

No. 353—8 Oz. COLONIAL STAR BOTTOM

No. 353—9 Oz. COLONIAL STAR BOTTOM

No. 353—10 Oz. COLONIAL STAR BOTTOM

No. 353—12 Oz. COLONIAL STAR BOTTOM

No. 353½—12 Oz. COLONIAL CUPPED STAR BOTTOM

No. 353½—10 Oz. COLONIAL CUPPED STAR BOTTOM

No. 353½—9 Oz. COLONIAL CUPPED STAR BOTTOM

No. 353½—8 Oz. COLONIAL CUPPED STAR BOTTOM

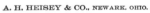

ALL SODAS ON THIS PAGE HAVE GROUND BOTTOMS

No. 396—8 Oz. FLARED PLAIN BOTTOM

No. 396—10 Oz. FLARED PLAIN BOTTOM

No. 396—12 Oz. FLARED PLAIN BOTTOM

No. 396—12 Oz. CUPPED PLAIN BOTTOM

No. 396—10 Oz. CUPPED PLAIN BOTTOM

No. 396—8 Oz. CUPPED PLAIN BOTTOM

No. 433—8 Oz. STAR BOTTOM

No. 433—12 Oz. STAR BOTTOM

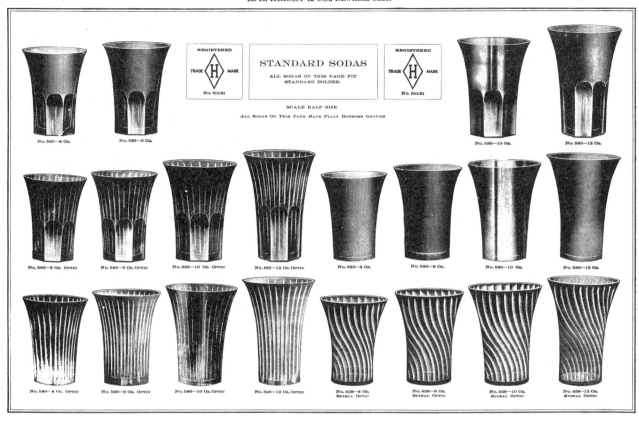

REGISTERED
TRADE H MARK
No. 50121

STANDARD SODAS
ALL SODAS ON THIS PAGE FIT
STANDARD HOLDER.

REGISTERED
TRADE H MARK
No. 50121

SCALE HALF SIZE
ALL SODAS ON THIS PAGE HAVE PLAIN BOTTOMS GROUND

No. 585—8 Oz.   No. 585—9 Oz.   No. 585—10 Oz.   No. 585—12 Oz.

No. 585—8 Oz. Optic   No. 585—9 Oz. Optic   No. 585—10 Oz. Optic   No. 585—12 Oz. Optic   No. 586—8 Oz.   No. 586—9 Oz.   No. 586—10 Oz.   No. 586—12 Oz.

No. 586—8 Oz. Optic   No. 586—9 Oz. Optic   No. 586—10 Oz. Optic   No. 586—12 Oz. Optic   No. 438—8 Oz. Spiral Optic   No. 438—9 Oz. Spiral Optic   No. 438—10 Oz. Spiral Optic   No. 438—12 Oz. Spiral Optic

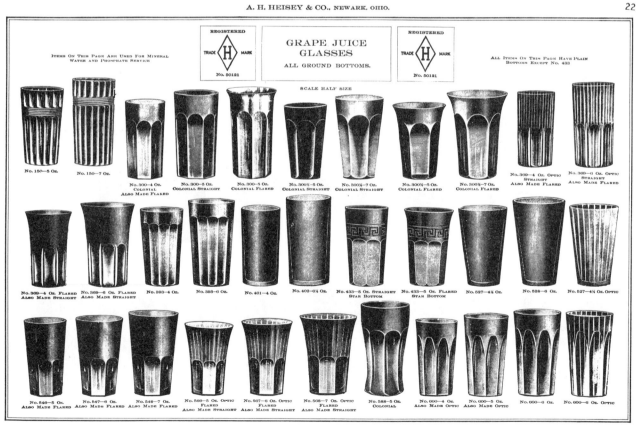

ITEMS ON THIS PAGE ARE USED FOR MINERAL
WATER AND PHOSPHATE SERVICE

REGISTERED
TRADE H MARK
No. 50121

GRAPE JUICE GLASSES
ALL GROUND BOTTOMS.

REGISTERED
TRADE H MARK
No. 50121

ALL ITEMS ON THIS PAGE HAVE PLAIN
BOTTOMS EXCEPT NO. 433

SCALE HALF SIZE

No. 150—5 Oz.   No. 150—7 Oz.   No. 300—4 Oz. COLONIAL ALSO MADE FLARED   No. 300—5 Oz. COLONIAL STRAIGHT   No. 300—5 Oz. COLONIAL FLARED   No. 300½—5 Oz. COLONIAL STRAIGHT   No. 300½—7 Oz. COLONIAL STRAIGHT   No. 300½—5 Oz. COLONIAL FLARED   No. 300½—7 Oz. COLONIAL FLARED   No. 369—4 Oz. OPTIC STRAIGHT ALSO MADE FLARED   No. 369—6 Oz. OPTIC STRAIGHT ALSO MADE FLARED

No. 369—4 Oz. FLARED ALSO MADE STRAIGHT   No. 369—6 Oz. FLARED ALSO MADE STRAIGHT   No. 393—4 Oz.   No. 393—6 Oz.   No. 401—4 Oz.   No. 402—6½ Oz.   No. 433—5 Oz. STRAIGHT STAR BOTTOM   No. 433—5 Oz. FLARED STAR BOTTOM   No. 527—4½ Oz.   No. 528—6 Oz.   No. 527—4½ Oz. OPTIC

No. 546—5 Oz. ALSO MADE FLARED   No. 547—6 Oz. ALSO MADE FLARED   No. 548—7 Oz. ALSO MADE FLARED   No. 566—5 Oz. OPTIC FLARED ALSO MADE STRAIGHT   No. 567—6 Oz. OPTIC FLARED ALSO MADE STRAIGHT   No. 568—7 Oz. OPTIC FLARED ALSO MADE STRAIGHT   No. 588—5 Oz. COLONIAL   No. 600—4 Oz. ALSO MADE OPTIC   No. 600—5 Oz. ALSO MADE OPTIC   No. 600—6 Oz.   No. 600—6 Oz. OPTIC

HOFFMAN HOUSE GOBLETS
ALSO MADE IN
No. 811½—12 Oz.
No. 811½—14 Oz., 15 Oz., 16 Oz. SIZES

REGISTERED
TRADE H MARK
No. 50121

HOFFMAN HOUSE
STEMWARE
PLAIN AND OPTIC.

REGISTERED
TRADE H MARK
No. 50121

SCALE HALF SIZE

No. 805—½ Oz. CORDIAL.   No. 806—2 Oz. WINE   No. 807—3 Oz. WINE   No. 808—4½ Oz. CLARET   No. 809—6 Oz. CHAMPAGNE   No. 810—8 Oz. GOBLET   No. 811—10 Oz. GOBLET   No. 811½—13 Oz. GOBLET   No. 811½—17 Oz. GOBLET

HOFFMAN HOUSE GOBLETS
ALSO MADE OPTIC IN
No. 862—12 Oz.
No. 864—14 Oz. 865—15 Oz. 866—16 Oz. SIZES

No. 867—17 Oz. GOBLET OPTIC   No. 863—13 Oz. GOBLET OPTIC   No. 861—10 Oz. GOBLET OPTIC   No. 860—8 Oz. GOBLET OPTIC   No. 859—6 Oz. CHAMPAGNE OPTIC   No. 858—4½ Oz. CLARET OPTIC   No. 857—3 Oz. WINE OPTIC   No. 856—2 Oz. WINE OPTIC   No. 855—½ Oz. CORDIAL OPTIC

REGISTERED
TRADE H MARK
No. 50121

No. 1055
STEMWARE
PLAIN AND OPTIC.

REGISTERED
TRADE H MARK
No. 50121

SCALE HALF SIZE

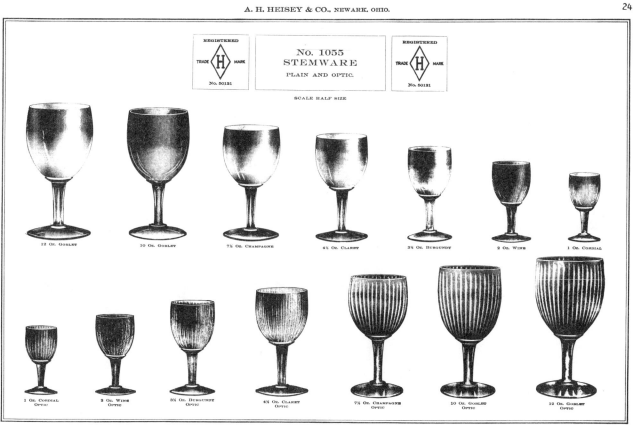

12 Oz. GOBLET   10 Oz. GOBLET   7½ Oz. CHAMPAGNE   4½ Oz. CLARET   3½ Oz. BURGUNDY   2 Oz. WINE   1 Oz. CORDIAL

1 Oz. CORDIAL OPTIC   2 Oz. WINE OPTIC   3½ Oz. BURGUNDY OPTIC   4½ Oz. CLARET OPTIC   7½ Oz. CHAMPAGNE OPTIC   10 Oz. GOBLET OPTIC   12 Oz. GOBLET OPTIC

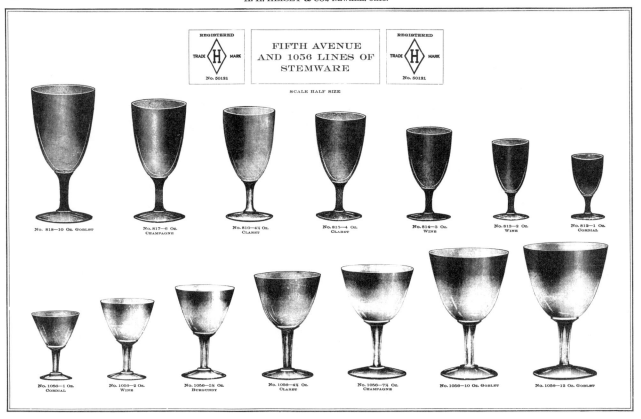

REGISTERED TRADE H MARK No. 50121

FIFTH AVENUE AND 1056 LINES OF STEMWARE

REGISTERED TRADE H MARK No. 50121

SCALE HALF SIZE

No. 818—10 Oz. GOBLET

No. 817—6 Oz. CHAMPAGNE

No. 816—4½ Oz. CLARET

No. 815—4 Oz. CLARET

No. 814—3 Oz. WINE

No. 813—2 Oz. WINE

No. 812—1 Oz. CORDIAL

No. 1056—1 Oz. CORDIAL

No. 1056—2 Oz. WINE

No. 1056—3½ Oz. BURGUNDY

No. 1056—4½ Oz. CLARET

No. 1056—7½ Oz. CHAMPAGNE

No. 1056—10 Oz. GOBLET

No. 1056—12 Oz. GOBLET

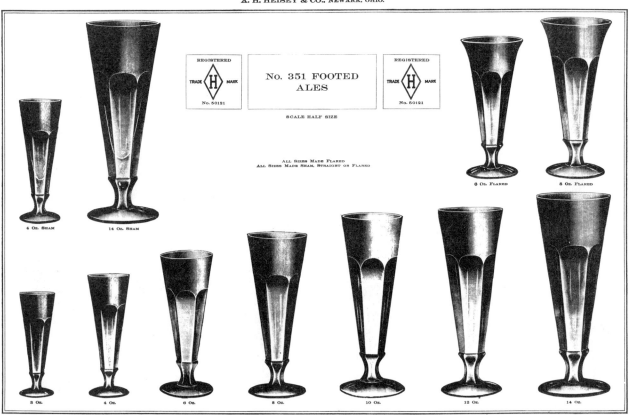

REGISTERED TRADE H MARK No. 50121

No. 351 FOOTED ALES

REGISTERED TRADE H MARK No. 50121

SCALE HALF SIZE

ALL SIZES MADE FLARED
ALL SIZES MADE SHAM, STRAIGHT OR FLARED

4 Oz. SHAM

14 Oz. SHAM

6 Oz. FLARED

8 Oz. FLARED

3 Oz.

4 Oz.

6 Oz.

8 Oz.

10 Oz.

12 Oz.

14 Oz.

REGISTERED
TRADE **H** MARK
No. 50121

GOBLETS
PLAIN AND OPTIC.

REGISTERED
TRADE **H** MARK
No. 50121

SCALE HALF SIZE

No. 337—8 Oz.

No. 707—10 Oz.

No. 708—10 Oz.

No. 818—10 Oz.

No. 1049—11 Oz.

No. 1050—11 Oz.

No. 1185—9 Oz.

No. 1187—9 Oz.

No. 337—8 Oz. Optic

No. 438—8 Oz.
SPIRAL OPTIC

No. 368—7½ Oz. Optic

No. 369—10 Oz. Optic

No. 370—12 Oz. Optic

No. 1186—9 Oz. Optic

No. 1188—9 Oz. Optic

No. 1525A—10 Oz.
WIDE OPTIC

REGISTERED
TRADE **H** MARK
No. 50121

GOBLETS

REGISTERED
TRADE **H** MARK
No. 50121

SCALE HALF SIZE

No. 150—7 Oz.
ALSO MAKE 9 Oz.

No. 300—7 Oz. COLONIAL

No. 300—9 Oz. COLONIAL

No. 300—10 Oz. COLONIAL

No. 341—9 Oz. COLONIAL

No. 347—10 Oz. COLONIAL

No. 348—10 Oz. COLONIAL

No. 349—10 Oz. COLONIAL

No. 351—8 Oz. COLONIAL

No. 359—7 Oz. COLONIAL

No. 359—7 Oz. COLONIAL
OPTIC

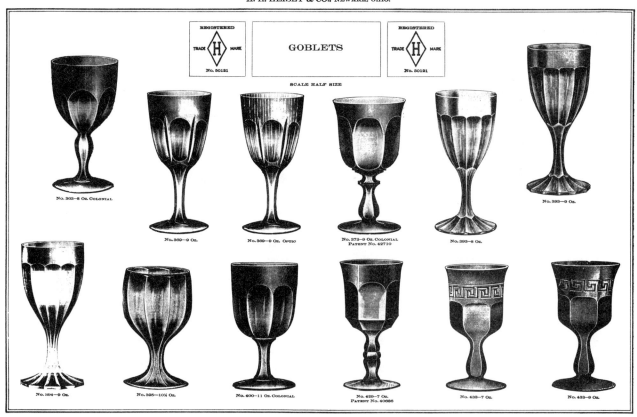

REGISTERED
TRADE (H) MARK
No. 50121

GOBLETS

REGISTERED
TRADE (H) MARK
No. 50121

SCALE HALF SIZE

No. 363—8 Oz. COLONIAL

No. 369—9 Oz.

No. 369—9 Oz. OPTIC

No. 373—9 Oz. COLONIAL
PATENT No. 42710

No. 393—8 Oz.

No. 393—9 Oz.

No. 394—9 Oz.

No. 395—10¼ Oz.

No. 400—11 Oz. COLONIAL

No. 429—7 Oz.
PATENT No. 40686

No. 433—7 Oz.

No. 433—9 Oz.

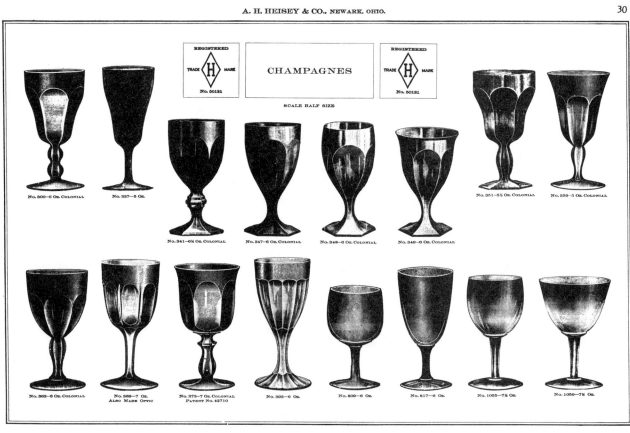

REGISTERED
TRADE (H) MARK
No. 50121

CHAMPAGNES

REGISTERED
TRADE (H) MARK
No. 50121

SCALE HALF SIZE

No. 300—6 Oz. COLONIAL

No. 337—5 Oz.

No. 341—6¼ Oz. COLONIAL

No. 347—6 Oz. COLONIAL

No. 348—6 Oz. COLONIAL

No. 349—6 Oz. COLONIAL

No. 351—5½ Oz. COLONIAL

No. 359—5 Oz. COLONIAL

No. 363—6 Oz. COLONIAL

No. 369—7 Oz.
ALSO MADE OPTIC

No. 373—7 Oz. COLONIAL
PATENT No. 42710

No. 393—6 Oz.

No. 809—6 Oz.

No. 817—6 Oz.

No. 1055—7½ Oz.

No. 1050—7½ Oz.

CHAMPAGNES
AND
PARFAITS

SCALE HALF SIZE

CLARETS
PLAIN AND OPTIC.

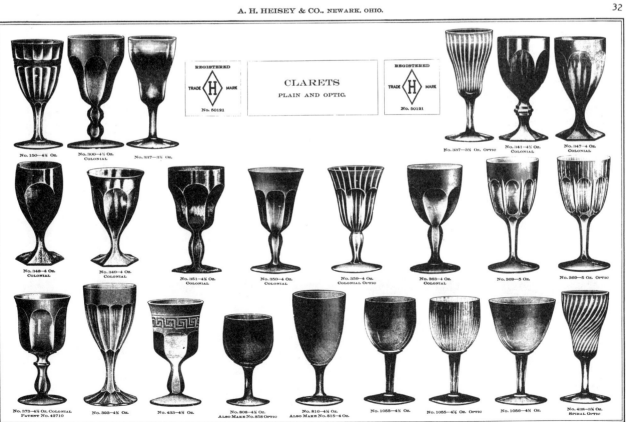

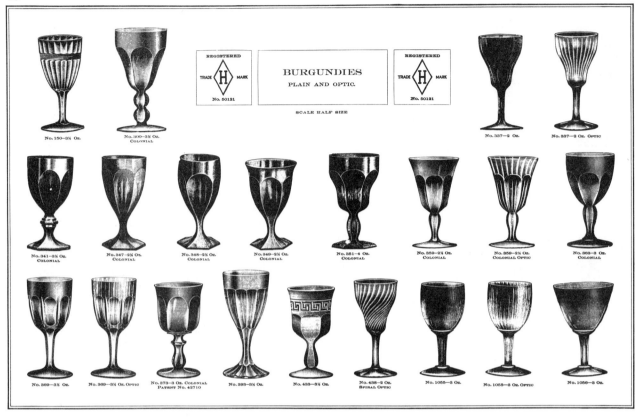

REGISTERED TRADE H MARK No. 50121

BURGUNDIES
PLAIN AND OPTIC.

REGISTERED TRADE H MARK No. 50121

SCALE HALF SIZE

No. 150—3½ Oz.

No. 300—3½ Oz.
COLONIAL

No. 337—2 Oz.

No. 337—2 Oz. OPTIC

No. 341—3½ Oz.
COLONIAL

No. 347—2½ Oz.
COLONIAL

No. 348—2½ Oz.
COLONIAL

No. 349—2½ Oz.
COLONIAL

No. 351—4 Oz.
COLONIAL

No. 359—2½ Oz.
COLONIAL

No. 359—2½ Oz.
COLONIAL OPTIC

No. 363—3 Oz.
COLONIAL

No. 369—3½ Oz.

No. 369—3½ Oz. OPTIC

No. 373—3 Oz. COLONIAL
PATENT No. 42710

No. 393—3½ Oz.

No. 433—3½ Oz.

No. 438—2 Oz.
SPIRAL OPTIC

No. 1055—3 Oz.

No. 1055—3 Oz. OPTIC

No. 1056—3 Oz.

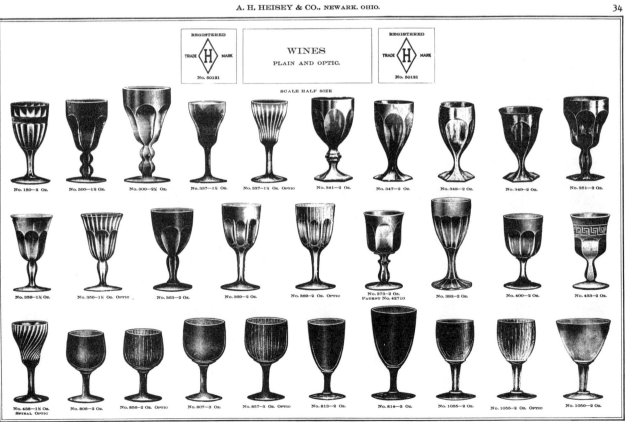

REGISTERED TRADE H MARK No. 50121

WINES
PLAIN AND OPTIC.

REGISTERED TRADE H MARK No. 50121

SCALE HALF SIZE

No. 150—2 Oz.

No. 300—1½ Oz.

No. 300—2½ Oz.

No. 337—1½ Oz.

No. 337—1½ Oz. OPTIC

No. 341—2 Oz.

No. 347—2 Oz.

No. 348—2 Oz.

No. 349—2 Oz.

No. 351—2 Oz.

No. 359—1½ Oz.

No. 359—1½ Oz. OPTIC

No. 363—2 Oz.

No. 369—2 Oz.

No. 369—2 Oz. OPTIC

No. 373—2 Oz.
PATENT No. 42710

No. 393—2 Oz.

No. 400—2 Oz.

No. 433—2 Oz.

No. 438—1½ Oz.
SPIRAL OPTIC

No. 806—2 Oz.

No. 856—2 Oz. OPTIC

No. 807—3 Oz.

No. 857—3 Oz. OPTIC

No. 813—2 Oz.

No. 814—3 Oz.

No. 1055—2 Oz.

No. 1055—2 Oz. OPTIC

No. 1056—2 Oz.

CORDIALS, SHERRIES
AND
PONY BRANDIES
PLAIN AND OPTIC.

SCALE HALF SIZE

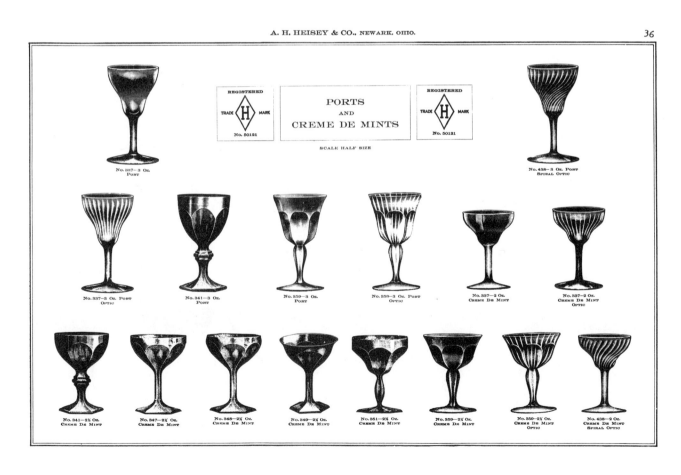

PORTS
AND
CREME DE MINTS

SCALE HALF SIZE

REGISTERED
TRADE **H** MARK
No. 50121

SAUCER
CHAMPAGNES

REGISTERED
TRADE **H** MARK
No. 50121

SCALE HALF SIZE

No. 337—6 Oz.

No. 337—6 Oz.
OPTIC

No. 438—6 Oz.
SPIRAL OPTIC

No. 1212—4½ Oz.

No. 1212—4½ Oz.
SHALLOW

No. 1213—6 Oz.

No. 1213—6 Oz.
SHALLOW

No. 1214—5 Oz.

No. 1214—5 Oz.
SHALLOW

No. 1215—6 Oz. SAUCER CHAMPAGNE
WITH
No. 1125—6 IN. PLATE GROUND BOTTOM

No. 1215—6 Oz.

No. 1215—6 Oz.
SHALLOW

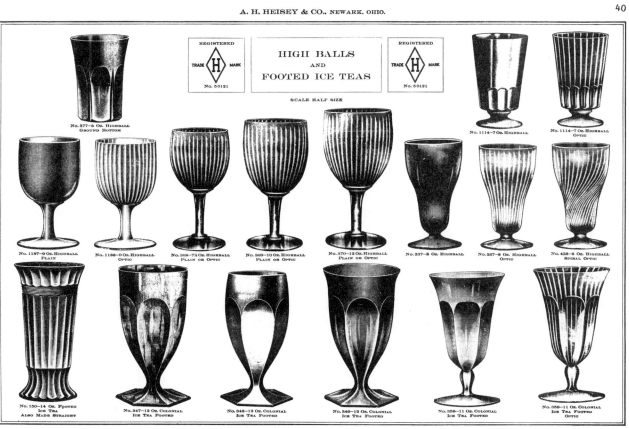

REGISTERED
TRADE **H** MARK
No. 50121

HIGH BALLS
AND
FOOTED ICE TEAS

REGISTERED
TRADE **H** MARK
No. 50121

SCALE HALF SIZE

No. 377—8 Oz. HIGHBALL
GROUND BOTTOM

No. 1114—7 Oz. HIGHBALL

No. 1114—7 Oz. HIGHBALL
OPTIC

No. 1187—9 Oz. HIGHBALL
PLAIN

No. 1188—9 Oz. HIGHBALL
OPTIC

No. 368—7½ Oz. HIGHBALL
PLAIN OR OPTIC

No. 369—10 Oz. HIGHBALL
PLAIN OR OPTIC

No. 370—12 Oz. HIGHBALL
PLAIN OR OPTIC

No. 337—8 Oz. HIGHBALL

No. 337—8 Oz. HIGHBALL
OPTIC

No. 438—8 Oz. HIGHBALL
SPIRAL OPTIC

No. 150—14 Oz. FOOTED
ICE TEA
ALSO MADE STRAIGHT

No. 347—12 Oz. COLONIAL
ICE TEA FOOTED

No. 348—12 Oz. COLONIAL
ICE TEA FOOTED

No. 349—12 Oz. COLONIAL
ICE TEA FOOTED

No. 359—11 Oz. COLONIAL
ICE TEA FOOTED

No. 359—11 Oz. COLONIAL
ICE TEA FOOTED
OPTIC

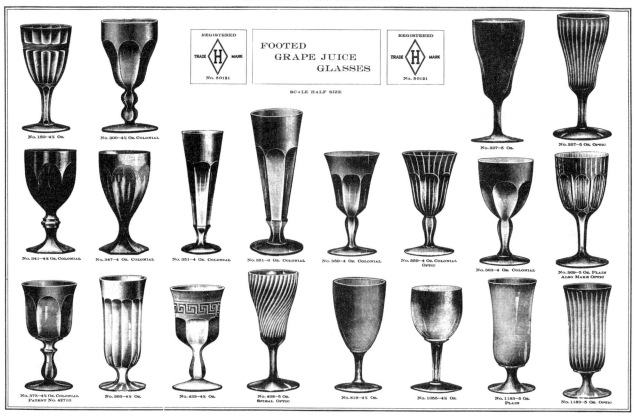

REGISTERED TRADE H MARK No. 50121

FOOTED
GRAPE JUICE
GLASSES

REGISTERED TRADE H MARK No. 50121

SCALE HALF SIZE

No. 150—4½ Oz.   No. 300—4½ Oz. Colonial   No. 337—5 Oz.   No. 337—5 Oz. Optic

No. 341—4½ Oz. Colonial   No. 347—4 Oz. Colonial   No. 351—4 Oz. Colonial   No. 351—6 Oz. Colonial   No. 359—4 Oz. Colonial   No. 359—4 Oz. Colonial Optic   No. 363—4 Oz. Colonial   No. 369—5 Oz. Plain Also Make Optic

No. 373—4½ Oz. Colonial Patent No. 42710   No. 393—4½ Oz.   No. 433—4½ Oz.   No. 438—5 Oz. Spiral Optic   No. 816—4½ Oz.   No. 1055—4½ Oz.   No. 1183—5 Oz. Plain   No. 1183—5 Oz. Optic

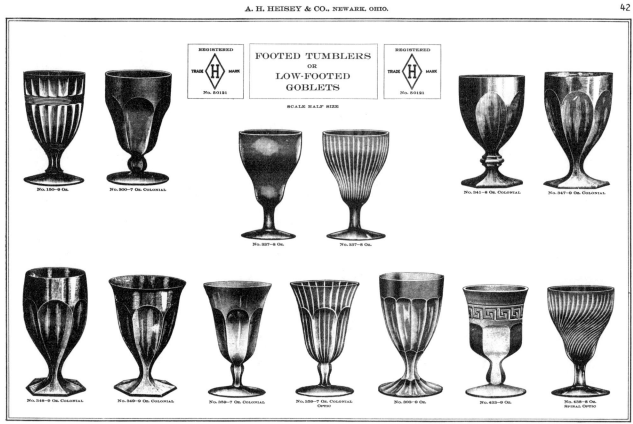

REGISTERED TRADE H MARK No. 50121

FOOTED TUMBLERS
OR
LOW-FOOTED
GOBLETS

REGISTERED TRADE H MARK No. 50121

SCALE HALF SIZE

No. 150—9 Oz.   No. 300—7 Oz. Colonial   No. 337—8 Oz.   No. 337—8 Oz.   No. 341—8 Oz. Colonial   No. 347—9 Oz. Colonial

No. 348—9 Oz. Colonial   No. 349—9 Oz. Colonial   No. 359—7 Oz. Colonial   No. 359—7 Oz. Colonial Optic   No. 393—9 Oz.   No. 433—9 Oz.   No. 438—8 Oz. Spiral Optic

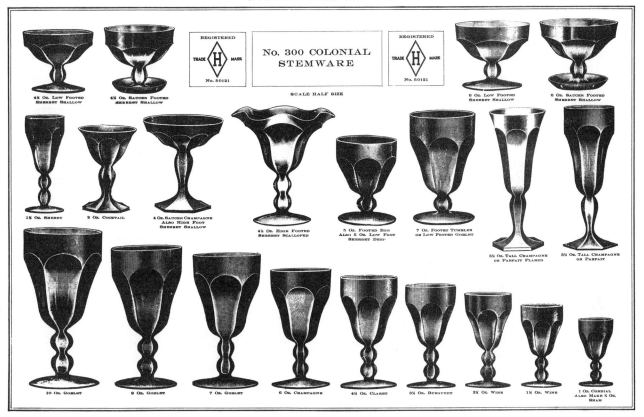

REGISTERED TRADE H MARK No. 50121

No. 300 COLONIAL STEMWARE

REGISTERED TRADE H MARK No. 50121

SCALE HALF SIZE

4½ Oz. LOW FOOTED SHERBET SHALLOW

4½ Oz. SAUCER FOOTED SHERBET SHALLOW

6 Oz. LOW FOOTED SHERBET SHALLOW

6 Oz. SAUCER FOOTED SHERBET SHALLOW

1½ Oz. SHERRY

2 Oz. COCKTAIL

4 Oz. SAUCER CHAMPAGNE ALSO HIGH FOOT SHERBET SHALLOW

4½ Oz. HIGH FOOTED SHERBET SCALLOPED

5 Oz. FOOTED EGG ALSO 5 Oz. LOW FOOT SHERBET DEEP

7 Oz. FOOTED TUMBLER OR LOW FOOTED GOBLET

3½ Oz. TALL CHAMPAGNE OR PARFAIT FLARED

3½ Oz. TALL CHAMPAGNE OR PARFAIT

10 Oz. GOBLET

9 Oz. GOBLET

7 Oz. GOBLET

6 Oz. CHAMPAGNE

4½ Oz. CLARET

3½ Oz. BURGUNDY

2½ Oz. WINE

1½ Oz. WINE

1 Oz. CORDIAL ALSO MAKE ½ Oz. SHAM

REGISTERED TRADE H MARK No. 50121

No. 337 PLAIN STEMWARE

REGISTERED TRADE H MARK No. 50121

SCALE HALF SIZE

4 Oz. LOW FOOTED SHERBET

4½ Oz. LOW FOOTED SHERBET

4 Oz. SAUCER FOOTED SHERBET

4½ Oz. SAUCER FOOTED SHERBET

2 Oz. CREME DE MINT

2½ Oz. COCKTAIL

6 Oz. SAUCER CHAMPAGNE

5 Oz. EGG OR OYSTER COCKTAIL

8 Oz. HIGHBALL

8 Oz. LOW FOOTED GOBLET OR FOOTED TUMBLER

3½ Oz. TALL CHAMPAGNE OR PARFAIT

8 Oz. GOBLET

5 Oz. CHAMPAGNE

3½ Oz. CLARET

2 Oz. BURGUNDY

1½ Oz. WINE

½ Oz. CORDIAL

3 Oz. PORT

5 Oz. SAUTERNE

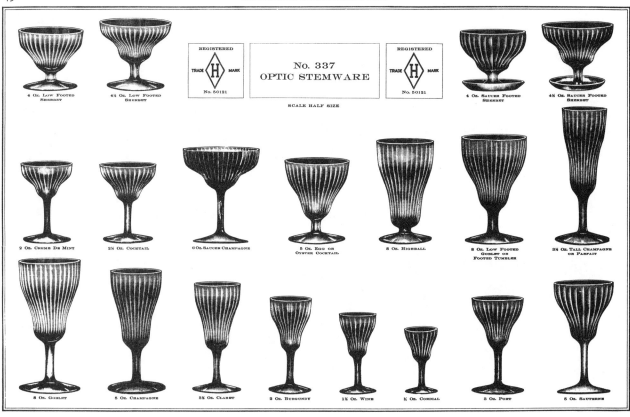

REGISTERED TRADE H MARK No. 50121

No. 337 OPTIC STEMWARE

REGISTERED TRADE H MARK No. 50121

SCALE HALF SIZE

4 Oz. Low Footed Sherbet

4½ Oz. Low Footed Sherbet

4 Oz. Saucer Footed Sherbet

4½ Oz. Saucer Footed Sherbet

2 Oz. Creme De Mint

2½ Oz. Cocktail

6 Oz. Saucer Champagne

5 Oz. Egg or Oyster Cocktail

8 Oz. Highball

8 Oz. Low Footed Goblet or Footed Tumbler

3½ Oz. Tall Champagne or Parfait

8 Oz. Goblet

5 Oz. Champagne

3½ Oz. Claret

2 Oz. Burgundy

1½ Oz. Wine

¾ Oz. Cordial

3 Oz. Port

5 Oz. Sauterne

REGISTERED TRADE H MARK No. 50121

No. 341 COLONIAL STEMWARE

REGISTERED TRADE H MARK No. 50121

SCALE HALF SIZE

3 Oz. Low Footed Sherbet

4½ Oz. Low Footed Sherbet

3 Oz. Low Footed Sherbet Scalloped

4½ Oz. Low Footed Sherbet Scalloped Also Make 6 Oz. Sherbet Like Above

2½ Oz. Creme De Mint

2 Oz. Cocktail

3 Oz. Cocktail

4½ Oz. Saucer Champagne Also High Footed Sherbet Shallow

6 Oz. Footed Egg Also 6 Oz. Oyster Cocktail

8 Oz. Footed Tumbler or Low Footed Goblet

3½ Oz. Parfait Straight or Tall Champagne

3½ Oz. Parfait Flared or Tall Champagne

9 Oz. Goblet

6½ Oz. Champagne

4½ Oz. Claret

3½ Oz. Burgundy

2 Oz. Wine

1 Oz. Cordial

2 Oz. Sherry

2 Oz. Sherry Flared

3 Oz. Port

REGISTERED
TRADE (H) MARK
No. 50121

No. 347 COLONIAL
STEMWARE

REGISTERED
TRADE (H) MARK
No. 50121

SCALE HALF SIZE

4 Oz. Low Footed Sherbet
Scalloped
Also Make 3 Oz. Sherbet Like Above

6 Oz. Low Footed Sherbet
Scalloped

5 Oz. High Footed Sherbet
Scalloped
Also Make 4 Oz. Like Above

3 Oz. Low Footed
Sherbet Shallow
Also Oyster Cocktail

3 Oz. Low Footed
Sherbet Deep

4 Oz. Low Footed
Sherbet Deep
Also Make 6 Oz. Like Above

6 Oz. Egg
Also 6 Oz. Oyster
Cocktail

4½ Oz. High Footed Sherbet
Shallow

9 Oz. Footed Tumbler
or Low Footed Goblet

12 Oz. Low Footed Ice Tea

10 Oz. Goblet

6 Oz. Champagne

4 Oz. Claret

2½ Oz. Burgundy

2 Oz. Wine

1 Oz. Cordial

2½ Oz. Creme De Mint

3 Oz. Cocktail

4½ Oz. Saucer Champagne

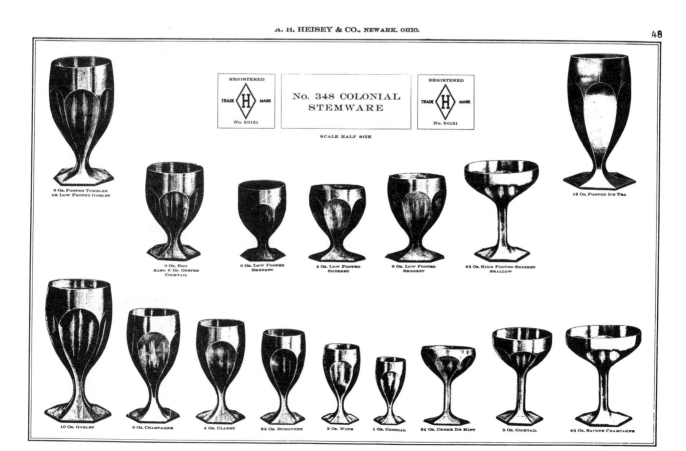

REGISTERED
TRADE (H) MARK
No. 50121

No. 348 COLONIAL
STEMWARE

REGISTERED
TRADE (H) MARK
No. 50121

SCALE HALF SIZE

9 Oz. Footed Tumbler
or Low Footed Goblet

6 Oz. Egg
Also 6 Oz. Oyster
Cocktail

3 Oz. Low Footed
Sherbet

4 Oz. Low Footed
Sherbet

6 Oz. Low Footed
Sherbet

4½ Oz. High Footed Sherbet
Shallow

12 Oz. Footed Ice Tea

10 Oz. Goblet

6 Oz. Champagne

4 Oz. Claret

2½ Oz. Burgundy

2 Oz. Wine

1 Oz. Cordial

2½ Oz. Creme De Mint

3 Oz. Cocktail

4½ Oz. Saucer Champagne

REGISTERED TRADE MARK No. 50121

No. 349 COLONIAL STEMWARE

REGISTERED TRADE MARK No. 50121

SCALE HALF SIZE

5 Oz. High Footed Sherbet Scalloped Also Make 4 Oz. Sherbet Like Above

4 Oz. Low Footed Sherbet Scalloped Also Make 3 Oz. Sherbet Like Above

6 Oz. Low Footed Sherbet Scalloped

3 Oz. Low Footed Sherbet

4 Oz. Low Footed Sherbet Also Make 6 Oz. Sherbet Like Above

6 Oz. Egg Also 6 Oz. Oyster Cocktail

4½ Oz. High Footed Sherbet Shallow

9 Oz. Footed Tumbler or Low Footed Goblet

12 Oz. Low Footed Ice Tea

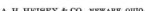

10 Oz. Goblet | 6 Oz. Champagne | 4 Oz. Claret | 2½ Oz. Burgundy | 2 Oz. Wine | 1 Oz. Cordial | 2½ Oz. Creme De Mint | 3 Oz. Cocktail | 4½ Oz. Saucer Champagne

REGISTERED TRADE MARK No. 50121

No. 351 COLONIAL STEMWARE

REGISTERED TRADE MARK No. 50121

SCALE HALF SIZE

4 Oz. Low Foot Also Make 3 Oz. Sherbet Like Above

5 Oz. Low Foot Sherbet Scalloped

3 Oz. Low Footed Sherbet | 4 Oz. Low Footed Sherbet | 5 Oz. Low Footed Sherbet | 5 Oz. Egg Also 5 Oz. Oyster Cocktail | 4 Oz. High Footed Sherbet Shallow

8 Oz. Goblet | 5½ Oz. Champagne | 4½ Oz. Claret | 3 Oz. Burgundy | 2 Oz. Wine | 1 Oz. Cordial | 2½ Oz. Creme De Mint | 2½ Oz. Cocktail | 4 Oz. Saucer Champagne

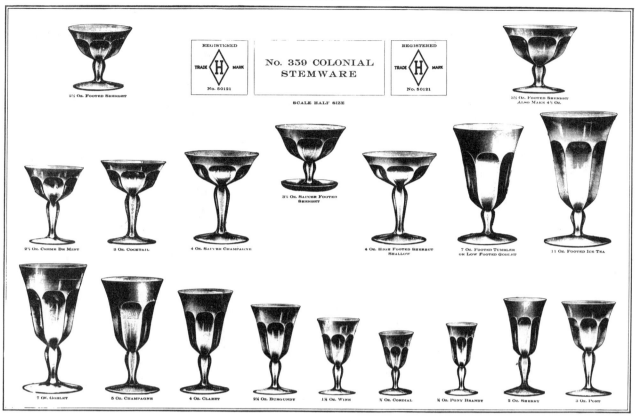

No. 359 COLONIAL STEMWARE

REGISTERED TRADE H MARK No. 50121

REGISTERED TRADE H MARK No. 50121

SCALE HALF SIZE

2½ Oz. Footed Sherbet

3½ Oz. Footed Sherbet Also Made 4½ Oz.

3½ Oz. Saucer Footed Sherbet

2½ Oz. Creme De Mint

3 Oz. Cocktail

4 Oz. Saucer Champagne

4 Oz. High Footed Sherbet Shallow

7 Oz. Footed Tumbler or Low Footed Goblet

11 Oz. Footed Ice Tea

7 Oz. Goblet

5 Oz. Champagne

4 Oz. Claret

2½ Oz. Burgundy

1½ Oz. Wine

¾ Oz. Cordial

¾ Oz. Pony Brandy

2 Oz. Sherry

3 Oz. Port

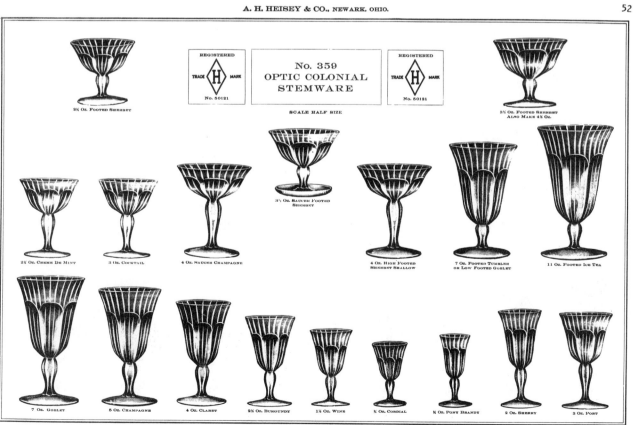

No. 359 OPTIC COLONIAL STEMWARE

REGISTERED TRADE H MARK No. 50121

REGISTERED TRADE H MARK No. 50121

SCALE HALF SIZE

2½ Oz. Footed Sherbet

3½ Oz. Footed Sherbet Also Made 4½ Oz.

3½ Oz. Saucer Footed Sherbet

2½ Oz. Creme De Mint

3 Oz. Cocktail

4 Oz. Saucer Champagne

4 Oz. High Footed Sherbet Shallow

7 Oz. Footed Tumbler or Low Footed Goblet

11 Oz. Footed Ice Tea

7 Oz. Goblet

5 Oz. Champagne

4 Oz. Claret

2½ Oz. Burgundy

1½ Oz. Wine

¾ Oz. Cordial

¾ Oz. Pony Brandy

2 Oz. Sherry

3 Oz. Port

No. 369 STEMWARE
PLAIN AND OPTIC.

SCALE HALF SIZE

9 Oz. Goblet   7 Oz. Champagne   5 Oz. Claret   3½ Oz. Burgundy   2 Oz. Wine   1 Oz. Cordial   3 Oz. Cocktail   4½ Oz. Saucer Champagne   4½ Oz. High Footed Sherbet Shallow

9 Oz. Goblet Optic   7 Oz. Champagne Optic   5 Oz. Claret Optic   3½ Oz. Burgundy Optic   2 Oz. Wine Optic   1 Oz. Cordial Optic   3 Oz. Cocktail Optic   4½ Oz. Saucer Champagne Optic   4½ Oz. High Footed Sherbet Shallow Optic

No. 363 COLONIAL
STEMWARE

SCALE HALF SIZE

8 Oz. Goblet   6 Oz. Champagne   4 Oz. Claret   3 Oz. Burgundy   2 Oz. Wine   1 Oz. Cordial

4½ Oz. Saucer Champagne   4½ Oz. High Footed Sherbet Shallow

5 Oz. High Footed Sherbet Shallow   6 Oz. Egg Cup

No. 373 COLONIAL
STEMWARE
PATENT No. 42710

9 Oz. Goblet   7 Oz. Champagne   4½ Oz. Claret   3 Oz. Burgundy   1½ Oz. Wine   ¾ Oz. Cordial   5 Oz. Low Footed Sherbet   3 Oz. Cocktail   5 Oz. Saucer Champagne

REGISTERED
TRADE (H) MARK
No. 50121

No. 393 AND 393½ STEMWARE

REGISTERED
TRADE (H) MARK
No. 50121

SCALE HALF SIZE

No. 393½—4½ Oz.
Low Footed Sherbet

No. 393½—4½ Oz.
Low Footed Sherbet
Cupped

No. 393½—4½ Oz. Low Footed Sherbet
Flared

9 Oz. Footed Tumbler
or Low Footed Goblet

4½ Oz. Parfait

5 Oz. Low Footed
Sherbet Shallow

5 Oz. Low Footed
Water Ice Flared

4 Oz. Low Footed
Sherbet Deep

5 Oz. Egg

4½ Oz. Hollow Stem
Champagne Straight

4½ Oz. Hollow Stem
Champagne Flared

9 Oz. Goblet

8 Oz. Goblet

6 Oz. Champagne

5 Oz. Claret

3 Oz. Burgundy

2 Oz. Wine

1 Oz. Cordial

2 Oz. Sherry

3 Oz. Cocktail

5 Oz. Saucer Champagne
Also High Footed
Sherbet Shallow

REGISTERED
TRADE (H) MARK
No. 50121

No. 433 STEMWARE

REGISTERED
TRADE (H) MARK
No. 50121

SCALE HALF SIZE

4½ Oz. Low Footed Sherbet

4½ Oz. Low Footed Sherbet
Shallow

4½ Oz. Low Footed Sherbet
Flared

4½ Oz. Low Footed Sherbet
Cupped

6 Oz. Low Footed Sherbet

6 Oz. Low Footed Sherbet
Flared

6 Oz. Low Footed Sherbet
Cupped

6 Oz. Low Footed Sherbet
Shallow

4½ Oz. High Footed Sherbet
Shallow

5 Oz. Egg

9 Oz. Footed Tumbler
or Low Footed Goblet

9 Oz. Goblet

7 Oz. Goblet

4½ Oz. Claret

3½ Oz. Burgundy

2 Oz. Wine

¾ Oz. Cordial

2 Oz. Sherry

3 Oz. Cocktail

4½ Oz. Saucer Champagne

REGISTERED
TRADE H MARK
No. 50121

No. 438
SPIRAL OPTIC
STEMWARE

REGISTERED
TRADE H MARK
No. 50121

SCALE HALF SIZE

4 Oz. Low Footed Sherbet — 4½ Oz. Low Footed Sherbet — 4 Oz. Saucer Footed Sherbet — 4½ Oz. Saucer Footed Sherbet

No. 438½—4½ Oz. Low Footed Sherbet

2 Oz. Creme De Mint — 2½ Oz. Cocktail — 6 Oz. Saucer Champagne — 5 Oz. Egg or Oyster Cocktail — 8 Oz. Highball — 8 Oz. Low Footed Goblet or Footed Tumbler — 5½ Oz. Tall Champagne or Parfait

8 Oz. Goblet — 5 Oz. Champagne — 3½ Oz. Claret — 2 Oz. Burgundy — 1½ Oz. Wine — ¾ Oz. Cordial — 3 Oz. Port — 5 Oz. Sauterne

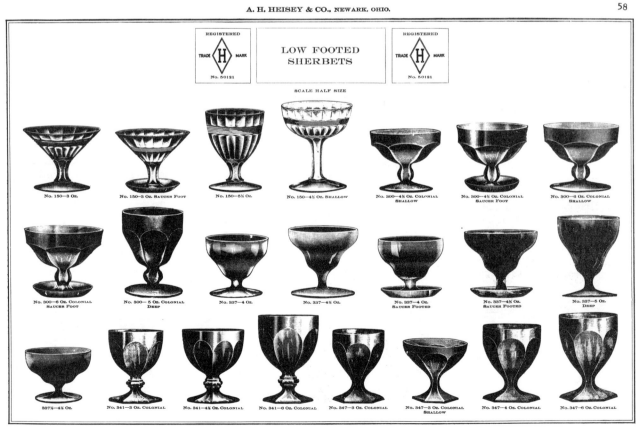

REGISTERED
TRADE H MARK
No. 50121

LOW FOOTED
SHERBETS

REGISTERED
TRADE H MARK
No. 50121

SCALE HALF SIZE

No. 150—3 Oz. — No. 150—3 Oz. Saucer Foot — No. 150—5½ Oz. — No. 150—4½ Oz. Shallow — No. 300—4½ Oz. Colonial Shallow — No. 300—4½ Oz. Colonial Saucer Foot — No. 300—6 Oz. Colonial Shallow

No. 300—6 Oz. Colonial Saucer Foot — No. 300—5 Oz. Colonial Deep — No. 337—4 Oz. — No. 337—4½ Oz. — No. 337—4 Oz. Saucer Footed — No. 337—4½ Oz. Saucer Footed — No. 337—5 Oz. Deep

337½—4½ Oz. — No. 341—3 Oz. Colonial — No. 341—4½ Oz. Colonial — No. 341—6 Oz. Colonial — No. 347—3 Oz. Colonial — No. 347—3 Oz. Colonial Shallow — No. 347—4 Oz. Colonial — No. 347—6 Oz. Colonial

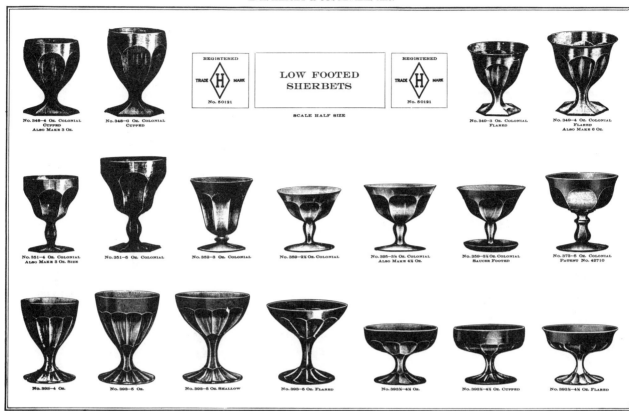

REGISTERED	LOW FOOTED	REGISTERED
TRADE H MARK	SHERBETS	TRADE H MARK
No. 50121		No. 50121

SCALE HALF SIZE

No. 348—4 Oz. Colonial Cupped Also Make 3 Oz.   No. 348—6 Oz. Colonial Cupped   No. 349—3 Oz. Colonial Flared   No. 349—4 Oz. Colonial Flared Also Make 6 Oz.

No. 351—4 Oz. Colonial Also Make 3 Oz. Size   No. 351—5 Oz. Colonial   No. 352—3 Oz. Colonial   No. 359—2½ Oz. Colonial   No. 395—3½ Oz. Colonial Also Make 4½ Oz.   No. 359—3½ Oz. Colonial Saucer Footed   No. 373—5 Oz. Colonial Patent No. 42710

No. 393—4 Oz.   No. 393—5 Oz.   No. 393—5 Oz. Shallow   No. 393—5 Oz. Flared   No. 393½—4½ Oz.   No. 393½—4½ Oz. Cupped   No. 393½—4½ Oz. Flared

---

REGISTERED	LOW FOOTED	REGISTERED
TRADE H MARK	SHERBETS	TRADE H MARK
No. 50121		No. 50121

SCALE HALF SIZE

No. 400—4 Oz. Colonial   No. 400—6 Oz. Colonial Deep   No. 429—4 Oz. Straight Patent No. 40686   No. 429—4 Oz. Flared Patent No. 40686

No. 433—5 Oz. Deep   No. 433—4½ Oz. Straight Patent No. 41533   No. 433—6 Oz. Straight Patent No. 41533   No. 433—4½ Oz. Flared Patent No. 41533   No. 433—6 Oz. Flared Patent No. 41533   No. 433—4½ Oz. Shallow Patent No. 41533   No. 433—6 Oz. Shallow Patent No. 41533

No. 433—4½ Oz. Cupped Patent No. 41533   No. 433—6 Oz. Cupped Patent No. 41533   No. 1109—4 Oz. Deep   No. 1110—4 Oz.   No. 1111—6 Oz.   No. 1112—3½ Oz. Deep Also Make 3 Oz.   No. 1112—4 Oz. Deep   No. 1112—4½ Oz. Deep Also Make 5 Oz.

1112 Sherbets Are Also Made Optic

No. 1113—4½ Oz. Saucer Footed Also Make Optic   No. 1216—2½ Oz. Roman Punch   No. 1217—3½ Oz.   No. 1218—3½ Oz.   No. 1219—3½ Oz. Handled   No. 1220—3½ Oz. Handled   No. 1221—6 Oz. Flared Also Make Straight

REGISTERED
TRADE H MARK
No. 50121

LOW FOOTED
SHERBETS

REGISTERED
TRADE H MARK
No. 50121

SCALE HALF SIZE

No. 1222—6 Oz. Straight

No. 1222—6 Oz. Flared

No. 1223—6 Oz. Colonial Straight

No. 1223—6 Oz. Colonial Flared

No. 1224—5 Oz. Straight

No. 1224—5 Oz. Flared

No. 1225—5¼ Oz. Colonial Straight

No. 1225—5¼ Oz. Colonial Flared

No. 1226—5¼ Oz. Colonial Straight

No. 1226—5¼ Oz. Colonial Flared

No. 1227—7 Oz. Plain Also Made Optic

No. 1234—4½ Oz. Colonial

No. 1239—8 Oz.

No. 1243—6 Oz. Plain Also Made Optic

No. 1248—4 Oz. Colonial

No. 1250—4 Oz. Colonial

No. 1253—3½ Oz. Colonial

No. 1253—5 Oz. Colonial

No. 1254—5½ Oz. Colonial Straight

No. 1254—5½ Oz. Colonial Flared

No. 1255—4½ Oz. Colonial

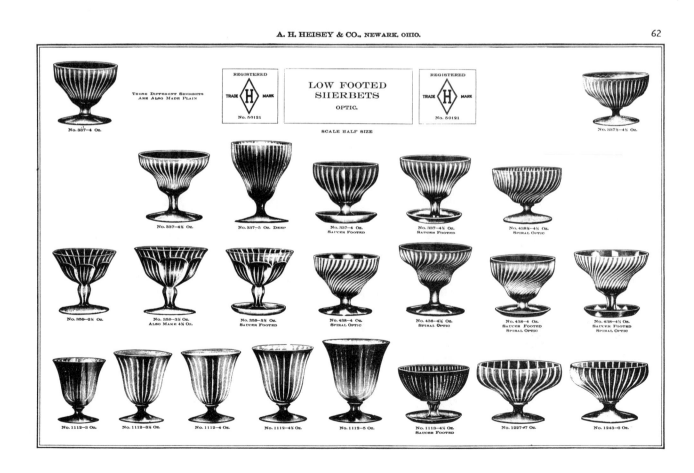

THESE DIFFERENT SHERBETS ARE ALSO MADE PLAIN

REGISTERED
TRADE H MARK
No. 50121

LOW FOOTED
SHERBETS
OPTIC.

REGISTERED
TRADE H MARK
No. 50121

SCALE HALF SIZE

No. 337—4 Oz.

No. 337½—4½ Oz.

No. 337—4½ Oz.

No. 337—5 Oz. Deep

No. 337—4 Oz. Saucer Footed

No. 337—4½ Oz. Saucer Footed

No. 438½—4½ Oz. Spiral Optic

No. 350—2½ Oz.

No. 350—3½ Oz. Also Made 4½ Oz.

No. 350—3½ Oz. Saucer Footed

No. 438—4 Oz. Spiral Optic

No. 438—4½ Oz. Spiral Optic

No. 438—4 Oz. Saucer Footed Spiral Optic

No. 438—4½ Oz. Saucer Footed Spiral Optic

No. 1112—3 Oz.

No. 1112—3½ Oz.

No. 1112—4 Oz.

No. 1112—4½ Oz.

No. 1112—5 Oz.

No. 1113—4½ Oz. Saucer Footed

No. 1227—7 Oz.

No. 1243—6 Oz.

LOW FOOTED
SHERBETS
WITH PLATES.

REGISTERED
TRADE **H** MARK
No. 50121

REGISTERED
TRADE **H** MARK
No. 50121

SCALE HALF SIZE
ALL PLATES ON THIS PAGE HAVE GROUND BOTTOMS

No. 150—5 Oz. SHERBET DEEP
No. 150—6-IN. PLATE

No. 300—4½ Oz. SHERBET SHALLOW
No. 1150—5-IN. PLATE

No. 300—5 Oz. SHERBET DEEP
No. 1150—6-IN. PLATE

No. 339—5 Oz. SHERBET DEEP
No. 1150—6-IN. PLATE

No. 352—3 Oz. SHERBET
No. 1150—4½-IN. PLATE

No. 393—5 Oz. SHERBET
No. 393—5½-IN. PLATE

No. 429—4½ Oz. SHERBET FLARED
No. 1150—5-IN. PLATE

No. 433—5 Oz. SHERBET DEEP
No. 433—5½-IN. PLATE

No. 1112—4 Oz. SHERBET
No. 1125—4½-IN. PLATE

No. 1217—3½ Oz. SHERBET
No. 1150—4½-IN. PLATE

No. 1218—3½ Oz. SHERBET
No. 1150—4½-IN. PLATE

No. 1223—6 Oz. SHERBET
No. 1150—5½-IN. PLATE

No. 1226—5 Oz. SHERBET
No. 1150—6-IN. PLATE

No. 1227—7 Oz. SHERBET OPTIC
No. 1125—5½-IN. PLATE

No. 1243—6 Oz. SHERBET
No. 1125—5½-IN. PLATE

No. 1253—5 Oz. SHERBET
No. 1150—5½-IN. PLATE

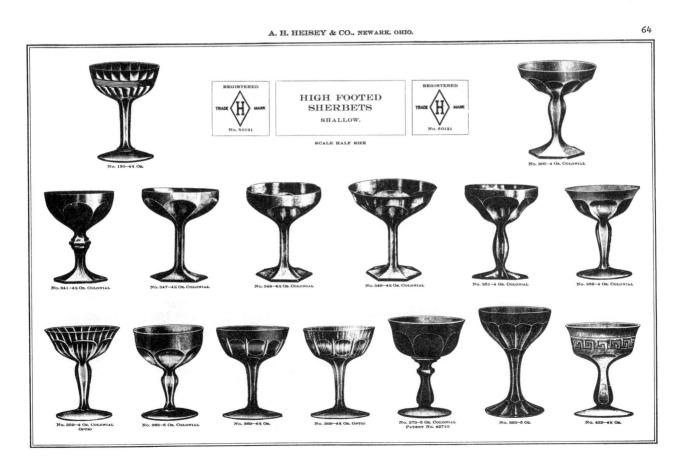

HIGH FOOTED
SHERBETS
SHALLOW.

REGISTERED
TRADE **H** MARK
No. 50121

REGISTERED
TRADE **H** MARK
No. 50121

SCALE HALF SIZE

No. 150—4½ Oz.

No. 300—4 Oz. COLONIAL

No. 341—4½ Oz. COLONIAL

No. 347—4½ Oz. COLONIAL

No. 348—4½ Oz. COLONIAL

No. 349—4½ Oz. COLONIAL

No. 351—4 Oz. COLONIAL

No. 359—4 Oz. COLONIAL

No. 359—4 Oz. COLONIAL
OPTIC

No. 363—5 Oz. COLONIAL

No. 369—4½ Oz.

No. 369—4½ Oz. OPTIC

No. 373—5 Oz. COLONIAL
PATENT NO. 42710

No. 393—5 Oz.

No. 433—4½ Oz.

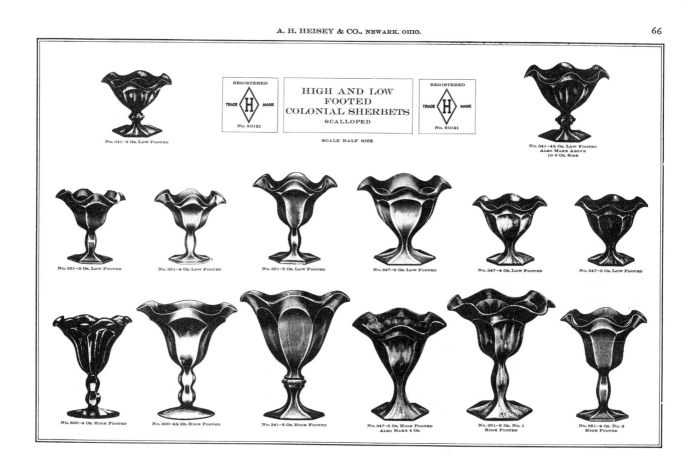

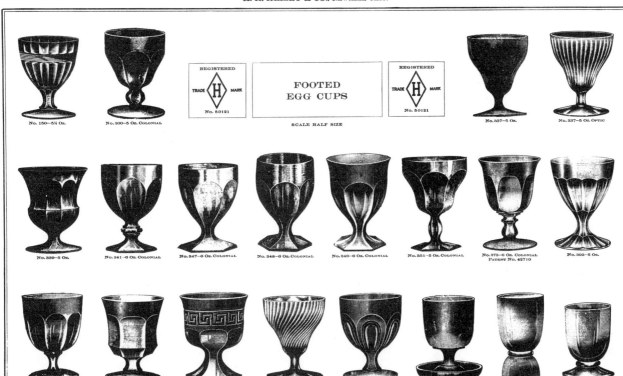

REGISTERED
TRADE H MARK
No. 50121

FOOTED
EGG CUPS

REGISTERED
TRADE H MARK
No. 50121

SCALE HALF SIZE

No. 150—5½ Oz.

No. 300—5 Oz. Colonial

No. 337—5 Oz.

No. 337—5 Oz. Optic

No. 339—5 Oz.

No. 341—6 Oz. Colonial

No. 347—6 Oz. Colonial

No. 348—6 Oz. Colonial

No. 349—6 Oz. Colonial

No. 351—5 Oz. Colonial

No. 373—6 Oz. Colonial
Patent No. 42710

No. 393—5 Oz.

No. 400—6 Oz. Colonial

No. 429—5 Oz.
Patent No. 40686

No. 433—5 Oz.

No. 438—5 Oz.
Spiral Optic

No. 439—5 Oz.
Also Mark Cupped
Patent No. 42200

No. 1108—5 Oz.
Saucer Footed

No. 1228

No. 1229

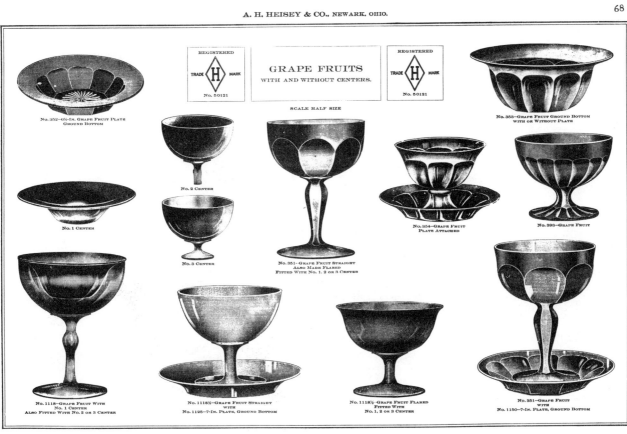

REGISTERED
TRADE H MARK
No. 50121

GRAPE FRUITS
WITH AND WITHOUT CENTERS.

REGISTERED
TRADE H MARK
No. 50121

SCALE HALF SIZE

No. 352—6½-In. Grape Fruit Plate
Ground Bottom

No. 353—Grape Fruit Ground Bottom
with or without Plate

No. 1 Center

No. 2 Center

No. 3 Center

No. 351—Grape Fruit Straight
Also Made Flared
Fitted With No. 1, 2 or 3 Center

No. 354—Grape Fruit
Plate Attached

No. 393—Grape Fruit

No. 1118—Grape Fruit With
No. 1 Center
Also Fitted With No. 2 or 3 Center

No. 1118½—Grape Fruit Straight
with
No. 1125—7-In. Plate, Ground Bottom

No. 1118½—Grape Fruit Flared
Fitted With
No. 1, 2 or 3 Center

No. 351—Grape Fruit
with
No. 1150—7-In. Plate, Ground Bottom

PRESSED
HANDLED CUSTARDS
ALL GROUND BOTTOMS.

SCALE HALF SIZE

No. 150—4 Oz.

No. 300—4 Oz.
COLONIAL

No. 331—4½ Oz.
COLONIAL

No. 337—5 Oz.

No. 339—4 Oz.
COLONIAL

No. 341—3 Oz.
COLONIAL

No. 341—4½ Oz.
COLONIAL

No. 341—4½ Oz.
COLONIAL SHALLOW

No. 341½—3 Oz.
COLONIAL

No. 343—4 Oz.

No. 343½—5 Oz.

No. 350—4½ Oz.

No. 351—5 Oz.
COLONIAL

No. 365—5 Oz.

No. 400—3½ Oz.
COLONIAL

No. 393—4½ Oz.

No. 429—4½ Oz.
PATENT NO. 40680

No. 433—4½ Oz.

No. 439—4½ Oz.
PATENT NO. 42260

No. 1101—5 Oz.

No. 1101—5 Oz.
OPTIC

No. 1103—5 Oz.
COLONIAL

No. 1238—4 Oz.
COLONIAL

PRESSED
HANDLED CUSTARDS
ALL GROUND BOTTOMS.

SCALE HALF SIZE

No. 1211—5 Oz.

No. 1212—4½ Oz.

No. 1151—2½ Oz.

No. 1152—3½ Oz.

No. 1153—4½ Oz.

No. 1154—5½ Oz.

No. 1155—6 Oz.

No. 1156—3 Oz.

No. 1157—3½ Oz.

No. 1158—4½ Oz.

No. 1159—5 Oz.

No. 1160—6½ Oz.

No. 1161—2½ Oz. FLUTED

No. 1162—3 Oz. FLUTED

No. 1163—3½ Oz. FLUTED

No. 1164—5 Oz. FLUTED

No. 1165—6 Oz. FLUTED

No. 1165—6 Oz. FLARED

STUCK
HANDLED CUSTARDS
ALL GROUND BOTTOMS.

REGISTERED TRADE H MARK No. 50121

REGISTERED TRADE H MARK No. 50121

SCALE HALF SIZE

No. 300½—4 Oz.
COLONIAL

No. 337—5 Oz.

No. 341—4 Oz.
COLONIAL

No. 389—4½ Oz.

No. 1100—5 Oz.

No. 1102—4 Oz.

No. 1104—4 Oz.

No. 1105 FLARED

No. 1106—4½ Oz.

No. 1166—2½ Oz.

No. 1167—3½ Oz.

No. 1168—4 Oz.

No. 1169—5 Oz.

No. 1170—6½ Oz.

No. 1171—2½ Oz.

No. 1172—3½ Oz.

No. 1173—4 Oz.

No. 1174—5 Oz.

No. 1175—6 Oz.

No. 1200—5½ Oz. FLARED

No. 1207—3 Oz.

No. 1209—3 Oz.

No. 1210—7 Oz.

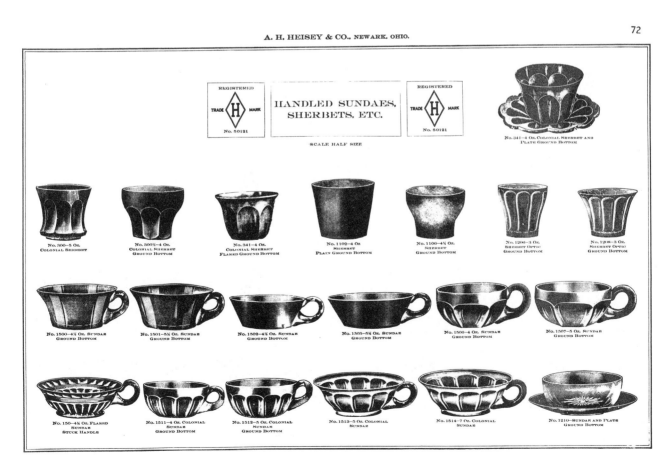

REGISTERED TRADE H MARK No. 50121

HANDLED SUNDAES,
SHERBETS, ETC.

REGISTERED TRADE H MARK No. 50121

SCALE HALF SIZE

No. 341—4 Oz. COLONIAL SHERBET AND
PLATE GROUND BOTTOM

No. 300—5 Oz.
COLONIAL SHERBET

No. 300½—4 Oz.
COLONIAL SHERBET
GROUND BOTTOM

No. 341—4 Oz.
COLONIAL SHERBET
FLARED GROUND BOTTOM

No. 1102—4 Oz
SHERBET
PLAIN GROUND BOTTOM

No. 1106—4½ Oz.
SHERBET
GROUND BOTTOM

No. 1206—3 Oz.
SHERBET OPTIC
GROUND BOTTOM

No. 1208—3 Oz.
SHERBET OPTIC
GROUND BOTTOM

No. 1500—4½ Oz. SUNDAE
GROUND BOTTOM

No. 1501—5½ Oz. SUNDAE
GROUND BOTTOM

No. 1502—4½ Oz. SUNDAE
GROUND BOTTOM

No. 1503—5½ Oz. SUNDAE
GROUND BOTTOM

No. 1506—4 Oz. SUNDAE
GROUND BOTTOM

No. 1507—5 Oz. SUNDAE
GROUND BOTTOM

No. 150—4½ Oz. FLARED
SUNDAE
STUCK HANDLE

No. 1511—4 Oz. COLONIAL
SUNDAE
GROUND BOTTOM

No. 1512—5 Oz. COLONIAL
SUNDAE
GROUND BOTTOM

No. 1513—5 Oz. COLONIAL
SUNDAE

No. 1514—7 Oz. COLONIAL
SUNDAE

No. 1210—SUNDAE AND PLATE
GROUND BOTTOM

No. 150—5½ Oz.

FOOTED
OYSTER COCKTAILS

SCALE HALF SIZE

No. 300—5 Oz. Colonial

No. 337—5 Oz.   No. 337—5 Oz. Optic   No. 339—5 Oz. Colonial   No. 341—4½ Oz. Colonial   No. 341—6 Oz. Colonial   No. 347—6 Oz. Colonial   No. 348—6 Oz. Colonial

No. 349—6 Oz. Colonial   No. 351—5 Oz. Colonial   No. 393—5 Oz.   No. 400—6 Oz. Colonial   No. 429—5 Oz. Patent No. 40686   No. 433—5 Oz.   No. 438—5 Oz. Spiral Optic   No. 439—5 Oz. Also Make Cupped Patent No. 42280

TWO PIECE
FOOTED
OYSTER COCKTAILS

SCALE HALF SIZE
ALL PLATES ON THIS PAGE HAVE GROUND BOTTOMS

No. 150
No. 150—5 Oz. Oyster Cocktail
AND
No. 150—6-Inch Plate

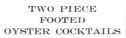

No. 352
No. 352—3½ Oz. Oyster Cocktail
AND
No. 1150—4½-Inch Plate

No. 393
No. 393—5 Oz. Oyster Cocktail
AND
No. 393—5½-Inch Plate

No. 300
No. 300—5 Oz. Oyster Cocktail
AND
No. 1150—5½-Inch Plate

No. 433
No. 433—5 Oz. Oyster Cocktail
AND
No. 433—5½-Inch Plate

No. 1112
No. 1112—4½ Oz. Oyster Cocktail
AND
No. 1125—4½-Inch Plate

No. 1217
No. 1217—3½ Oz. Oyster Cocktail
AND
No. 1150—4½-Inch Plate

No. 1218
No. 1218—3½ Oz. Oyster Cocktail
AND
No. 1150—4½-Inch Plate

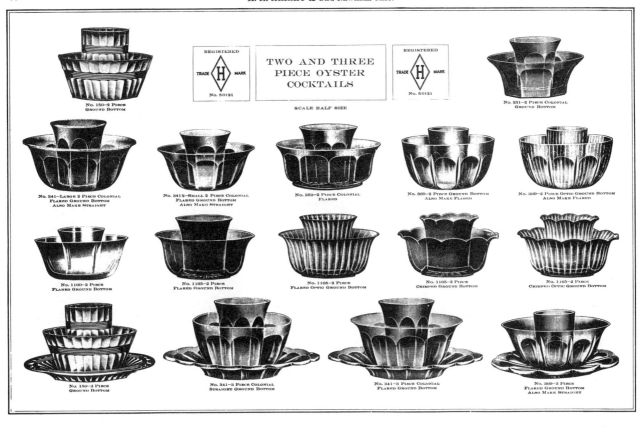

TWO AND THREE PIECE OYSTER COCKTAILS

REGISTERED TRADE H MARK No. 50121

REGISTERED TRADE H MARK No. 50121

SCALE HALF SIZE

No. 150—2 PIECE GROUND BOTTOM

No. 331—2 PIECE COLONIAL GROUND BOTTOM

No. 341—LARGE 2 PIECE COLONIAL FLARED GROUND BOTTOM ALSO MAKE STRAIGHT

No. 341½—SMALL 2 PIECE COLONIAL FLARED GROUND BOTTOM ALSO MAKE STRAIGHT

No. 353—2 PIECE COLONIAL FLARED

No. 369—2 PIECE GROUND BOTTOM ALSO MAKE FLARED

No. 369—2 PIECE OPTIC GROUND BOTTOM ALSO MAKE FLARED

No. 1160—2 PIECE FLARED GROUND BOTTOM

No. 1165—2 PIECE FLARED GROUND BOTTOM

No. 1165—2 PIECE FLARED OPTIC GROUND BOTTOM

No. 1165—2 PIECE CRIMPED GROUND BOTTOM

No. 1165—2 PIECE CRIMPED OPTIC GROUND BOTTOM

No. 150—3 PIECE GROUND BOTTOM

No. 341—3 PIECE COLONIAL STRAIGHT GROUND BOTTOM

No. 341—3 PIECE COLONIAL FLARED GROUND BOTTOM

No. 369—3 PIECE FLARED GROUND BOTTOM ALSO MAKE STRAIGHT

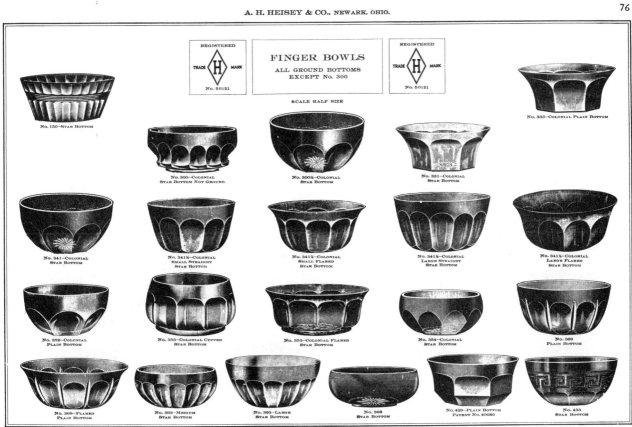

FINGER BOWLS

ALL GROUND BOTTOMS EXCEPT No. 300

REGISTERED TRADE H MARK No. 50121

REGISTERED TRADE H MARK No. 50121

SCALE HALF SIZE

No. 150—STAR BOTTOM

No. 333—COLONIAL PLAIN BOTTOM

No. 300—COLONIAL STAR BOTTOM NOT GROUND

No. 300½—COLONIAL STAR BOTTOM

No. 331—COLONIAL STAR BOTTOM

No. 341—COLONIAL STAR BOTTOM

No. 341½—COLONIAL SMALL STRAIGHT STAR BOTTOM

No. 341½—COLONIAL SMALL FLARED STAR BOTTOM

No. 341½—COLONIAL LARGE STRAIGHT STAR BOTTOM

No. 341½—COLONIAL LARGE FLARED STAR BOTTOM

No. 352—COLONIAL PLAIN BOTTOM

No. 353—COLONIAL CUPPED STAR BOTTOM

No. 353—COLONIAL FLARED STAR BOTTOM

No. 354—COLONIAL STAR BOTTOM

No. 369 PLAIN BOTTOM

No. 369—FLARED PLAIN BOTTOM

No. 393—MEDIUM STAR BOTTOM

No. 393—LARGE STAR BOTTOM

No. 398 STAR BOTTOM

No. 429—PLAIN BOTTOM PATENT No. 46686

No. 433 STAR BOTTOM

FINGER BOWLS

REGISTERED TRADE H MARK No. 50121

REGISTERED TRADE H MARK No. 50121

SCALE HALF SIZE

No. 1160—Plain Bottom Ground

No. 1161—Plain Bottom Ground

No. 1162—Plain Bottom Ground

No. 1163—Plain Bottom Ground

No. 1104—Plain Bottom Ground

No. 1104—Flared, Star Bottom Ground

No. 1104—Crimped, Star Bottom Ground

No. 1216—Plain Bottom Ground

No. 1217—Star Bottom Ground

No. 1230—Star Bottom Ground

No. 1231—Star Bottom Ground

No. 1232—Star Bottom Ground

No. 1232½—Star Bottom Ground

No. 1233—Star Bottom Ground

No. 1242—Plain Bottom Ground

No. 1244—Plain Bottom

No. 1244—Flared, Plain Bottom

No. 1245—Star Bottom

No. 1245—Flared, Star Bottom

No. 1246—Plain Bottom

No. 1246—Flared, Plain Bottom

No. 1247—Star Bottom

No. 1247—Flared, Star Bottom

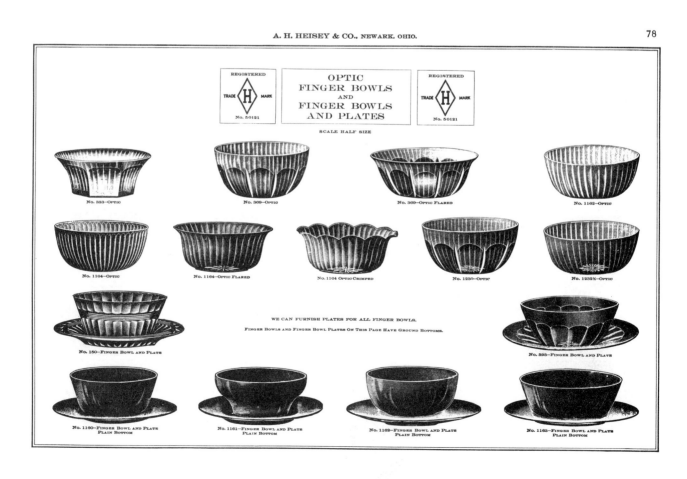

REGISTERED TRADE H MARK No. 50121

OPTIC FINGER BOWLS AND FINGER BOWLS AND PLATES

REGISTERED TRADE H MARK No. 50121

SCALE HALF SIZE

No. 333—Optic

No. 369—Optic

No. 369—Optic Flared

No. 1162—Optic

No. 1104—Optic

No. 1104—Optic Flared

No. 1104 Optic Crimped

No. 1230—Optic

No. 1232½—Optic

No. 150—Finger Bowl and Plate

WE CAN FURNISH PLATES FOR ALL FINGER BOWLS.

FINGER BOWLS AND FINGER BOWL PLATES ON THIS PAGE HAVE GROUND BOTTOMS.

No. 393—Finger Bowl and Plate

No. 1160—Finger Bowl and Plate Plain Bottom

No. 1161—Finger Bowl and Plate Plain Bottom

No. 1162—Finger Bowl and Plate Plain Bottom

No. 1163—Finger Bowl and Plate Plain Bottom

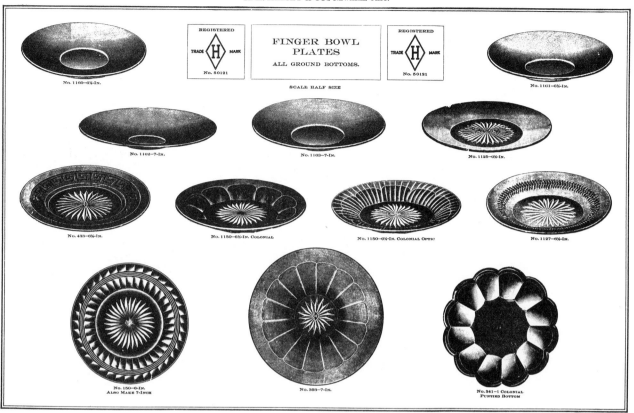

FINGER BOWL
PLATES
ALL GROUND BOTTOMS.

REGISTERED TRADE H MARK No. 50121

REGISTERED TRADE H MARK No. 50121

SCALE HALF SIZE

No. 1100—6½-In.

No. 1161—6½-In.

No. 1162—7-In.

No. 1163—7-In.

No. 1125—6½-In.

No. 433—6½-In.

No. 1150—6½-In. Colonial

No. 1150—6½-In. Colonial Optic

No. 1127—6½-In.

No. 150—6-In.
Also Make 7-Inch

No. 393—7-In.

No. 341—1 Colonial
Punted Bottom

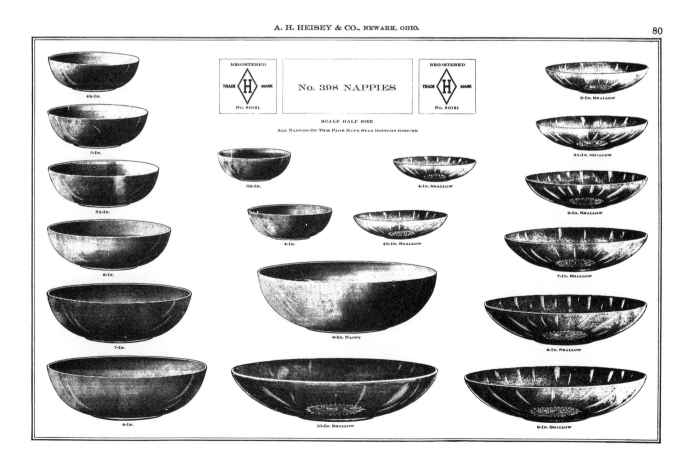

No. 398 NAPPIES

REGISTERED TRADE H MARK No. 50121

REGISTERED TRADE H MARK No. 50121

SCALE HALF SIZE
ALL NAPPIES ON THIS PAGE HAVE STAR BOTTOMS GROUND

4½-In.

5-In.

5½-In.

6-In.

7-In.

8-In.

3½-In.

4-In.

9-In. Nappy

10-In. Shallow

4-In. Shallow

4½-In. Shallow

5-In. Shallow

5½-In. Shallow

6-In. Shallow

7-In. Shallow

8-In. Shallow

9-In. Shallow

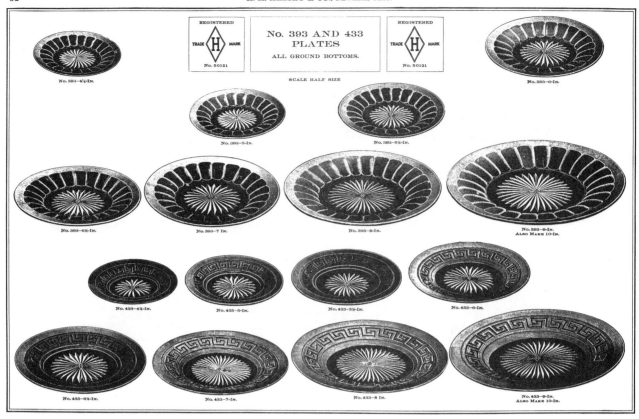

REGISTERED TRADE MARK No. 50121

No. 393 AND 433
PLATES
ALL GROUND BOTTOMS.

REGISTERED TRADE MARK No. 50121

SCALE HALF SIZE

No. 393—4½-In.

No. 393—6-In.

No. 393—5-In.

No. 393—5½-In.

No. 393—6½-In.

No. 393—7 In.

No. 393—8-In.

No. 393—9-In.
ALSO MAKE 10-In.

No. 433—4½-In.

No. 433—5-In.

No. 433—5½-In.

No. 433—6-In.

No. 433—6½-In.

No. 433—7-In.

No. 433—8 In.

No. 433—9-In.
ALSO MAKE 10-In.

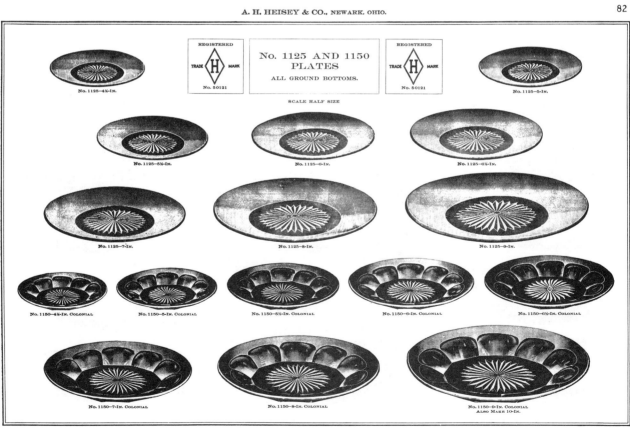

REGISTERED TRADE MARK No. 50121

No. 1125 AND 1150
PLATES
ALL GROUND BOTTOMS.

REGISTERED TRADE MARK No. 50121

SCALE HALF SIZE

No. 1125—4½-In.

No. 1125—5-In.

No. 1125—5½-In.

No. 1125—6-In.

No. 1125—6½-In.

No. 1125—7-In.

No. 1125—8-In.

No. 1125—9-In.

No. 1150—4½-In. COLONIAL

No. 1150—5-In. COLONIAL

No. 1150—5½-In. COLONIAL

No. 1150—6-In. COLONIAL

No. 1150—6½-In. COLONIAL

No. 1150—7-In. COLONIAL

No. 1150—8-In. COLONIAL

No. 1150—9-In. COLONIAL
ALSO MAKE 10-In.

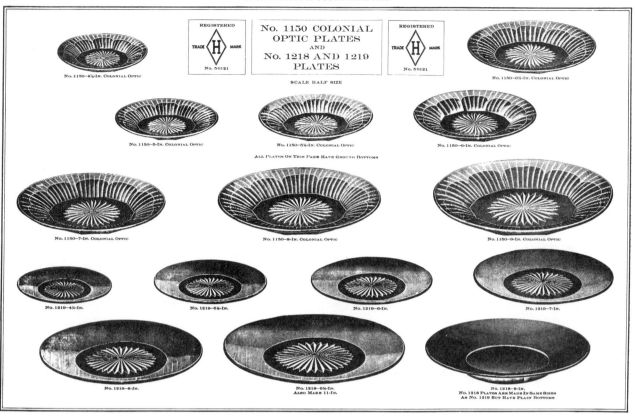

REGISTERED
TRADE **H** MARK
No. 50121

No. 1150 COLONIAL
OPTIC PLATES
AND
No. 1218 AND 1219
PLATES

REGISTERED
TRADE **H** MARK
No. 50121

SCALE HALF SIZE

No. 1150—4½-In. Colonial Optic

No. 1150—6½-In. Colonial Optic

No. 1150—5-In. Colonial Optic

No. 1150—5½-In. Colonial Optic

No. 1150—6-In. Colonial Optic

ALL PLATES ON THIS PAGE HAVE GROUND BOTTOMS

No. 1150—7-In. Colonial Optic

No. 1150—8-In. Colonial Optic

No. 1150—9-In. Colonial Optic

No. 1219—4½-In.

No. 1219—5½-In.

No. 1219—6-In.

No. 1219—7-In.

No. 1219—8-In.

No. 1219—9½-In.
Also Make 11-In.

No. 1218—8-In.
No. 1218 Plates Are Made In Same Sizes
As No. 1219 But Have Plain Bottoms

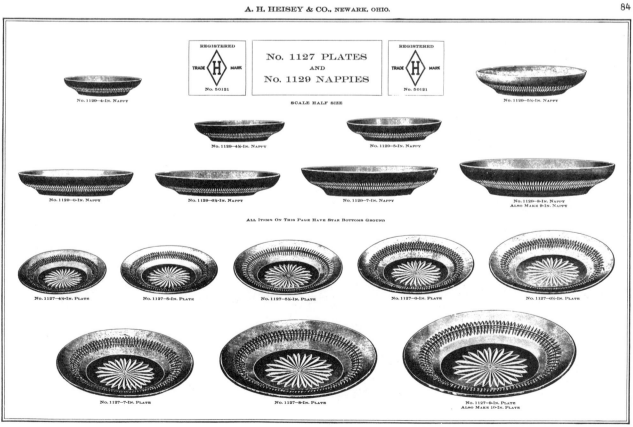

REGISTERED
TRADE **H** MARK
No. 50121

No. 1127 PLATES
AND
No. 1129 NAPPIES

REGISTERED
TRADE **H** MARK
No. 50121

No. 1129—4-In. Nappy

No. 1129—5½-In. Nappy

SCALE HALF SIZE

No. 1129—4½-In. Nappy

No. 1129—5-In. Nappy

No. 1129—6-In. Nappy

No. 1129—6½-In. Nappy

No. 1129—7-In. Nappy

No. 1129—8-In. Nappy
Also Make 9-In. Nappy

ALL ITEMS ON THIS PAGE HAVE STAR BOTTOMS GROUND

No. 1127—4½-In. Plate

No. 1127—5-In. Plate

No. 1127—5½-In. Plate

No. 1127—6-In. Plate

No. 1127—6½-In. Plate

No. 1127—7-In. Plate

No. 1127—8-In. Plate

No. 1127—9-In. Plate
Also Make 10-In. Plate

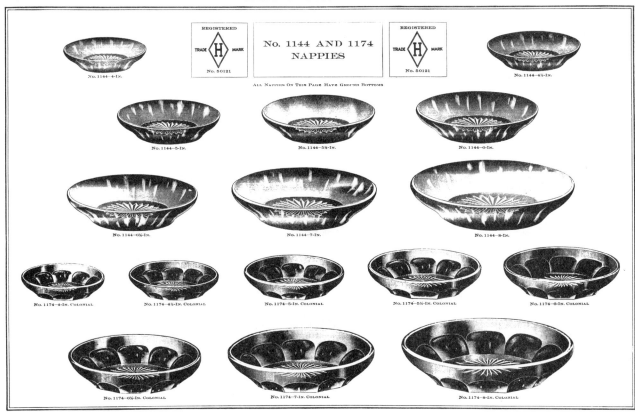

No. 1144 AND 1174 NAPPIES

REGISTERED TRADE H MARK No. 50121

REGISTERED TRADE H MARK No. 50121

All Nappies On This Page Have Ground Bottoms

No. 1144—4-In.

No. 1144—4½-In.

No. 1144—5-In.

No. 1144—5½-In.

No. 1144—6-In.

No. 1144—6½-In.

No. 1144—7-In.

No. 1144—8-In.

No. 1174—4-In. Colonial

No. 1174—4½-In. Colonial

No. 1174—5-In. Colonial

No. 1174—5½-In. Colonial

No. 1174—6-In. Colonial

No. 1174—6½-In. Colonial

No. 1174—7-In. Colonial

No. 1174—8-In. Colonial

WINE AND WHISKEY SETS

REGISTERED TRADE H MARK No. 50121

REGISTERED TRADE H MARK No. 50121

SCALE HALF SIZE

No. 333 Wine Set Consists Of
1 20 oz. Decanter
1 10-In. (352) Tray
6 1¾ oz. (353) Wines

No. 351 Wine Set

No. 351 Whiskey Set

No. 351 Wine Set Consists Of
1 Pint Decanter
1 12-In. (352) Tray Fire Polished
6 2 oz. Wines
Also Furnished With 1 Qt. Decanter

No. 351 Whiskey Set Consists Of
1 Pint Decanter
1 12-In. (352) Tray Fire Polished
6 2½ oz. (300½) Bars
Also Furnished With 1 Qt. Decanter

No. 333 Wine Set

A. H. HEISEY & CO., NEWARK, OHIO.

WATER SETS

SCALE HALF SIZE

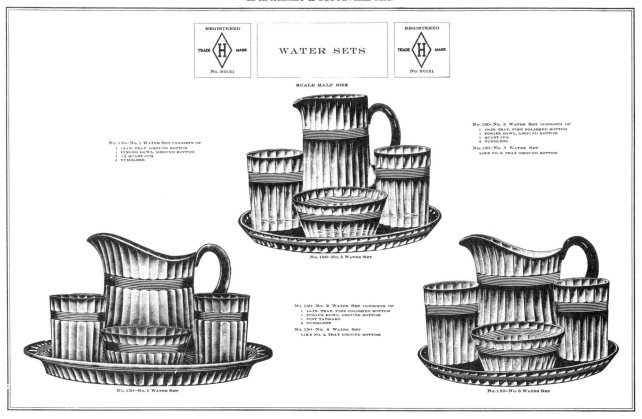

No. 150—No. 1 Water Set consists of
1 10-IN. TRAY, GROUND BOTTOM
1 FINGER BOWL, GROUND BOTTOM
1 1½ QUART JUG
2 TUMBLERS

No. 150—No. 3 Water Set consists of
1 10-IN. TRAY, FIRE POLISHED BOTTOM
1 FINGER BOWL, GROUND BOTTOM
1 QUART JUG
2 TUMBLERS

No. 150—No. 5 Water Set
LIKE NO. 3, TRAY GROUND BOTTOM

No. 150—No. 2 Water Set consists of
1 10-IN. TRAY, FIRE POLISHED BOTTOM
1 FINGER BOWL, GROUND BOTTOM
1 PINT TANKARD
2 TUMBLERS

No. 150—No. 4 Water Set
LIKE NO. 2, TRAY GROUND BOTTOM

No. 150—No. 2 Water Set

No. 150—No. 1 Water Set

No. 150—No. 3 Water Set

A. H. HEISEY & CO., NEWARK, OHIO.

COLONIAL
WATER SETS

SCALE HALF SIZE

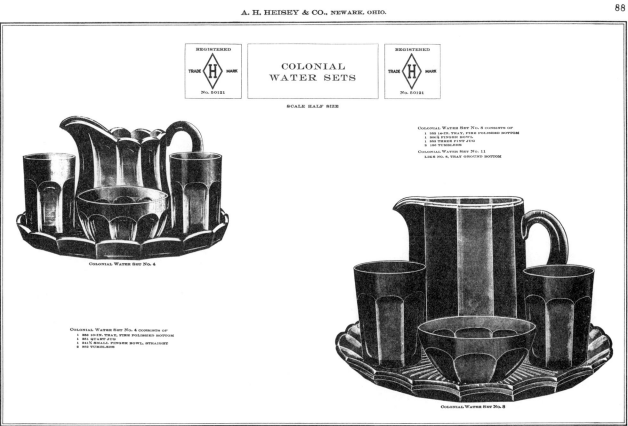

Colonial Water Set No. 8 consists of
1 352 14-IN. TRAY, FIRE POLISHED BOTTOM
1 300½ FINGER BOWL
1 353 THREE PINT JUG
2 150 TUMBLERS

Colonial Water Set No. 11
LIKE NO. 8, TRAY GROUND BOTTOM

Colonial Water Set No. 4

Colonial Water Set No. 4 consists of
1 352 10-IN. TRAY, FIRE POLISHED BOTTOM
1 351 QUART JUG
1 341½ SMALL FINGER BOWL, STRAIGHT
2 352 TUMBLERS

Colonial Water Set No. 8

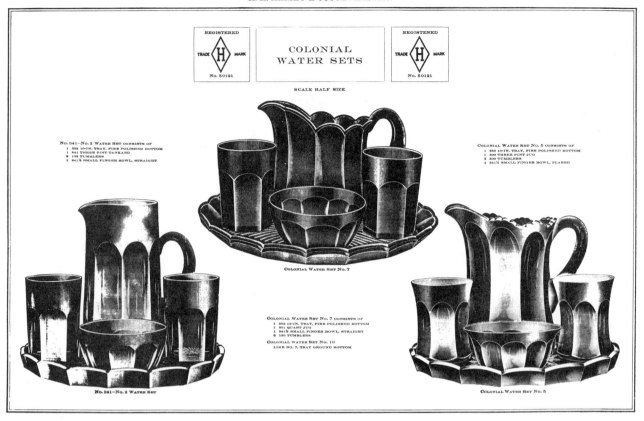

REGISTERED
TRADE **H** MARK
No. 50121

COLONIAL
WATER SETS

REGISTERED
TRADE **H** MARK
No. 50121

SCALE HALF SIZE

No. 341—No. 2 Water Set consists of
1   353 10-IN. TRAY, FIRE POLISHED BOTTOM
1   341 THREE PINT TANKARD
3   153 TUMBLERS
1   341½ SMALL FINGER BOWL, STRAIGHT

Colonial Water Set No. 5 consists of
1   353 10-IN. TRAY, FIRE POLISHED BOTTOM
1   300 THREE PINT JUG
3   300 TUMBLERS
1   341½ SMALL FINGER BOWL, FLARED

Colonial Water Set No. 7

Colonial Water Set No. 7 consists of
1   353 10-IN. TRAY, FIRE POLISHED BOTTOM
1   351 QUART JUG
1   341½ SMALL FINGER BOWL, STRAIGHT
3   130 TUMBLERS

Colonial Water Set No. 10
LIKE NO. 7, TRAY GROUND BOTTOM

No. 341—No. 2 Water Set

Colonial Water Set No. 5

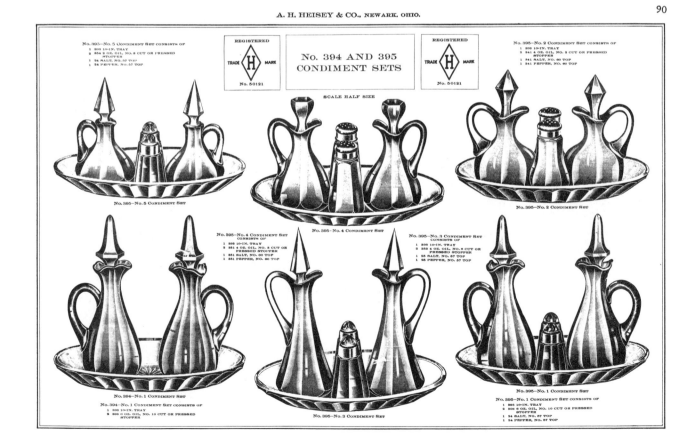

No. 395—No. 5 Condiment Set consists of
1   353 10-IN. TRAY
3   354 2 OZ. OIL, NO. 3 CUT OR PRESSED
       STOPPER
1   34 SALT, NO. 57 TOP
1   34 PEPPER, NO. 57 TOP

REGISTERED
TRADE **H** MARK
No. 50121

No. 394 AND 395
CONDIMENT SETS

REGISTERED
TRADE **H** MARK
No. 50121

No. 395—No. 2 Condiment Set consists of
1   353 10-IN. TRAY
3   341 4 OZ. OIL, NO. 3 CUT OR PRESSED
       STOPPER
1   341 SALT, NO. 60 TOP
1   341 PEPPER, NO. 60 TOP

SCALE HALF SIZE

No. 395—No. 5 Condiment Set

No. 395—No. 4 Condiment Set

No. 395—No. 2 Condiment Set

No. 395—No. 4 Condiment Set
CONSISTS OF
1   353 10-IN. TRAY
3   351 4 OZ. OIL, NO. 3 CUT OR
       PRESSED STOPPER
1   351 SALT, NO. 60 TOP
1   351 PEPPER, NO. 60 TOP

No. 395—No. 3 Condiment Set
CONSISTS OF
1   353 10-IN. TRAY
3   353 4 OZ. OIL, NO. 3 CUT OR
       PRESSED STOPPER
1   35 SALT, NO. 57 TOP
1   35 PEPPER, NO. 57 TOP

No. 394—No. 1 Condiment Set

No. 394—No. 1 Condiment Set consists of
1   353 10-IN. TRAY
3   353 8 OZ. OIL, NO. 10 CUT OR PRESSED
       STOPPER

No. 395—No. 3 Condiment Set

No. 395—No. 1 Condiment Set

No. 395—No. 1 Condiment Set consists of
1   353 10-IN. TRAY
3   353 8 OZ. OIL, NO. 10 CUT OR PRESSED
       STOPPER
1   34 SALT, NO. 57 TOP
1   34 PEPPER, NO. 57 TOP

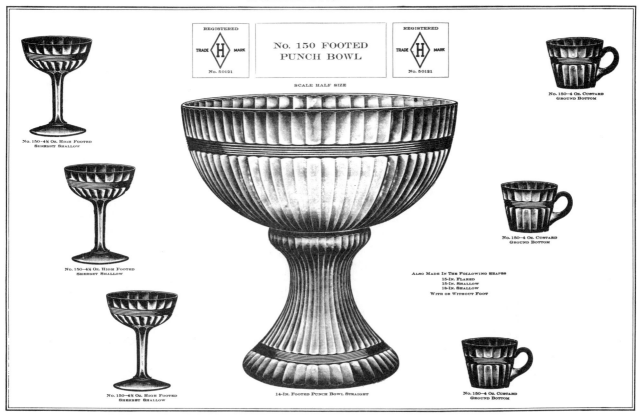

REGISTERED
TRADE H MARK
No. 50121

No. 150 FOOTED
PUNCH BOWL

REGISTERED
TRADE H MARK
No. 50121

SCALE HALF SIZE

No. 150—4½ Oz. HIGH FOOTED
SHERBET SHALLOW

No. 150—4½ Oz. HIGH FOOTED
SHERBET SHALLOW

No. 150—4½ Oz. HIGH FOOTED
SHERBET SHALLOW

14-IN. FOOTED PUNCH BOWL STRAIGHT

No. 150—4 Oz. CUSTARD
GROUND BOTTOM

No. 150—4 Oz. CUSTARD
GROUND BOTTOM

ALSO MADE IN THE FOLLOWING SHAPES
15-IN. FLARED
15-IN. SHALLOW
18-IN. SHALLOW
WITH OR WITHOUT FOOT

No. 150—4 Oz. CUSTARD
GROUND BOTTOM

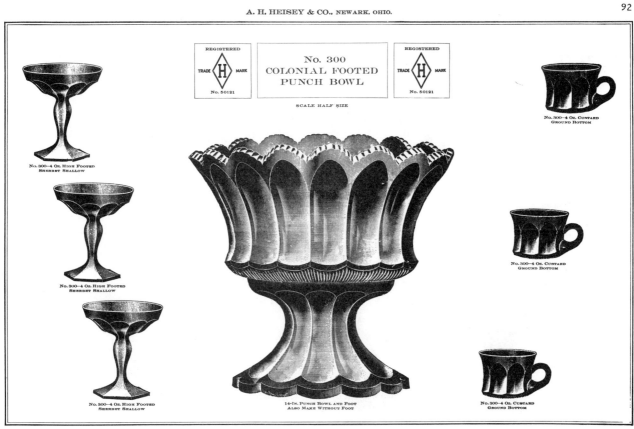

REGISTERED
TRADE H MARK
No. 50121

No. 300
COLONIAL FOOTED
PUNCH BOWL

REGISTERED
TRADE H MARK
No. 50121

SCALE HALF SIZE

No. 300—4 Oz. HIGH FOOTED
SHERBET SHALLOW

No. 300—4 Oz. HIGH FOOTED
SHERBET SHALLOW

No. 300—4 Oz. HIGH FOOTED
SHERBET SHALLOW

14-IN. PUNCH BOWL AND FOOT
ALSO MAKE WITHOUT FOOT

No. 300—4 Oz. CUSTARD
GROUND BOTTOM

No. 300—4 Oz. CUSTARD
GROUND BOTTOM

No. 300—4 Oz. CUSTARD
GROUND BOTTOM

No. 341—4½ Oz. High Footed
Sherbet Shallow

No. 341—4½ Oz. High Footed
Sherbet Shallow

No. 341—4½ Oz. High Footed
Sherbet Shallow

REGISTERED
TRADE H MARK
No. 50121

No. 341 COLONIAL
LOW FOOTED
PUNCH BOWL

REGISTERED
TRADE H MARK
No. 50121

SCALE HALF SIZE

Also Made In The Following Shapes
12-In. Cupped
14-In. Flared
10½-In. Shallow
With or Without Foot

No. 341—4½ Oz. Custard
Ground Bottom

No. 341—4½ Oz. Custard
Ground Bottom

13-In. Punch Bowl Straight and Low Foot

No. 341—4½ Oz. Custard
Ground Bottom

No. 341—4½ Oz. High Footed
Sherbet Shallow

No. 341—4½ Oz. High Footed
Sherbet Shallow

No. 341—4½ Oz. High Footed
Sherbet Shallow

REGISTERED
TRADE H MARK
No. 50121

No. 341 COLONIAL
HIGH FOOTED
PUNCH BOWL

REGISTERED
TRADE H MARK
No. 50121

SCALE HALF SIZE

13-In. Punch Bowl
Straight
and High Foot

Also Made In The Following Shapes
12-In. Cupped
14-In. Flared
10½-In. Shallow
With or Without Foot

No. 341—4½ Oz. Custard
Ground Bottom

No. 341—4½ Oz. Custard
Ground Bottom

No. 341—4½ Oz. Custard
Ground Bottom

REGISTERED
TRADE H MARK
No. 50121

No. 341½ COLONIAL
FOOTED
PUNCH BOWL

REGISTERED
TRADE H MARK
No. 50121

SCALE HALF SIZE

No. 341—4½ Oz.
LOW FOOTED SHERBET

No. 341—4½ Oz.
LOW FOOTED SHERBET

No. 341—4½ Oz.
LOW FOOTED SHERBET

No. 341—3 Oz. CUSTARD
GROUND BOTTOM

No. 341—3 Oz. CUSTARD
GROUND BOTTOM

No. 341—3 Oz. CUSTARD
GROUND BOTTOM

12-IN. PUNCH BOWL FLARED AND FOOT
10-IN. PUNCH BOWL
ALSO MAKE { 13-IN. PUNCH BOWL
13-IN. PUNCH BOWL SHALLOW
WITH OR WITHOUT FOOT

REGISTERED
TRADE H MARK
No. 50121

No. 343
FOOTED PUNCH BOWL

REGISTERED
TRADE H MARK
No. 50121

SCALE HALF SIZE

No. 343—4 Oz. CUSTARD
GROUND BOTTOM

No. 343—4 Oz. CUSTARD
GROUND BOTTOM

No. 343—4 Oz. CUSTARD
GROUND BOTTOM

No. 343—4 Oz. CUSTARD
GROUND BOTTOM

No. 343—4 Oz. CUSTARD
GROUND BOTTOM

No. 343—4 Oz. CUSTARD
GROUND BOTTOM

14-IN. PUNCH BOWL AND FOOT
ALSO MAKE WITHOUT FOOT

REGISTERED
TRADE H MARK
No. 50121

No. 350
FOOTED PUNCH BOWL

REGISTERED
TRADE H MARK
No. 50121

SCALE HALF SIZE

No. 350—4½ Oz. Custard
Ground Bottom

No. 350—4½ Oz. Custard
Ground Bottom

No. 350—4½ Oz. Custard
Ground Bottom

No. 350—4½ Oz. Custard
Ground Bottom

No. 350—4½ Oz. Custard
Ground Bottom

No. 350—4½ Oz. Custard
Ground Bottom

14-In. Punch Bowl and High Foot
Also Made Without Foot

REGISTERED
TRADE H MARK
No. 50121

No. 365
FOOTED PUNCH BOWL

REGISTERED
TRADE H MARK
No. 50121

SCALE HALF SIZE

No. 365—5 Oz. Custard
Ground Bottom

No. 365—5 Oz. Custard
Ground Bottom

No. 365—5 Oz. Custard
Ground Bottom

No. 365—5 Oz. Custard
Ground Bottom

No. 365—5 Oz. Custard
Ground Bottom

No. 365—5 Oz. Custard
Ground Bottom

15-In. Punch Bowl and Foot
Also Made 17-In. Flared
Both Shapes Also Made Without Foot

A. H. HEISEY & CO., NEWARK, OHIO.

REGISTERED
TRADE H MARK
No. 50121

No. 393
FOOTED PUNCH BOWL

REGISTERED
TRADE H MARK
No. 50121

SCALE HALF SIZE

No. 393—5 Oz. Footed
Sherbet Shallow

No. 393—5 Oz. Footed
Sherbet Shallow

No. 393—5 Oz. Footed
Sherbet Shallow

No. 393—4½ Oz. Custard
Ground Bottom

No. 393—4½ Oz. Custard
Ground Bottom

No. 393—4½ Oz. Custard
Ground Bottom

14-In. Punch Bowl and High Foot
Also Make 16-In. Flared and 18-In. Shallow Shapes
All Shapes Made With or Without Foot

A. H. HEISEY & CO., NEWARK, OHIO.

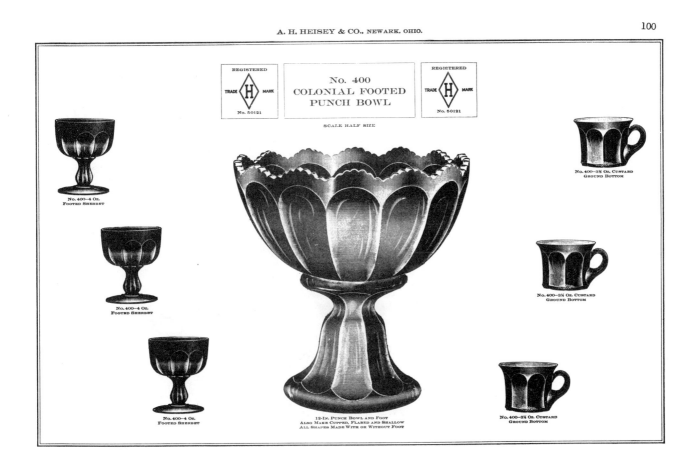

REGISTERED
TRADE H MARK
No. 50121

No. 400
COLONIAL FOOTED
PUNCH BOWL

REGISTERED
TRADE H MARK
No. 50121

SCALE HALF SIZE

No. 400—4 Oz.
Footed Sherbet

No. 400—4 Oz.
Footed Sherbet

No. 400—4 Oz.
Footed Sherbet

No. 400—3½ Oz. Custard
Ground Bottom

No. 400—3½ Oz. Custard
Ground Bottom

No. 400—3½ Oz. Custard
Ground Bottom

12-In. Punch Bowl and Foot
Also Make Cupped, Flared and Shallow
All Shapes Made With or Without Foot

REGISTERED
TRADE **H** MARK
No. 50121

No. 433
FOOTED PUNCH BOWL

REGISTERED
TRADE **H** MARK
No. 50121

SCALE HALF SIZE

No. 433—4½ Oz. High Footed
Sherbet Shallow

No. 433—4½ Oz. High Footed
Sherbet Shallow

No. 433—4½ Oz. High Footed
Sherbet Shallow

No. 433—4½ Oz. Custard
Ground Bottom

No. 433—4½ Oz. Custard
Ground Bottom

No. 433—4½ Oz. Custard
Ground Bottom

15-In. Punch Bowl and High Foot
Also Make 12-In. Cupped and 18-In. Shallow
All Shapes Made With or Without Foot

No. 300—Colonial Cream

No. 300—Colonial Sugar

REGISTERED
TRADE **H** MARK
No. 50121

INDIVIDUAL
CREAMS, SUGARS
AND BUTTERS

SCALE HALF SIZE

REGISTERED
TRADE **H** MARK
No. 50121

No. 352—Cream
Ground Bottom

No. 352—Sugar and Cover
Ground Bottom
Also Furnished Without Cover

No. 355—Cream
Ground Bottom
Patent No. 42752

No. 355—Sugar
Ground Bottom
Patent No. 42752

No. 393—Cream

No. 393—Sugar

No. 433—Oval Cream
Ground Bottom
Patent No. 41704

No. 433—Oval Sugar
Ground Bottom
Patent No. 41704

No. 351—Individual
Almond

No. 351—Butter
Ground Bottom

No. 433—Butter
Ground Bottom

No. 1181—Cream
Ground Bottom

No. 1181—Sugar
Ground Bottom

No. 1182—Cream
Ground Bottom

No. 393—Butter
Ground Bottom

No. 1184—Butter
Ground Bottom

No. 1183—Cream
Ground Bottom

No. 1183—Sugar
Ground Bottom

No. 1183½—Sugar and Cover
Ground Bottom

No. 1185—Cream
Ground Bottom

No. 1185—Sugar
Ground Bottom

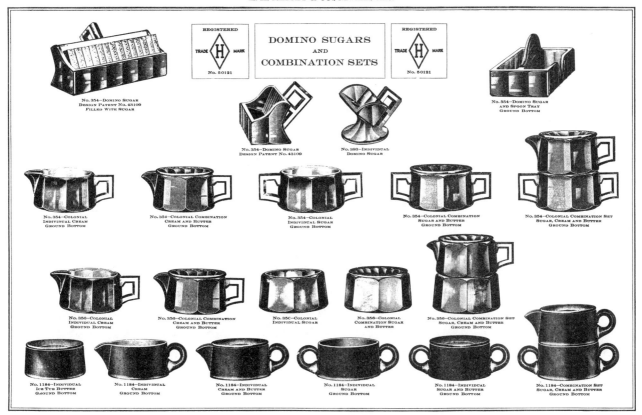

No. 354—DOMINO SUGAR
DESIGN PATENT NO. 43109
FILLED WITH SUGAR

REGISTERED
TRADE MARK
No. 50121

DOMINO SUGARS
AND
COMBINATION SETS

REGISTERED
TRADE MARK
No. 50121

No. 354—DOMINO SUGAR
AND SPOON TRAY
GROUND BOTTOM

No. 354—DOMINO SUGAR
DESIGN PATENT No. 43109

No. 393—INDIVIDUAL
DOMINO SUGAR

No. 354—COLONIAL
INDIVIDUAL CREAM
GROUND BOTTOM

No. 354—COLONIAL COMBINATION
CREAM AND BUTTER
GROUND BOTTOM

No. 354—COLONIAL
INDIVIDUAL SUGAR
GROUND BOTTOM

No. 354—COLONIAL COMBINATION
SUGAR AND BUTTER
GROUND BOTTOM

No. 354—COLONIAL COMBINATION SET
SUGAR, CREAM AND BUTTER
GROUND BOTTOM

No. 356—COLONIAL
INDIVIDUAL CREAM
GROUND BOTTOM

No. 356—COLONIAL COMBINATION
CREAM AND BUTTER
GROUND BOTTOM

No. 356—COLONIAL
INDIVIDUAL SUGAR

No. 356—COLONIAL
COMBINATION SUGAR
AND BUTTER

No. 356—COLONIAL COMBINATION SET
SUGAR, CREAM AND BUTTER
GROUND BOTTOM

No. 1184—INDIVIDUAL
ICE TUB BUTTER
GROUND BOTTOM

No. 1184—INDIVIDUAL
CREAM
GROUND BOTTOM

No. 1184—INDIVIDUAL
CREAM AND BUTTER
GROUND BOTTOM

No. 1184—INDIVIDUAL
SUGAR
GROUND BOTTOM

No. 1184—INDIVIDUAL
SUGAR AND BUTTER
GROUND BOTTOM

No. 1184—COMBINATION SET
SUGAR, CREAM AND BUTTER
GROUND BOTTOM

REGISTERED
TRADE MARK
No. 50121

HOTEL
CREAMS AND SUGARS

REGISTERED
TRADE MARK
No. 50121

SCALE HALF SIZE

No. 150—SUGAR AND COVER

No. 300½—COLONIAL SUGAR

No. 300½—COLONIAL CREAM
STUCK HANDLE

No. 150—CREAM

No. 300—COLONIAL SUGAR

No. 300—COLONIAL CREAM

No. 351—COLONIAL TAPER
SUGAR FLARED AND PLATE
GROUND BOTTOM
ALSO FURNISHED WITHOUT PLATE

No. 341—COLONIAL OVAL SUGAR
GROUND BOTTOM

No. 341—COLONIAL OVAL CREAM
GROUND BOTTOM

No. 350—SUGAR
GROUND BOTTOM

No. 350—CREAM
GROUND BOTTOM

No. 351—COLONIAL TAPER
CREAM FLARED AND PLATE
GROUND BOTTOM
ALSO FURNISHED WITHOUT PLATE

No. 351—COLONIAL SUGAR
CUT SHUT PONTIED NECK
GROUND BOTTOM

No. 351—COLONIAL CREAM
CUT SHUT
CUT TOP AND GROUND BOTTOM

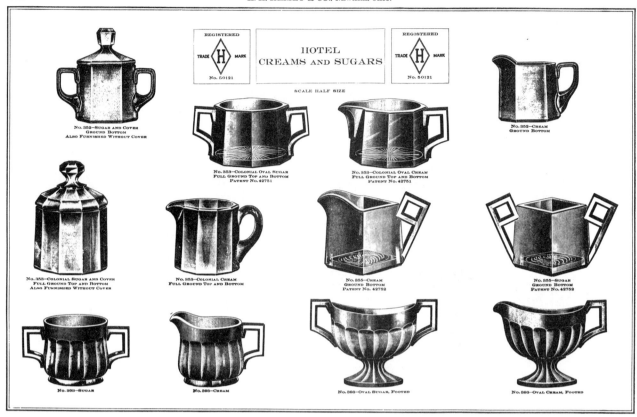

REGISTERED TRADE **H** MARK No. 50121

HOTEL
CREAMS AND SUGARS

REGISTERED TRADE **H** MARK No. 50121

SCALE HALF SIZE

No. 352—Sugar and Cover
Ground Bottom
Also Furnished Without Cover

No. 353—Colonial Oval Sugar
Full Ground Top and Bottom
Patent No. 42751

No. 353—Colonial Oval Cream
Full Ground Top and Bottom
Patent No. 42751

No. 352—Cream
Ground Bottom

No. 353—Colonial Sugar and Cover
Full Ground Top and Bottom
Also Furnished Without Cover

No. 353—Colonial Cream
Full Ground Top and Bottom

No. 355—Cream
Ground Bottom
Patent No. 42752

No. 355—Sugar
Ground Bottom
Patent No. 42752

No. 393—Sugar

No. 393—Cream

No. 393—Oval Sugar, Footed

No. 393—Oval Cream, Footed

REGISTERED TRADE **H** MARK No. 50121

HOTEL
CREAMS AND SUGARS

REGISTERED TRADE **H** MARK No. 50121

SCALE HALF SIZE

ALL ITEMS ON THIS PAGE HAVE GROUND BOTTOMS
EXCEPTING No. 400 CREAM AND SUGAR

No. 400—Colonial Cream

No. 400—Colonial Sugar

No. 429—Cream
Design Patent No. 40686

No. 429—Sugar and Cover
Design Patent No. 40686

No. 433—Round Cream

No. 433—Round Sugar

No. 433—Oval Cream
Design Patent No. 41764

No. 433—Oval Sugar
Design Patent No. 41764

No. 439—Cream
Design Patent No. 42260

No. 439—Sugar
Design Patent No. 42260

No. 1185—Cream

No. 1185—Sugar

A. H. HEISEY & CO., NEWARK. OHIO.

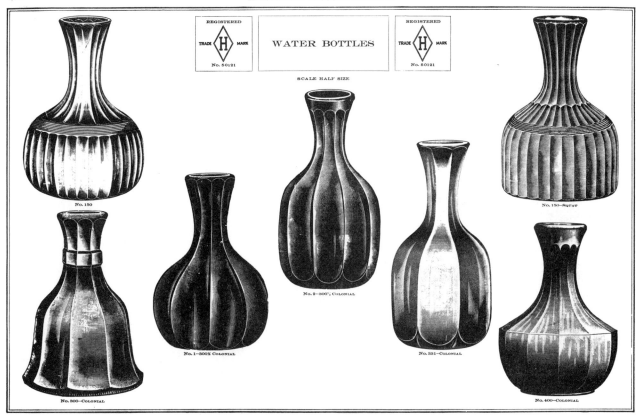

REGISTERED
TRADE **H** MARK
No. 50121

WATER BOTTLES

REGISTERED
TRADE **H** MARK
No. 50121

SCALE HALF SIZE

No. 150

No. 300—Colonial

No. 1—300½ Colonial

No. 2—300½ Colonial

No. 331—Colonial

No. 150—Squat

No. 400—Colonial

A. H. HEISEY & CO., NEWARK. OHIO.

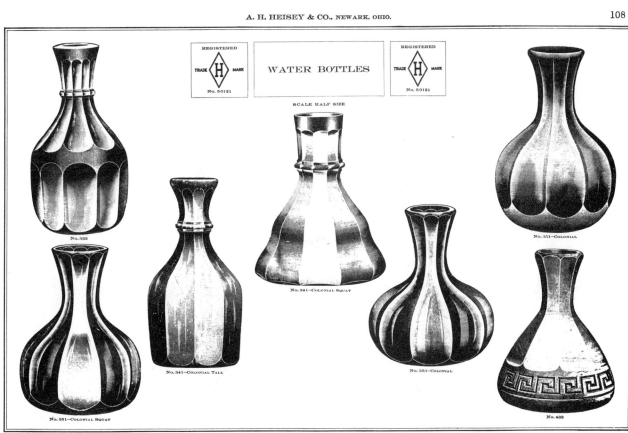

REGISTERED
TRADE **H** MARK
No. 50121

WATER BOTTLES

REGISTERED
TRADE **H** MARK
No. 50121

SCALE HALF SIZE

No. 333

No. 351—Colonial Squat

No. 341—Colonial Tall

No. 341—Colonial Squat

No. 353—Colonial

No. 351—Colonial

No. 433

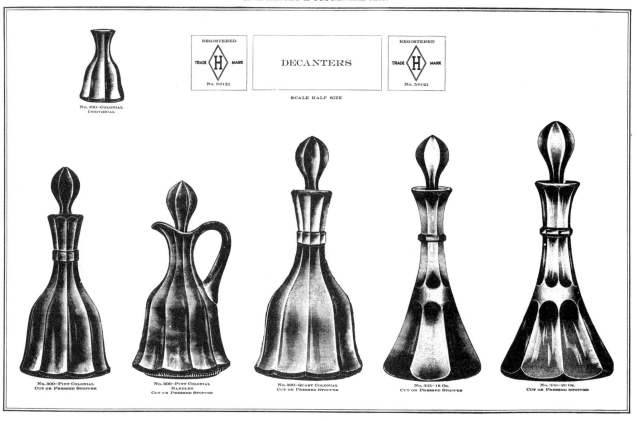

No. 300—Colonial
Individual

REGISTERED
TRADE H MARK
No. 50121

DECANTERS

REGISTERED
TRADE H MARK
No. 50121

SCALE HALF SIZE

No. 300—Pint Colonial
Cut or Pressed Stopper

No. 300—Pint Colonial
Handled
Cut or Pressed Stopper

No. 300—Quart Colonial
Cut or Pressed Stopper

No. 333—18 Oz.
Cut or Pressed Stopper

No. 333—20 Oz.
Cut or Pressed Stopper

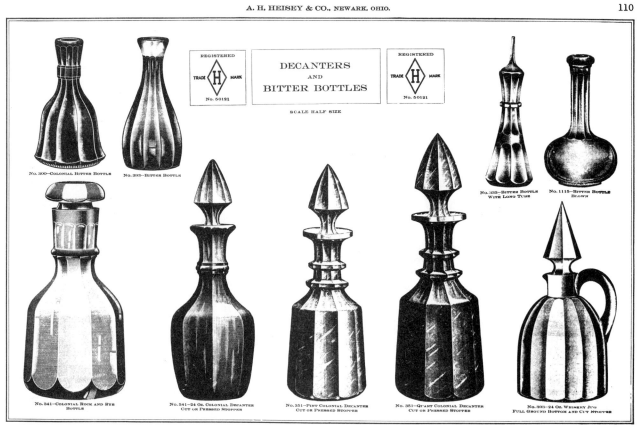

REGISTERED
TRADE H MARK
No. 50121

DECANTERS
AND
BITTER BOTTLES

REGISTERED
TRADE H MARK
No. 50121

SCALE HALF SIZE

No. 300—Colonial Bitter Bottle

No. 393—Bitter Bottle

No. 333—Bitter Bottle
With Long Tube

No. 1115—Bitter Bottle
Blown

No. 341—Colonial Rock and Rye
Bottle

No. 341—24 Oz. Colonial Decanter
Cut or Pressed Stopper

No. 351—Pint Colonial Decanter
Cut or Pressed Stopper

No. 351—Quart Colonial Decanter
Cut or Pressed Stopper

No. 393—24 Oz. Whiskey Jug
Full Ground Bottom and Cut Stopper

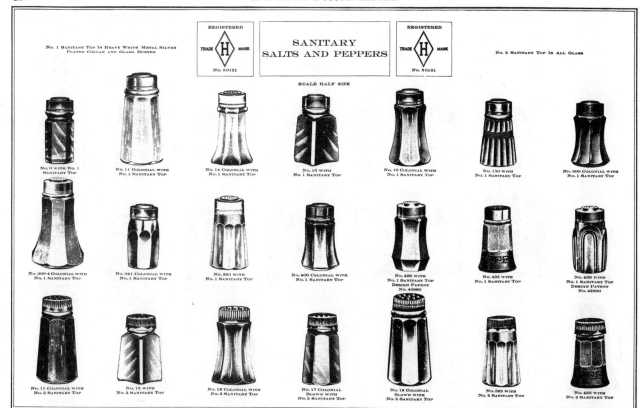

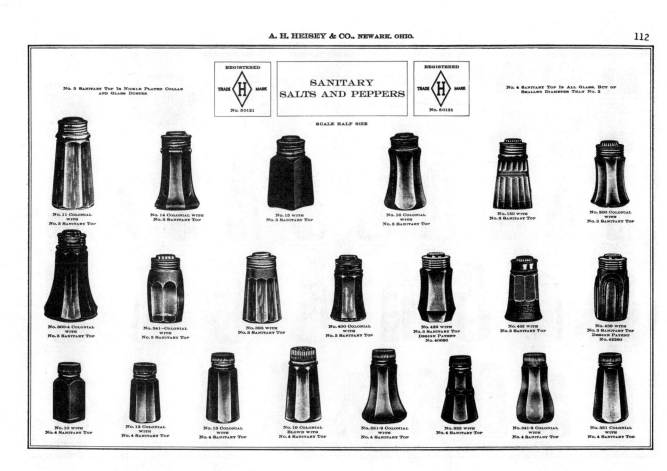

REGISTERED TRADE H MARK No. 50121

SALTS AND PEPPERS
WITH
METAL TOPS

REGISTERED TRADE H MARK No. 50121

NICKEL TOP IS OF SPUN NICKEL

No. 43 TOP IS WHITE METAL WITH HEAVY SILVER PLATED

SCALE HALF SIZE

No. 18 COLONIAL BLOWN WITH NICKEL TOP

No. 150 WITH NICKEL TOP

No. 300 COLONIAL WITH NICKEL TOP

No. 341 COLONIAL WITH NICKEL TOP

No. 400 COLONIAL WITH NICKEL TOP

No. 429 WITH NICKEL TOP DESIGN PATENT No. 40686

No. 433 WITH NICKEL TOP

No. 439 WITH NICKEL TOP DESIGN PATENT No. 42280

No. 9 WITH No. 43 TOP

No. 11 COLONIAL WITH No. 43 TOP

No. 14 COLONIAL WITH No. 43 TOP

No. 15 WITH No. 43 TOP

No. 16 COLONIAL WITH No. 43 TOP

No. 18 COLONIAL BLOWN SALT WITH No. 43 TOP

No. 150 WITH No. 43 TOP

No. 300 COLONIAL WITH No. 43 TOP

No. 300-4 COLONIAL WITH No. 43 TOP

No. 341 COLONIAL WITH No. 43 TOP

No. 393 WITH No. 43 TOP

No. 400 COLONIAL WITH No. 43 TOP

No. 429 WITH No. 43 TOP DESIGN PATENT No. 40686

No. 433 WITH No. 43 TOP

No. 439 WITH No. 43 TOP DESIGN PATENT No. 42260

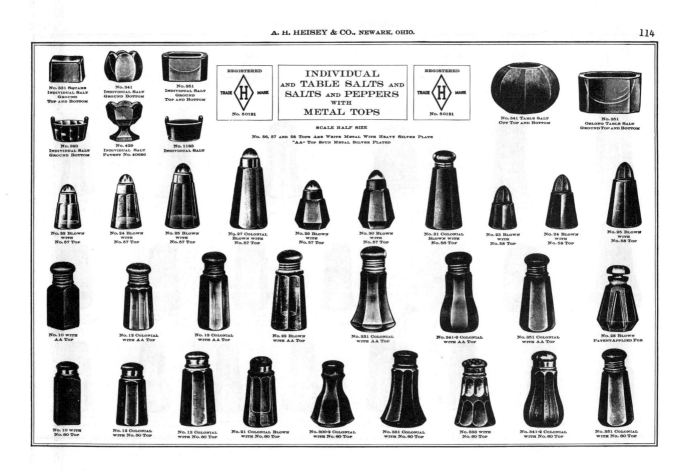

No. 331 SQUARE INDIVIDUAL SALT GROUND TOP AND BOTTOM

No. 341 INDIVIDUAL SALT GROUND BOTTOM

No. 351 INDIVIDUAL SALT GROUND TOP AND BOTTOM

REGISTERED TRADE H MARK No. 50121

INDIVIDUAL
AND TABLE SALTS AND
SALTS AND PEPPERS
WITH
METAL TOPS

REGISTERED TRADE H MARK No. 50121

No. 341 TABLE SALT CUT TOP AND BOTTOM

No. 351 OBLONG TABLE SALT GROUND TOP AND BOTTOM

No. 393 INDIVIDUAL SALT GROUND BOTTOM

No. 429 INDIVIDUAL SALT PATENT No. 40686

No. 1183 INDIVIDUAL SALT

SCALE HALF SIZE

No. 56, 57 AND 58 TOPS ARE WHITE METAL WITH HEAVY SILVER PLATE
"AA" TOP SPUN METAL SILVER PLATED

No. 23 BLOWN WITH No. 57 TOP

No. 24 BLOWN WITH No. 57 TOP

No. 25 BLOWN WITH No. 57 TOP

No. 27 COLONIAL BLOWN WITH No. 57 TOP

No. 29 BLOWN WITH No. 57 TOP

No. 30 BLOWN WITH No. 57 TOP

No. 31 COLONIAL BLOWN WITH No. 56 TOP

No. 23 BLOWN WITH No. 58 TOP

No. 24 BLOWN WITH No. 58 TOP

No. 25 BLOWN WITH No. 58 TOP

No. 10 WITH AA TOP

No. 12 COLONIAL WITH AA TOP

No. 13 COLONIAL WITH AA TOP

No. 22 BLOWN WITH AA TOP

No. 331 COLONIAL WITH AA TOP

No. 341-2 COLONIAL WITH AA TOP

No. 351 COLONIAL WITH AA TOP

No. 28 BLOWN PATENT APPLIED FOR

No. 10 WITH No. 60 TOP

No. 12 COLONIAL WITH No. 60 TOP

No. 13 COLONIAL WITH No. 60 TOP

No. 21 COLONIAL BLOWN WITH No. 60 TOP

No. 300-2 COLONIAL WITH No. 60 TOP

No. 331 COLONIAL WITH No. 60 TOP

No. 333 WITH No. 60 TOP

No. 341-2 COLONIAL WITH No. 60 TOP

No. 351 COLONIAL WITH No. 60 TOP

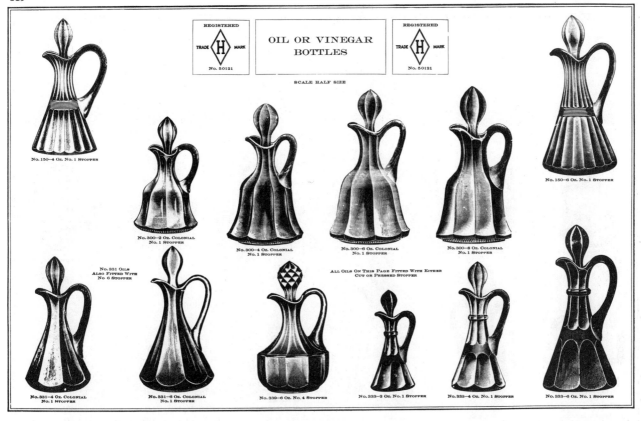

REGISTERED
TRADE H MARK
No. 50121

OIL OR VINEGAR BOTTLES

SCALE HALF SIZE

REGISTERED
TRADE H MARK
No. 50121

No. 150—4 Oz. No. 1 Stopper

No. 150—6 Oz. No. 1 Stopper

No. 300—2 Oz. Colonial No. 1 Stopper

No. 300—4 Oz. Colonial No. 1 Stopper

No. 300—6 Oz. Colonial No. 1 Stopper

No. 300—8 Oz. Colonial No. 1 Stopper

No. 331 Oils Also Fitted With No 6 Stopper

All Oils On This Page Fitted With Either Cut or Pressed Stopper

No. 331—4 Oz. Colonial No. 1 Stopper

No. 331—6 Oz. Colonial No. 1 Stopper

No. 339—6 Oz. No. 4 Stopper

No. 333—2 Oz. No. 1 Stopper

No. 333—4 Oz. No. 1 Stopper

No. 333—6 Oz. No. 1 Stopper

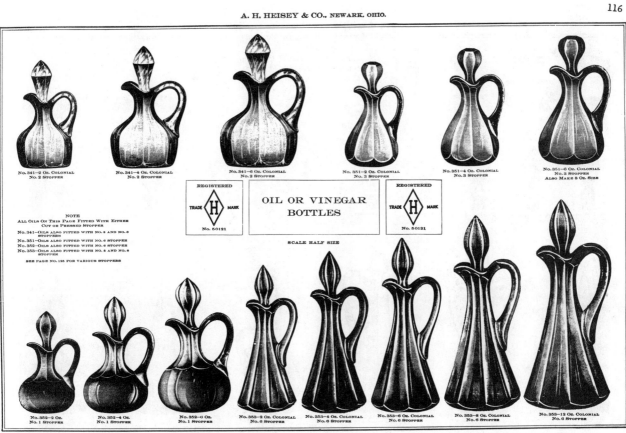

No. 341—2 Oz. Colonial No. 2 Stopper

No. 341—4 Oz. Colonial No. 2 Stopper

No. 341—6 Oz. Colonial No. 2 Stopper

No. 351—2 Oz. Colonial No. 3 Stopper

No. 351—4 Oz. Colonial No. 3 Stopper

No. 351—6 Oz. Colonial No. 3 Stopper Also Make 8 Oz. Size

NOTE
All Oils On This Page Fitted With Either Cut or Pressed Stopper
No. 341—Oils also fitted with No. 3 and No. 6 Stoppers
No. 351—Oils also fitted with No. 6 Stopper
No. 352—Oils also fitted with No. 6 Stopper
No. 353—Oils also fitted with No. 5 and No. 6 Stopper

SEE PAGE No. 135 FOR VARIOUS STOPPERS

REGISTERED
TRADE H MARK
No. 50121

OIL OR VINEGAR BOTTLES

REGISTERED
TRADE H MARK
No. 50121

SCALE HALF SIZE

No. 352—2 Oz. No. 1 Stopper

No. 352—4 Oz. No. 1 Stopper

No. 352—6 Oz. No. 1 Stopper

No. 353—2 Oz. Colonial No. 6 Stopper

No. 353—4 Oz. Colonial No. 6 Stopper

No. 353—6 Oz. Colonial No. 6 Stopper

No. 353—8 Oz. Colonial No. 6 Stopper

No. 353—12 Oz. Colonial No. 6 Stopper

No. 354 Oils Design Patent No. 42594

REGISTERED TRADE H MARK No. 50121

OIL OR VINEGAR
BOTTLES

REGISTERED TRADE H MARK No. 50121

All Oils On This Page Fitted With
Cut or Pressed Stoppers

SCALE HALF SIZE

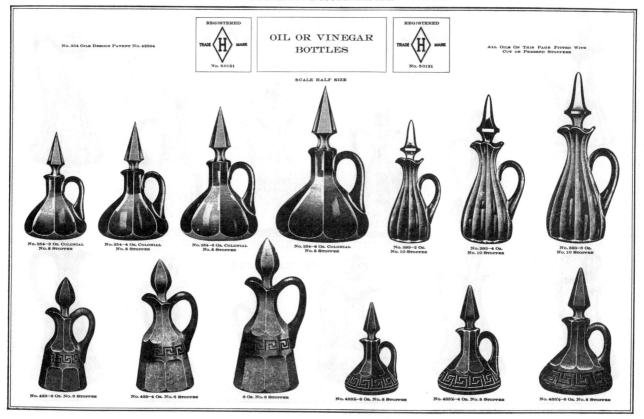

No. 354—2 Oz. Colonial
No. 8 Stopper

No. 354—4 Oz. Colonial
No. 8 Stopper

No. 354—6 Oz. Colonial
No. 8 Stopper

No. 354—8 Oz. Colonial
No. 8 Stopper

No. 393—2 Oz.
No. 10 Stopper

No. 393—4 Oz.
No. 10 Stopper

No. 393—6 Oz.
No. 10 Stopper

No. 433—2 Oz. No. 6 Stopper

No. 433—4 Oz. No. 6 Stopper

6 Oz. No. 6 Stopper

No. 433½—2 Oz. No. 8 Stopper

No. 433½—4 Oz. No. 8 Stopper

No. 433½—6 Oz. No. 8 Stopper

Nickel Top

Plated
Sugar Sifter Top

No. 43 Top

REGISTERED TRADE H MARK No. 50121

SALT TOPS AND OIL
STOPPERS AND
MISCELLANEOUS
OIL OR VINEGAR
BOTTLES

REGISTERED TRADE H MARK No. 50121

No. 1 Sanitary
Sugar Sifter Top

No. 60 Top

No. 57 Top

No. 58 Top

AA Top

SCALE HALF SIZE
ALL STOPPERS MADE EITHER CUT OR PRESSED

No. 1 Sanitary
Top

No. 3 Sanitary
Top

No. 2 Sanitary
Top

No. 4 Sanitary
Top

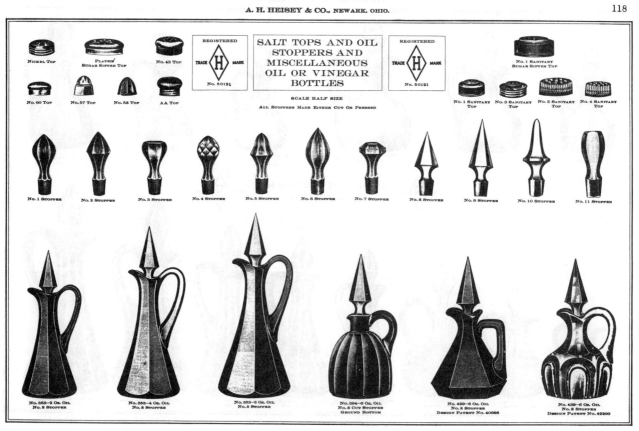

No. 1 Stopper

No. 2 Stopper

No. 3 Stopper

No. 4 Stopper

No. 5 Stopper

No. 6 Stopper

No. 7 Stopper

No. 8 Stopper

No. 9 Stopper

No. 10 Stopper

No. 11 Stopper

No. 353—2 Oz. Oil.
No. 8 Stopper

No. 353—4 Oz. Oil.
No. 8 Stopper

No. 353—6 Oz. Oil.
No. 8 Stopper

No. 394—6 Oz. Oil.
No. 8 Cut Stopper
Ground Bottom

No. 429—6 Oz. Oil.
No. 8 Stopper
Design Patent No. 40686

No. 439—6 Oz. Oil.
No. 8 Stopper
Design Patent No. 42290

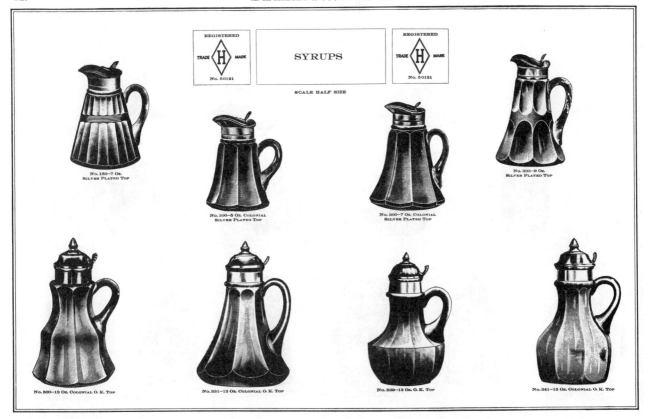

SYRUPS

REGISTERED
TRADE **H** MARK
No. 50121

REGISTERED
TRADE **H** MARK
No. 50121

SCALE HALF SIZE

No. 150—7 Oz.
SILVER PLATED TOP

No. 300—5 Oz. COLONIAL
SILVER PLATED TOP

No. 300—7 Oz. COLONIAL
SILVER PLATED TOP

No. 333—9 Oz.
SILVER PLATED TOP

No. 300—13 Oz. COLONIAL O. K. TOP

No. 331—13 Oz. COLONIAL O. K. TOP

No. 339—13 Oz. O. K. TOP

No. 341—13 Oz. COLONIAL O. K. TOP

SANITARY SYRUPS

REGISTERED
TRADE **H** MARK
No. 50121

REGISTERED
TRADE **H** MARK
No. 50121

SCALE HALF SIZE

No. 353—7 Oz. SANITARY SYRUP
WITH
No. 1150—5½-IN. PLATE, GROUND BOTTOM
PATENT NO. 40000

No. 357—7 Oz.
PATENT NO. 40001

No. 353—5 Oz.
PATENT NO. 40000

No. 359—12 Oz.
PATENT NO. 40001

No. 353—12 Oz. WITH TOP REMOVED
PATENT NO. 40000

THE TOPS CAN BE EASILY REMOVED FROM THESE SANITARY SYRUPS
FOR CLEANING, THUS INSURING AN ABSOLUTE SANITARY CONDITION

No. 355—24 Oz.
PATENT NO. 40000

No. 355—32 Oz.
PATENT NO. 40000

No. 355—32 Oz. CHOCOLATE POT
SHOWING REMOVABLE RUBBER SHOE
PATENT NO. 40000

No. 354—16 Oz.
PATENT NO. 40000

No. 354—12 Oz.
PATENT NO. 40000

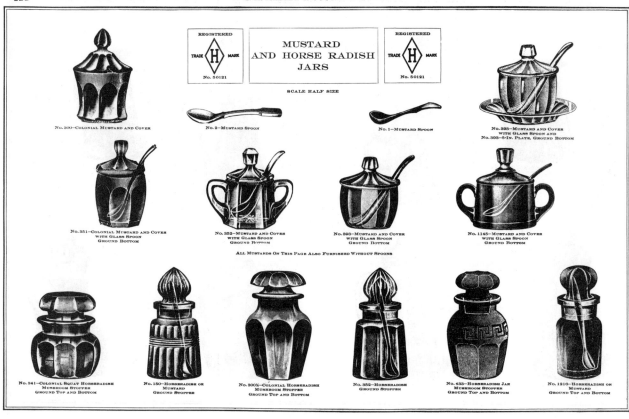

REGISTERED
TRADE **H** MARK
No. 50121

MUSTARD
AND HORSE RADISH
JARS

REGISTERED
TRADE **H** MARK
No. 50121

SCALE HALF SIZE

No. 300—Colonial Mustard and Cover

No. 2—Mustard Spoon

No. 1—Mustard Spoon

No. 393—Mustard and Cover
with Glass Spoon and
No. 393—5-In. Plate, Ground Bottom

No. 351—Colonial Mustard and Cover
with Glass Spoon
Ground Bottom

No. 352—Mustard and Cover
with Glass Spoon
Ground Bottom

No. 393—Mustard and Cover
with Glass Spoon
Ground Bottom

No. 1145—Mustard and Cover
with Glass Spoon
Ground Bottom

All Mustards On This Page Also Furnished Without Spoons

No. 341—Colonial Squat Horseradish
Mushroom Stopper
Ground Top and Bottom

No. 150—Horseradish or
Mustard
Ground Stopper

No. 300½—Colonial Horseradish
Mushroom Stopper
Ground Top and Bottom

No. 352—Horseradish
Ground Stopper

No. 433—Horseradish Jar
Mushroom Stopper
Ground Top and Bottom

No. 1216—Horseradish or
Mustard
Ground Top and Bottom

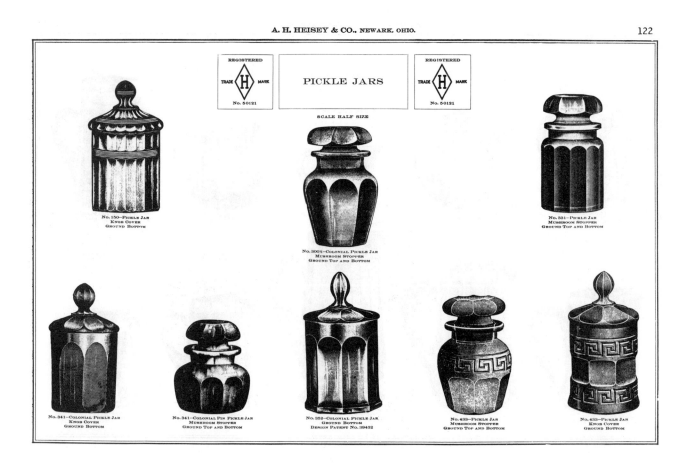

REGISTERED
TRADE **H** MARK
No. 50121

PICKLE JARS

REGISTERED
TRADE **H** MARK
No. 50121

SCALE HALF SIZE

No. 150—Pickle Jar
Knob Cover
Ground Bottom

No. 300½—Colonial Pickle Jar
Mushroom Stopper
Ground Top and Bottom

No. 331—Pickle Jar
Mushroom Stopper
Ground Top and Bottom

No. 341—Colonial Pickle Jar
Knob Cover
Ground Bottom

No. 341—Colonial Pin Pickle Jar
Mushroom Stopper
Ground Top and Bottom

No. 352—Colonial Pickle Jar
Ground Bottom
Design Patent No. 39432

No. 433—Pickle Jar
Mushroom Stopper
Ground Top and Bottom

No. 433—Pickle Jar
Knob Cover
Ground Bottom

A. H. HEISEY & CO., NEWARK, OHIO.

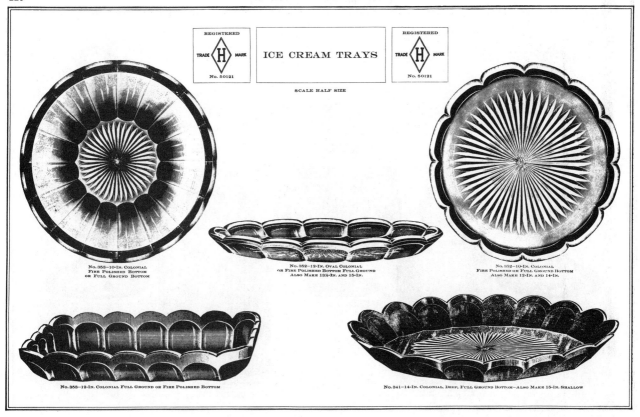

ICE CREAM TRAYS

SCALE HALF SIZE

No. 353—10-In. Colonial
Fire Polished Bottom
or Full Ground Bottom

No. 352—12-In. Oval Colonial
or Fire Polished Bottom Full Ground
Also Make 13½-In. and 15-In.

No. 352—10-In. Colonial
Fire Polished or Full Ground Bottom
Also Make 12-In. and 14-In.

No. 353—12-In. Colonial Full Ground or Fire Polished Bottom

No. 341—14-In. Colonial, Deep, Full Ground Bottom—Also Make 15-In. Shallow

---

A. H. HEISEY & CO., NEWARK, OHIO.

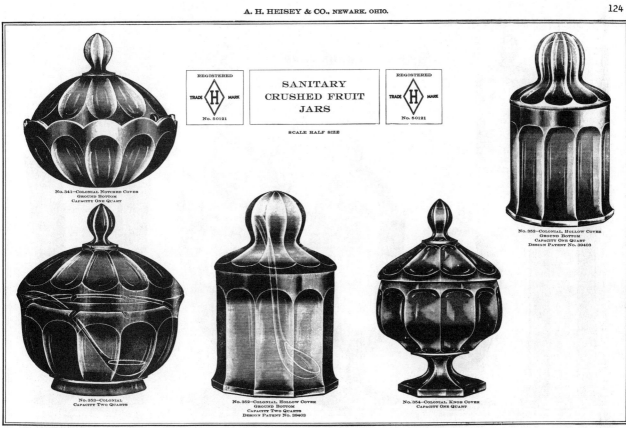

SANITARY
CRUSHED FRUIT
JARS

SCALE HALF SIZE

No. 341—Colonial Notched Cover
Ground Bottom
Capacity One Quart

No. 352—Colonial, Hollow Cover
Ground Bottom
Capacity One Quart
Design Patent No. 39403

No. 353—Colonial
Capacity Two Quarts

No. 352—Colonial, Hollow Cover
Ground Bottom
Capacity Two Quarts
Design Patent No. 39403

No. 354—Colonial, Knob Cover
Capacity One Quart

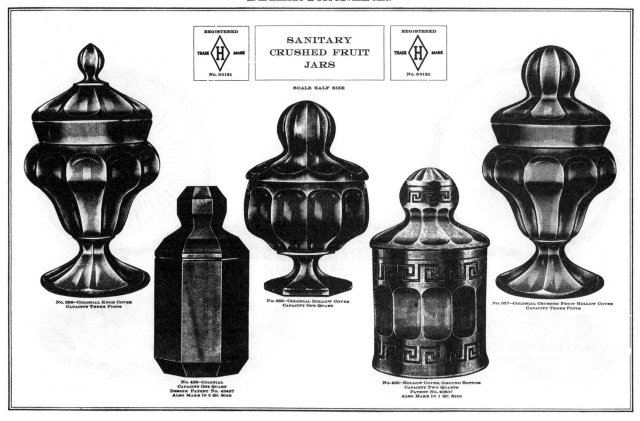

REGISTERED
TRADE **H** MARK
No. 50121

SANITARY
CRUSHED FRUIT
JARS

REGISTERED
TRADE **H** MARK
No. 50121

SCALE HALF SIZE

No. 356—Colonial Knob Cover
Capacity Three Pints

No. 429—Colonial
Capacity One Quart
Design Patent No. 43437
Also Made In 2 Qt. Size

No. 355—Colonial Hollow Cover
Capacity One Quart

No. 433—Hollow Cover, Ground Bottom
Capacity Two Quarts
Patent No. 40837
Also Made In 1 Qt. Size

No. 357—Colonial Crushed Fruit Hollow Cover
Capacity Three Pints

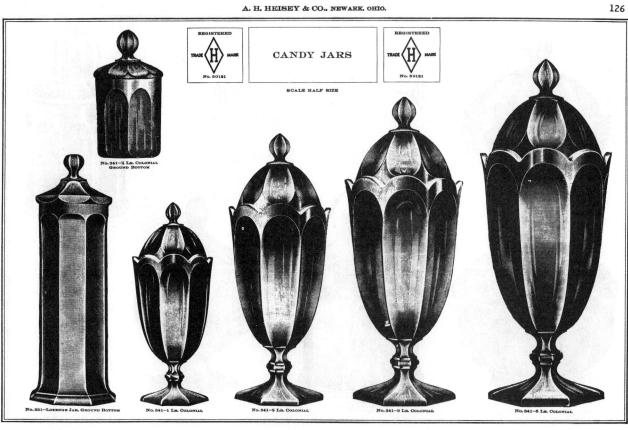

REGISTERED
TRADE **H** MARK
No. 50121

CANDY JARS

REGISTERED
TRADE **H** MARK
No. 50121

SCALE HALF SIZE

No. 341—½ Lb. Colonial
Ground Bottom

No. 331—Lozenge Jar, Ground Bottom

No. 341—1 Lb. Colonial

No. 341—2 Lb. Colonial

No. 341—3 Lb. Colonial

No. 341—5 Lb. Colonial

REGISTERED
TRADE H MARK
No. 50121

CANDY JARS

REGISTERED
TRADE H MARK
No. 50121

SCALE HALF SIZE

No. 352—½ Lb. Colonial
Ground Bottom
Design Patent No. 39432

No. 352—1 Lb. Colonial
Ground Bottom
Design Patent No. 39432

No. 352—2 Lb. Colonial
Ground Bottom
Design Patent No. 39432

No. 352—4 Lb. Colonial
Ground Bottom
Design Patent No. 39432

No. 433—4 Lb.
Ground Bottom
Patent No. 40837

No. 433—½ Lb.
Ground Bottom
Patent No. 40837

No. 433—1 Lb.
Ground Bottom
Patent No. 40837

No. 433—2 Lb.
Ground Bottom
Patent No. 40837

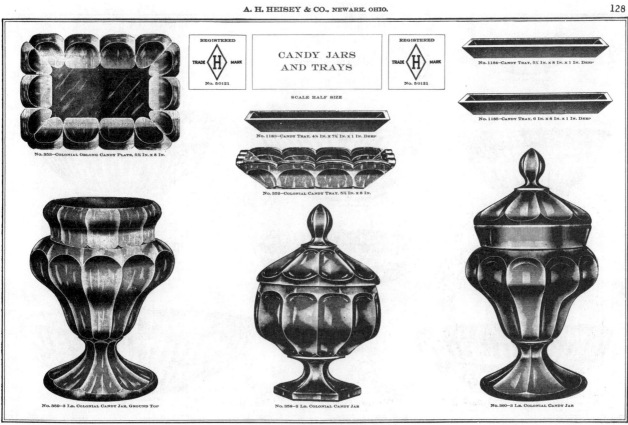

REGISTERED
TRADE H MARK
No. 50121

CANDY JARS
AND TRAYS

REGISTERED
TRADE H MARK
No. 50121

SCALE HALF SIZE

No. 353—Colonial Oblong Candy Plate, 5½ In. x 8 In.

No. 1183—Candy Tray, 4½ In. x 7½ In. x 1 In. Deep

No. 352—Colonial Candy Tray, 5½ In. x 8 In.

No. 1184—Candy Tray, 5½ In. x 8 In. x 1 In. Deep

No. 1185—Candy Tray, 6 In. x 8 In. x 1 In. Deep

No. 359—3 Lb. Colonial Candy Jar, Ground Top

No. 358—2 Lb. Colonial Candy Jar

No. 360—3 Lb. Colonial Candy Jar

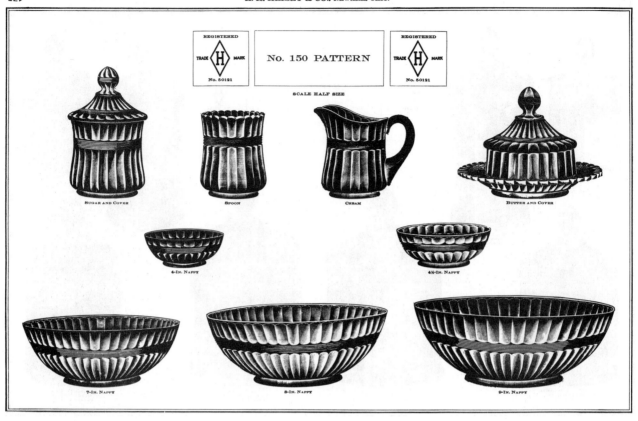

REGISTERED TRADE MARK No. 50121

No. 150 PATTERN

REGISTERED TRADE MARK No. 50121

SCALE HALF SIZE

SUGAR AND COVER

SPOON

CREAM

BUTTER AND COVER

4-IN. NAPPY

4½-IN. NAPPY

7-IN. NAPPY

8-IN. NAPPY

9-IN. NAPPY

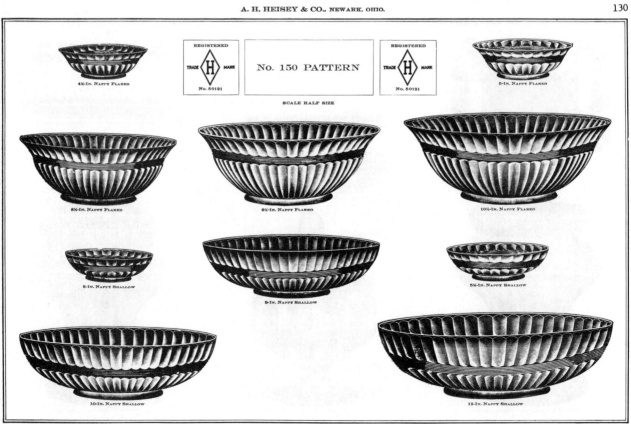

4½-IN. NAPPY FLARED

REGISTERED TRADE MARK No. 50121

No. 150 PATTERN

REGISTERED TRADE MARK No. 50121

5-IN. NAPPY FLARED

SCALE HALF SIZE

8½-IN. NAPPY FLARED

9½-IN. NAPPY FLARED

10½-IN. NAPPY FLARED

5-IN. NAPPY SHALLOW

9-IN. NAPPY SHALLOW

5½-IN. NAPPY SHALLOW

10-IN. NAPPY SHALLOW

12-IN. NAPPY SHALLOW

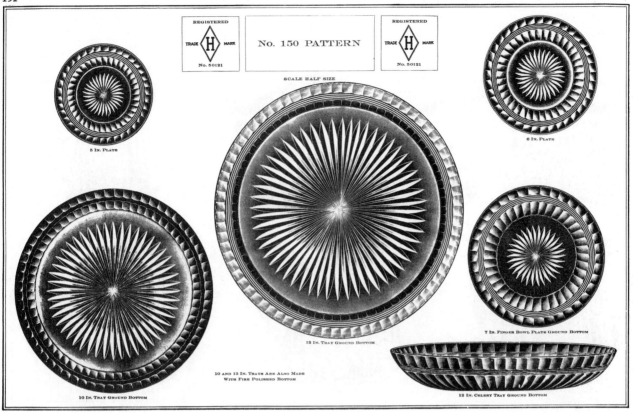

No. 150 PATTERN

SCALE HALF SIZE

5 IN. PLATE

6 IN. PLATE

13 IN. TRAY GROUND BOTTOM

7 IN. FINGER BOWL PLATE GROUND BOTTOM

10 AND 13 IN. TRAYS ARE ALSO MADE
WITH FIRE POLISHED BOTTOM

10 IN. TRAY GROUND BOTTOM

12 IN. CELERY TRAY GROUND BOTTOM

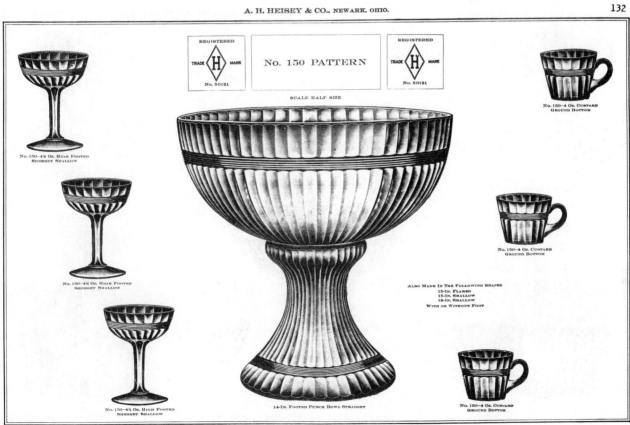

No. 150 PATTERN

SCALE HALF SIZE

No. 150—4 OZ. CUSTARD
GROUND BOTTOM

No. 150—4½ OZ. HIGH FOOTED
SHERBET SHALLOW

No. 150—4½ OZ. HIGH FOOTED
SHERBET SHALLOW

No. 150—4 OZ. CUSTARD
GROUND BOTTOM

ALSO MADE IN THE FOLLOWING SHAPES
15-IN. FLARED
15-IN. SHALLOW
18-IN. SHALLOW
WITH OR WITHOUT FOOT

No. 150—4½ OZ. HIGH FOOTED
SHERBET SHALLOW

14-IN. FOOTED PUNCH BOWL STRAIGHT

No. 150—4 OZ. CUSTARD
GROUND BOTTOM

REGISTERED
TRADE **H** MARK
No. 50121

No. 150 JUGS
STUCK HANDLES

REGISTERED
TRADE **H** MARK
No. 50121

SCALE HALF SIZE

PINT
ALSO MAKE ½ PINT SIZE

1½ PINT

QUART

1½ QUART

3 PINT

½ GALLON

3 QUART

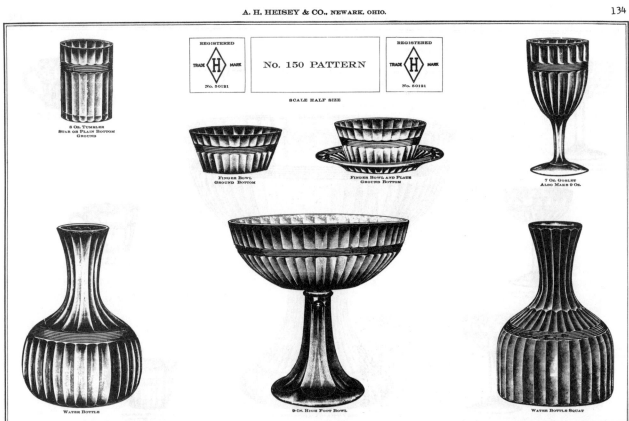

8 OZ. TUMBLER
STAR OR PLAIN BOTTOM
GROUND

REGISTERED
TRADE **H** MARK
No. 50121

No. 150 PATTERN

REGISTERED
TRADE **H** MARK
No. 50121

SCALE HALF SIZE

FINGER BOWL
GROUND BOTTOM

FINGER BOWL AND PLATE
GROUND BOTTOM

7 OZ. GOBLET
ALSO MAKE 9 OZ.

WATER BOTTLE

9-IN. HIGH FOOT BOWL

WATER BOTTLE SQUAT

A. H. HEISEY & CO., NEWARK, OHIO.

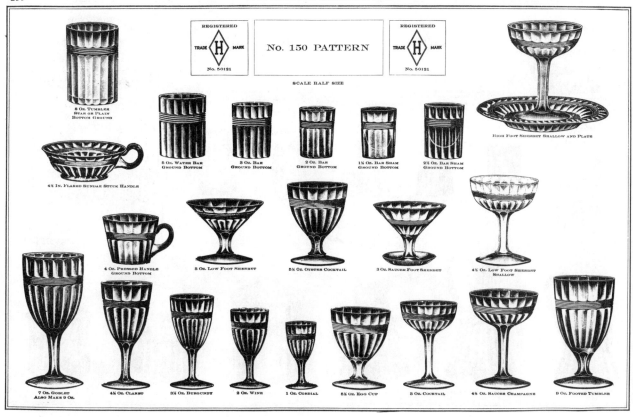

| REGISTERED TRADE **H** MARK No. 50121 | No. 150 PATTERN | REGISTERED TRADE **H** MARK No. 50121 |

SCALE HALF SIZE

8 OZ. TUMBLER STAR OR PLAIN BOTTOM GROUND

5 OZ. WATER BAR GROUND BOTTOM

3 OZ. BAR GROUND BOTTOM

2 OZ. BAR GROUND BOTTOM

1½ OZ. BAR SHAM GROUND BOTTOM

2½ OZ. BAR SHAM GROUND BOTTOM

HIGH FOOT SHERBET SHALLOW AND PLATE

4½ IN. FLARED SUNDAE STUCK HANDLE

4 OZ. PRESSED HANDLE GROUND BOTTOM

3 OZ. LOW FOOT SHERBET

5½ OZ. OYSTER COCKTAIL

3 OZ. SAUCER FOOT SHERBET

4½ OZ. LOW FOOT SHERBET SHALLOW

7 OZ. GOBLET ALSO MAKE 9 OZ.

4½ OZ. CLARET

3½ OZ. BURGUNDY

2 OZ. WINE

1 OZ. CORDIAL

5½ OZ. EGG CUP

3 OZ. COCKTAIL

4½ OZ. SAUCER CHAMPAGNE

9 OZ. FOOTED TUMBLER

A. H. HEISEY & CO., NEWARK, OHIO.

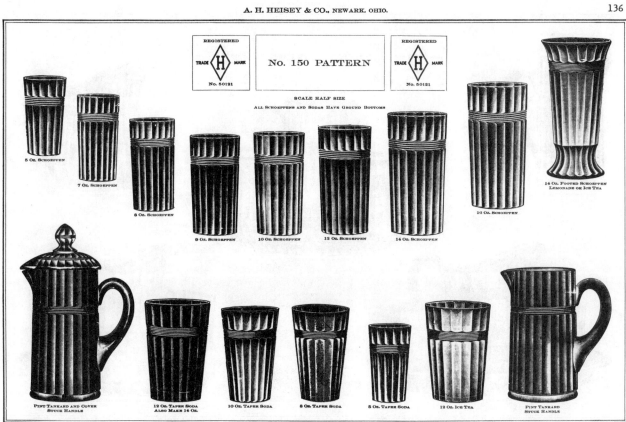

| REGISTERED TRADE **H** MARK No. 50121 | No. 150 PATTERN | REGISTERED TRADE **H** MARK No. 50121 |

SCALE HALF SIZE

ALL SCHOEPPENS AND SODAS HAVE GROUND BOTTOMS

5 OZ. SCHOEPPEN

7 OZ. SCHOEPPEN

8 OZ. SCHOEPPEN

9 OZ. SCHOEPPEN

10 OZ. SCHOEPPEN

12 OZ. SCHOEPPEN

14 OZ. SCHOEPPEN

16 OZ. SCHOEPPEN

14 OZ. FOOTED SCHOEPPEN LEMONADE OR ICE TEA

PINT TANKARD AND COVER STUCK HANDLE

12 OZ. TAPER SODA ALSO MAKE 14 OZ.

10 OZ. TAPER SODA

8 OZ. TAPER SODA

5 OZ. TAPER SODA

12 OZ. ICE TEA

PINT TANKARD STUCK HANDLE

**2-PIECE OYSTER COCKTAIL
GROUND BOTTOMS**

REGISTERED TRADE **H** MARK No. 50121

No. 150 PATTERN

REGISTERED TRADE **H** MARK No. 50121

SCALE HALF SIZE

NO. 1 SANITARY TOP IS HEAVY WHITE METAL SILVER PLATED COLLAR AND GLASS DUSTER

NO. 3 SANITARY TOP IS NICKEL PLATED COLLAR AND GLASS DUSTER

NO. 43 TOP IS WHITE METAL WITH HEAVY SILVER PLATE "NT" TOP IS OF SPUN NICKEL

**3-PIECE OYSTER COCKTAIL
GROUND BOTTOMS**

**HORSERADISH OR MUSTARD JAR
GROUND-IN STOPPER**

**TOOTHPICK
GROUND BOTTOM**

**SALT OR PEPPER WITH
NO. 1 SANITARY TOP**

**SALT OR PEPPER WITH
NO. 3 SANITARY TOP**

**SALT OR PEPPER
WITH NO. 43 TOP**

**SALT OR PEPPER
WITH NT TOP**

**SUGAR SIFTER
NO. 1 SANITARY TOP**

**SUGAR SIFTER
SILVER PLATED TOP**

NO. 1 MUSTARD SPOON

**4 OZ. OIL
PRESSED OR CUT STOPPER**

**6 OZ. OIL
PRESSED OR CUT STOPPER**

**7 OZ. SYRUP
SILVER PLATED TOP**

**PICKLE JAR KNOB COVER
GROUND BOTTOM**

HOTEL CREAM

HOTEL SUGAR

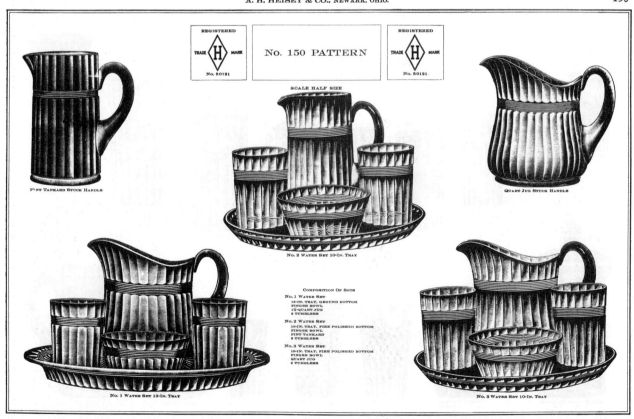

REGISTERED TRADE **H** MARK No. 50121

No. 150 PATTERN

REGISTERED TRADE **H** MARK No. 50121.

SCALE HALF SIZE

PINT TANKARD STUCK HANDLE

QUART JUG STUCK HANDLE

NO. 2 WATER SET 10-IN. TRAY

COMPOSITION OF SETS

NO. 1 WATER SET
13-IN. TRAY, GROUND BOTTOM
FINGER BOWL
1½-QUART JUG
2 TUMBLERS

NO. 2 WATER SET
10-IN. TRAY, FIRE POLISHED BOTTOM
FINGER BOWL
PINT TANKARD
2 TUMBLERS

NO. 3 WATER SET
10-IN. TRAY, FIRE POLISHED BOTTOM
FINGER BOWL
QUART JUG
2 TUMBLERS

NO. 1 WATER SET 13-IN. TRAY

NO. 3 WATER SET 10-IN. TRAY

REGISTERED TRADE **H** MARK No. 50121

No. 150 PATTERN

REGISTERED TRADE **H** MARK No. 50121

SCALE HALF SIZE

HANDLED CANDLESTICK

MATCH BOX STAND

SAUCER FOOT CANDLESTICK

MATCH BOX AND COVER

No. 1 BED ROOM SET

No. 2 BED ROOM SET

No. 3 BED ROOM SET

COMPOSITION OF SETS

No. 1 BED ROOM SET
13-IN. TRAY, GROUND BOTTOM
HDL. CANDLESTICK
1¼-QUART JUG
TUMBLER

No. 2 BED ROOM SET
10-IN. TRAY, FIRE POLISHED BOTTOM
PINT TANKARD AND COVER
TUMBLER
MATCH BOX AND COVER
SAUCER FOOT CANDLESTICK

No. 3 BED ROOM SET
10-IN. TRAY, FIRE POLISHED BOTTOM
PINT TANKARD AND COVER
TUMBLER
MATCH STAND
SAUCER FOOT CANDLESTICK

5-IN. PLATE

REGISTERED TRADE **H** MARK No. 50121

No. 300 COLONIAL PATTERN

REGISTERED TRADE **H** MARK No. 50121

6-IN. PLATE

SCALE HALF SIZE

4-IN. NAPPY

4½-IN. NAPPY

4½-IN. NAPPY SHALLOW

5-IN. NAPPY SHALLOW

8-IN. BERRY NAPPY

9-IN. BERRY NAPPY

8½-IN. BERRY NAPPY FLARED

9½-IN. BERRY NAPPY FLARED

9-IN. BERRY NAPPY SHALLOW

10-IN. BERRY NAPPY SHALLOW

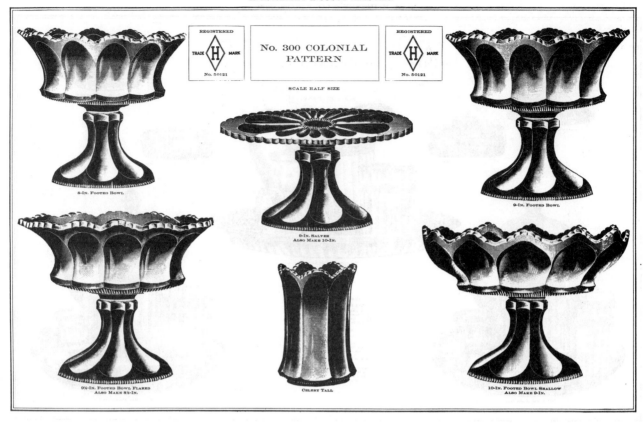

REGISTERED TRADE MARK No. 50121

No. 300 COLONIAL
PATTERN

REGISTERED TRADE MARK No. 50121

SCALE HALF SIZE

8-In. Footed Bowl

9-In. Salver
Also Make 10-In.

9-In. Footed Bowl

9½-In. Footed Bowl Flared
Also Make 8½-In.

Celery Tall

10-In. Footed Bowl Shallow
Also Make 9-In.

REGISTERED TRADE MARK No. 50121

No. 300
COLONIAL FOOTED
PUNCH BOWL

REGISTERED TRADE MARK No. 50121

SCALE HALF SIZE

No. 300—4 Oz. High Footed
Sherbet Shallow

No. 300—4 Oz. Custard
Ground Bottom

No. 300—4 Oz. High Footed
Sherbet Shallow

No. 300—4 Oz. Custard
Ground Bottom

No. 300—4 Oz. High Footed
Sherbet Shallow

14-In. Punch Bowl and Foot
Also Make Without Foot

No. 300—4 Oz. Custard
Ground Bottom

REGISTERED TRADE H MARK No. 50121

No. 300 COLONIAL PATTERN

REGISTERED TRADE H MARK No. 50121

SCALE HALF SIZE

7 OZ. TUMBLER
STAR OR PLAIN BOTTOM GROUND

8 OZ. TUMBLER
PLAIN BOTTOM GROUND

8½ OZ. TUMBLER
STAR BOTTOM GROUND

12 OZ. ICE TEA TUMBLER
STAR BOTTOM GROUND

QUART JUG

THREE PINT JUG

HALF GALLON JUG

THREE QUART JUG

REGISTERED TRADE H MARK No. 50121

No. 300 COLONIAL PATTERN

REGISTERED TRADE H MARK No. 50121

SCALE HALF SIZE

4½ OZ. LOW FOOTED
SHERBET SHALLOW

4¼ OZ. SAUCER FOOTED
SHERBET SHALLOW

6 OZ. LOW FOOTED
SHERBET SHALLOW

6 OZ. SAUCER FOOTED
SHERBET SHALLOW

1¼ OZ. SHERRY

2 OZ. COCKTAIL

4 OZ. SAUCER CHAMPAGNE
ALSO HIGH FOOT
SHERBET SHALLOW

4½ OZ. HIGH FOOTED
SHERBET SCALLOPED

5 OZ. FOOTED EGG
ALSO 5 OZ. LOW FOOT
SHERBET DEEP

7 OZ. FOOTED TUMBLER
OR LOW FOOTED GOBLET

3½ OZ. TALL CHAMPAGNE
OR PARFAIT FLARED

3½ OZ. TALL CHAMPAGNE
OR PARFAIT

10 OZ. GOBLET

9 OZ. GOBLET

7 OZ. GOBLET

6 OZ. CHAMPAGNE

4½ OZ. CLARET

3½ OZ. BURGUNDY

2½ OZ. WINE

1½ OZ. WINE

1 OZ. CORDIAL
ALSO MAKE ¾ OZ.
SHAM

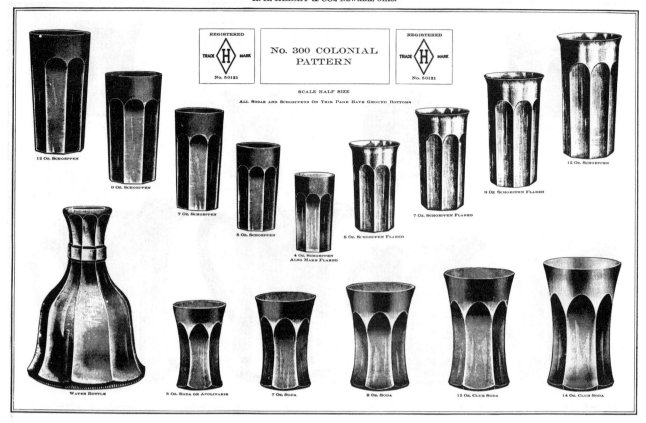

REGISTERED
TRADE **H** MARK
No. 50121

No. 300 COLONIAL PATTERN

REGISTERED
TRADE **H** MARK
No. 50121

SCALE HALF SIZE

ALL SODAS AND SCHOEPPENS ON THIS PAGE HAVE GROUND BOTTOMS

12 OZ. SCHOEPPEN

9 OZ. SCHOEPPEN

7 OZ. SCHOEPPEN

5 OZ. SCHOEPPEN

4 OZ. SCHOEPPEN
ALSO MAKE FLARED

5 OZ. SCHOEPPEN FLARED

7 OZ. SCHOEPPEN FLARED

9 OZ. SCHOEPPEN FLARED

12 OZ. SCHOEPPEN

WATER BOTTLE

5 OZ. SODA OR APOLINARIS

7 OZ. SODA

9 OZ. SODA

12 OZ. CLUB SODA

14 OZ. CLUB SODA

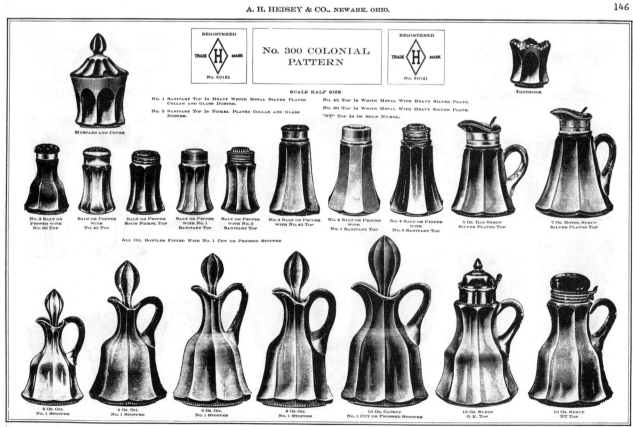

REGISTERED
TRADE **H** MARK
No. 50121

No. 300 COLONIAL PATTERN

REGISTERED
TRADE **H** MARK
No. 50121

SCALE HALF SIZE

TOOTHPICK

NO. 1 SANITARY TOP IS HEAVY WHITE METAL SILVER PLATED COLLAR AND GLASS DUSTER.

NO. 3 SANITARY TOP IS NICKEL PLATED COLLAR AND GLASS DUSTER.

NO. 43 TOP IS WHITE METAL WITH HEAVY SILVER PLATE.

NO. 60 TOP IS WHITE METAL WITH HEAVY SILVER PLATE.

"NT" TOP IS OF SPUN NICKEL.

MUSTARD AND COVER

NO. 2 SALT OR PEPPER WITH NO. 60 TOP

SALT OR PEPPER WITH NO. 43 TOP

SALT OR PEPPER SPUN NICKEL TOP

SALT OR PEPPER WITH NO. 1 SANITARY TOP

SALT OR PEPPER WITH NO. 3 SANITARY TOP

NO. 4 SALT OR PEPPER WITH NO. 43 TOP

NO. 4 SALT OR PEPPER WITH NO. 1 SANITARY TOP

NO. 4 SALT OR PEPPER WITH NO. 3 SANITARY TOP

5 OZ. BAR SYRUP SILVER PLATED TOP

7 OZ. HOTEL SYRUP SILVER PLATED TOP

ALL OIL BOTTLES FITTED WITH NO. 1 CUT OR PRESSED STOPPER

2 OZ. OIL NO. 1 STOPPER

4 OZ. OIL NO. 1 STOPPER

6 OZ. OIL NO. 1 STOPPER

8 OZ. OIL NO. 1 STOPPER

10 OZ. CATSUP NO. 1 CUT OR PRESSED STOPPER

13 OZ. SYRUP O. K. TOP

13 OZ. SYRUP NT TOP

INDIVIDUAL CREAM

REGISTERED
TRADE H MARK
No. 50121

No. 300 COLONIAL
PATTERN

REGISTERED
TRADE H MARK
No. 50121

INDIVIDUAL SUGAR

SCALE HALF SIZE

6-IN. PLATE

4 OZ. CUSTARD
GROUND BOTTOM

2½ OZ. BAR
GROUND BOTTOM

SHERBET

FINGER BOWL

INDIVIDUAL DECANTER

HOTEL SUGAR

HOTEL CREAM

BITTER BOTTLE

PINT DECANTER
NO. 1 CUT OR PRESSED STOPPER

QUART DECANTER
NO. 1 CUT OR PRESSED STOPPER

A. H. HEISEY & CO., NEWARK. OHIO.

REGISTERED
TRADE H MARK
No. 50121

No. 300 1-2 COLONIAL
PATTERN

REGISTERED
TRADE H MARK
No. 50121

SCALE HALF SIZE

NO. 1-6-IN. ICE CREAM PLATE
PUNTIED BOTTOM

HOTEL SUGAR

HOTEL CREAM
STUCK HANDLE

NO. 2-6-IN. ICE CREAM PLATE SHALLOW
PUNTIED BOTTOM

6-IN. JELLY
PATENT LOW FOOT

NO. 1 WATER BOTTLE

2 OZ. BAR
GROUND BOTTOM

8 OZ. TUMBLER
GROUND BOTTOM

HALF GALLON JUG
STUCK HANDLE

2 OZ. BAR FLARED
GROUND BOTTOM

NO. 300½—12 OZ. ICE TEA FLARED
ALSO MAKE STRAIGHT
GROUND BOTTOM

NO. 2 WATER BOTTLE

REGISTERED
TRADE H MARK
No. 50121

REGISTERED
TRADE H MARK
No. 50121

No. 300 1-2 COLONIAL PATTERN

SCALE HALF SIZE

ALL ITEMS ON THIS PAGE HAVE GROUND BOTTOMS

FINGER BOWL
STAR BOTTOM

No. 1—6-IN. FINGER BOWL PLATE
PUNTIED BOTTOM

No. 2—6-IN. FINGER BOWL PLATE
PUNTIED BOTTOM

4 OZ. SHERBET

4 OZ. CUSTARD
STUCK HANDLE

No. 1 TEA CADDY
FULL CUT MUSHROOM STOPPER

No. 2 TEA CADDY
FULL CUT MUSHROOM STOPPER

PICKLE JAR
MUSHROOM STOPPER, GROUND TOP

HORSERADISH JAR
MUSHROOM STOPPER, GROUND TOP

5 OZ. TAPER
CHAMPAGNE

7 OZ. TAPER
CHAMPAGNE

9 OZ. TAPER
CHAMPAGNE

12 OZ. TAPER SODA
ALSO MAKE 10 OZ. SODA

12 OZ. TAPER SODA FLARED
ALSO MAKE 10 OZ. SODA FLARED

9 OZ. TAPER
CHAMPAGNE FLARED

7 OZ. TAPER
CHAMPAGNE FLARED

5 OZ. TAPER
CHAMPAGNE FLARED

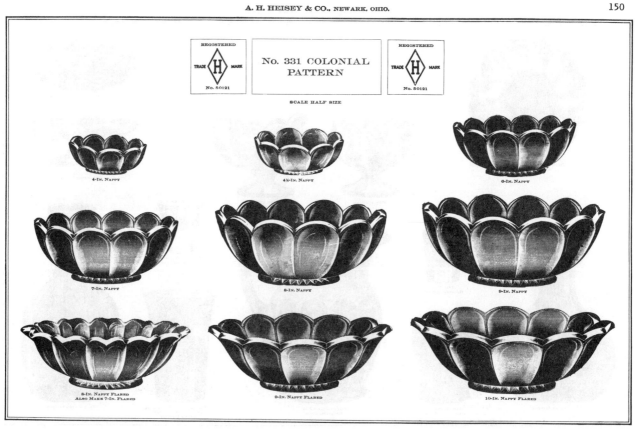

REGISTERED
TRADE H MARK
No. 50121

REGISTERED
TRADE H MARK
No. 50121

No. 331 COLONIAL PATTERN

SCALE HALF SIZE

4-IN. NAPPY

4½-IN. NAPPY

6-IN. NAPPY

7-IN. NAPPY

8-IN. NAPPY

9-IN. NAPPY

8-IN. NAPPY FLARED
ALSO MAKE 7-IN. FLARED

9-IN. NAPPY FLARED

10-IN. NAPPY FLARED

REGISTERED
TRADE **H** MARK
No. 50121

No. 331 COLONIAL PATTERN

REGISTERED
TRADE **H** MARK
No. 50121

SCALE HALF SIZE

4½-In. Nappy Shallow

5-In. Nappy Shallow

7-In. Nappy Shallow

9-In. Nappy Shallow

10-In. Nappy Shallow

11-In. Nappy Shallow

Pint Jug Stuck Handle

Quart Jug Stuck Handle

Three Pint Jug Stuck Handle

Half Gallon Jug Stuck Handle

REGISTERED
TRADE **H** MARK
No. 50121

No. 331 COLONIAL PATTERN

REGISTERED
TRADE **H** MARK
No. 50121

SCALE HALF SIZE

Finger Bowl
Plain or Star Bottom Ground
Also Make Optic

2 Piece Oyster Cocktail
Ground Bottom
Also Make 3 Piece Oyster Cocktail
consisting of
Bar, Finger Bowl and Finger Bowl Plate

Square
Individual Salt
Ground
Top and Bottom

Salt or Pepper No. 4
All Glass Sanitary Top

Salt or Pepper No. 60
Silver Plated Top

Mustard and Cover

4½ Oz. Custard
Ground Bottom

7 Oz. 8 Flute Tumbler
Ground Bottom

Toothpick

These Oils Also Furnished With No. 6 Stoppers

Water Bottle

4 Oz. Oil
No. 1 Pressed or Cut Stopper

6 Oz. Oil
No. 1 Pressed or Cut Stopper

Pickle Jar Mushroom Stopper Ground
Top and Bottom

13 Oz. Syrup O. K. Top

Straw Jar and Cover

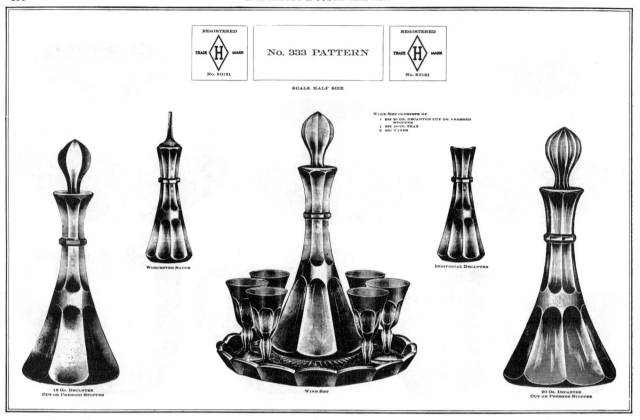

REGISTERED
TRADE MARK
No. 50121

No. 333 PATTERN

REGISTERED
TRADE MARK
No. 50121

SCALE HALF SIZE

WINE SET CONSISTS OF
1 333 20 OZ. DECANTER CUT OR PRESSED
    STOPPER
1 333 10-IN. TRAY
6 350 WINES

WORCESTER SAUCE

INDIVIDUAL DECANTER

18 OZ. DECANTER
CUT OR PRESSED STOPPER

WINE SET

20 OZ. DECANTER
CUT OR PRESSED STOPPER

REGISTERED
TRADE MARK
No. 50121

No. 333 PATTERN

REGISTERED
TRADE MARK
No. 50121

SCALE HALF SIZE

8½ OZ. TUMBLER
PLAIN BOTTOM GROUND

SALT OR PEPPER
WITH No. 60
SILVER PLATED TOP

SALT OR PEPPER
WITH No. 4
ALL GLASS SANITARY TOP

No. 333½—9 OZ. TUMBLER
PLAIN BOTTOM GROUND

FINGER BOWL.
PLAIN OR STAR BOTTOM GROUND

6½-IN. FINGER BOWL PLATE
GROUND BOTTOM
ALSO MAKE OPTIC

OPTIC FINGER BOWL
PLAIN OR STAR BOTTOM GROUND

ALSO MAKE 3 PIECE OYSTER COCKTAIL
CONSISTING OF BAR, FINGER BOWL
AND FINGER BOWL PLATE

2 PIECE OYSTER COCKTAIL
GROUND BOTTOM

9 OZ. SYRUP
SILVER PLATED TOP

WATER BOTTLE

2 OZ. OIL
No. 1 CUT OR PRESSED STOPPER

4 OZ. OIL
No. 1 CUT OR PRESSED STOPPER

6 OZ. OIL
No. 1 CUT OR PRESSED STOPPER

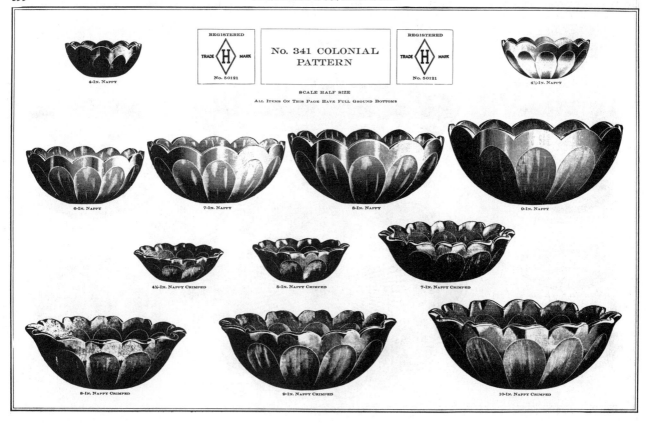

No. 341 COLONIAL PATTERN

SCALE HALF SIZE

ALL ITEMS ON THIS PAGE HAVE FULL GROUND BOTTOMS

4-IN. NAPPY

4½-IN. NAPPY

6-IN. NAPPY

7-IN. NAPPY

8-IN. NAPPY

9-IN. NAPPY

4½-IN. NAPPY CRIMPED

5-IN. NAPPY CRIMPED

7-IN. NAPPY CRIMPED

8-IN. NAPPY CRIMPED

9-IN. NAPPY CRIMPED

10-IN. NAPPY CRIMPED

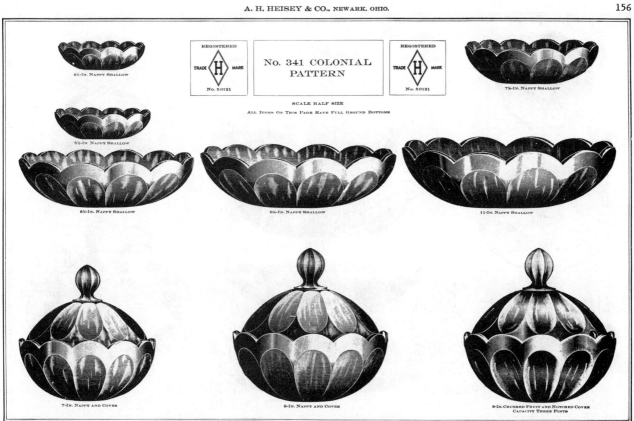

No. 341 COLONIAL PATTERN

SCALE HALF SIZE

ALL ITEMS ON THIS PAGE HAVE FULL GROUND BOTTOMS

4½-IN. NAPPY SHALLOW

7½-IN. NAPPY SHALLOW

5½-IN. NAPPY SHALLOW

8½-IN. NAPPY SHALLOW

9½-IN. NAPPY SHALLOW

11-IN. NAPPY SHALLOW

7-IN. NAPPY AND COVER

8-IN. NAPPY AND COVER

8-IN. CRUSHED FRUIT AND NOTCHED COVER
CAPACITY THREE PINTS

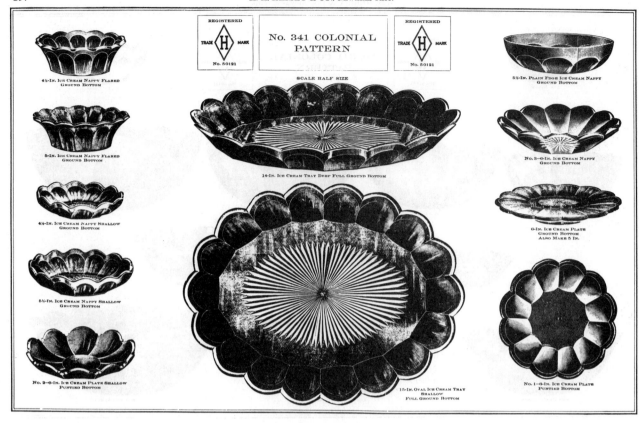

REGISTERED TRADE H MARK No. 50121

No. 341 COLONIAL PATTERN

REGISTERED TRADE H MARK No. 50121

SCALE HALF SIZE

4¼-In. Ice Cream Nappy Flared Ground Bottom

5-In. Ice Cream Nappy Flared Ground Bottom

4½-In. Ice Cream Nappy Shallow Ground Bottom

5½-In. Ice Cream Nappy Shallow Ground Bottom

No. 2—6-In. Ice Cream Plate Shallow Puntied Bottom

14-In. Ice Cream Tray Deep Full Ground Bottom

15-In. Oval Ice Cream Tray Shallow Full Ground Bottom

5½-In. Plain Edge Ice Cream Nappy Ground Bottom

No. 3—6-In. Ice Cream Nappy Ground Bottom

6-In. Ice Cream Plate Ground Bottom Also Make 5 In.

No. 1—6-In. Ice Cream Plate Puntied Bottom

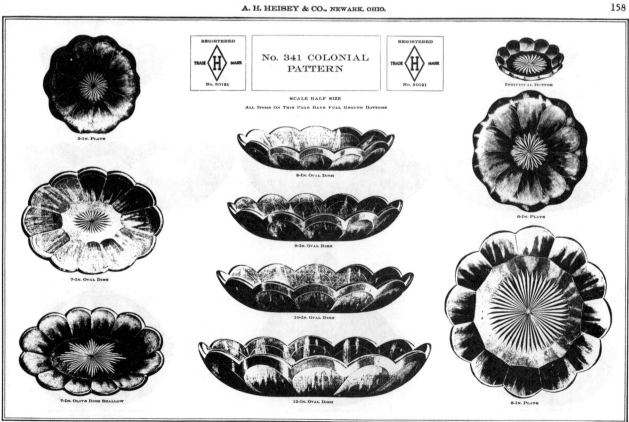

REGISTERED TRADE H MARK No. 50121

No. 341 COLONIAL PATTERN

REGISTERED TRADE H MARK No. 50121

SCALE HALF SIZE

All Items On This Page Have Full Ground Bottoms

5-In. Plate

7-In. Oval Dish

7-In. Olive Dish Shallow

8-In. Oval Dish

9-In. Oval Dish

10-In. Oval Dish

12-In. Oval Dish

Individual Butter

6-In. Plate

8-In. Plate

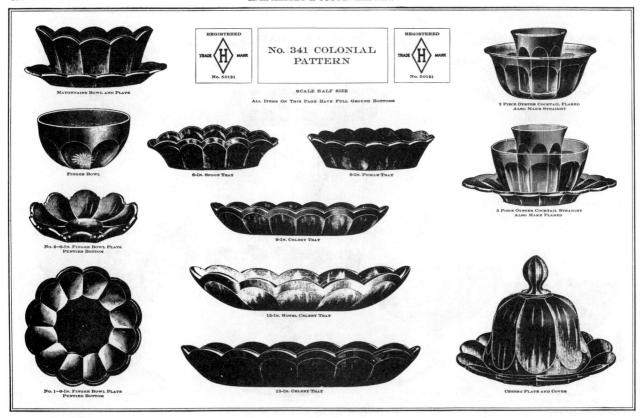

REGISTERED
TRADE H MARK
No. 50121

No. 341 COLONIAL
PATTERN

REGISTERED
TRADE H MARK
No. 50121

SCALE HALF SIZE

ALL ITEMS ON THIS PAGE HAVE FULL GROUND BOTTOMS

MAYONNAISE BOWL AND PLATE

2 PIECE OYSTER COCKTAIL FLARED
ALSO MADE STRAIGHT

FINGER BOWL

6-IN. SPOON TRAY

6-IN. PICKLE TRAY

3 PIECE OYSTER COCKTAIL STRAIGHT
ALSO MADE FLARED

NO. 2—6-IN. FINGER BOWL PLATE
PUNTIED BOTTOM

9-IN. CELERY TRAY

12-IN. HOTEL CELERY TRAY

NO. 1—6-IN. FINGER BOWL PLATE
PUNTIED BOTTOM

13-IN. CELERY TRAY

CHEESE PLATE AND COVER

REGISTERED
TRADE H MARK
No. 50121

No. 341 COLONIAL
PATTERN

REGISTERED
TRADE H MARK
No. 50121

SCALE HALF SIZE

5-IN. HANDLED JELLY
GROUND BOTTOM

5-IN. HANDLED JELLY THREE-CORNERED
GROUND BOTTOM

4-IN. LOW FOOTED JELLY

4½ LOW FOOTED JELLY

5-IN. LOW FOOTED JELLY CRIMPED
ALSO MADE 4½-IN.

4½-IN. LOW FOOTED JELLY SHALLOW

5-IN. LOW FOOTED JELLY SHALLOW

4½-IN. HIGH FOOTED JELLY

5-IN. HIGH FOOTED JELLY

5-IN. HIGH FOOTED JELLY CRIMPED

5½-IN. HIGH FOOTED JELLY CRIMPED

5-IN. HIGH FOOTED JELLY SHALLOW

5½-IN. HIGH FOOTED JELLY SHALLOW

REGISTERED TRADE MARK No. 50121

No. 341 COLONIAL PATTERN

REGISTERED TRADE MARK No. 50121

SCALE HALF SIZE

9-In. High Footed Bowl Crimped Also Made 10-In.

7-In. High Footed Bowl Crimped

8-In. High Footed Bowl Crimped

6-In. High Footed Bowl

7-In. High Footed Bowl

8-In. High Footed Bowl

9-In. High Footed Bowl

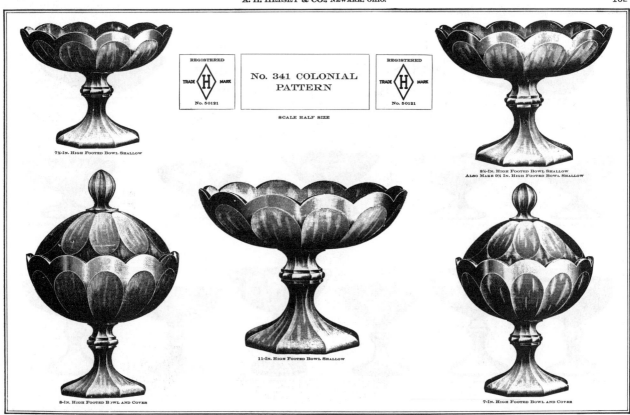

REGISTERED TRADE MARK No. 50121

No. 341 COLONIAL PATTERN

REGISTERED TRADE MARK No. 50121

SCALE HALF SIZE

7½-In. High Footed Bowl Shallow

8½-In. High Footed Bowl Shallow Also Made 9½ In. High Footed Bowl Shallow

8-In. High Footed Bowl and Cover

11-In. High Footed Bowl Shallow

7-In. High Footed Bowl and Cover

REGISTERED TRADE MARK No. 50121

No. 341 COLONIAL PATTERN

SCALE HALF SIZE

Also Made In The Following Shapes
12-In. Cupped
14-In. Flared
16½-In. Shallow
With or Without Foot

REGISTERED TRADE MARK No. 50121

No. 341—4½ Oz. High Footed
Sherbet Shallow

No. 341—4½ Oz. High Footed
Sherbet Shallow

No. 341—4½ Oz. High Footed
Sherbet Shallow

13-In. Punch Bowl Straight and Low Foot

No. 341—4½ Oz. Custard
Ground Bottom

No. 341—4½ Oz. Custard
Ground Bottom

No. 341—4½ Oz. Custard
Ground Bottom

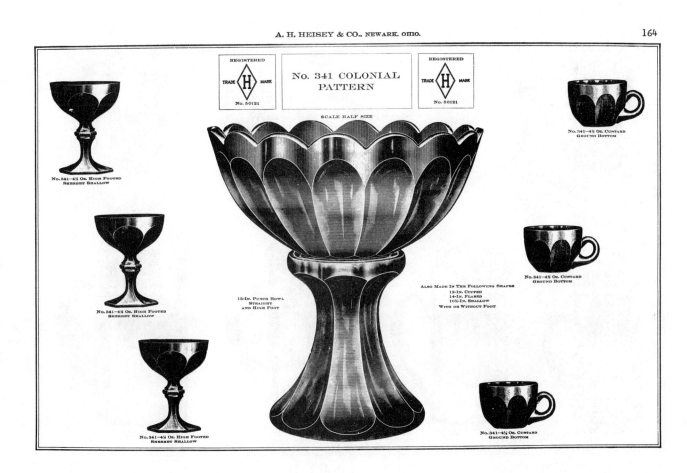

REGISTERED TRADE MARK No. 50121

No. 341 COLONIAL PATTERN

SCALE HALF SIZE

REGISTERED TRADE MARK No. 50121

No. 341—4½ Oz. High Footed
Sherbet Shallow

No. 341—4½ Oz. High Footed
Sherbet Shallow

No. 341—4½ Oz. High Footed
Sherbet Shallow

13-In. Punch Bowl
Straight
and High Foot

Also Made In The Following Shapes
12-In. Cupped
14-In. Flared
16½-In. Shallow
With or Without Foot

No. 341—4½ Oz. Custard
Ground Bottom

No. 341—4½ Oz. Custard
Ground Bottom

No. 341—4½ Oz. Custard
Ground Bottom

REGISTERED
TRADE **H** MARK
No. 50121

No. 341 COLONIAL PATTERN

SCALE HALF SIZE

REGISTERED
TRADE **H** MARK
No. 50121

24 Oz. Decanter
Cut or Pressed Stopper

13 Oz. Ice Tea Tumbler
Ground Bottom

10 Oz. Tumbler
Ground Bottom

Water Bottle

One Pint Tankard, Stuck Handle

Quart Tankard
Stuck Handle

30 Oz. Rock and Rye Bottle
Mushroom Stopper, Ground Top

Three Pint Tankard
Stuck Handle

Half Gallon Tankard, Stuck Handle

REGISTERED
TRADE **H** MARK
No. 50121

No. 341 COLONIAL PATTERN

SCALE HALF SIZE

REGISTERED
TRADE **H** MARK
No. 50121

Ice Tub, Drainer and Plate
Ground Bottom

No. 341½—8 Oz. Tumbler
Star Bottom Ground

Pint Tankard and Cover
Stuck Handle

Quart Tankard and Cover
Stuck Handle

3 Pint Tankard and Cover
Stuck Handle

Half Gallon Tankard and Cover
Stuck Handle

REGISTERED
TRADE H MARK
No. 50121

No. 341 COLONIAL PATTERN

REGISTERED
TRADE H MARK
No. 50121

SCALE HALF SIZE

3 Oz. Low Footed Sherbet   4½ Oz. Low Footed Sherbet   3 Oz. Low Footed Sherbet Scalloped   4½ Oz. Low Footed Sherbet Scalloped Also Made 6 Oz. Sherbet Like Above

2½ Oz. Creme De Mint   2 Oz. Cocktail   3 Oz. Cocktail   4½ Oz. Saucer Champagne Also High Footed Sherbet Shallow   6 Oz. Footed Egg Also 6 Oz. Oyster Cocktail   8 Oz. Footed Tumbler or Low Footed Goblet   3½ Oz. Parfait Straight or Tall Champagne   3½ Oz. Parfait Flared or Tall Champagne

9 Oz. Goblet   6½ Oz. Champagne   4½ Oz. Claret   3½ Oz. Burgundy   2 Oz. Wine   1 Oz. Cordial   2 Oz. Sherry   2 Oz. Sherry Flared   3 Oz. Port

REGISTERED
TRADE H MARK
No. 50121

No. 341 COLONIAL PATTERN

REGISTERED
TRADE H MARK
No. 50121

SCALE HALF SIZE

DESCRIPTION OF SALT AND PEPPER TOPS

"AA" Top Is Spun Metal Silver Plated.
No. 43 Top Is White Metal With Heavy Silver Plate.
No. 60 Top Is White Metal With Heavy Silver Plate.
NT Top Is Of Spun Nickel.

No. 1 Sanitary Top Is Heavy White Metal Silver Plated Collar and Glass Duster.
No. 3 Sanitary Top Is Nickel Plated Collar and Glass Duster.
No. 4 Sanitary Top Is All Glass.

Individual Salt Ground Bottom   Toothpick Footed   Table Salt Cut Top and Bottom

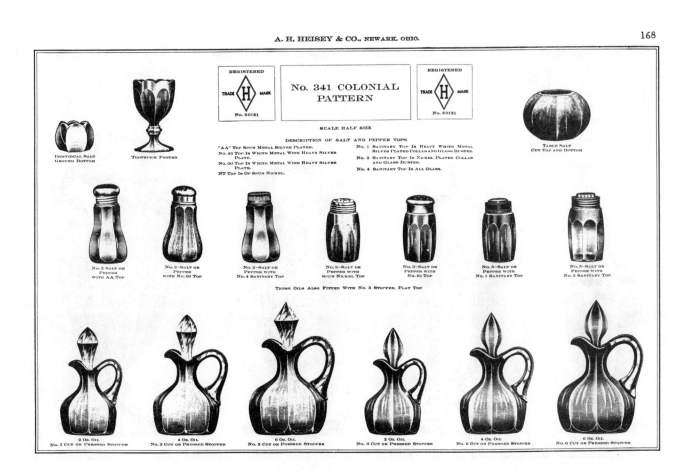

No. 2 Salt or Pepper With AA Top   No. 2 Salt or Pepper With No. 60 Top   No. 2 Salt or Pepper With No. 4 Sanitary Top   No. 3 Salt or Pepper With Spun Nickel Top   No. 3 Salt or Pepper With No. 43 Top   No. 3 Salt or Pepper With No. 1 Sanitary Top   No. 3 Salt or Pepper With No. 3 Sanitary Top

These Oils Also Fitted With No. 3 Stopper, Flat Top

2 Oz. Oil No. 2 Cut or Pressed Stopper   4 Oz. Oil No. 2 Cut or Pressed Stopper   6 Oz. Oil No. 2 Cut or Pressed Stopper   2 Oz. Oil No. 6 Cut or Pressed Stopper   4 Oz. Oil No. 6 Cut or Pressed Stopper   6 Oz. Oil No. 6 Cut or Pressed Stopper

OVAL HOTEL CREAM GROUND BOTTOM

REGISTERED
TRADE H MARK
No. 50121

No. 341 COLONIAL
PATTERN

REGISTERED
TRADE H MARK
No. 50121

SCALE HALF SIZE

OVAL HOTEL SUGAR GROUND BOTTOM

SMALL TEA CADDY
GROUND BOTTOM
MUSHROOM STOPPER, FULL CUT

LARGE TEA CADDY
GROUND BOTTOM
MUSHROOM STOPPER, FULL CUT

SQUAT HORSERADISH
OR COLD CREAM JAR
GROUND BOTTOM
MUSHROOM STOPPER, GROUND TOP

PIN PICKLE JAR
OR SMALL MARMALADE JAR
GROUND BOTTOM
MUSHROOM STOPPER, GROUND TOP

MEDIUM MARMALADE JAR
GROUND BOTTOM
MUSHROOM STOPPER, GROUND TOP

LARGE MARMALADE JAR
GROUND BOTTOM
MUSHROOM STOPPER, GROUND TOP

PICKLE JAR KNOB COVER
GROUND BOTTOM

PICKLE JAR, GROUND BOTTOM
MUSHROOM STOPPER, GROUND TOP

TALL HORSERADISH JAR
GROUND BOTTOM
MUSHROOM STOPPER, GROUND TOP

SMALL CHERRY JAR
GROUND BOTTOM
MUSHROOM STOPPER, GROUND TOP

LARGE CHERRY JAR
GROUND BOTTOM
MUSHROOM STOPPER, GROUND TOP

13 OZ. SYRUP
O. K. BRITTANIA TOP

REGISTERED
TRADE H MARK
No. 50121

No. 341 COLONIAL
PATTERN

REGISTERED
TRADE H MARK
No. 50121

SCALE HALF SIZE

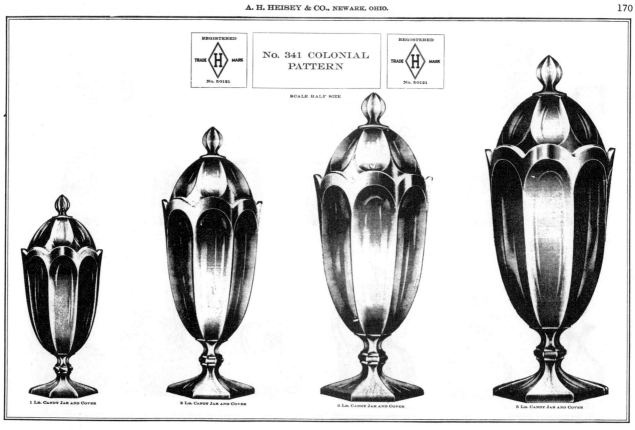

1 LB. CANDY JAR AND COVER

2 LB. CANDY JAR AND COVER

3 LB. CANDY JAR AND COVER

5 LB. CANDY JAR AND COVER

REGISTERED
TRADE **H** MARK
No. 50121

No. 341 COLONIAL PATTERN

REGISTERED
TRADE **H** MARK
No. 50121

SCALE HALF SIZE

SHERBET AND PLATE
GROUND BOTTOM

4½ OZ. HANDLED WATER ICE
SHALLOW, GROUND BOTTOM

3 OZ. CUSTARD
GROUND BOTTOM

4 OZ. CUSTARD FLARED
STUCK HANDLE GROUND BOTTOM

No. 1 WATER SET CONSISTS OF
1 130 13-IN. TRAY
1 341 THREE PINT TANKARD
5 341½ TUMBLERS
1 341½ SMALL FINGER BOWL, FLARED

No. 2 WATER SET CONSISTS OF
1 353 10-IN. TRAY
1 341 THREE PINT TANKARD
2 153 TUMBLERS
1 341½ SMALL FINGER BOWL, STRAIGHT

4½ OZ. CUSTARD
GROUND BOTTOM

4 OZ. SHERBET
GROUND BOTTOM

NO. 1 WATER SET 13-IN. TRAY

NO. 2 WATER SET 10-IN. TRAY

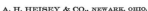
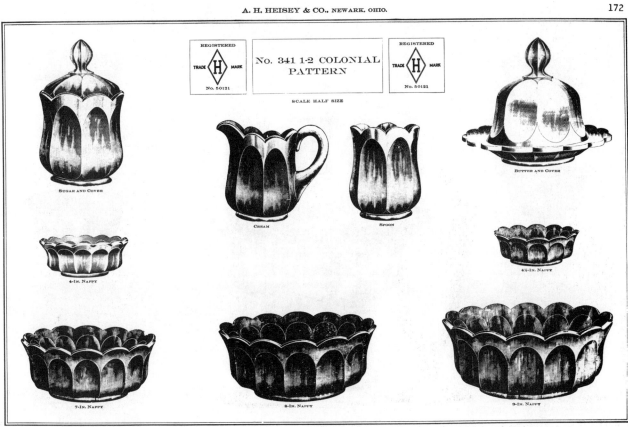

REGISTERED
TRADE **H** MARK
No. 50121

No. 341 1-2 COLONIAL PATTERN

REGISTERED
TRADE **H** MARK
No. 50121

SCALE HALF SIZE

SUGAR AND COVER

CREAM

SPOON

BUTTER AND COVER

4-IN. NAPPY

4½-IN. NAPPY

7-IN. NAPPY

8-IN. NAPPY

9-IN. NAPPY

No. 341 1-2 COLONIAL PATTERN

SCALE HALF SIZE

5-In. Plate

6-In. Plate

4½-In. Nappy Flared

8½-In. Nappy Flared

5-In. Nappy Flared

9½-In. Nappy Flared

5½-In. Nappy Shallow
ALSO MAKE 5-IN. NAPPY, SHALLOW

10½-In. Nappy Flared

9-In. Nappy Shallow

10-In. Nappy Shallow

11-In. Nappy Shallow

No. 341 1-2 COLONIAL PATTERN

SCALE HALF SIZE

SMALL FINGER BOWL STRAIGHT
GROUND BOTTOM

LARGE FINGER BOWL STRAIGHT
GROUND BOTTOM

3 OZ. CUSTARD
GROUND BOTTOM

SMALL FINGER BOWL FLARED
GROUND BOTTOM

LARGE FINGER BOWL FLARED
GROUND BOTTOM

9-IN. CHEESE PLATE AND COVER
GROUND BOTTOM

THIS PUNCH BOWL
ALSO MADE WITHOUT FOOT, STRAIGHT,
FLARED AND SHALLOW.

12-IN. FOOTED PUNCH BOWL FLARED
ALSO MAKE | 10-IN. FOOTED PUNCH BOWL
| 13-IN. FOOTED PUNCH BOWL SHALLOW

SMALL 2 PIECE OYSTER COCKTAIL
FLARED GROUND BOTTOM
ALSO MAKE STRAIGHT

REGISTERED
TRADE **H** MARK
No. 50121

No. 341 1-2 COLONIAL
PATTERN

REGISTERED
TRADE **H** MARK
No. 50121

SCALE HALF SIZE

ONE PINT SQUAT JUG
STUCK HANDLE

8 OZ. TUMBLER
STAR BOTTOM GROUND

ONE QUART SQUAT JUG
STUCK HANDLE

THREE PINT SQUAT JUG
STUCK HANDLE

HALF GALLON SQUAT JUG
STUCK HANDLE

THREE QUART SQUAT JUG
STUCK HANDLE

REGISTERED
TRADE **H** MARK
No. 50121

No. 350 PATTERN

REGISTERED
TRADE **H** MARK
No. 50121

SCALE HALF SIZE

HOTEL CREAM
GROUND BOTTOM

HOTEL SUGAR
GROUND BOTTOM

8 OZ. TUMBLER
GROUND BOTTOM

4½ OZ. CUSTARD
GROUND BOTTOM

5-IN. NAPPY SHALLOW
GROUND BOTTOM

4½-IN. NAPPY
GROUND BOTTOM

3 PINT JUG—STUCK HANDLE

14-IN. PUNCH BOWL AND HIGH FOOT
ALSO MAKE WITHOUT FOOT

8-IN. NAPPY
GROUND BOTTOM

REGISTERED
TRADE **H** MARK
No. 50121

No. 351 COLONIAL PATTERN

REGISTERED
TRADE **H** MARK
No. 50121

SCALE HALF SIZE

HOTEL CREAM CUT SHUT
CUT TOP AND BOTTOM

HOTEL SUGAR CUT SHUT
CUT TOP AND BOTTOM

HOTEL CREAM FLARED AND PLATE
GROUND BOTTOM
ALSO MAKE WITHOUT PLATE

HOTEL SUGAR FLARED AND PLATE
GROUND BOTTOM
ALSO MAKE WITHOUT PLATE

MAYONNAISE DISH AND PLATE
GROUND BOTTOM

6½-IN. PLATE FULL GROUND BOTTOM
THESE PLATES ALSO MADE IN 4½ IN., 5 IN.,
8 IN., 10 IN. AND 11 IN. SIZES

4½-IN. NAPPY
FULL GROUND BOTTOM

5-IN. NAPPY
FULL GROUND BOTTOM

6-IN. NAPPY
FULL GROUND BOTTOM

9-IN. CELERY TRAY GROUND BOTTOM
ALSO MAKE 12-IN. CELERY TRAY, OVAL, GROUND BOTTOM

9-IN. PLATE FULL GROUND BOTTOM

13-IN. CELERY TRAY GROUND BOTTOM

9-IN. NAPPY
ALSO MAKE 7, 8 AND 10 IN.
FULL GROUND BOTTOM

REGISTERED
TRADE **H** MARK
No. 50121

No. 351 COLONIAL PATTERN

REGISTERED
TRADE **H** MARK
No. 50121

SCALE HALF SIZE

FINGER BOWL
PLAIN OR STAR BOTTOM GROUND
ALSO MAKE OPTIC

2 PIECE OYSTER COCKTAIL
GROUND BOTTOM

6-IN. JELLY PATENT LOW FOOT
PUNTIED BOTTOM

NO. 1 GRAPE FRUIT CENTER
GROUND BOTTOM

6-IN. JELLY 2 HANDLES
PUNTIED BOTTOM

GRAPE FRUIT STRAIGHT
ALSO MAKE FLARED
FITTED WITH NO. 1, 2 OR 3 CENTER

NO. 3 GRAPE FRUIT CENTER

10-IN. EXTRA HIGH FOOTED BOWL SHALLOW
PUNTIED BOTTOM

NO. 2 GRAPE FRUIT CENTER

SWEETMEAT CRIMPED

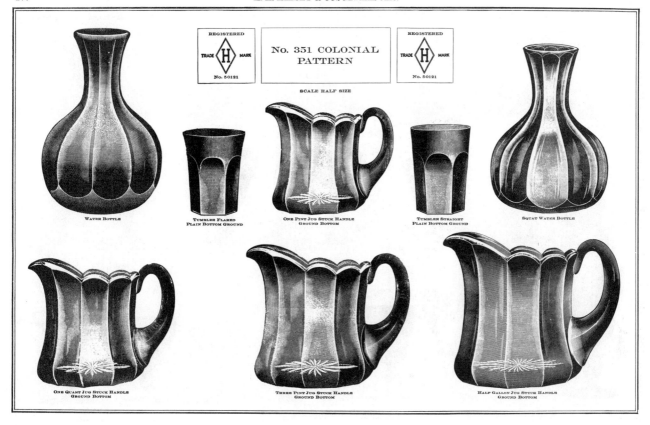

No. 351 COLONIAL
PATTERN

SCALE HALF SIZE

WATER BOTTLE

TUMBLER FLARED
PLAIN BOTTOM GROUND

ONE PINT JUG STUCK HANDLE
GROUND BOTTOM

TUMBLER STRAIGHT
PLAIN BOTTOM GROUND

SQUAT WATER BOTTLE

ONE QUART JUG STUCK HANDLE
GROUND BOTTOM

THREE PINT JUG STUCK HANDLE
GROUND BOTTOM

HALF GALLON JUG STUCK HANDLE
GROUND BOTTOM

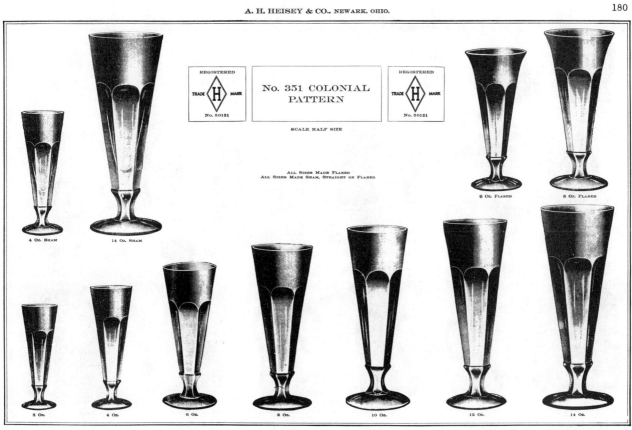

No. 351 COLONIAL
PATTERN

SCALE HALF SIZE

ALL SIZES MADE FLARED
ALL SIZES MADE SHAM, STRAIGHT OR FLARED

4 OZ. SHAM

14 OZ. SHAM

6 OZ. FLARED

8 OZ. FLARED

3 OZ.   4 OZ.   6 OZ.   8 OZ.   10 OZ.   12 OZ.   14 OZ.

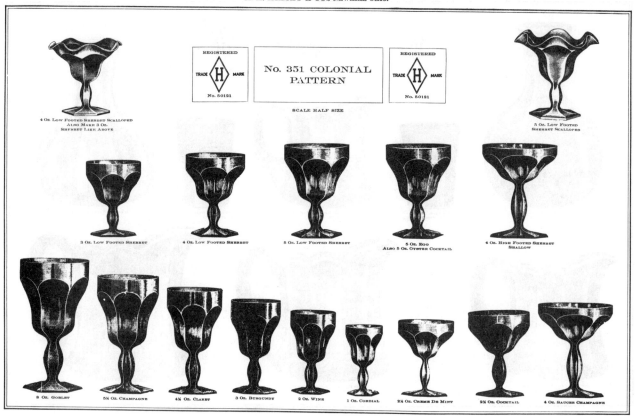

REGISTERED
TRADE **H** MARK
No. 50121

No. 351 COLONIAL
PATTERN

REGISTERED
TRADE **H** MARK
No. 50121

SCALE HALF SIZE

4 Oz. Low Footed Sherbet Scalloped
Also Make 3 Oz.
Sherbet Like Above

5 Oz. Low Footed
Sherbet Scalloped

3 Oz. Low Footed Sherbet

4 Oz. Low Footed Sherbet

5 Oz. Low Footed Sherbet

5 Oz. Egg
Also 5 Oz. Oyster Cocktail

4 Oz. High Footed Sherbet
Shallow

8 Oz. Goblet

5½ Oz. Champagne

4½ Oz. Claret

3 Oz. Burgundy

2 Oz. Wine

1 Oz. Cordial

2½ Oz. Creme De Mint

2½ Oz. Cocktail

4 Oz. Saucer Champagne

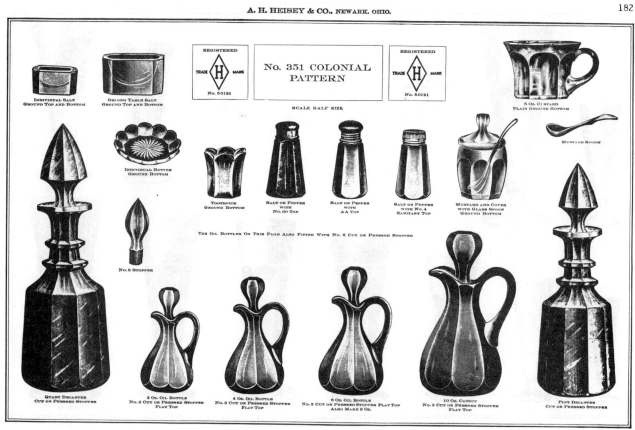

REGISTERED
TRADE **H** MARK
No. 50121

No. 351 COLONIAL
PATTERN

REGISTERED
TRADE **H** MARK
No. 50121

SCALE HALF SIZE

Individual Salt
Ground Top and Bottom

Oblong Table Salt
Ground Top and Bottom

5 Oz. Custard
Plain Ground Bottom

Individual Butter
Ground Bottom

Mustard Spoon

Toothpick
Ground Bottom

Salt or Pepper
With
No. 60 Top

Salt or Pepper
With
AA Top

Salt or Pepper
With No. 4
Sanitary Top

Mustard and Cover
With Glass Spoon
Ground Bottom

No. 6 Stopper

The Oil Bottles On This Page Also Fitted With No. 6 Cut or Pressed Stopper

Quart Decanter
Cut or Pressed Stopper

2 Oz. Oil Bottle
No. 3 Cut or Pressed Stopper
Flat Top

4 Oz. Oil Bottle
No. 3 Cut or Pressed Stopper
Flat Top

6 Oz. Oil Bottle
No. 3 Cut or Pressed Stopper Flat Top
Also Makes 8 Oz.

10 Oz. Catsup
No. 3 Cut or Pressed Stopper
Flat Top

Pint Decanter
Cut or Pressed Stopper

2 Oz. Bar Straight
Ground Bottom

REGISTERED
TRADE **H** MARK
No. 50121

No. 351 COLONIAL
PATTERN

REGISTERED
TRADE **H** MARK
No. 50121

2 Oz. Bar Flared
Ground Bottom

SCALE HALF SIZE

No. 351 Wine Set consists of
1 Pint Decanter P-S
1 12-In. (352) Tray Fire Polished
6 2 Oz. Wines

No. 351 Whiskey Set consists of
1 Pint Decanter P-S
1 12-In. (352) Tray Fire Polished
6 2½ Oz. (300½) Bars

Either Of Above Sets Furnished With
1 Qt. Decanter P-S or
Full Ground Bottom Trays
And Cut Stopper Decanters

2 Oz. Wine

Wine Set

Whiskey Set

4½-In. Nappy
Ground Bottom

REGISTERED
TRADE **H** MARK
No. 50121

No. 352 PATTERN
DESIGN PATENT No. 39432

REGISTERED
TRADE **H** MARK
No. 50121

5-In. Low Foot Jelly

5½-In. Nappy
Ground Bottom

SCALE HALF SIZE

7½-In. Nappy
Ground Bottom

Hotel Sugar and Cover
Furnished With or Without Cover
Ground Bottom

Hotel Cream
Ground Bottom

Individual Sugar and Cover
Furnished With or Without Cover
Ground Bottom

Individual Cream
Ground Bottom

9-In. Nappy
Ground Bottom

7½-In. Oval Ground Bottom

10-In. Strawberry Plate and Drainer

10-In. Nappy
Ground Bottom
Also Makes 11 In.

8-In. Strawberry Dish and Drainer

Two-Piece Cheese and Cracker Plate

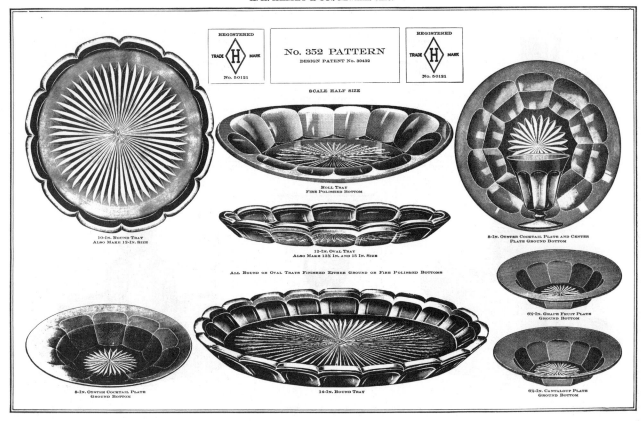

REGISTERED
TRADE H MARK
No. 50121

No. 352 PATTERN
DESIGN PATENT No. 39432

REGISTERED
TRADE H MARK
No. 50121

SCALE HALF SIZE

10-IN. ROUND TRAY
ALSO MAKE 12-IN. SIZE

ROLL TRAY
FIRE POLISHED BOTTOM

12-IN. OVAL TRAY
ALSO MAKE 13½ IN. AND 15 IN. SIZE

ALL ROUND OR OVAL TRAYS FINISHED EITHER GROUND OR FIRE POLISHED BOTTOMS

8-IN. OYSTER COCKTAIL PLATE AND CENTER
PLATE GROUND BOTTOM

6½-IN. GRAPE FRUIT PLATE
GROUND BOTTOM

8-IN. OYSTER COCKTAIL PLATE
GROUND BOTTOM

14-IN. ROUND TRAY

6½-IN. CANTALOUP PLATE
GROUND BOTTOM

REGISTERED
TRADE H MARK
No. 50121

No. 352 PATTERN
DESIGN PATENT No. 39432

REGISTERED
TRADE H MARK
No. 50121

SCALE HALF SIZE

FINGER BOWL. GROUND BOTTOM

3½ OZ. FOOTED SHERBET

TWO PIECE OYSTER COCKTAIL

6½ OZ. TUMBLER
GROUND BOTTOM

TOOTHPICK
PUNTIED BOTTOM

SUGAR SIFTER
WITH SILVER PLATED TOP

SUGAR SIFTER
WITH NO. 1 SANITARY TOP

MUSTARD AND COVER. GROUND BOTTOM
WITH OR WITHOUT SPOON

HORSERADISH
WITH OR WITHOUT SPOON

OILS FITTED WITH EITHER CUT OR PRESSED STOPPER

2 OZ. OIL
WITH NO. 1 STOPPER

4 OZ. OIL
WITH NO. 1 STOPPER

6 OZ. OIL
WITH NO. 1 STOPPER

PICKLE JAR
GROUND BOTTOM

INDIVIDUAL CELERY
GROUND BOTTOM

HALF GALLON JUG STUCK HANDLE

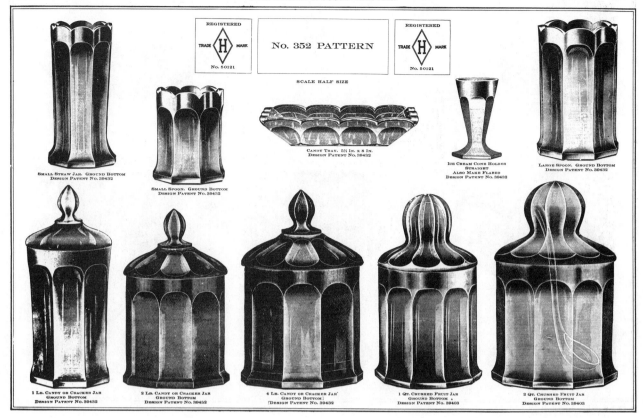

REGISTERED TRADE H MARK No. 50121

No. 352 PATTERN

REGISTERED TRADE H MARK No. 50121

SCALE HALF SIZE

SMALL STRAW JAR. GROUND BOTTOM
DESIGN PATENT No. 39432

SMALL SPOON. GROUND BOTTOM
DESIGN PATENT No. 39432

CANDY TRAY. 5½ IN. x 8 IN.
DESIGN PATENT No. 39432

ICE CREAM CONE HOLDER
STRAIGHT
ALSO MADE FLARED
DESIGN PATENT No. 39432

LARGE SPOON. GROUND BOTTOM
DESIGN PATENT No. 39432

1 LB. CANDY OR CRACKER JAR
GROUND BOTTOM
DESIGN PATENT No. 39432

2 LB. CANDY OR CRACKER JAR
GROUND BOTTOM
DESIGN PATENT No. 39432

4 LB. CANDY OR CRACKER JAR
GROUND BOTTOM
DESIGN PATENT No. 39432

1 QT. CRUSHED FRUIT JAR
GROUND BOTTOM
DESIGN PATENT No. 39403

2 QT. CRUSHED FRUIT JAR
GROUND BOTTOM
DESIGN PATENT No. 39403

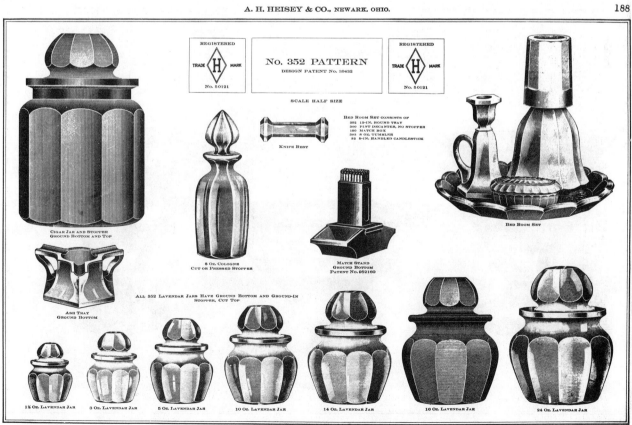

REGISTERED TRADE H MARK No. 50121

No. 352 PATTERN
DESIGN PATENT No. 39432

REGISTERED TRADE H MARK No. 50121

SCALE HALF SIZE

CIGAR JAR AND STOPPER
GROUND BOTTOM AND TOP

KNIFE REST

BED ROOM SET CONSISTS OF
352 12-IN. ROUND TRAY
300 PINT DECANTER, NO STOPPER
150 MATCH BOX
303 8 OZ. TUMBLER
33 8-IN. HANDLED CANDLESTICK

8 OZ. COLOGNE
CUT OR PRESSED STOPPER

MATCH STAND
GROUND BOTTOM
PATENT No. 052160

BED ROOM SET

ASH TRAY
GROUND BOTTOM

ALL 352 LAVENDAR JARS HAVE GROUND BOTTOM AND GROUND-IN
STOPPER, CUT TOP

1½ OZ. LAVENDAR JAR

3 OZ. LAVENDAR JAR

5 OZ. LAVENDAR JAR

10 OZ. LAVENDAR JAR

14 OZ. LAVENDAR JAR

16 OZ. LAVENDAR JAR

24 OZ. LAVENDAR JAR

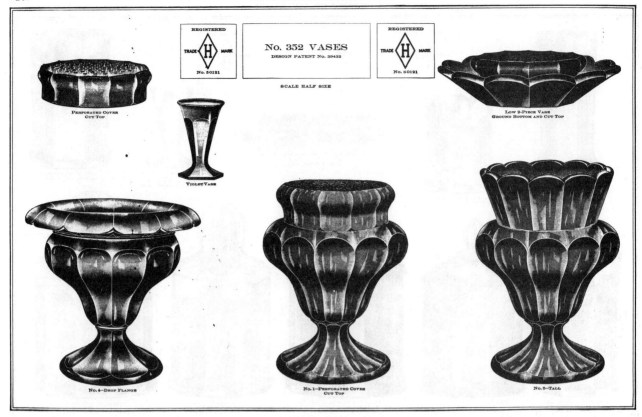

REGISTERED

TRADE H MARK

No. 50121

No. 352 VASES
DESIGN PATENT No. 39432

REGISTERED

TRADE H MARK

No. 50121

SCALE HALF SIZE

PERFORATED COVER
CUT TOP

VIOLET VASE

LOW 2-PIECE VASE
GROUND BOTTOM AND CUT TOP

No. 4—DROP FLANGE

No. 1—PERFORATED COVER
CUT TOP

No. 5—TALL

REGISTERED

TRADE H MARK

No. 50121

No. 352 PATTERN
DESIGN PATENT No. 39432

REGISTERED

TRADE H MARK

No. 50121

SCALE HALF SIZE

No. 2—VASE, MEDIUM FLARE

ORANGE BOWL

No. 3—VASE, WIDE FLARE

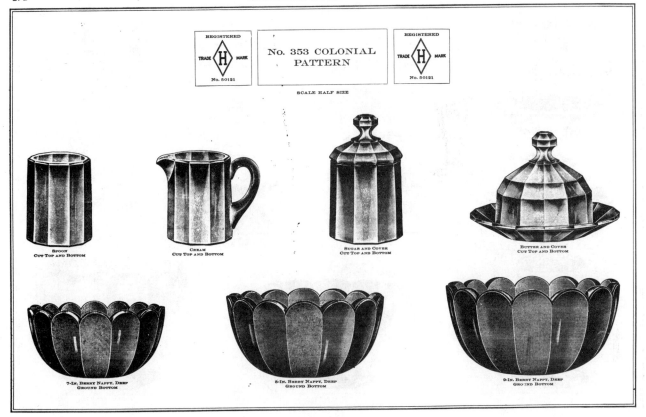

REGISTERED TRADE MARK No. 50121

No. 353 COLONIAL
PATTERN

REGISTERED TRADE MARK No. 50121

SCALE HALF SIZE

SPOON
CUT TOP AND BOTTOM

CREAM
CUT TOP AND BOTTOM

SUGAR AND COVER
CUT TOP AND BOTTOM

BUTTER AND COVER
CUT TOP AND BOTTOM

7-IN. BERRY NAPPY, DEEP
GROUND BOTTOM

8-IN. BERRY NAPPY, DEEP
GROUND BOTTOM

9-IN. BERRY NAPPY, DEEP
GROUND BOTTOM

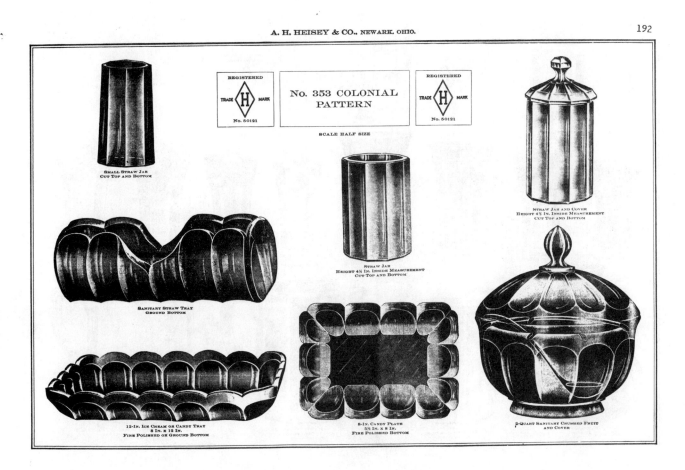

REGISTERED TRADE MARK No. 50121

No. 353 COLONIAL
PATTERN

REGISTERED TRADE MARK No. 50121

SCALE HALF SIZE

SMALL STRAW JAR
CUT TOP AND BOTTOM

STRAW JAR AND COVER
HEIGHT 4½ IN. INSIDE MEASUREMENT
CUT TOP AND BOTTOM

STRAW JAR
HEIGHT 4½ IN. INSIDE MEASUREMENT
CUT TOP AND BOTTOM

SANITARY STRAW TRAY
GROUND BOTTOM

12-IN. ICE CREAM OR CANDY TRAY
8 IN. x 12 IN.
FIRE POLISHED OR GROUND BOTTOM

8-IN. CANDY PLATE
5½ IN. x 8 IN.
FIRE POLISHED BOTTOM

2-QUART SANITARY CRUSHED FRUIT
AND COVER

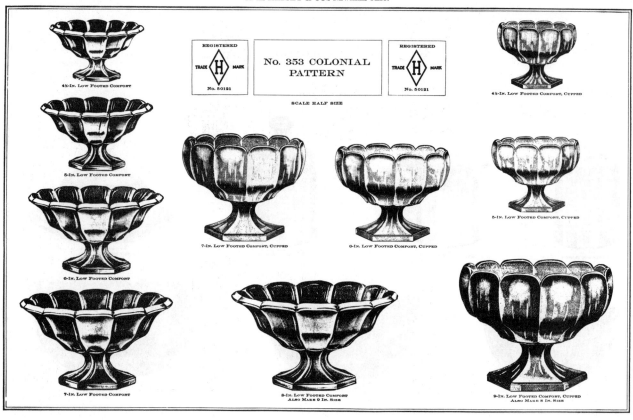

| REGISTERED TRADE **H** MARK No. 50121 | No. 353 COLONIAL PATTERN | REGISTERED TRADE **H** MARK No. 50121 |

SCALE HALF SIZE

4½-In. Low Footed Comfort

4½-In. Low Footed Comfort, Cupped

5-In. Low Footed Comfort

7-In. Low Footed Comfort, Cupped

6-In. Low Footed Comfort, Cupped

5-In. Low Footed Comfort, Cupped

6-In. Low Footed Comfort

7-In. Low Footed Comfort

8-In. Low Footed Comfort
Also Make 9 In. Size

9-In. Low Footed Comfort, Cupped
Also Make 8 In. Size

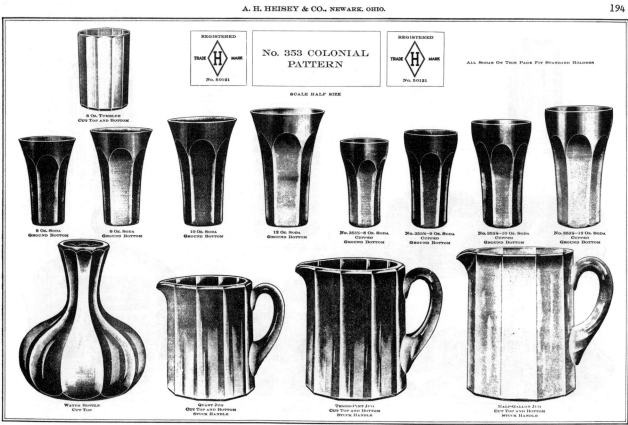

| REGISTERED TRADE **H** MARK No. 50121 | No. 353 COLONIAL PATTERN | REGISTERED TRADE **H** MARK No. 50121 |

SCALE HALF SIZE

All Sodas On This Page Fit Standard Holders

8 Oz. Tumbler
Cut Top and Bottom

8 Oz. Soda
Ground Bottom

9 Oz. Soda
Ground Bottom

10 Oz. Soda
Ground Bottom

12 Oz. Soda
Ground Bottom

No. 353½—8 Oz. Soda
Cupped
Ground Bottom

No. 353½—9 Oz. Soda
Cupped
Ground Bottom

No. 353½—10 Oz. Soda
Cupped
Ground Bottom

No. 353½—12 Oz. Soda
Cupped
Ground Bottom

Water Bottle
Cut Top

Quart Jug
Cut Top and Bottom
Stuck Handle

Three-Pint Jug
Cut Top and Bottom
Stuck Handle

Half-Gallon Jug
Cut Top and Bottom
Stuck Handle

REGISTERED TRADE MARK No. 50121

No. 353 COLONIAL PATTERN

REGISTERED TRADE MARK No. 50121

SCALE HALF SIZE

HOTEL SUGAR AND COVER
CUT TOP AND BOTTOM

HOTEL CREAM
CUT TOP AND BOTTOM

OVAL HOTEL SUGAR
CUT TOP AND BOTTOM
DESIGN PATENT No. 42751

OVAL HOTEL CREAM
CUT TOP AND BOTTOM
DESIGN PATENT No. 42751

ALL OILS ON THIS PAGE FITTED WITH No. 6 OR No. 8 CUT OR PRESSED STOPPERS

2 OZ. OIL No. 8 STOPPER   4 OZ. OIL No. 8 STOPPER   6 OZ. OIL No. 8 STOPPER   2 OZ. OIL No. 6 STOPPER   4 OZ. OIL No. 6 STOPPER   6 OZ. OIL No. 6 STOPPER   8 OZ. OIL No. 6 STOPPER   12 OZ. OIL No. 6 STOPPER

REGISTERED TRADE MARK No. 50121

No. 353 COLONIAL PATTERN

REGISTERED TRADE MARK No. 50121

SCALE HALF SIZE

No. 353—SANITARY SYRUP PATENT No. 40600

5 OZ. SANITARY SYRUP

5 OZ. SANITARY SYRUP
WITH
No. 1150—5¼-IN. PLATE, GROUND BOTTOM

7 OZ. SANITARY SYRUP

12 OZ. SANITARY SYRUP

SANITARY SYRUP
SHOWING COVER REMOVED

12 OZ. SANITARY SYRUP
WITH
No. 1150—6-IN. PLATE, GROUND BOTTOM

7 OZ. SANITARY SYRUP
WITH
No. 1150—5¼-IN. PLATE, GROUND BOTTOM

INDIVIDUAL CELERY
CUT TOP AND BOTTOM

TALL CELERY
CUT TOP AND BOTTOM

MAYONNAISE DISH AND PLATE
GROUND BOTTOM

MARMALADE JAR AND COVER
GROUND TOP AND BOTTOM
COVER NOTCHED FOR SPOON

INDIVIDUAL ALMOND

6-IN. FOOTED ALMOND

REGISTERED TRADE MARK No. 50121

No. 353 COLONIAL PATTERN

REGISTERED TRADE MARK No. 50121

SCALE HALF SIZE

GRAPE FRUIT
GROUND BOTTOM

GRAPE FRUIT AND PLATE
GROUND BOTTOM

9-IN. OYSTER COCKTAIL PLATE
GROUND BOTTOM

CRUSHED ICE BOWL
GROUND BOTTOM

10-IN. SPICE TRAY
FIRE POLISHED BOTTOM

ICE BOWL AND PLATE
GROUND BOTTOM

10-IN. TRAY
FIRE POLISHED BOTTOM

CHEESE AND CRACKER PLATE
GROUND BOTTOM

REGISTERED TRADE MARK No. 50121

No. 353 COLONIAL PATTERN

REGISTERED TRADE MARK No. 50121

SCALE HALF SIZE

FINGER BOWL FLARED
STAR BOTTOM

TWO PIECE OYSTER COCKTAIL

FINGER BOWL CUPPED
STAR BOTTOM

TOOTHPICK TRAY
GROUND BOTTOM

KNIFE REST

6½-IN. MUSHROOM COVER

5½-IN. MUSHROOM COVER

4½-IN. MUSHROOM COVER

4½-IN. MUSHROOM COVER AND 7-IN. PLATE
GROUND BOTTOM

6½-IN. MUSHROOM COVER AND 10-IN. PLATE
GROUND BOTTOM
ALSO 10-IN. CHEESE PLATE AND COVER

5½-IN. MUSHROOM COVER AND 8-IN. PLATE
GROUND BOTTOM

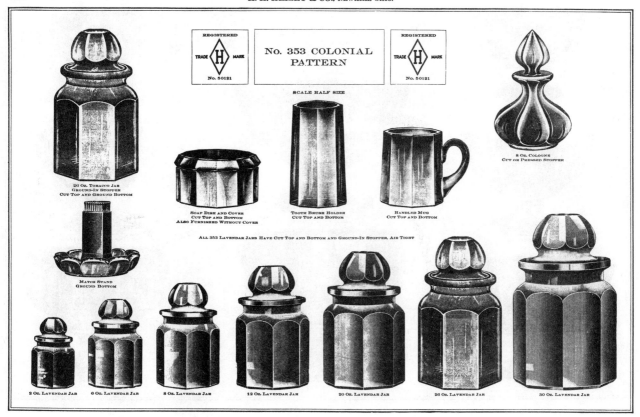

REGISTERED
TRADE **H** MARK
No. 50121

No. 353 COLONIAL PATTERN

REGISTERED
TRADE **H** MARK
No. 50121

SCALE HALF SIZE

26 OZ. TOBACCO JAR
GROUND-IN STOPPER
CUT TOP AND GROUND BOTTOM

SOAP DISH AND COVER
CUT TOP AND BOTTOM
ALSO FURNISHED WITHOUT COVER

TOOTH BRUSH HOLDER
CUT TOP AND BOTTOM

HANDLED MUG
CUT TOP AND BOTTOM

8 OZ. COLOGNE
CUT OR PRESSED STOPPER

MATCH STAND
GROUND BOTTOM

ALL 353 LAVENDAR JARS HAVE CUT TOP AND BOTTOM AND GROUND-IN STOPPER, AIR TIGHT

2 OZ. LAVENDAR JAR   6 OZ. LAVENDAR JAR   8 OZ. LAVENDAR JAR   12 OZ. LAVENDAR JAR   20 OZ. LAVENDAR JAR   26 OZ. LAVENDAR JAR   30 OZ. LAVENDAR JAR

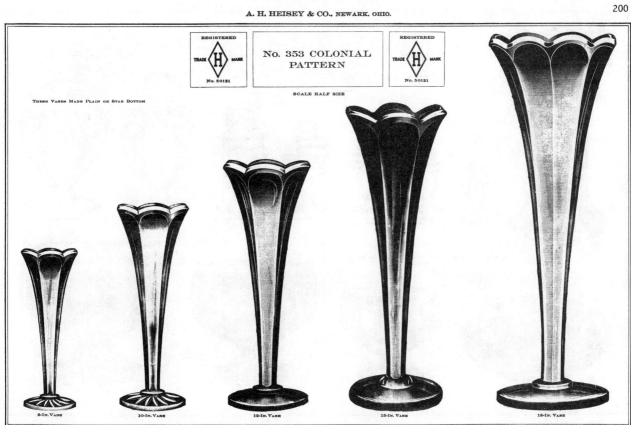

THESE VASES MADE PLAIN OR STAR BOTTOM

REGISTERED
TRADE **H** MARK
No. 50121

No. 353 COLONIAL PATTERN

REGISTERED
TRADE **H** MARK
No. 50121

SCALE HALF SIZE

8-IN. VASE   10-IN. VASE   12-IN. VASE   15-IN. VASE   18-IN. VASE

REGISTERED
TRADE **H** MARK
No. 50121

No. 354 COLONIAL PATTERN

REGISTERED
TRADE **H** MARK
No. 50121

SCALE HALF SIZE

6-In. Low Footed Bowl

7-In. Low Footed Bowl

9-In. Low Footed Bowl

8-In. Low Footed Bowl

9-In. Low Footed Bowl, Cupped

6-In. Low Footed Bowl, Cupped

7-In. Low Footed Bowl, Cupped

8-In. Low Footed Bowl, Cupped

REGISTERED
TRADE **H** MARK
No. 50121

No. 354 COLONIAL PATTERN

REGISTERED
TRADE **H** MARK
No. 50121

SCALE HALF SIZE

10-In. Vase

1 Oz. Lavendar Jar

2¼ Oz. Lavendar Jar

4½ Oz. Lavendar Jar

7 Oz. Lavendar Jar

11 Oz. Lavendar Jar

16 Oz. Lavendar Jar

27 Oz. Lavendar Jar

All No. 354 Lavendar Jars Have Cut Top Stopper, Ground-In Air Tight

8-In. Nappy
Ground Bottom

No. 1 Fern Dish
With
Silver Plated Liner

No. 2 Fern Dish
With
Silver Plated Liner

No. 3 Fern Dish
With
Silver Plated Liner

A. H. HEISEY & CO., NEWARK, OHIO.

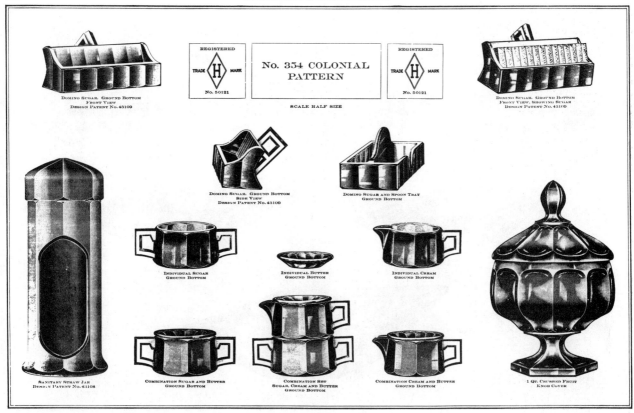

REGISTERED
TRADE **H** MARK
No. 50121

No. 354 COLONIAL
PATTERN

SCALE HALF SIZE

REGISTERED
TRADE **H** MARK
No. 50121

DOMINO SUGAR, GROUND BOTTOM
FRONT VIEW
DESIGN PATENT No. 43109

DOMINO SUGAR, GROUND BOTTOM
FRONT VIEW, SHOWING SUGAR
DESIGN PATENT No. 43109

DOMINO SUGAR, GROUND BOTTOM
SIDE VIEW
DESIGN PATENT No. 43109

DOMINO SUGAR AND SPOON TRAY
GROUND BOTTOM

INDIVIDUAL SUGAR
GROUND BOTTOM

INDIVIDUAL BUTTER
GROUND BOTTOM

INDIVIDUAL CREAM
GROUND BOTTOM

SANITARY STRAW JAR
DESIGN PATENT No. 43108

COMBINATION SUGAR AND BUTTER
GROUND BOTTOM

COMBINATION SET
SUGAR, CREAM AND BUTTER
GROUND BOTTOM

COMBINATION CREAM AND BUTTER
GROUND BOTTOM

1 QT. CRUSHED FRUIT
KNOB COVER

A. H. HEISEY & CO., NEWARK, OHIO.

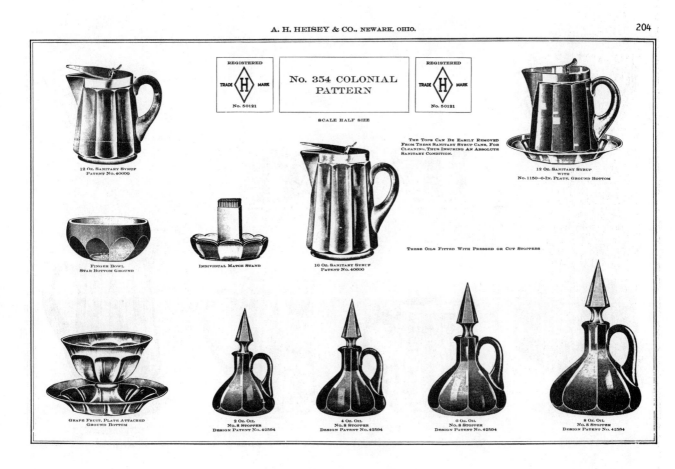

REGISTERED
TRADE **H** MARK
No. 50121

No. 354 COLONIAL
PATTERN

SCALE HALF SIZE

REGISTERED
TRADE **H** MARK
No. 50121

12 OZ. SANITARY SYRUP
PATENT No. 40000

THE TOPS CAN BE EASILY REMOVED
FROM THESE SANITARY SYRUP CANS, FOR
CLEANING, THUS INSURING AN ABSOLUTE
SANITARY CONDITION.

12 OZ. SANITARY SYRUP
WITH
No. 1150—6-IN. PLATE, GROUND BOTTOM

FINGER BOWL
STAR BOTTOM GROUND

INDIVIDUAL MATCH STAND

16 OZ. SANITARY SYRUP
PATENT No. 40000

THESE OILS FITTED WITH PRESSED OR CUT STOPPERS

GRAPE FRUIT, PLATE ATTACHED
GROUND BOTTOM

2 OZ. OIL
No. 8 STOPPER
DESIGN PATENT No. 42594

4 OZ. OIL
No. 8 STOPPER
DESIGN PATENT No. 42594

6 OZ. OIL
No. 8 STOPPER
DESIGN PATENT No. 42594

8 OZ. OIL
No. 8 STOPPER
DESIGN PATENT No. 42594

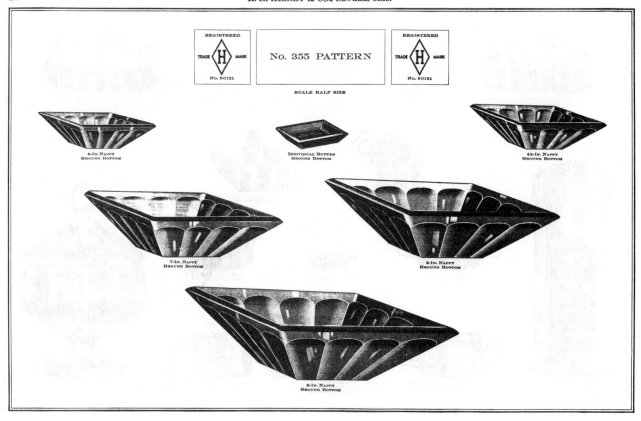

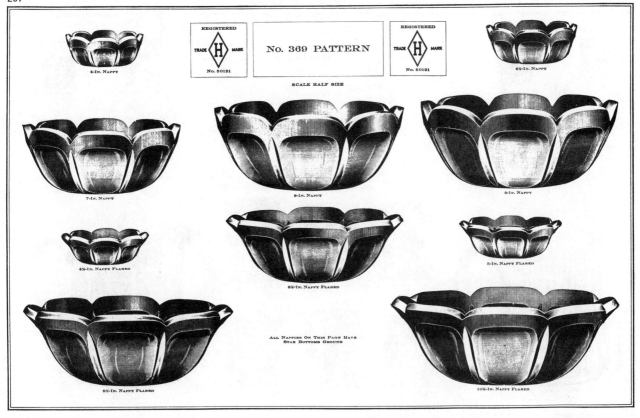

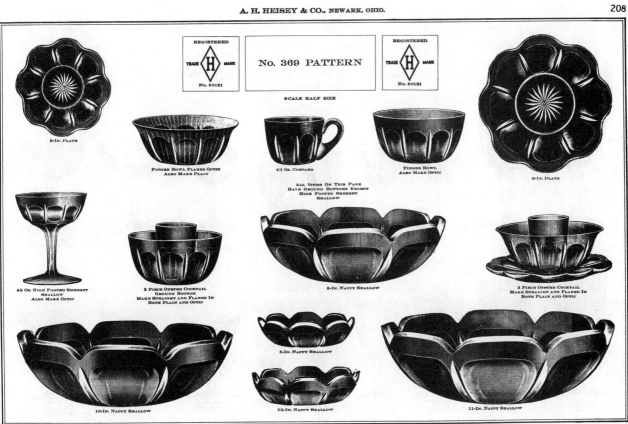

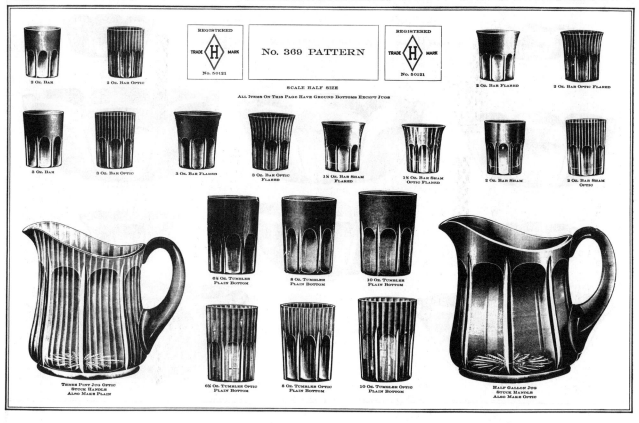

REGISTERED TRADE **H** MARK No. 50121

No. 369 PATTERN

REGISTERED TRADE **H** MARK No. 50121

SCALE HALF SIZE

ALL ITEMS ON THIS PAGE HAVE GROUND BOTTOMS EXCEPT JUGS

2 OZ. BAR

2 OZ. BAR OPTIC

2 OZ. BAR FLARED

2 OZ. BAR OPTIC FLARED

3 OZ. BAR

3 OZ. BAR OPTIC

3 OZ. BAR FLARED

3 OZ. BAR OPTIC FLARED

1½ OZ. BAR SHAM FLARED

1½ OZ. BAR SHAM OPTIC FLARED

2 OZ. BAR SHAM

2 OZ. BAR SHAM OPTIC

THREE PINT JUG OPTIC STUCK HANDLE ALSO MADE PLAIN

6½ OZ. TUMBLER PLAIN BOTTOM

8 OZ. TUMBLER PLAIN BOTTOM

10 OZ. TUMBLER PLAIN BOTTOM

6½ OZ. TUMBLER OPTIC PLAIN BOTTOM

8 OZ. TUMBLER OPTIC PLAIN BOTTOM

10 OZ. TUMBLER OPTIC PLAIN BOTTOM

HALF GALLON JUG STUCK HANDLE ALSO MADE OPTIC

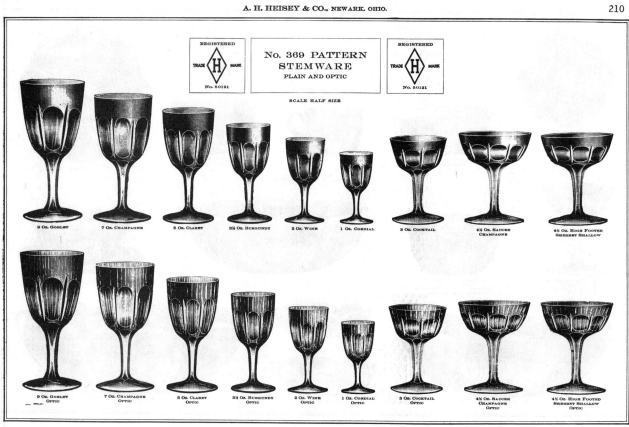

REGISTERED TRADE **H** MARK No. 50121

No. 369 PATTERN STEMWARE PLAIN AND OPTIC

REGISTERED TRADE **H** MARK No. 50121

SCALE HALF SIZE

9 OZ. GOBLET

7 OZ. CHAMPAGNE

5 OZ. CLARET

3½ OZ. BURGUNDY

2 OZ. WINE

1 OZ. CORDIAL

3 OZ. COCKTAIL

4½ OZ. SAUCER CHAMPAGNE

4½ OZ. HIGH FOOTED SHERBET SHALLOW

9 OZ. GOBLET OPTIC

7 OZ. CHAMPAGNE OPTIC

5 OZ. CLARET OPTIC

3½ OZ. BURGUNDY OPTIC

2 OZ. WINE OPTIC

1 OZ. CORDIAL OPTIC

3 OZ. COCKTAIL OPTIC

4½ OZ. SAUCER CHAMPAGNE OPTIC

4½ OZ. HIGH FOOTED SHERBET SHALLOW OPTIC

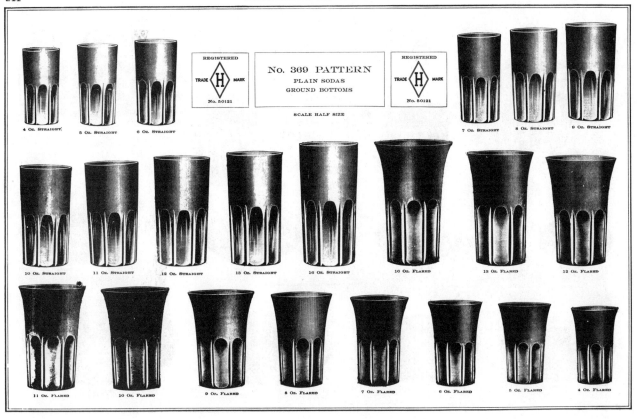

No. 369 PATTERN
PLAIN SODAS
GROUND BOTTOMS

SCALE HALF SIZE

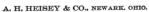

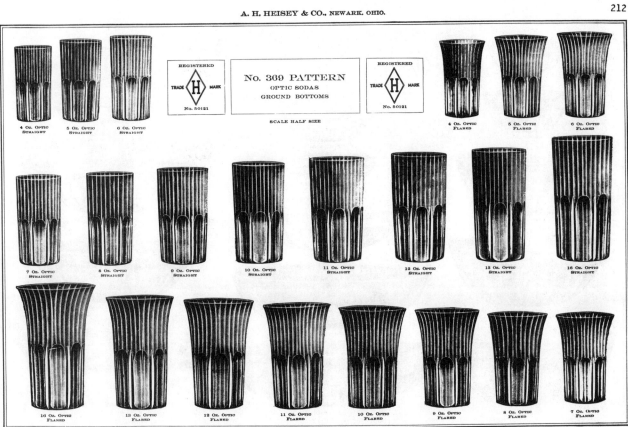

No. 369 PATTERN
OPTIC SODAS
GROUND BOTTOMS

SCALE HALF SIZE

REGISTERED TRADE H MARK No. 50121

No. 393 PATTERN

REGISTERED TRADE H MARK No. 50121

SCALE HALF SIZE

SUGAR AND COVER

CREAM

SPOON

BUTTER AND COVER
GROUND BOTTOM
DESIGN PATENT No. 42711

4-IN. NAPPY

4½-IN. NAPPY

5-IN. NAPPY

5½-IN. NAPPY

ALL THESE NAPPIES HAVE GROUND BOTTOMS

6-IN. NAPPY

6½-IN. NAPPY

7-IN. NAPPY

8-IN. NAPPY
ALSO MAKES 9 IN.

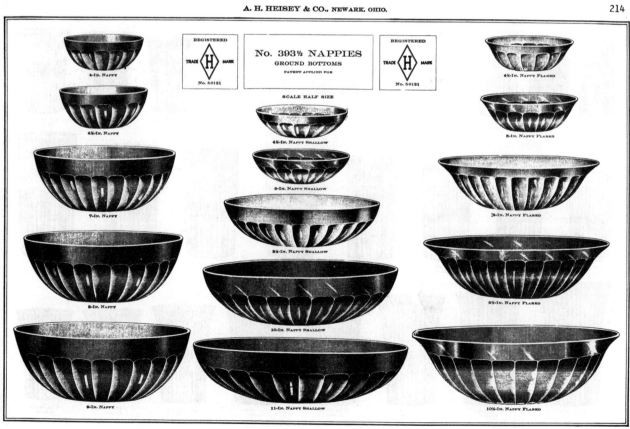

REGISTERED TRADE H MARK No. 50121

No. 393½ NAPPIES
GROUND BOTTOMS
PATENT APPLIED FOR

REGISTERED TRADE H MARK No. 50121

SCALE HALF SIZE

4-IN. NAPPY

4½-IN. NAPPY

7-IN. NAPPY

8-IN. NAPPY

9-IN. NAPPY

4½-IN. NAPPY SHALLOW

5-IN. NAPPY SHALLOW

8½-IN. NAPPY SHALLOW

10-IN. NAPPY SHALLOW

11-IN. NAPPY SHALLOW

4½-IN. NAPPY FLARED

5-IN. NAPPY FLARED

8-IN. NAPPY FLARED

9½-IN. NAPPY FLARED

10½-IN. NAPPY FLARED

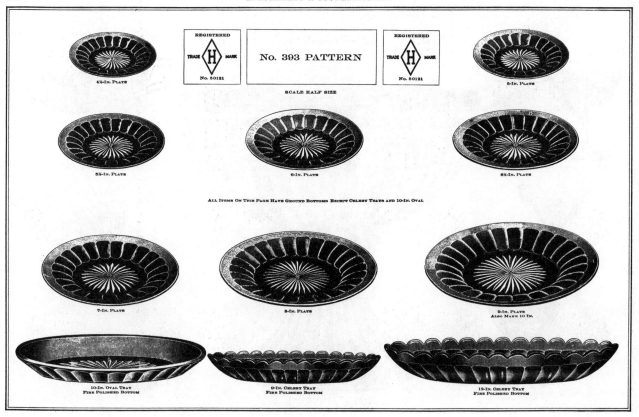

No. 393 PATTERN

SCALE HALF SIZE

4½-In. Plate

5-In. Plate

5½-In. Plate

6-In. Plate

6½-In. Plate

All Items On This Page Have Ground Bottoms Except Celery Trays and 10-In. Oval

7-In. Plate

8-In. Plate

9-In. Plate
Also Made 10 In.

10-In. Oval Tray
Fire Polished Bottom

9-In. Celery Tray
Fire Polished Bottom

12-In. Celery Tray
Fire Polished Bottom

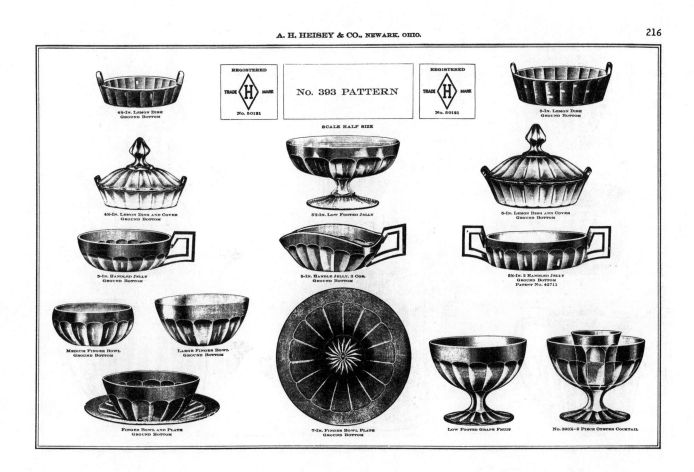

No. 393 PATTERN

SCALE HALF SIZE

4½-In. Lemon Dish
Ground Bottom

5-In. Lemon Dish
Ground Bottom

4½-In. Lemon Dish and Cover
Ground Bottom

5½-In. Low Footed Jelly

5-In. Lemon Dish and Cover
Ground Bottom

5-In. Handled Jelly
Ground Bottom

5-In. Handle Jelly, 3 Cor.
Ground Bottom

5½-In. 2 Handled Jelly
Ground Bottom
Patent No. 42711

Medium Finger Bowl
Ground Bottom

Large Finger Bowl
Ground Bottom

Finger Bowl and Plate
Ground Bottom

7-In. Finger Bowl Plate
Ground Bottom

Low Footed Grape Fruit

No. 393½—2 Piece Oyster Cocktail

REGISTERED
TRADE **H** MARK
No. 50121

No. 393 PATTERN

REGISTERED
TRADE **H** MARK
No. 50121

SCALE HALF SIZE

No. 393—5 Oz. Footed
SHERBET SHALLOW

No. 393—5 Oz. Footed
SHERBET SHALLOW

No. 393—5 Oz. Footed
SHERBET SHALLOW

No. 393—4½ Oz. Custard
GROUND BOTTOM

No. 393—4½ Oz. Custard
GROUND BOTTOM

No. 393—4½ Oz. Custard
GROUND BOTTOM

14-In. PUNCH BOWL AND HIGH FOOT
ALSO MAKE 16-IN. FLARED AND 18-IN. SHALLOW SHAPES
ALL SHAPES MADE WITH OR WITHOUT FOOT

REGISTERED
TRADE **H** MARK
No. 50121

No. 393 PATTERN

REGISTERED
TRADE **H** MARK
No. 50121

SCALE HALF SIZE

ALL ITEMS ON THIS PAGE HAVE STUCK HANDLE WITH EXCEPTION OF 8 OZ. JUG

DESIGN PATENT No. 42665

10 Oz. JUG

1 PINT JUG

3 PINT JUG

8 OZ. JUG

HALF GALLON TANKARD

12 OZ. JUG

1 QUART JUG

HALF GALLON JUG

REGISTERED
TRADE **H** MARK
No. 50121

No. 393 PATTERN

REGISTERED
TRADE **H** MARK
No. 50121

SCALE HALF SIZE

24 OZ. WHISKEY JUG.
CUT STOPPER AND FULL GROUND BOTTOM

10-IN. 2 PIECE CHEESE AND CRACKER PLATE
FIRE POLISHED BOTTOM

MARMALADE JAR
GROUND BOTTOM

1 PINT HOTEL JUG
GROUND BOTTOM
PATENT NO. 43854

1 QUART HOTEL JUG
GROUND BOTTOM
PATENT NO. 43854

3 PINT HOTEL JUG
GROUND BOTTOM
PATENT NO. 43854

½ GALLON HOTEL JUG
GROUND BOTTOM
PATENT NO. 43854

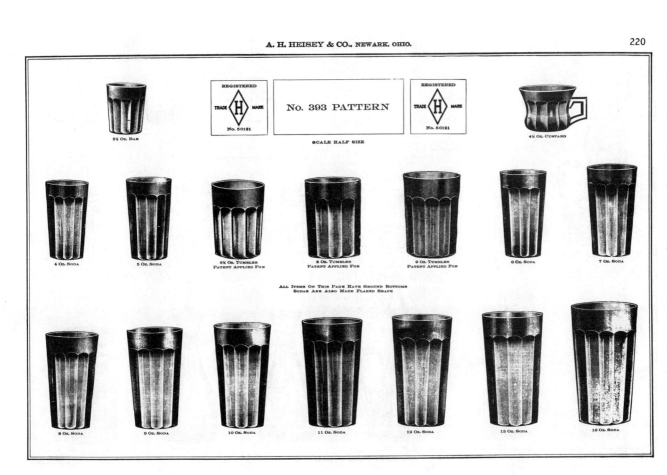

2½ OZ. BAR

REGISTERED
TRADE **H** MARK
No. 50121

No. 393 PATTERN

REGISTERED
TRADE **H** MARK
No. 50121

SCALE HALF SIZE

4½ OZ. CUSTARD

4 OZ. SODA

5 OZ. SODA

6½ OZ. TUMBLER
PATENT APPLIED FOR

8 OZ. TUMBLER
PATENT APPLIED FOR

9 OZ. TUMBLER
PATENT APPLIED FOR

6 OZ. SODA

7 OZ. SODA

ALL ITEMS ON THIS PAGE HAVE GROUND BOTTOMS
SODAS ARE ALSO MADE FLARED SHAPE

8 OZ. SODA

9 OZ. SODA

10 OZ. SODA

11 OZ. SODA

12 OZ. SODA

13 OZ. SODA

16 OZ. SODA

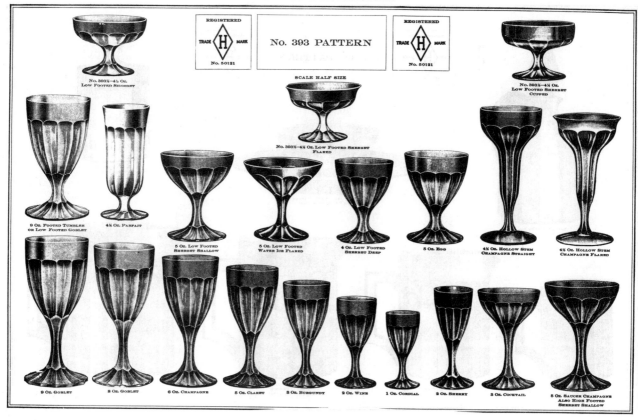

No. 393¼—4½ Oz.
LOW FOOTED SHERBET

REGISTERED
TRADE H MARK
No. 50121

No. 393 PATTERN

SCALE HALF SIZE

REGISTERED
TRADE H MARK
No. 50121

No. 393¼—4½ Oz.
LOW FOOTED SHERBET
CUPPED

No. 393¼—4½ Oz. LOW FOOTED SHERBET
FLARED

9 Oz. FOOTED TUMBLER
OR LOW FOOTED GOBLET

4½ Oz. PARFAIT

5 Oz. LOW FOOTED
SHERBET SHALLOW

5 Oz. LOW FOOTED
WATER ICE FLARED

4 Oz. LOW FOOTED
SHERBET DEEP

5 Oz. EGG

4½ Oz. HOLLOW STEM
CHAMPAGNE STRAIGHT

4½ Oz. HOLLOW STEM
CHAMPAGNE FLARED

9 Oz. GOBLET

8 Oz. GOBLET

6 Oz. CHAMPAGNE

5 Oz. CLARET

3 Oz. BURGUNDY

2 Oz. WINE

1 Oz. CORDIAL

2 Oz. SHERRY

3 Oz. COCKTAIL

5 Oz. SAUCER CHAMPAGNE
ALSO HIGH FOOTED
SHERBET SHALLOW

A. H. HEISEY & CO., NEWARK, OHIO.

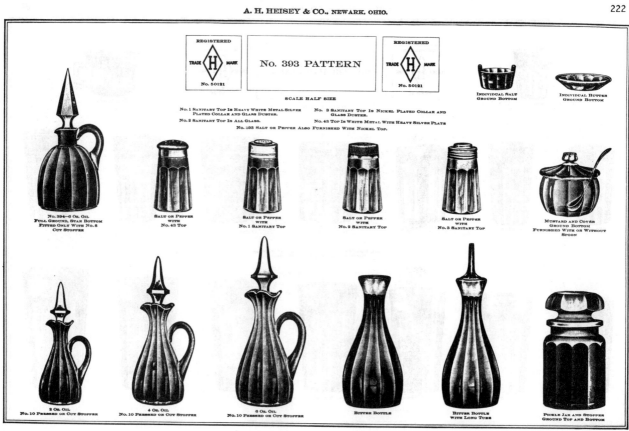

REGISTERED
TRADE H MARK
No. 50121

No. 393 PATTERN

REGISTERED
TRADE H MARK
No. 50121

SCALE HALF SIZE

No. 1 SANITARY TOP IS HEAVY WHITE METAL SILVER
PLATED COLLAR AND GLASS DUSTER.

No. 2 SANITARY TOP IS ALL GLASS.

No. 3 SANITARY TOP IS NICKEL PLATED COLLAR AND
GLASS DUSTER.

No. 43 TOP IS WHITE METAL WITH HEAVY SILVER PLATE

No. 393 SALT OR PEPPER ALSO FURNISHED WITH NICKEL TOP.

INDIVIDUAL SALT
GROUND BOTTOM

INDIVIDUAL BUTTER
GROUND BOTTOM

No. 394—6 Oz. OIL
FULL GROUND, STAR BOTTOM
FITTED ONLY WITH No. 5
CUT STOPPER

SALT OR PEPPER
WITH
No. 43 TOP

SALT OR PEPPER
WITH
No. 1 SANITARY TOP

SALT OR PEPPER
WITH
No. 2 SANITARY TOP

SALT OR PEPPER
WITH
No. 3 SANITARY TOP

MUSTARD AND COVER
GROUND BOTTOM
FURNISHED WITH OR WITHOUT
SPOON

2 Oz. OIL
No. 10 PRESSED OR CUT STOPPER

4 Oz. OIL
No. 10 PRESSED OR CUT STOPPER

6 Oz. OIL
No. 10 PRESSED OR CUT STOPPER

BITTER BOTTLE

BITTER BOTTLE
WITH LONG TUBE

PICKLE JAR AND STOPPER
GROUND TOP AND BOTTOM

REGISTERED
TRADE **H** MARK
No. 50121

No. 393 PATTERN

REGISTERED
TRADE **H** MARK
No. 50121

SCALE HALF SIZE

HOTEL SUGAR

HOTEL CREAM

DOMINO SUGAR
PATENT APPLIED FOR

OVAL HOTEL SUGAR FOOTED

OVAL HOTEL CREAM FOOTED

INDIVIDUAL
CREAM

INDIVIDUAL ICE TUB AND BUTTER
GROUND BOTTOM

FRENCH DRESSING BOAT

FRENCH DRESSING BOAT AND PLATE

INDIVIDUAL
SUGAR

THIS FRENCH DRESSING BOAT ALSO USED FOR MINT SAUCE AND MAYONNAISE DRESSING

HOTEL ICE TUB. GROUND BOTTOM

10-IN. OVAL TRAY AND SHERBET
TRAY WITH FIRE POLISHED BOTTOM

9-IN. FOOTED BANANA SPLIT

REGISTERED
TRADE **H** MARK
No. 50121

No. 400 COLONIAL
PATTERN

REGISTERED
TRADE **H** MARK
No. 50121

SCALE HALF SIZE

SUGAR AND COVER

SPOON

CREAM

BUTTER AND COVER

4-IN. NAPPY

4½-IN. NAPPY SHALLOW

7½-IN. NAPPY

4½-IN. NAPPY

5-IN. NAPPY SHALLOW

8-IN. NAPPY SHALLOW

8½-IN. NAPPY
ALSO MAKE 9½-IN. NAPPY

9-IN. NAPPY SHALLOW
ALSO MAKE 10-IN. NAPPY SHALLOW

REGISTERED
TRADE **H** MARK
No. 50121

No. 400 COLONIAL PATTERN

REGISTERED
TRADE **H** MARK
No. 50121

SCALE HALF SIZE

WATER BOTTLE

EGG CUP

8 OZ. TUMBLER

2 OZ. WINE

11 OZ. GOBLET

QUART JUG

THREE PINT JUG

HALF GALLON JUG

THREE QUART JUG

REGISTERED
TRADE **H** MARK
No. 50121

No. 400 COLONIAL PATTERN

REGISTERED
TRADE **H** MARK
No. 50121

SCALE HALF SIZE

No. 1 SANITARY TOP IS HEAVY WHITE METAL SILVER PLATED COLLAR AND GLASS DUSTER.
No. 3 SANITARY TOP IS NICKEL PLATED COLLAR AND GLASS DUSTER.

"NT" TOP IS OF SPUN NICKEL.
No. 43 TOP IS WHITE METAL WITH HEAVY SILVER PLATE

6 OZ. OIL
PRESSED OR CUT STOPPER

TOOTHPICK

SALT OR PEPPER
WITH
No. 1 SANITARY TOP

SALT OR PEPPER
WITH
No. 3 SANITARY TOP

2 HANDLED LOW FOOTED JELLY

SALT OR PEPPER
WITH
NT TOP

SALT OR PEPPER
WITH
No. 43 TOP

5-IN. FOOTED JELLY
ALSO MAKE 5½ IN. SHALLOW

No. 2 SALT OR PEPPER
WITH
No. 60 TOP

13 OZ. SYRUP. O. K. TOP

HOTEL SUGAR

9-IN. SALVER
ALSO MAKE 10 IN.

HOTEL CREAM

TALL CELERY

REGISTERED TRADE H MARK No. 50121

No. 400 COLONIAL PATTERN

REGISTERED TRADE H MARK No. 50121

SCALE HALF SIZE

No. 400—4 Oz. FOOTED SHERBET

No. 400—4 Oz. FOOTED SHERBET

No. 400—4 Oz. FOOTED SHERBET

No. 400—3½ Oz. CUSTARD GROUND BOTTOM

No. 400—3½ Oz. CUSTARD GROUND BOTTOM

No. 400—3½ Oz. CUSTARD GROUND BOTTOM

12-IN. PUNCH BOWL AND FOOT
ALSO MAKE CUPPED, FLARED AND SHALLOW
ALL SHAPES MADE WITH OR WITHOUT FOOT

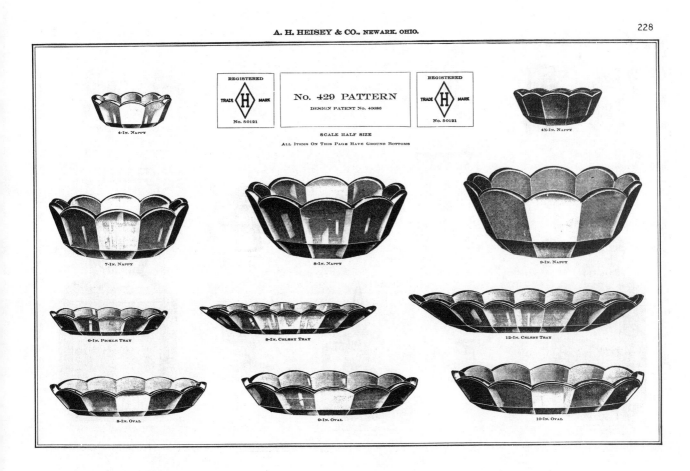

REGISTERED TRADE H MARK No. 50121

No. 429 PATTERN
DESIGN PATENT No. 40086

REGISTERED TRADE H MARK No. 50121

SCALE HALF SIZE
ALL ITEMS ON THIS PAGE HAVE GROUND BOTTOMS

4-IN. NAPPY

4½-IN. NAPPY

7-IN. NAPPY

8-IN. NAPPY

9-IN. NAPPY

6-IN. PICKLE TRAY

9-IN. CELERY TRAY

12-IN. CELERY TRAY

8-IN. OVAL

9-IN. OVAL

10-IN. OVAL

REGISTERED
TRADE **H** MARK
No. 50121

No. 429 PATTERN
DESIGN PATENT No. 40086

REGISTERED
TRADE **H** MARK
No. 50121

SCALE HALF SIZE

ALL ITEMS ON THIS PAGE HAVE GROUND BOTTOMS EXCEPT THE GOBLET

8 OZ. TUMBLER
DESIGN PATENT No. 43703

7 OZ. GOBLET

4 OZ. CUSTARD

HOTEL CREAM

12 OZ. ICE TEA
DESIGN PATENT No. 43703

HOTEL SUGAR AND COVER

PINT JUG. STUCK HANDLE

QUART JUG. STUCK HANDLE

THREE PINT JUG. STUCK HANDLE

HALF GALLON JUG. STUCK HANDLE

REGISTERED
TRADE **H** MARK
No. 50121

No. 429 PATTERN
DESIGN PATENT No. 40086

REGISTERED
TRADE **H** MARK
No. 50121

SCALE HALF SIZE

No. 1 SALT AND PEPPER
WITH
NT TOP

No. 3 SALT AND PEPPER
WITH
No. 43 TOP

No. 1 SALT AND PEPPER
WITH
No. 1 SANITARY TOP

No. 3 SALT AND PEPPER
WITH
No. 3 SANITARY TOP

"NT" TOP IS OF SPUN NICKEL.
No. 43 TOP IS WHITE METAL WITH HEAVY SILVER PLATE
No. 57 TOP IS WHITE METAL WITH HEAVY SILVER PLATE

No. 1 SANITARY TOP IS HEAVY WHITE METAL SILVER
PLATED COLLAR AND GLASS DUSTER.
No. 3 SANITARY TOP IS NICKEL PLATED COLLAR AND
GLASS DUSTER.

5 OZ. EGG

INDIVIDUAL
SALT

FINGER BOWL
GROUND BOTTOM

ONE QUART CRUSHED FRUIT
GROUND BOTTOM
DESIGN PATENT No. 43437

4 OZ. LOW FOOTED
SHERBET STRAIGHT

6 OZ. OIL
No. 8 PRESSED OR CUT STOPPER
DESIGN PATENT No. 43853

4 OZ. LOW FOOTED
SHERBET FLARED

TWO QUART CRUSHED FRUIT
GROUND BOTTOM
DESIGN PATENT No. 43437

A. H. HEISEY & CO., NEWARK. OHIO.

REGISTERED TRADE MARK No. 50121

NO. 433 PATTERN

REGISTERED TRADE MARK No. 50121

SCALE HALF SIZE
ALL ITEMS ON THIS PAGE HAVE GROUND BOTTOMS

6-IN. NAPPY

4½-IN. NAPPY
ALSO MAKE 5 IN.

7-IN. NAPPY

8-IN. NAPPY

9-IN. NAPPY

CREAM

SPOON

SUGAR AND COVER

BUTTER AND COVER

4¾-IN. NAPPY SHALLOW

5½-IN. NAPPY SHALLOW
ALSO MAKE 6 IN.

8½-IN. NAPPY SHALLOW

9½-IN. NAPPY SHALLOW

11-IN. NAPPY SHALLOW

A. H. HEISEY & CO., NEWARK. OHIO.

REGISTERED TRADE MARK No. 50121

NO. 433 PATTERN

REGISTERED TRADE MARK No. 50121

SCALE HALF SIZE

5-IN. ALMOND DISH

INDIVIDUAL ALMOND DISH

4½-IN. NAPPY, SCALLOPED TOP
GROUND BOTTOM
DESIGN PATENT No. 42110

8-IN. NAPPY, SCALLOPED TOP
GROUND BOTTOM
DESIGN PATENT No. 42110

5-IN. ALMOND DISH AND COVER

HOTEL ICE TUB
GROUND BOTTOM

SMALL ICE TUB
GROUND BOTTOM

LARGE ICE TUB
GROUND BOTTOM
ALSO MAKE MEDIUM ICE TUB

HOTEL ICE TUB AND COVER
GROUND BOTTOM

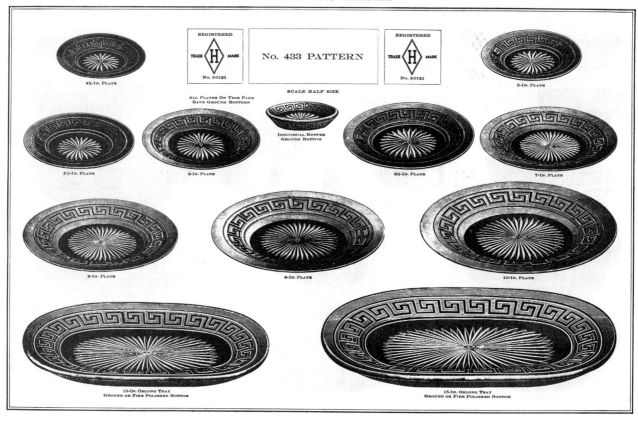

REGISTERED TRADE H MARK No. 50121

No. 433 PATTERN

REGISTERED TRADE H MARK No. 50121

SCALE HALF SIZE

ALL PLATES ON THIS PAGE HAVE GROUND BOTTOMS

4½-IN. PLATE

5-IN. PLATE

5½-IN. PLATE

6-IN. PLATE

INDIVIDUAL BUTTER GROUND BOTTOM

6¾-IN. PLATE

7-IN. PLATE

8-IN. PLATE

9-IN. PLATE

10-IN. PLATE

13-IN. OBLONG TRAY GROUND OR FIRE POLISHED BOTTOM

15-IN. OBLONG TRAY GROUND OR FIRE POLISHED BOTTOM

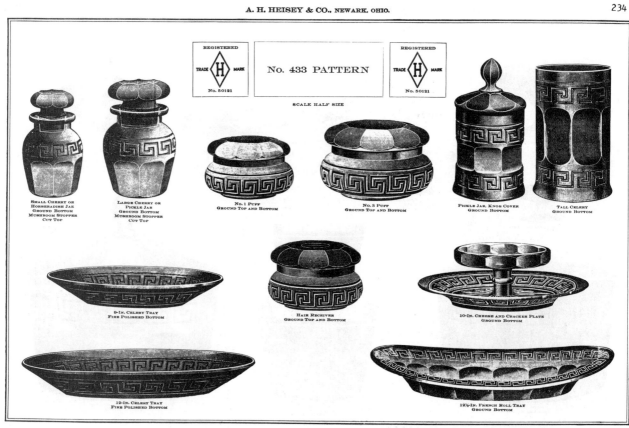

REGISTERED TRADE H MARK No. 50121

No. 433 PATTERN

REGISTERED TRADE H MARK No. 50121

SCALE HALF SIZE

SMALL CHERRY OR HORSERADISH JAR GROUND BOTTOM MUSHROOM STOPPER CUT TOP

LARGE CHERRY OR PICKLE JAR GROUND BOTTOM MUSHROOM STOPPER CUT TOP

NO. 1 PUFF GROUND TOP AND BOTTOM

NO. 3 PUFF GROUND TOP AND BOTTOM

PICKLE JAR, KNOB COVER GROUND BOTTOM

TALL CELERY GROUND BOTTOM

9-IN. CELERY TRAY FIRE POLISHED BOTTOM

HAIR RECEIVER GROUND TOP AND BOTTOM

10-IN. CHEESE AND CRACKER PLATE GROUND BOTTOM

12-IN. CELERY TRAY FIRE POLISHED BOTTOM

12½-IN. FRENCH ROLL TRAY GROUND BOTTOM

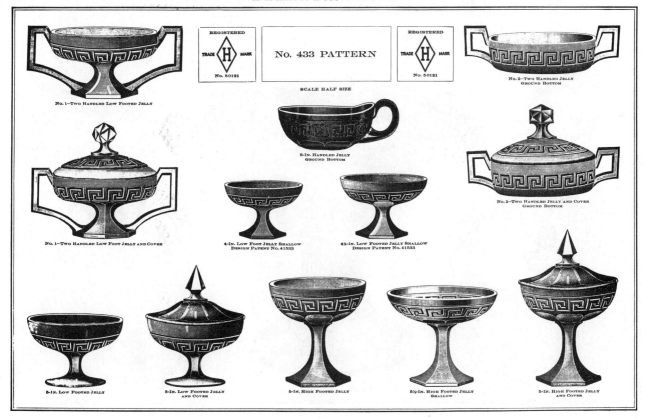

No. 1—Two Handled Low Footed Jelly

REGISTERED
TRADE MARK
No. 50121

No. 433 PATTERN

REGISTERED
TRADE MARK
No. 50121

No. 2—Two Handled Jelly
Ground Bottom

SCALE HALF SIZE

5-In. Handled Jelly
Ground Bottom

No. 1—Two Handled Low Foot Jelly and Cover

4-In. Low Foot Jelly Shallow
Design Patent No. 41533

4½-In. Low Footed Jelly Shallow
Design Patent No. 41533

No. 2—Two Handled Jelly and Cover
Ground Bottom

5-In. Low Footed Jelly

5-In. Low Footed Jelly
and Cover

5-In. High Footed Jelly

5½-In. High Footed Jelly
Shallow

5-In. High Footed Jelly
and Cover

REGISTERED
TRADE MARK
No. 50121

No. 433 PATTERN

REGISTERED
TRADE MARK
No. 50121

SCALE HALF SIZE

10-In. Low Footed Bowl, Shallow

9-In. Low Footed Bowl, Shallow

8-In. Low Footed Bowl, Shallow

7-In. Low Footed Bowl

8-In. Low Footed Bowl

9-In. Low Footed Bowl

REGISTERED
TRADE H MARK
No. 50121

No. 433 PATTERN

REGISTERED
TRADE H MARK
No. 50121

SCALE HALF SIZE

No. 433—4½ Oz. High Footed
Sherbet Shallow

No. 433—4½ Oz. High Footed
Sherbet Shallow

No. 433—4½ Oz. High Footed
Sherbet Shallow

No. 433—4½ Oz. Custard
Ground Bottom

No. 433—4½ Oz. Custard
Ground Bottom

No. 433—4½ Oz. Custard
Ground Bottom

15-In. Punch Bowl and High Foot
Also Make 12-In. Cupped and 16-In. Shallow
All Shapes Made With or Without Foot

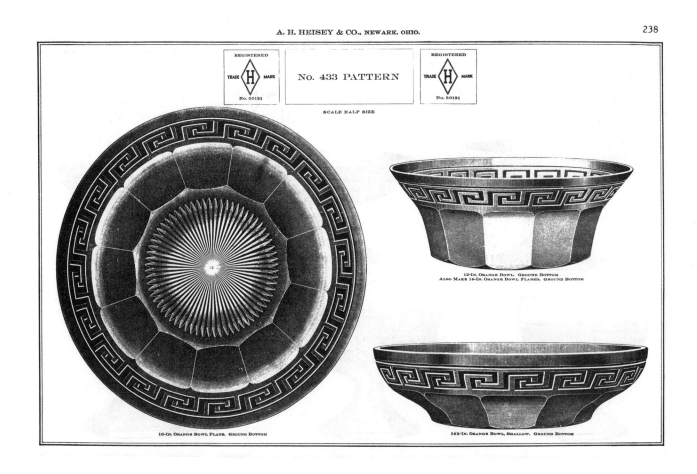

REGISTERED
TRADE H MARK
No. 50121

No. 433 PATTERN

REGISTERED
TRADE H MARK
No. 50121

SCALE HALF SIZE

12-In. Orange Bowl. Ground Bottom
Also Make 14-In. Orange Bowl Flared. Ground Bottom

16-In. Orange Bowl Plate. Ground Bottom

14½-In. Orange Bowl, Shallow. Ground Bottom

REGISTERED TRADE H MARK No. 50121

No. 433 PATTERN

REGISTERED TRADE H MARK No. 50121

SCALE HALF SIZE

PINT JUG
GROUND BOTTOM

2½ OZ. BAR
GROUND BOTTOM

5½ OZ. WATER BAR
GROUND BOTTOM

8 OZ. TUMBLER
GROUND BOTTOM

WATER BOTTLE

ALL JUGS ON THIS PAGE HAVE STUCK HANDLES

QUART JUG
GROUND BOTTOM

THREE PINT JUG
GROUND BOTTOM

HALF GALLON JUG
GROUND BOTTOM

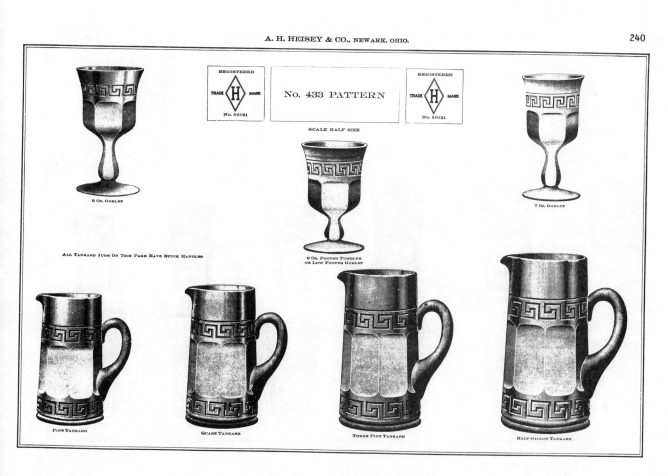

REGISTERED TRADE H MARK No. 50121

No. 433 PATTERN

REGISTERED TRADE H MARK No. 50121

SCALE HALF SIZE

9 OZ. GOBLET

7 OZ. GOBLET

ALL TANKARD JUGS ON THIS PAGE HAVE STUCK HANDLES

9 OZ. FOOTED TUMBLER
OR LOW FOOTED GOBLET

PINT TANKARD

QUART TANKARD

THREE PINT TANKARD

HALF GALLON TANKARD

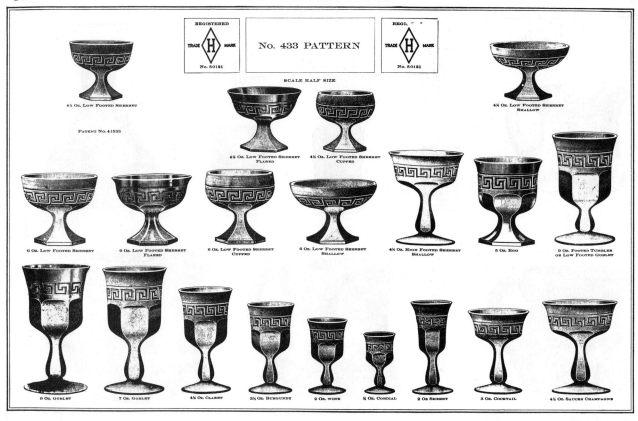

No. 433 PATTERN

SCALE HALF SIZE

4½ Oz. Low Footed Sherbet

Patent No. 41533

4½ Oz. Low Footed Sherbet Flared

4½ Oz. Low Footed Sherbet Cupped

4½ Oz. Low Footed Sherbet Shallow

6 Oz. Low Footed Sherbet

6 Oz. Low Footed Sherbet Flared

6 Oz. Low Footed Sherbet Cupped

6 Oz. Low Footed Sherbet Shallow

4½ Oz. High Footed Sherbet Shallow

5 Oz. Egg

9 Oz. Footed Tumbler or Low Footed Goblet

9 Oz. Goblet

7 Oz. Goblet

4½ Oz. Claret

3½ Oz. Burgundy

2 Oz. Wine

¾ Oz. Cordial

2 Oz. Sherry

3 Oz. Cocktail

4½ Oz. Saucer Champagne

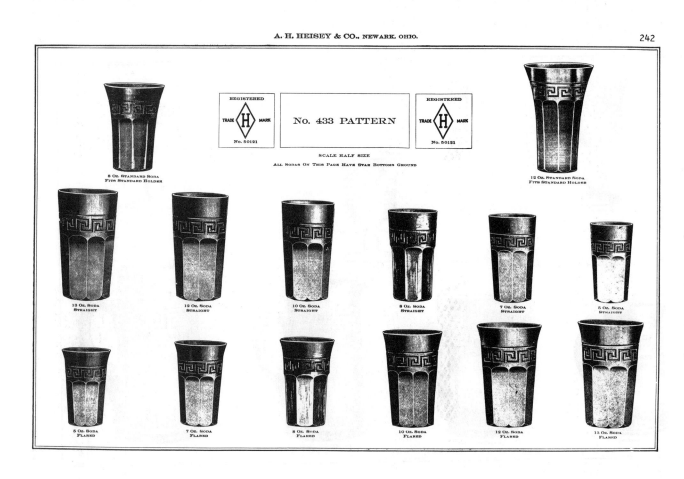

No. 433 PATTERN

SCALE HALF SIZE

ALL SODAS ON THIS PAGE HAVE STAR BOTTOMS GROUND

8 Oz. Standard Soda
Fits Standard Holder

12 Oz. Standard Soda
Fits Standard Holder

13 Oz. Soda Straight

12 Oz. Soda Straight

10 Oz. Soda Straight

8 Oz. Soda Straight

7 Oz. Soda Straight

5 Oz. Soda Straight

5 Oz. Soda Flared

7 Oz. Soda Flared

8 Oz. Soda Flared

10 Oz. Soda Flared

12 Oz. Soda Flared

13 Oz. Soda Flared

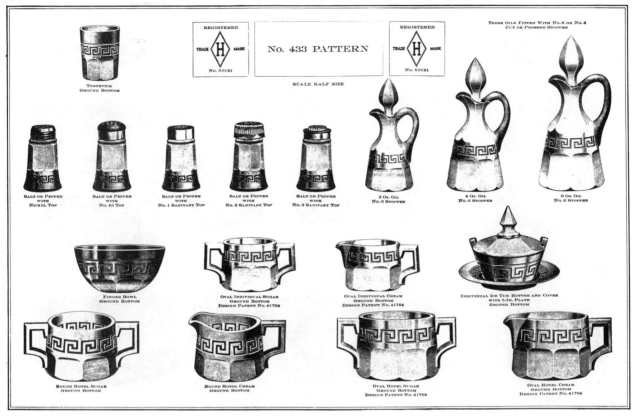

TOOTHPICK
GROUND BOTTOM

REGISTERED
TRADE H MARK
No. 50121

No. 433 PATTERN

REGISTERED
TRADE H MARK
No. 50121

THESE OILS FITTED WITH NO. 6 OR NO. 8
CUT OR PRESSED STOPPER

SCALE HALF SIZE

SALT OR PEPPER
WITH
NICKEL TOP

SALT OR PEPPER
WITH
NO. 43 TOP

SALT OR PEPPER
WITH
NO. 1 SANITARY TOP

SALT OR PEPPER
WITH
NO. 2 SANITARY TOP

SALT OR PEPPER
WITH
NO. 3 SANITARY TOP

2 OZ. OIL
NO. 6 STOPPER

4 OZ. OIL
NO. 6 STOPPER

6 OZ. OIL
NO. 6 STOPPER

FINGER BOWL
GROUND BOTTOM

OVAL INDIVIDUAL SUGAR
GROUND BOTTOM
DESIGN PATENT NO. 41764

OVAL INDIVIDUAL CREAM
GROUND BOTTOM
DESIGN PATENT NO. 41764

INDIVIDUAL ICE TUB BUTTER AND COVER
WITH 5-IN. PLATE
GROUND BOTTOM

ROUND HOTEL SUGAR
GROUND BOTTOM

ROUND HOTEL CREAM
GROUND BOTTOM

OVAL HOTEL SUGAR
GROUND BOTTOM
DESIGN PATENT NO. 41764

OVAL HOTEL CREAM
GROUND BOTTOM
DESIGN PATENT NO. 41764

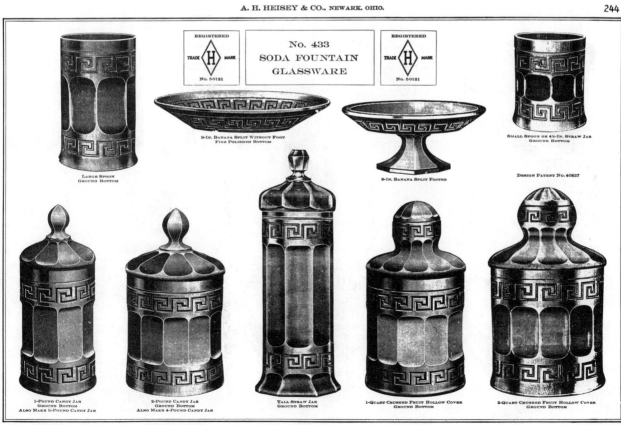

REGISTERED
TRADE H MARK
No. 50121

No. 433
SODA FOUNTAIN
GLASSWARE

REGISTERED
TRADE H MARK
No. 50121

LARGE SPOON
GROUND BOTTOM

9-IN. BANANA SPLIT WITHOUT FOOT
FIRE POLISHED BOTTOM

9-IN. BANANA SPLIT FOOTED

SMALL SPOON OR 4½-IN. STRAW JAR
GROUND BOTTOM

DESIGN PATENT NO. 40837

1-POUND CANDY JAR
GROUND BOTTOM
ALSO MAKE ½-POUND CANDY JAR

2-POUND CANDY JAR
GROUND BOTTOM
ALSO MAKE 4-POUND CANDY JAR

TALL STRAW JAR
GROUND BOTTOM

1-QUART CRUSHED FRUIT HOLLOW COVER
GROUND BOTTOM

2-QUART CRUSHED FRUIT HOLLOW COVER
GROUND BOTTOM

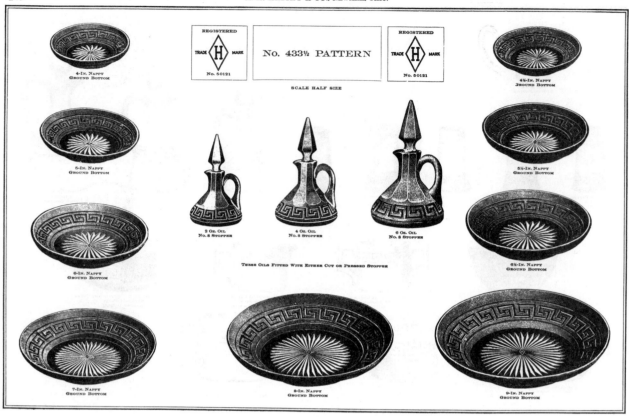

REGISTERED
TRADE **H** MARK
No. 50121

No. 433½ PATTERN

REGISTERED
TRADE **H** MARK
No. 50121

SCALE HALF SIZE

4-In. Nappy
Ground Bottom

5-In. Nappy
Ground Bottom

6-In. Nappy
Ground Bottom

7-In. Nappy
Ground Bottom

4¼-In. Nappy
Ground Bottom

5½-In. Nappy
Ground Bottom

6½-In. Nappy
Ground Bottom

2 Oz. Oil
No. 8 Stopper

4 Oz. Oil
No. 8 Stopper

6 Oz. Oil
No. 8 Stopper

These Oils Fitted With Either Cut or Pressed Stopper

8-In. Nappy
Ground Bottom

9-In. Nappy
Ground Bottom

REGISTERED
TRADE **H** MARK
No. 50121

No. 433½ PATTERN

REGISTERED
TRADE **H** MARK
No. 50121

SCALE HALF SIZE
All Items On This Page Have Ground Bottoms

Pint Jug
Stuck Handle

No. 433
8 Oz. Tumbler

No. 4 Puff
Also Furnished Without Cover

Quart Jug
Stuck Handle

Three Pint Jug
Stuck Handle

Half Gallon Jug
Stuck Handle

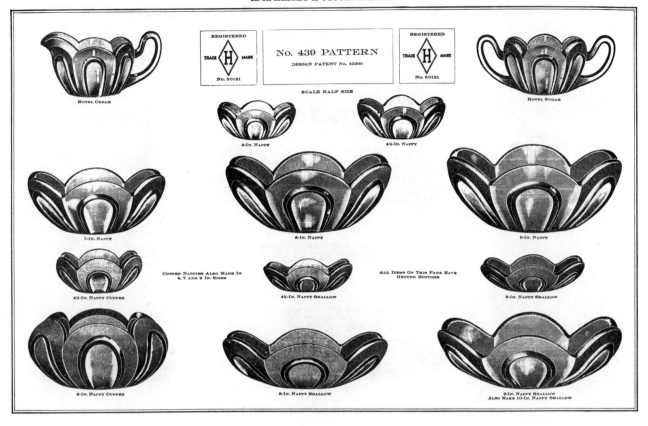

HOTEL CREAM

REGISTERED
TRADE H MARK
No. 50121

No. 439 PATTERN
DESIGN PATENT No. 42260

REGISTERED
TRADE H MARK
No. 50121

HOTEL SUGAR

SCALE HALF SIZE

4-IN. NAPPY

4½-IN. NAPPY

7-IN. NAPPY

8-IN. NAPPY

9-IN. NAPPY

4½-IN. NAPPY CUPPED

CUPPED NAPPIES ALSO MADE IN
4, 7 AND 9 IN. SIZES

4½-IN. NAPPY SHALLOW

ALL ITEMS ON THIS PAGE HAVE
GROUND BOTTOMS

5-IN. NAPPY SHALLOW

8-IN. NAPPY CUPPED

8-IN. NAPPY SHALLOW

9-IN. NAPPY SHALLOW
ALSO MAKE 10-IN. NAPPY SHALLOW

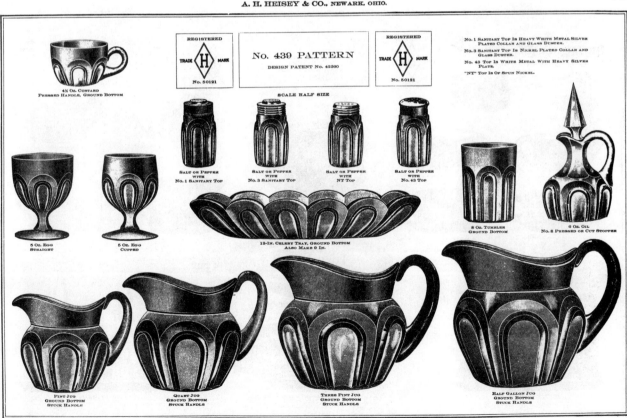

4½ OZ. CUSTARD
PRESSED HANDLE, GROUND BOTTOM

REGISTERED
TRADE H MARK
No. 50121

No. 439 PATTERN
DESIGN PATENT No. 42260

REGISTERED
TRADE H MARK
No. 50121

No. 1 SANITARY TOP IS HEAVY WHITE METAL SILVER
PLATED COLLAR AND GLASS DUSTER.
No. 3 SANITARY TOP IS NICKEL PLATED COLLAR AND
GLASS DUSTER.
No. 43 TOP IS WHITE METAL WITH HEAVY SILVER
PLATE.
"NT" TOP IS OF SPUN NICKEL.

SCALE HALF SIZE

5 OZ. EGG
STRAIGHT

5 OZ. EGG
CUPPED

SALT OR PEPPER
WITH
No. 1 SANITARY TOP

SALT OR PEPPER
WITH
No. 3 SANITARY TOP

SALT OR PEPPER
WITH
NT TOP

SALT OR PEPPER
WITH
No. 43 TOP

8 OZ. TUMBLER
GROUND BOTTOM

6 OZ. OIL
No. 2 PRESSED OR CUT STOPPER

12-IN. CELERY TRAY, GROUND BOTTOM
ALSO MAKE 9 IN.

PINT JUG
GROUND BOTTOM
STUCK HANDLE

QUART JUG
GROUND BOTTOM
STUCK HANDLE

THREE PINT JUG
GROUND BOTTOM
STUCK HANDLE

HALF GALLON JUG
GROUND BOTTOM
STUCK HANDLE

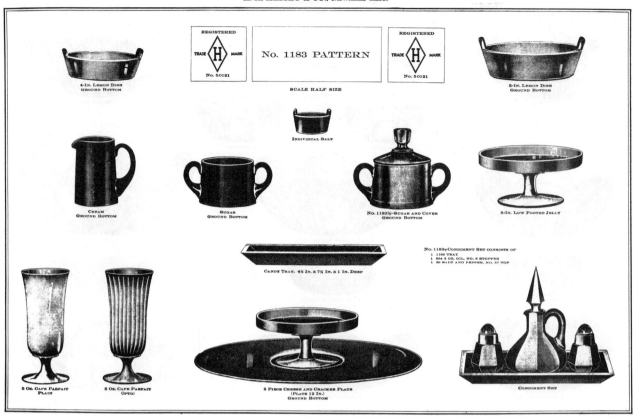

REGISTERED TRADE **H** MARK No. 50121

No. 1183 PATTERN

SCALE HALF SIZE

REGISTERED TRADE **H** MARK No. 50121

4-IN. LEMON DISH GROUND BOTTOM

5-IN. LEMON DISH GROUND BOTTOM

INDIVIDUAL SALT

CREAM GROUND BOTTOM

SUGAR GROUND BOTTOM

No. 1183½—SUGAR AND COVER GROUND BOTTOM

5-IN. LOW FOOTED JELLY

CANDY TRAY. 4½ IN. X 7½ IN. X 1 IN. DEEP

No. 1183—CONDIMENT SET CONSISTS OF
1 1183 TRAY
1 554 2 OZ. OIL, NO. 8 STOPPER
1 20 SALT AND PEPPER, NO. 57 TOP

5 OZ. CAFE PARFAIT PLAIN

5 OZ. CAFE PARFAIT OPTIC

2 PIECE CHEESE AND CRACKER PLATE (PLATE 12 IN.) GROUND BOTTOM

CONDIMENT SET

No. 1184—CANDY TRAY. 5¼ IN. X 8 IN. X 1 IN. DEEP

REGISTERED TRADE **H** MARK No. 50121

No. 1184 AND 1185 PATTERNS

SCALE HALF SIZE
ALL ITEMS ON THIS PAGE HAVE GROUND BOTTOMS

REGISTERED TRADE **H** MARK No. 50121

No. 1185—CANDY TRAY. 6 IN. X 8 IN. X 1 IN. DEEP

No. 1184—INDIVIDUAL BUTTER

No. 1184—ICE TUB AND BUTTER

No. 1185—INDIVIDUAL CREAM

No. 1185—INDIVIDUAL SUGAR

No. 1184—INDIVIDUAL CREAM

No. 1184—INDIVIDUAL CREAM AND BUTTER

No. 1184—COMBINATION SUGAR, CREAM AND BUTTER

No. 1184—INDIVIDUAL SUGAR

No. 1184—INDIVIDUAL SUGAR AND BUTTER

No. 1185—HOTEL CREAM

No. 1185—HOTEL SUGAR

No. 1184—CONDIMENT SET CONSISTS OF
1 1184 TRAY
2 551 4 OZ. OILS, NO. 8 STOPPER
1 20 SALT AND PEPPER, NO. 57 TOP

No. 1185—CONDIMENT SET CONSISTS OF
1 1185 TRAY
2 554 OILS, NO. 8 STOPPER
1 20 SALT AND PEPPER, NO. 57 TOP

No. 1184—8-IN. OYSTER COCKTAIL PLATE ALSO MAKE OPTIC

No. 1184—CONDIMENT SET

No. 1184—9-IN. OYSTER COCKTAIL PLATE ALSO MAKE OPTIC

No. 1185—CONDIMENT SET

REGISTERED TRADE H MARK No. 50121

Nos. 1216 - 1217 - 1218 - 1219 PATTERNS

REGISTERED TRADE H MARK No. 50121

SCALE HALF SIZE

No. 1217 Nappies Are Like No. 1216 But Have Star Instead Of Plain Bottoms
All Items On This Page Have Ground Bottoms Except Roman Punch

No. 1216—4-In. Nappy

No. 1216—4½-In. Nappy

No. 1216—5-In. Nappy

No. 1216—6-In. Nappy

No. 1216—7-In Nappy

No. 1216—8-In. Nappy

No. 1216—9-In. Nappy

No. 1216—Horseradish

No. 1216—Finger Bowl Plain Bottom

No. 1217—Finger Bowl Star Bottom

No. 1218—8-In. Plate
No. 1218 Plates Are Like 1219 But
Have Plain Instead Of Star Bottoms

No. 1216—8-In. Salad Set

No. 1216—7-In. Salad Set

No. 1216—2½ Oz. Roman Punch

No. 1219—4½-In. Plate

No. 1219—5½-In. Plate

No. 1219—6-In. Plate

No. 1219—7-In. Plate

No. 1219—8-In. Plate

No. 1219—9½-In. Plate
Also Make 1219—11-In. Plate

REGISTERED TRADE H MARK No. 50121

No. 440 AND 445 NAPPIES

REGISTERED TRADE H MARK No. 50121

SCALE HALF SIZE

All Items On This Page Have Ground Bottoms

No. 440—4½ In.

No. 440—8 In.

No. 440—5½ In. SHALLOW

No. 440—10 In. SHALLOW

No. 445—4 In.

No. 445—7 In.

No. 445—8 In.

No. 445—9 In.

No. 445—4½ In.

No. 445—4½-In. SHALLOW

No. 445—5½-In. SHALLOW

No. 445—8-In. SHALLOW

No. 445—9-In. SHALLOW

No. 445—10-In. SHALLOW

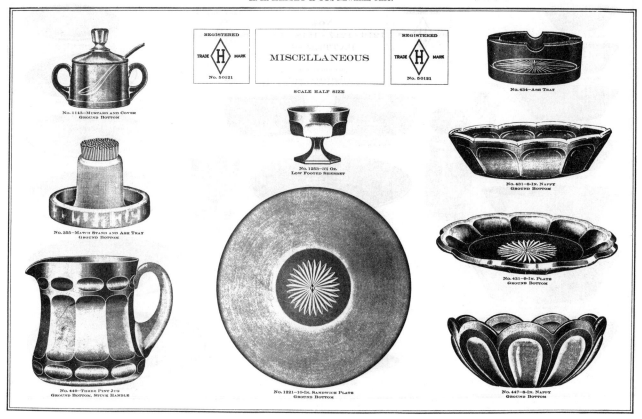

REGISTERED
TRADE H MARK
No. 50121

MISCELLANEOUS

REGISTERED
TRADE H MARK
No. 50121

SCALE HALF SIZE

No. 1145—Mustard and Cover
Ground Bottom

No. 355—Match Stand and Ash Tray
Ground Bottom

No. 440—Three Pint Jug
Ground Bottom, Stuck Handle

No. 1253—3½ Oz.
Low Footed Sherbet

No. 1221—10-In. Sandwich Plate
Ground Bottom

No. 434—Ash Tray

No. 431—8-In. Nappy
Ground Bottom

No. 431—9-In. Plate
Ground Bottom

No. 447—8-In. Nappy
Ground Bottom

REGISTERED
TRADE H MARK
No. 50121

MISCELLANEOUS

REGISTERED
TRADE H MARK
No. 50121

SCALE HALF SIZE

No. 10—Hair Receiver
Cut Top and Bottom
Design Patent No. 40460

No. 16—Puff Box and Cover
Cut Top and Bottom
Design Patent No. 40460

No. 17—Puff Box and Cover
Cut Top and Bottom
Design Patent No. 40460

No. 25—Puff Box and Cover
Cut Top and Bottom
Design Patent No. 40460

No. 356—Combination Set
Ground Bottom

No. 356—Individual Sugar
and Butter
Ground Bottom

No. 356—Individual
Sugar
Ground Bottom

No. 356—Combination Cream
and Butter
Ground Bottom

No. 356—Individual
Cream
Ground Bottom

No. 2—Mustard Spoon

No. 2—Salad Spoon

No. 2—Salad Fork

No. 385—Half Gallon Tankard
Stuck Handle

No. 385—9 Oz. Tumbler
Ground Bottom

No. 395—8-In. Low Foot Bowl

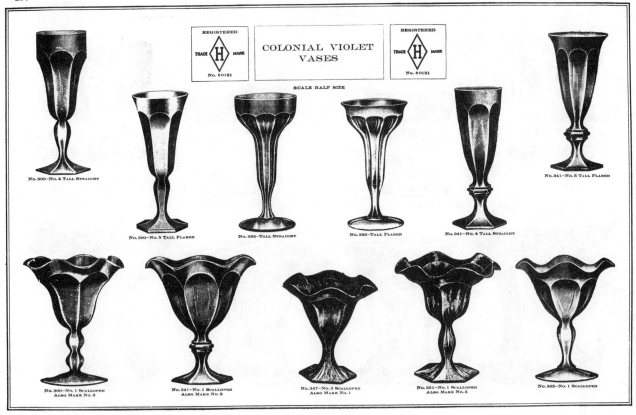

REGISTERED TRADE H MARK No. 50121

COLONIAL VIOLET VASES

REGISTERED TRADE H MARK No. 50121

SCALE HALF SIZE

No. 300—No. 4 Tall Straight

No. 341—No. 5 Tall Flared

No. 300—No. 5 Tall Flared

No. 393—Tall Straight

No. 393—Tall Flared

No. 341—No. 4 Tall Straight

No. 300—No. 1 Scalloped
Also Make No. 3

No. 341—No. 1 Scalloped
Also Make No. 3

No. 347—No. 3 Scalloped
Also Make No. 1

No. 351—No. 1 Scalloped
Also Make No. 3

No. 363—No. 1 Scalloped

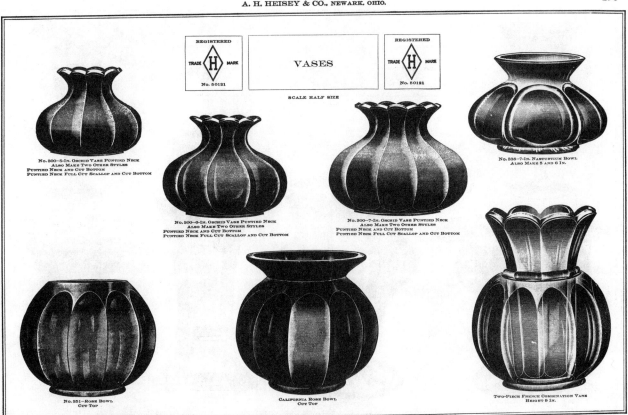

REGISTERED TRADE H MARK No. 50121

VASES

REGISTERED TRADE H MARK No. 50121

SCALE HALF SIZE

No. 300—5-In. Orchid Vase Puntied Neck
Also Make Two Other Styles
Puntied Neck and Cut Bottom
Puntied Neck Full Cut Scallop and Cut Bottom

No. 300—6-In. Orchid Vase Puntied Neck
Also Make Two Other Styles
Puntied Neck and Cut Bottom
Puntied Neck Full Cut Scallop and Cut Bottom

No. 300—7-In. Orchid Vase Puntied Neck
Also Make Two Other Styles
Puntied Neck and Cut Bottom
Puntied Neck Full Cut Scallop and Cut Bottom

No. 338—7-In. Nasturtium Bowl
Also Make 5 and 6 In.

No. 351—Rose Bowl
Cut Top

California Rose Bowl
Cut Top

Two-Piece French Combination Vase
Height 9 In.

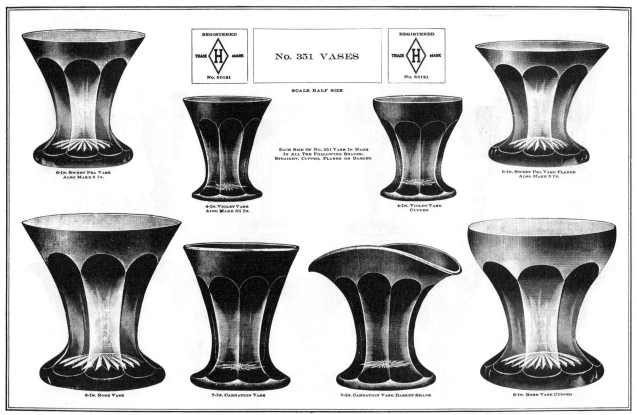

REGISTERED TRADE **H** MARK No. 50121

No. 351 VASES

REGISTERED TRADE **H** MARK No. 50121

SCALE HALF SIZE

EACH SIZE OF NO. 351 VASE IS MADE IN ALL THE FOLLOWING SHAPES: STRAIGHT, CUPPED, FLARED OR BASKET.

6-IN. SWEET PEA VASE ALSO MAKE 5 IN.

4-IN. VIOLET VASE ALSO MAKE 3½ IN.

4-IN. VIOLET VASE CUPPED

6-IN. SWEET PEA VASE FLARED ALSO MAKE 5 IN.

8-IN. ROSE VASE

7-IN. CARNATION VASE

7-IN. CARNATION VASE BASKET SHAPE

8-IN. ROSE VASE CUPPED

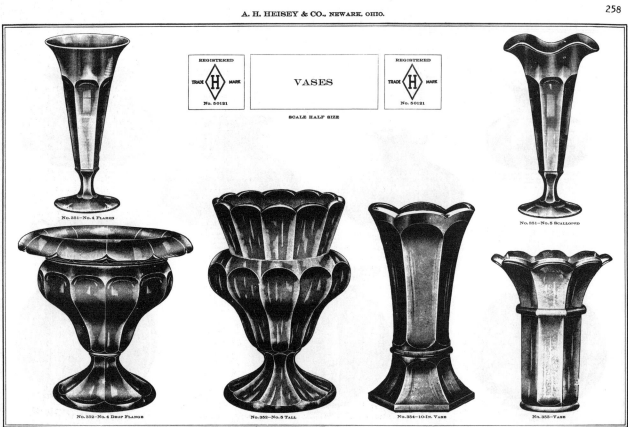

REGISTERED TRADE **H** MARK No. 50121

VASES

REGISTERED TRADE **H** MARK No. 50121

SCALE HALF SIZE

No. 351—No. 4 FLARED

No. 351—No. 5 SCALLOPED

No. 352—No. 4 DROP FLANGE

No. 352—No. 5 TALL

No. 354—10-IN. VASE

No. 355—VASE

A. H. HEISEY & CO., NEWARK, OHIO.

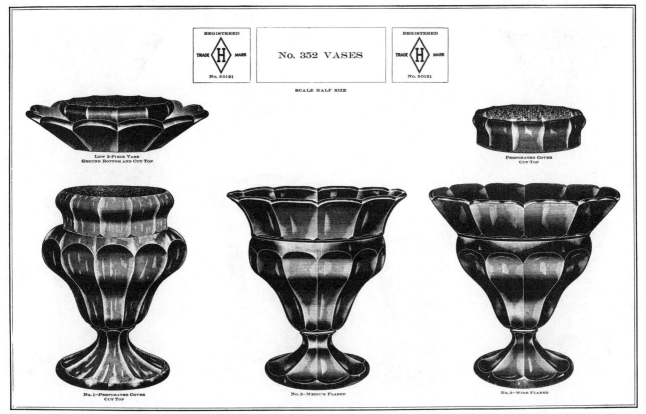

| REGISTERED TRADE (H) MARK No. 50121 | No. 352 VASES | REGISTERED TRADE (H) MARK No. 50121 |

SCALE HALF SIZE

Low 2-Piece Vase
Ground Bottom and Cut Top

Perforated Cover
Cut Top

No. 1—Perforated Cover
Cut Top

No. 2—Medium Flared

No. 3—Wide Flared

A. H. HEISEY & CO., NEWARK, OHIO.

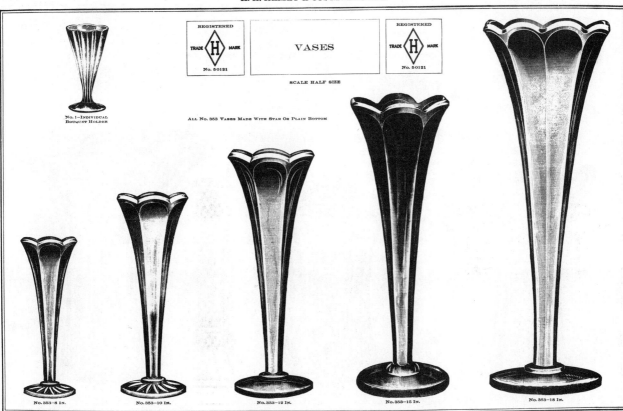
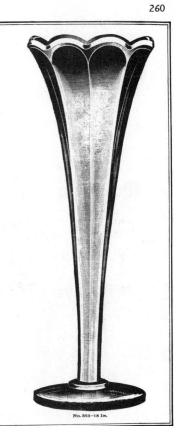

| REGISTERED TRADE (H) MARK No. 50121 | VASES | REGISTERED TRADE (H) MARK No. 50121 |

SCALE HALF SIZE

No. 1—Individual
Bouquet Holder

All No. 353 Vases Made With Star Or Plain Bottom

No. 353—8 In.

No. 353—10 In.

No. 353—12 In.

No. 353—15 In.

No. 353—18 In.

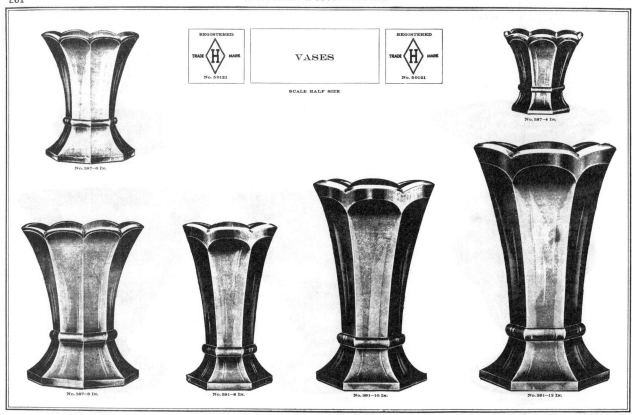

REGISTERED
TRADE **H** MARK
No. 50121

VASES

REGISTERED
TRADE **H** MARK
No. 50121

SCALE HALF SIZE

No. 387—6 In.

No. 387—4 In.

No. 387—8 In.

No. 391—8 In.

No. 391—10 In.

No. 391—12 In.

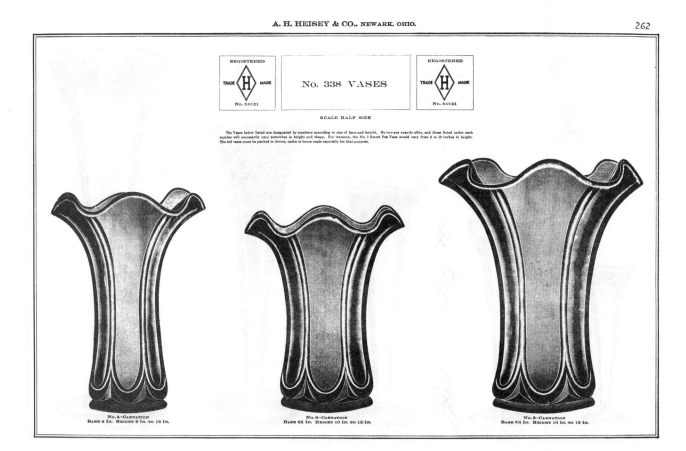

REGISTERED
TRADE **H** MARK
No. 50121

No. 338 VASES

REGISTERED
TRADE **H** MARK
No. 50121

SCALE HALF SIZE

The Vases below listed are designated by numbers according to size of base and height. No two are exactly alike, and those listed under each number will necessarily vary somewhat in height and shape. For instance, the No. 7 Sweet Pea Vase would vary from 8 to 10 inches in height. The tall vases must be packed in tierces, casks or boxes made especially for that purpose.

No. 4—CARNATION
BASE 4 IN. HEIGHT 9 IN. TO 13 IN.

No. 6—CARNATION
BASE 4½ IN. HEIGHT 10 IN. TO 13 IN.

No. 8—CARNATION
BASE 5½ IN. HEIGHT 10 IN. TO 13 IN.

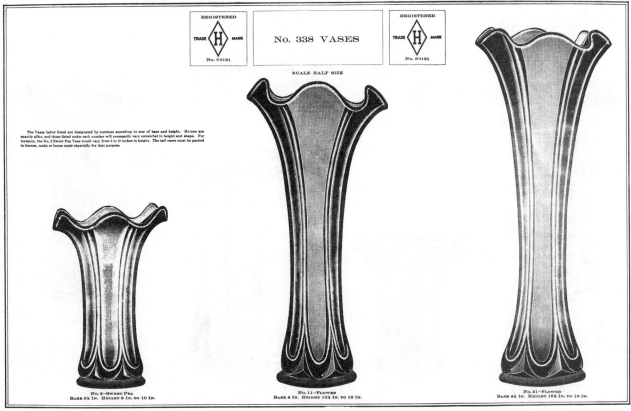

REGISTERED
TRADE **H** MARK
No. 50121

NO. 338 VASES

REGISTERED
TRADE **H** MARK
No. 50121

SCALE HALF SIZE

The Vases below listed are designated by numbers according to size of base and height. No two are exactly alike, and those listed under each number will necessarily vary somewhat in height and shape. For instance, the No. 2 Sweet Pea Vase would vary from 8 to 10 inches in height. The tall vases must be packed in tierces, casks or boxes made especially for that purpose.

NO. 2—SWEET PEA
BASE 3½ IN. HEIGHT 8 IN. TO 10 IN.

NO. 11—FLOWER
BASE 4 IN. HEIGHT 13½ IN. TO 16 IN.

NO. 21—FLOWER
BASE 4½ IN. HEIGHT 16½ IN. TO 19 IN.

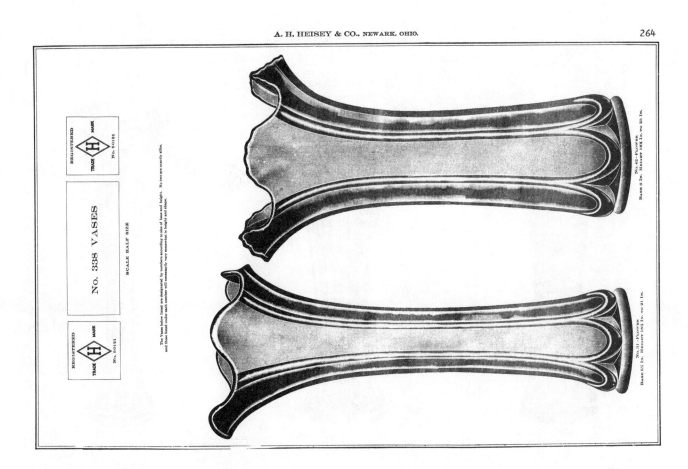

REGISTERED
TRADE **H** MARK
No. 50121

NO. 338 VASES

REGISTERED
TRADE **H** MARK
No. 50121

SCALE HALF SIZE

The Vases below listed are designated by numbers according to size of base and height. No two are exactly alike, and those listed under each number will necessarily vary somewhat in height and shape.

NO. 42—FLOWER
BASE 6 IN. HEIGHT 18½ IN. TO 23 IN.

NO. 31—FLOWER
BASE 5½ IN. HEIGHT 18½ IN. TO 21 IN.

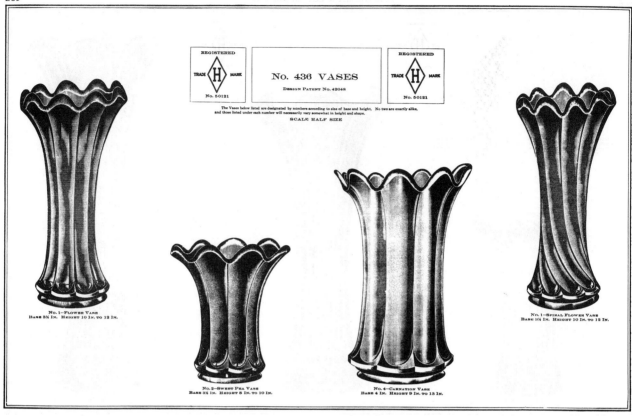

REGISTERED
TRADE H MARK
No. 50121

No. 436 VASES
DESIGN PATENT No. 42048

REGISTERED
TRADE H MARK
No. 50121

The Vases below listed are designated by numbers according to size of base and height. No two are exactly alike, and those listed under each number will necessarily vary somewhat in height and shape.

SCALE HALF SIZE

No. 1—FLOWER VASE
BASE 3½ IN. HEIGHT 10 IN. TO 12 IN.

No. 2—SWEET PEA VASE
BASE 3½ IN. HEIGHT 8 IN. TO 10 IN.

No. 4—CARNATION VASE
BASE 4 IN. HEIGHT 9 IN. TO 13 IN.

No. 1—SPIRAL FLOWER VASE
BASE 3½ IN. HEIGHT 10 IN. TO 12 IN.

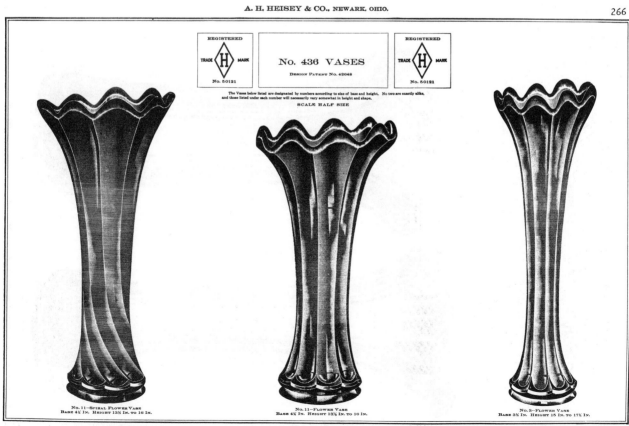

REGISTERED
TRADE H MARK
No. 50121

No. 436 VASES
DESIGN PATENT No. 42048

REGISTERED
TRADE H MARK
No. 50121

The Vases below listed are designated by numbers according to size of base and height. No two are exactly alike, and those listed under each number will necessarily vary somewhat in height and shape.

SCALE HALF SIZE

No. 11—SPIRAL FLOWER VASE
BASE 4½ IN. HEIGHT 13½ IN. TO 16 IN.

No. 11—FLOWER VASE
BASE 4½ IN. HEIGHT 13½ IN. TO 16 IN.

No. 3—FLOWER VASE
BASE 3½ IN. HEIGHT 15 IN. TO 17½ IN.

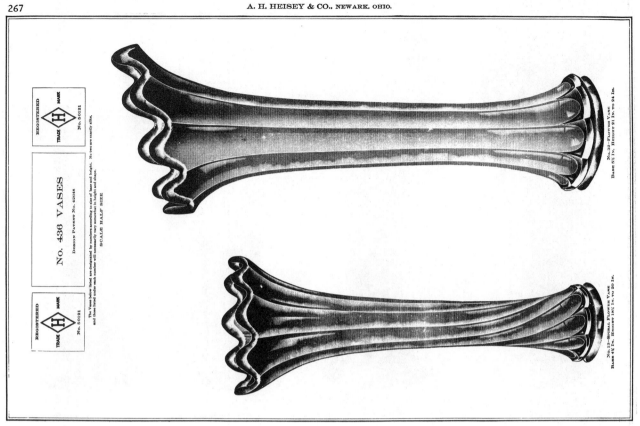

No. 436 VASES

DESIGN PATENT No. 42048

SCALE HALF SIZE

The Vases below listed are designated by numbers according to size of base and height. No two are exactly alike, and those listed under each number will necessarily vary somewhat in height and shape.

No. 32—FLOWER VASE. BASE 5⅝ IN. HEIGHT 21 IN. TO 24 IN.

No. 13—SPIRAL FLOWER VASE. BASE 4⅝ IN. HEIGHT 18½ IN. TO 20 IN.

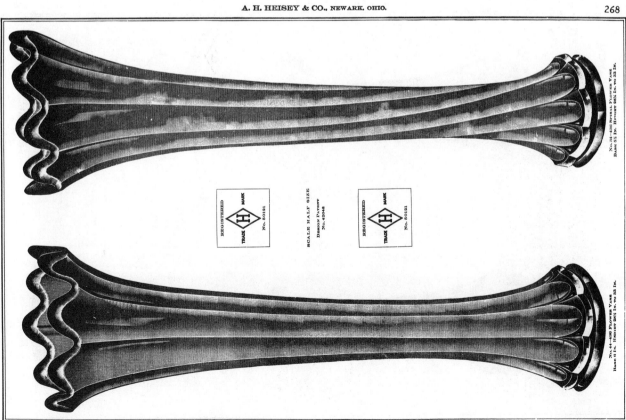

SCALE HALF SIZE

DESIGN PATENT No. 42048

No. 34—436 SPIRAL FLOWER VASE. BASE 5½ IN. HEIGHT 28½ IN. TO 33 IN.

No. 4—436 FLOWER VASE. BASE 6 IN. HEIGHT 28½ IN. TO 33 IN.

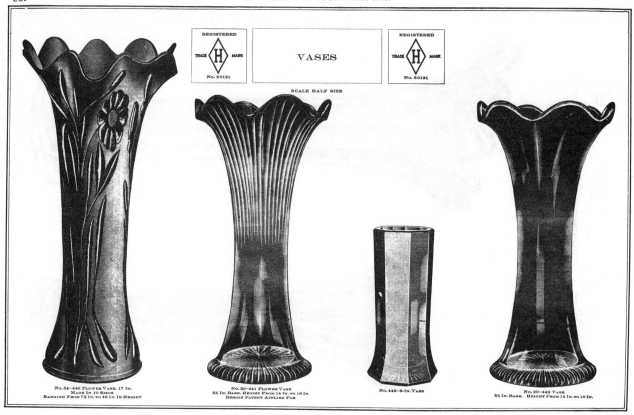

REGISTERED
TRADE **H** MARK
No. 50121

VASES

REGISTERED
TRADE **H** MARK
No. 50121

SCALE HALF SIZE

No. 54–440 Flower Vase, 17 In.
Made In 10 Sizes
Ranging From 7½ In. to 48 In. In Height

No. 20–441 Flower Vase
5¾ In. Base. Height From 14 In. to 16 In.
Design Patent Applied For

No. 442–8-In. Vase

No. 20–443 Vase
5¾ In. Base. Height From 14 In. to 16 In.

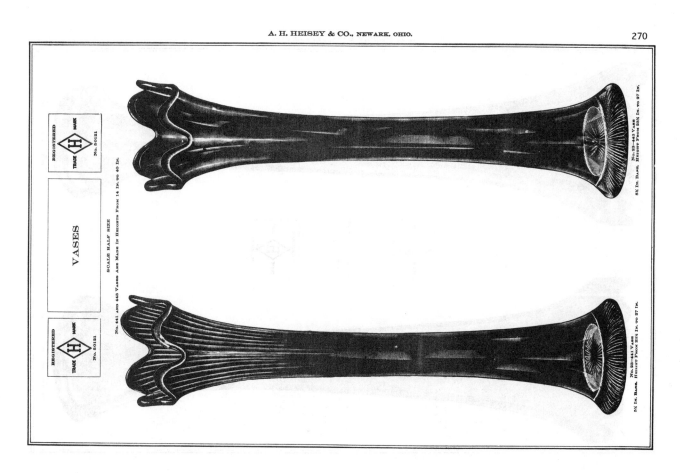

REGISTERED
TRADE **H** MARK
No. 50121

VASES

SCALE HALF SIZE

No. 441 and 443 Vases Are Made In Heights From 14 In. to 40 In.

REGISTERED
TRADE **H** MARK
No. 50121

No. 23–443 Vase
5¾ In. Base. Height From 25¾ In. to 27 In.

No. 23–441 Vase
5¾ In. Base. Height From 25¾ In. to 27 In.

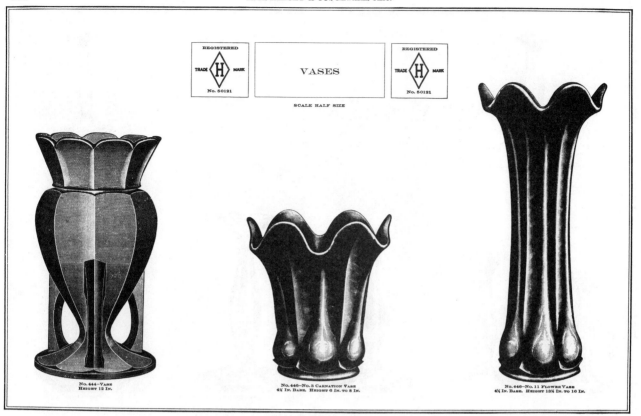

VASES

REGISTERED TRADE H MARK No. 50121

REGISTERED TRADE H MARK No. 50121

SCALE HALF SIZE

No. 444—Vase
Height 12 In.

No. 446—No. 3 Carnation Vase
4½ In. Base. Height 6 In. to 8 In.

No. 446—No. 11 Flower Vase
4½ In. Base. Height 13½ In. to 16 In.

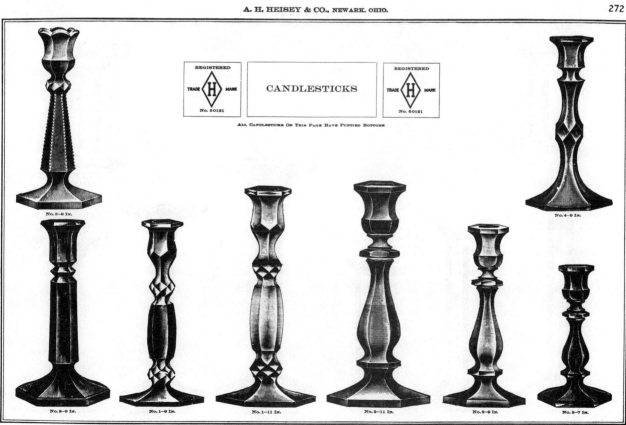

CANDLESTICKS

REGISTERED TRADE H MARK No. 50121

REGISTERED TRADE H MARK No. 50121

All Candlesticks On This Page Have Puntied Bottoms

No. 3—9 In.

No. 4—9 In.

No. 3—9 In.

No. 1—9 In.

No. 1—11 In.

No. 2—11 In.

No. 2—9 In.

No. 2—7 In.

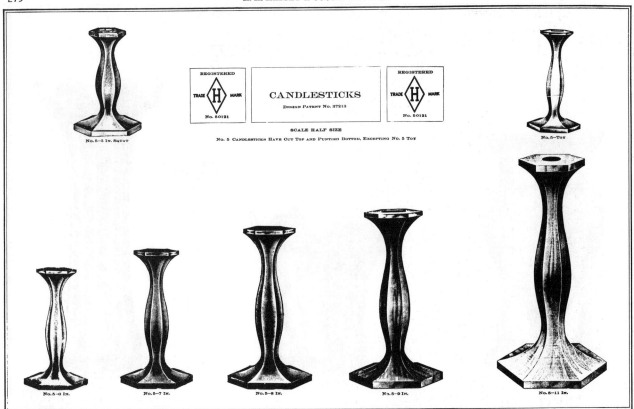

REGISTERED TRADE H MARK No. 50121

CANDLESTICKS

Design Patent No. 37213

REGISTERED TRADE H MARK No. 50121

SCALE HALF SIZE

No. 5 Candlesticks Have Cut Top and Puntied Bottom, Excepting No. 5 Toy

No. 5—5 In. Squat

No. 5—Toy

No. 5—6 In.

No. 5—7 In.

No. 5—8 In.

No. 5—9 In.

No. 5—11 In.

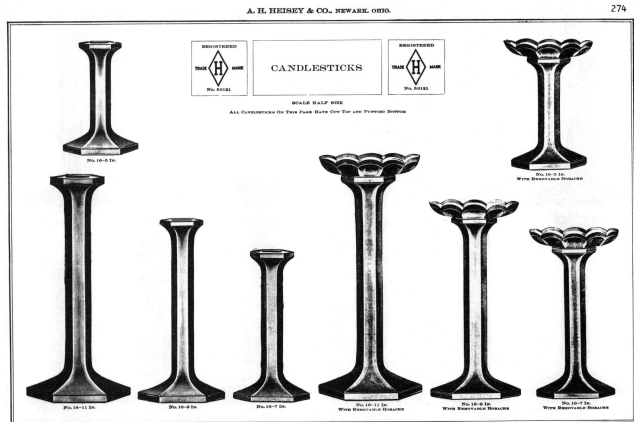

REGISTERED TRADE H MARK No. 50121

CANDLESTICKS

REGISTERED TRADE H MARK No. 50121

SCALE HALF SIZE

All Candlesticks On This Page Have Cut Top and Puntied Bottom

No. 16—5 In.

No. 16—5 In.
With Removable Bobache

No. 16—11 In.

No. 16—9 In.

No. 16—7 In.

No. 16—11 In.
With Removable Bobache

No. 16—9 In.
With Removable Bobache

No. 16—7 In.
With Removable Bobache

A. H. HEISEY & CO., NEWARK, OHIO.

REGISTERED
TRADE H MARK
No. 50121

CANDLESTICKS

REGISTERED
TRADE H MARK
No. 50121

SCALE HALF SIZE

ALL CANDLESTICKS ON THIS PAGE HAVE
CUT TOP AND PUNTIED BOTTOM

No. 20—7 IN.

No. 21—7 IN.

No. 21 CANDLESTICKS'
DESIGN PATENT No. 41520

No. 20—9 IN.

No. 20—11 IN.

No. 21—15 IN.

No. 21—11 IN.

No. 21—9 IN.

A. H. HEISEY & CO., NEWARK, OHIO.

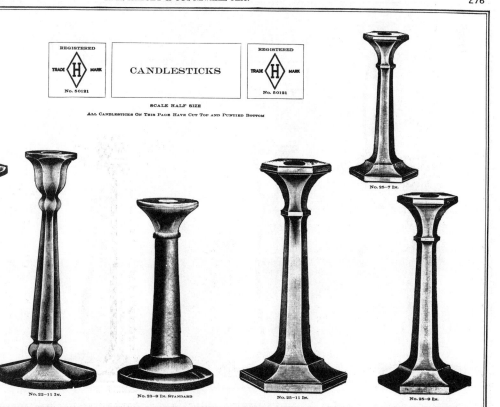

REGISTERED
TRADE H MARK
No. 50121

CANDLESTICKS

REGISTERED
TRADE H MARK
No. 50121

SCALE HALF SIZE
ALL CANDLESTICKS ON THIS PAGE HAVE CUT TOP AND PUNTIED BOTTOM

No. 22—7 IN.

No. 25—7 IN.

No. 22—9 IN.

No. 22—11 IN.

No. 23—9 IN. STANDARD

No. 25—11 IN.

No. 25—9 IN.

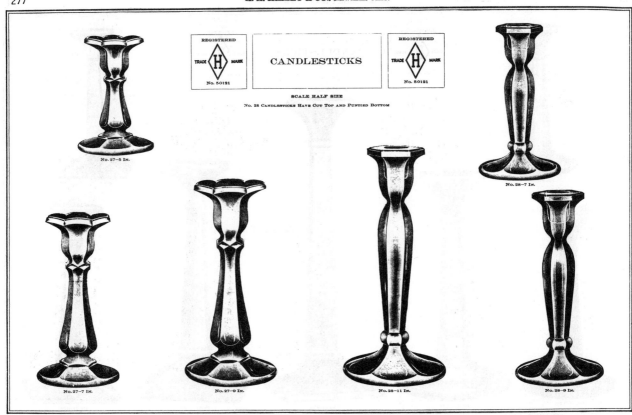

REGISTERED
TRADE (H) MARK
No. 50121

CANDLESTICKS

REGISTERED
TRADE (H) MARK
No. 50121

SCALE HALF SIZE

No. 28 Candlesticks Have Cut Top and Puntied Bottom

No. 27—5 In.

No. 28—7 In.

No. 27—7 In.

No. 27—9 In.

No. 28—11 In.

No. 28—9 In.

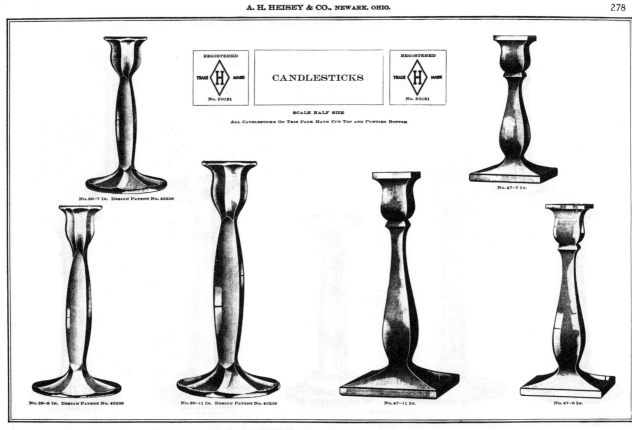

REGISTERED
TRADE (H) MARK
No. 50121

CANDLESTICKS

REGISTERED
TRADE (H) MARK
No. 50121

SCALE HALF SIZE

All Candlesticks On This Page Have Cut Top and Puntied Bottom

No. 29—7 In. Design Patent No. 43236

No. 47—7 In.

No. 29—9 In. Design Patent No. 43236

No. 29—11 In. Design Patent No. 43236

No. 47—11 In.

No. 47—9 In.

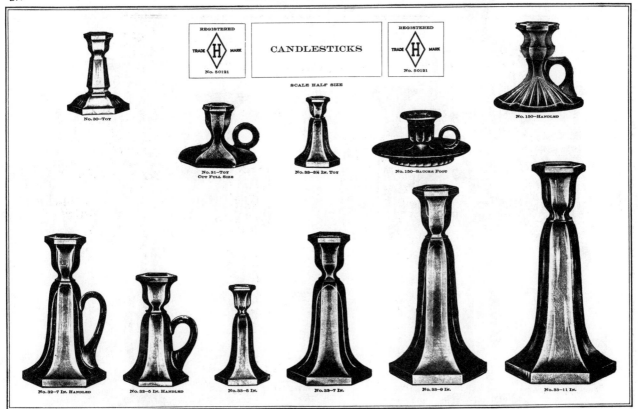

REGISTERED

TRADE (H) MARK

No. 50121

CANDLESTICKS

REGISTERED

TRADE (H) MARK

No. 50121

SCALE HALF SIZE

No. 30—TOY

No. 31—TOY
CUT FULL SIZE

No. 33—3½ IN. TOY

No. 150—SAUCER FOOT

No. 150—HANDLED

No. 32—7 IN. HANDLED

No. 32—5 IN. HANDLED

No. 33—5 IN.

No. 33—7 IN.

No. 33—9 IN.

No. 33—11 IN.

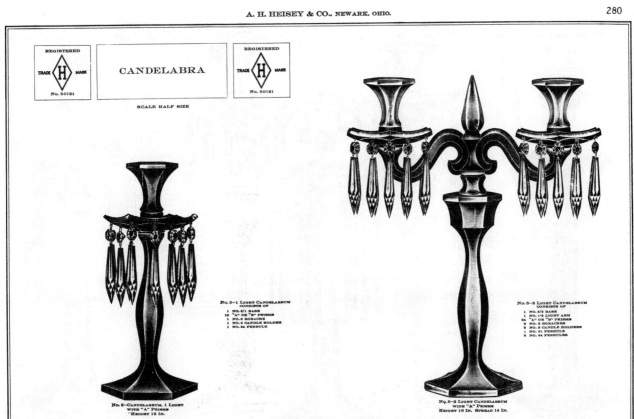

REGISTERED

TRADE (H) MARK

No. 50121

CANDELABRA

REGISTERED

TRADE (H) MARK

No. 50121

SCALE HALF SIZE

No. 5—1 LIGHT CANDELABRUM
CONSISTS OF

1 NO. 5/1 BASE
12 "A" OR "B" PRISMS
1 NO. 5 BOBACHE
1 NO. 5 CANDLE HOLDER
1 NO. 54 FERRULE

No. 5—2 LIGHT CANDELABRUM
CONSISTS OF

1 NO. 5/2 BASE
1 NO. 1-2 LIGHT ARM
24 "A" OR "B" PRISMS
2 NO. 5 BOBACHES
2 NO. 5 CANDLE HOLDERS
1 NO. 51 FERRULE
2 NO. 54 FERRULES

No. 5—CANDELABRUM, 1 LIGHT
WITH "A" PRISMS
HEIGHT 12 IN.

No. 5—2 LIGHT CANDELABRUM
WITH "A" PRISMS
HEIGHT 16 IN. SPREAD 14 IN.

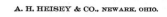

CANDELABRA

SCALE HALF SIZE

REGISTERED

TRADE H MARK

No. 50121

No. 5—CANDELABRUM. 2 ARMS, 3 LIGHTS
WITH "B" PRISMS
HEIGHT 21½ IN. SPREAD 14 IN.

No. 5—3 LIGHT CANDELABRUM
CONSISTS OF
1 NO. 5/3 BASE
1 NO. 1-3 LIGHT ARM
36 "A" OR "B" PRISMS
3 NO. 5 BOBACHES
3 NO. 5 CANDLE HOLDERS
1 NO. 51 FERRULE
1 NO. 54 FERRULES

No. 5—4 LIGHT CANDELABRUM
CONSISTS OF
1 NO. 5/4 BASE
1 NO. 1-4 LIGHT ARM
48 "A" OR "B" PRISMS
4 NO. 5 BOBACHES
4 NO. 5 CANDLE HOLDERS
1 NO. 51 FERRULE
1 NO. 54 FERRULES

No. 5—CANDELABRUM. 3 ARMS, 4 LIGHTS
WITH "A" PRISMS
HEIGHT 21½ IN. SPREAD 14 IN.

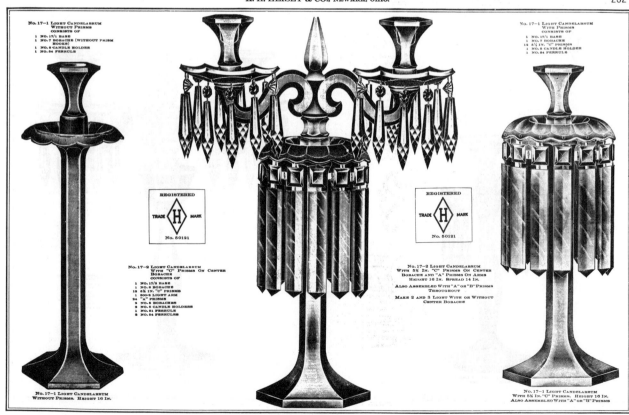

No. 17—1 LIGHT CANDELABRUM
WITHOUT PRISMS
CONSISTS OF
1 NO. 17/1 BASE
1 NO. 7 BOBACHE (WITHOUT PRISM
    HOOKS)
1 NO. 5 CANDLE HOLDER
1 NO. 54 FERRULE

No. 17—1 LIGHT CANDELABRUM
WITH PRISMS
CONSISTS OF
1 NO. 17/1 BASE
1 NO. 7 BOBACHE
12 5½ IN. "C" PRISMS
1 NO. 5 CANDLE HOLDER
1 NO. 54 FERRULE

REGISTERED

TRADE H MARK

No. 50121

REGISTERED

TRADE H MARK

No. 50121

No. 17—2 LIGHT CANDELABRUM
WITH "C" PRISMS ON CENTER
BOBACHE
CONSISTS OF
1 NO. 17/2 BASE
1 NO. 8 BOBACHE
12 5½ IN. "C" PRISMS
1 200-2 LIGHT ARM
24 "A" PRISMS
2 NO. 5 BOBACHES
2 NO. 5 CANDLE HOLDERS
1 NO. 51 FERRULE
2 NO. 54 FERRULES

No. 17—2 LIGHT CANDELABRUM
WITH 5½ IN. "C" PRISMS ON CENTER
BOBACHE AND "A" PRISMS ON ARMS
HEIGHT 16 IN. SPREAD 14 IN.

ALSO ASSEMBLED WITH "A" OR "B" PRISMS
THROUGHOUT

MAKE 2 AND 3 LIGHT WITH OR WITHOUT
CENTER BOBACHE

No. 17—1 LIGHT CANDELABRUM
WITHOUT PRISMS. HEIGHT 16 IN.

No. 17—1 LIGHT CANDELABRUM
WITH 5½ IN. "C" PRISMS. HEIGHT 16 IN.
ALSO ASSEMBLED WITH "A" OR "B" PRISMS

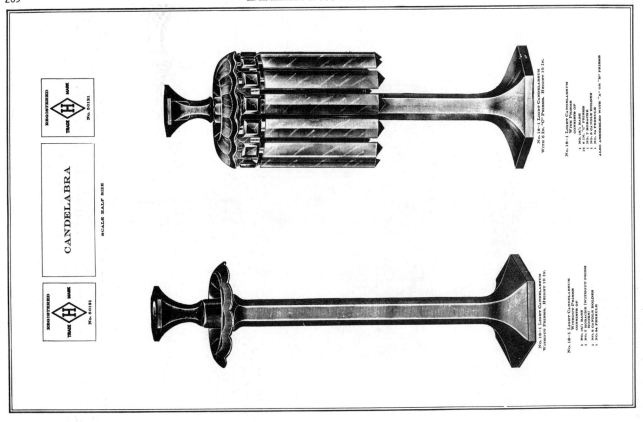

REGISTERED
TRADE H MARK
No. 50121

CANDELABRA

SCALE HALF SIZE

REGISTERED TRADE H MARK
No. 50121

No. 18-1 Light Candelabrum
With 6 In. "C" Prisms. Height 19 In.

No. 18-1 Light Candelabrum
With Prisms
Consists of
1 No. 18-1 Base
12 6 In. "C" Prisms
1 No. 7 Bobache
1 No. 5 Candle Holder
1 No. 54 Ferrule
Also Assembled with "A" or "B" Prisms

No. 18-1 Light Candelabrum
Without Prisms. Height 19 In.

No. 18-1 Light Candelabrum
Without Prisms
Consists of
1 No. 18-1 Base
1 No. 7 Bobache (Without Prism Holes)
1 No. 5 Candle Holder
1 No. 54 Ferrule

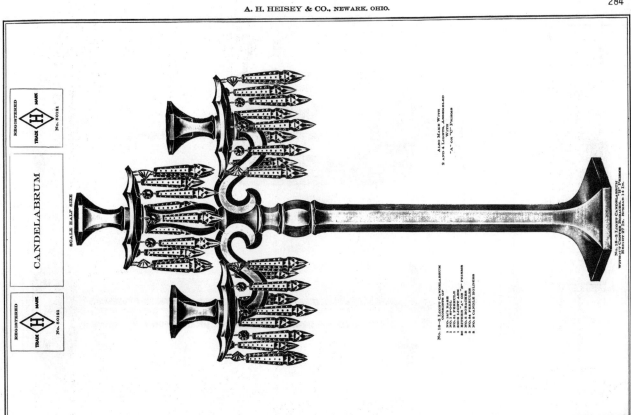

REGISTERED
TRADE H MARK
No. 50121

CANDELABRUM

SCALE HALF SIZE

REGISTERED TRADE H MARK
No. 50121

Also Made With
2 and 4 Lights Assembled
With
"A" or "C" Prisms

No. 18-3 Light Candelabrum
Consists of
1 No. 18-3 Base
1 No. 5 Ferrule
1 Son 3 Light Arm
30 6 In. "C" Prisms
2 No. 8 Bobaches
1 Either "A" or "B" Prisms
3 No. 64 Ferrules
3 No. 5 Candle Holders

No. 18-3 Light Candelabrum
Without Lower Bobache, "C" Prisms
Height 27 In., Spread 14 In.

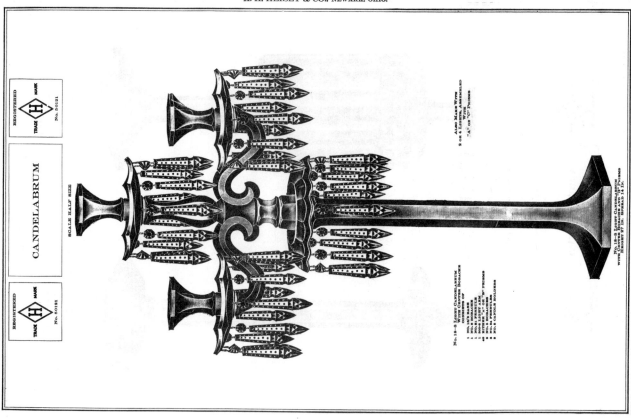

REGISTERED TRADE MARK No. 50121

CANDELABRUM

SCALE HALF SIZE

REGISTERED TRADE MARK No. 50121

REGISTERED TRADE MARK No. 50121

CANDELABRA

SCALE HALF SIZE

REGISTERED TRADE MARK No. 50121

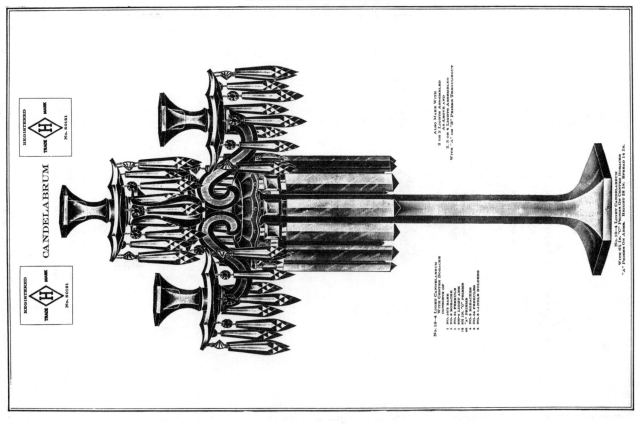

REGISTERED TRADE MARK No. 50121

CANDELABRUM

REGISTERED TRADE MARK No. 50121

No. 18–4 LIGHT CANDELABRUM
WITH CENTER BOBACHE
CONSISTS OF

1. NO. 10'S BASE
1. NO. 51 PRISMLE
1. 300-4 LIGHT ARM
12. 6½ IN. "C" PRISMS
4. NO. 5 BOBACHES
4. NO. 54 PRISMLES
4. NO. 5 CANDLE HOLDERS

ALSO MADE WITH
2 OR 3 LIGHTS ASSEMBLED
AS ABOVE AND
2, 3, OR 4 LIGHTS ASSEMBLED
WITH 6½ IN. "C" PRISMS THROUGHOUT

No. 18–4 LIGHT CANDELABRUM
WITH 6½ IN. "C" PRISMS ON CENTER BOBACHE
"A" PRISMS ON ARMS. HEIGHT 23 IN. SPREAD 14 IN.

REGISTERED TRADE MARK No. 50121

CANDELABRUM

SCALE HALF SIZE

REGISTERED TRADE MARK No. 50121

No. 34–1 LIGHT CANDELABRUM
WITH "A" OR "B"
PRISMS CONSISTS OF

1. NO. 34/1 BASE
1. NO. 34 PRISMLE
1. NO. 5 BOBACHE
12. "A" OR "B" PRISMS
1. NO. 5 CANDLE HOLDER

No. 34–1 LIGHT CANDELABRUM
WITH "A" PRISMS. HEIGHT 10 IN. BASE 12 IN.
ABOVE ALSO MADE IN FOLLOWING HEIGHTS:

No. 35–1 LIGHT CANDELABRUM
WITH "A" OR "B" PRISMS. HEIGHT 19 IN. BASE 15 IN.

No. 36–1 LIGHT CANDELABRUM
WITH "A" OR "B" PRISMS. HEIGHT 22 IN. BASE 18 IN.

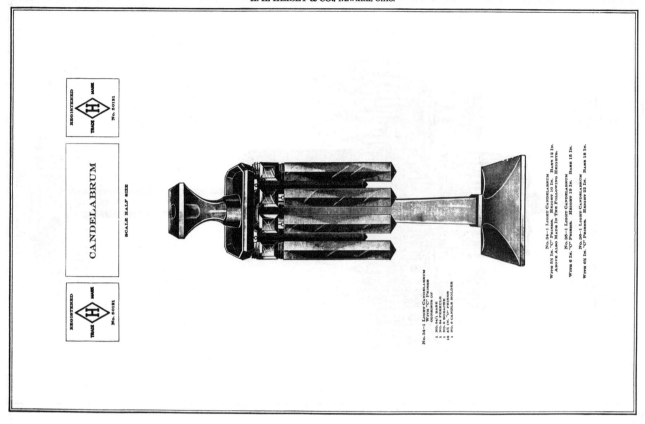

REGISTERED TRADE MARK H No. 50131

CANDELABRUM

SCALE HALF SIZE

REGISTERED TRADE MARK H No. 50131

No. 34—1 LIGHT CANDELABRUM WITH "C" PRISMS
CONSISTS OF

1   NO./1 BASE
1   NO. 84 PRISTICLE
1   NO. 9 BOBACHE
12   6½ IN. "C" PRISMS
1   NO. 6 CANDLE HOLDER

No. 34—1 LIGHT CANDELABRUM WITH "C" PRISMS. HEIGHT 10 IN. BASE 12 IN.
ABOVE ALSO MADE IN THE FOLLOWING HEIGHTS.

No. 35—1 LIGHT CANDELABRUM
WITH 6 IN. "O" PRISMS. HEIGHT 19 IN. BASE 15 IN.

No. 36—1 LIGHT CANDELABRUM
WITH 6½ IN. "C" PRISMS. HEIGHT 22 IN. BASE 18 IN.

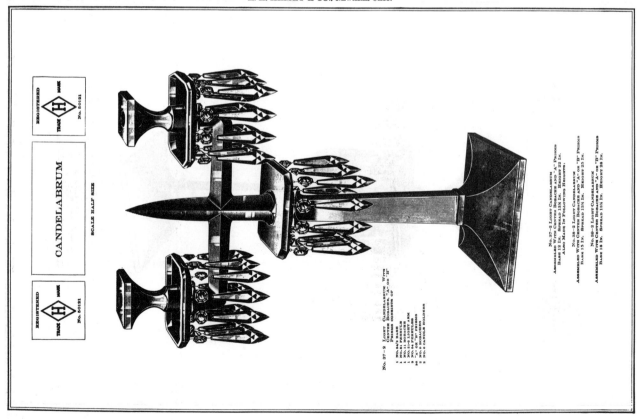

REGISTERED TRADE MARK H No. 50131

CANDELABRUM

SCALE HALF SIZE

REGISTERED TRADE MARK H No. 50131

No. 37—2 LIGHT CANDELABRUM WITH
CENTER BOBACHE, "A" OR "B"
PRISMS CONSISTS OF

1   NO./1 BASE
1   NO. 21 PRISTICLE
1   NO. 11 BOBACHE
2   NO. 212 LIGHT ARM
1   NO. 84 PRISTICLE
36   "A" OR "B" PRISMS
2   NO. 9 BOBACHE
2   NO. 6 CANDLE HOLDERS

No. 37—2 LIGHT CANDELABRUM
ASSEMBLED WITH CENTER BOBACHE AND "A" PRISMS
BASE 12 IN. SPREAD 13½ IN. HEIGHT 22 IN.
ALSO MADE IN FOLLOWING HEIGHTS.

No. 38—2 LIGHT CANDELABRUM
ASSEMBLED WITH CENTER BOBACHE AND "A" OR "B" PRISMS
BASE 15 IN. SPREAD 13½ IN. HEIGHT 25 IN.

No. 39—2 LIGHT CANDELABRUM
ASSEMBLED WITH CENTER BOBACHE AND "A" OR "B" PRISMS
BASE 18 IN. SPREAD 15½ IN. HEIGHT 28 IN.

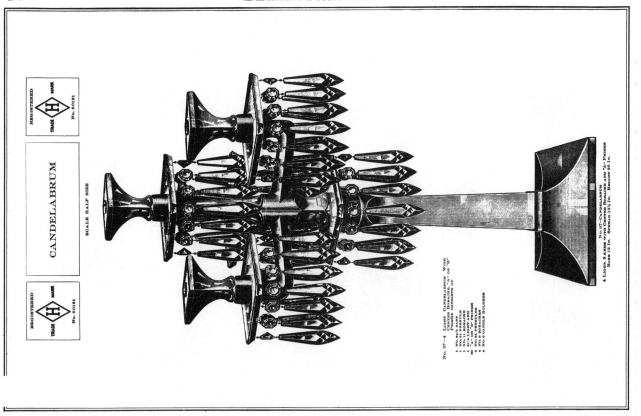

REGISTERED TRADE MARK [H] No. 50121

CANDELABRUM

REGISTERED TRADE MARK [H] No. 50121

SCALE HALF SIZE

No. 37-4 LIGHT CANDELABRUM WITH
CENTER BOBACHE "A" OR "B"
PRISMS CONSISTS OF

1   NO. 54/2 BASE
1   NO. 51 FERRULE
1   NO. 11 BOBACHE
2¼   "A" OR "B" PRISMS
60   "A" OR "B" PRISMS
4   NO. 54 FERRULES
4   NO. 8 BOBACHES
4   NO. 6 CANDLE HOLDERS

No. 37-CANDELABRUM WITH
4 LIGHT, 3 ARMS WITH CENTER BOBACHE AND "A" PRISMS
BASE 1/2 IN.   SPREAD 13¼ IN.   HEIGHT 25 IN.

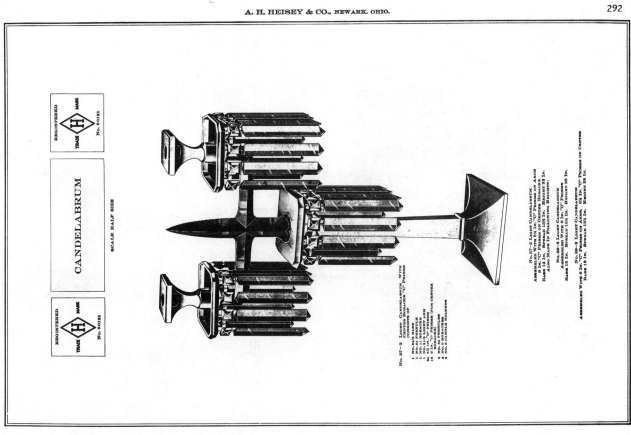

REGISTERED TRADE MARK [H] No. 50121

CANDELABRUM

REGISTERED TRADE MARK [H] No. 50121

SCALE HALF SIZE

No. 37-2 LIGHT CANDELABRUM WITH
CENTER BOBACHE "C" PRISMS
CONSISTS OF

1   NO. 54/2 BASE
1   NO. 51 FERRULE
1   NO. 11 BOBACHE
24   6½ IN. "C" PRISMS
54   6½ IN. "C" PRISMS (FOR CENTER
       BOBACHE)
2   NO. 54 FERRULES
2   NO. 8 BOBACHES
2   NO. 6 CANDLE HOLDERS

No. 37-2 LIGHT CANDELABRUM
ASSEMBLED WITH 6½ IN. "C" PRISMS ON ARMS
6 IN. "C" PRISMS ON CENTER BOBACHE
BASE 12 IN.   SPREAD 13⅜ IN.   HEIGHT 23 IN.
ALSO MADE IN FOLLOWING HEIGHTS:

No. 38-2 LIGHT CANDELABRUM
ASSEMBLED WITH 8 IN. "C" PRISMS
BASE 15 IN.   SPREAD 13¼ IN.   HEIGHT 25 IN.

No. 39-2 LIGHT CANDELABRUM
ASSEMBLED WITH 8 IN. "C" PRISMS ON ARMS   6½ IN. "C" PRISMS ON CENTER
BASE 18 IN.   SPREAD 13½ IN.   HEIGHT 28 IN.

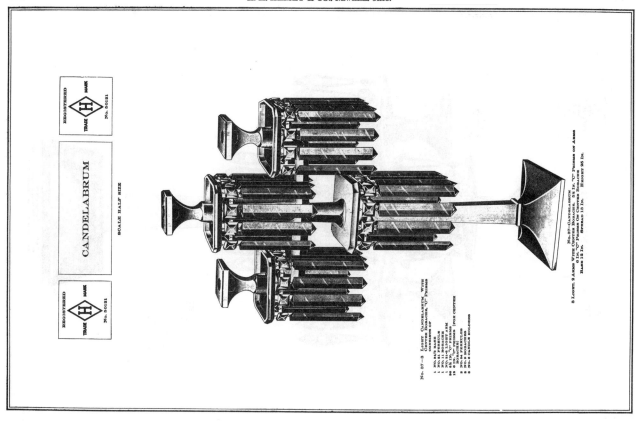

CANDELABRUM

SCALE HALF SIZE

No. 37—3 Light Candelabrum with Center Bobache, "C" Prisms consists of

1 No. 5½/3 Base
1 No. 41 Ferrule
1 No. 11 Bobache
1 No. 31—3 Light Arm
20 6½ In. "C" Prisms
12 6½ In. "C" Prisms (for center Bobache)
8 No. 9 Bobaches
8 No. 9 Bobaches
3 No. 6 Candle Holders

No. 37—Candelabrum
3 Light, 3 Arms with Center Bobache, 5¼ In. "C" Prisms on Arms
6 In. "C" Prisms on Center Bobache
Base 13 In. Spread 13 In. Height 25 In.

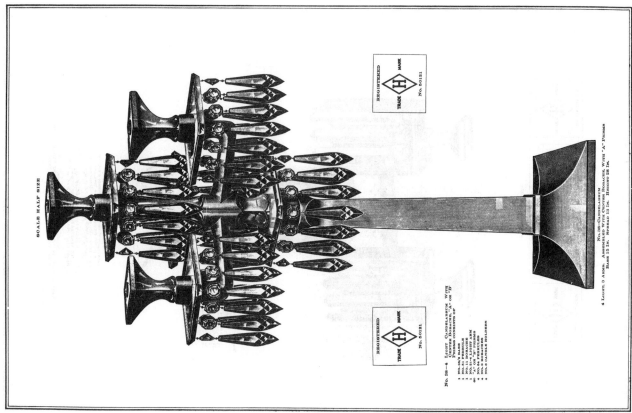

SCALE HALF SIZE

No. 38—4 Light Candelabrum with Center Bobache, "A" or "B" Prisms consists of

1 No. 5½/3 Base
1 No. 1 Ferrule
1 No. 11 Bobache
1 No. 31—4 Light Arm
80 "A" or "B" Prisms
4 No. 9 Ferrules
4 No. 9 Bobaches
4 No. 6 Candle Holders

No. 38—Candelabrum
4 Light, 3 Arms, Assembled With Center Bobache, With "A" Prisms
Base 13 In. Spread 13 In. Height 28 In.

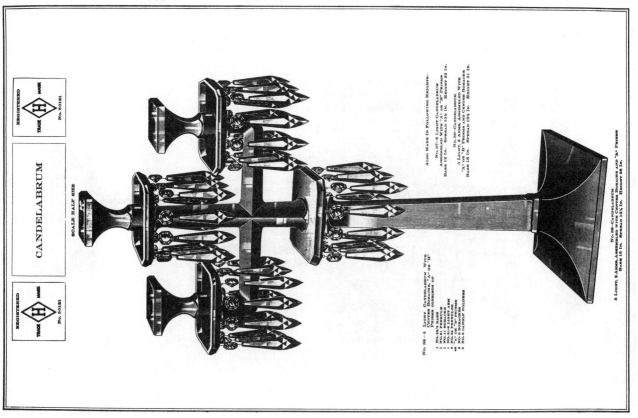

No. 50121 — CANDELABRUM

SCALE HALF SIZE

No. 38-3 LIGHT CANDELABRUM WITH
CENTER BOBACHE, "A" OR "B"
PRISMS CONSISTS OF

1   No. 38/3 BASE
1   No. 41 PRISMELTS
1   No. 11 BOBACHE
1   No. 3½ LIGHT ARM
46 "A" OR "B" PRISMS
8   No. 84 BOBACHES
8   No. 9 BOBACHES
8   No. 6 CANDLE HOLDERS

ALSO MADE IN FOLLOWING HEIGHTS.

No. 37-2 LIGHT CANDELABRUM
ASSEMBLED WITH "A" OR "B" PRISMS
BASE 12 IN.   SPREAD 13½ IN.   HEIGHT 22 IN.

No. 39 CANDELABRUM
3 LIGHT, 2 ARMS, ASSEMBLED WITH
"A" OR "B" PRISMS AND CENTER BOBACHE
BASE 18 IN.   SPREAD 13½ IN.   HEIGHT 31 IN.

No. 38 CANDELABRUM
3 LIGHT, 2 ARMS, ASSEMBLED WITH CENTER BOBACHE AND "A" PRISMS
BASE 15 IN.   SPREAD 13½ IN.   HEIGHT 28 IN.

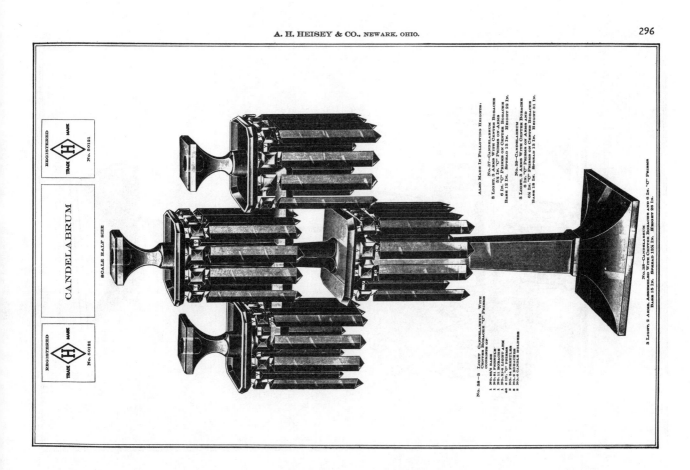

No. 50121 — CANDELABRUM

SCALE HALF SIZE

No. 38-3 LIGHT CANDELABRUM WITH
CENTER BOBACHE "C" PRISMS
CONSISTS OF

1   No. 38/3 BASE
1   No. 41 PRISMELTS
1   No. 11 BOBACHE
1   No. 3½ LIGHT ARM
46 "C" PRISMS
8   No. 84 BOBACHES
8   No. 9 BOBACHES
8   No. 6 CANDLE HOLDERS

ALSO MADE IN FOLLOWING HEIGHTS.

No. 37 CANDELABRUM
3 LIGHT, 2 ARMS WITH CENTER BOBACHE
5½ IN. "C" PRISMS ON ARMS
6 IN. "C" PRISMS ON CENTER BOBACHE
BASE 12 IN.   SPREAD 13 IN.   HEIGHT 22 IN.

No. 39 CANDELABRUM
3 LIGHT, 2 ARMS WITH CENTER BOBACHE
6 IN. "C" PRISMS ON ARMS AND
6½ IN. "C" PRISMS ON CENTER BOBACHE
BASE 18 IN.   SPREAD 13 IN.   HEIGHT 31 IN.

No. 38 CANDELABRUM
3 LIGHT, 2 ARMS, ASSEMBLED WITH CENTER BOBACHE AND 6 IN. "C" PRISMS
BASE 15 IN.   SPREAD 13½ IN.   HEIGHT 28 IN.

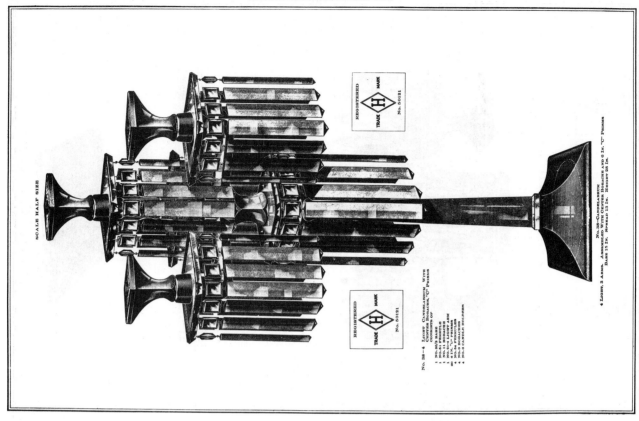

SCALE HALF SIZE

No. 38—4 Light Candelabrum With Center Bobache, "C" Prisms consists of

1 No. 38/3 Base
1 No. 61 Prickle
1 No. 11 Bobache
1 No. 31-4 Light Arm
60 6 In. "C" Prisms
4 No. 54 Prickles
4 No. 9 Bobaches
4 No. 6 Candle Holders

No. 38—Candelabrum
4 Light, 2 Arms. Assembled With Center Bobache and 6 In. "C" Prisms
Base 15 In. Spread 13 In. Height 23 In.

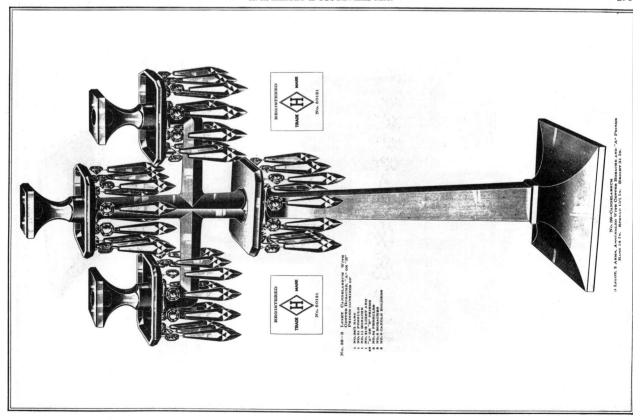

No. 39—3 Light Candelabrum With Center Bobache, "A" or "B" Prisms consists of

1 No. 39/3 Base
1 No. 61 Prickle
1 No. 11 Bobache
1 No. 31-3 Light Arm
48 "A" or "B" Prisms
3 No. 54 Prickles
3 No. 9 Bobaches
3 No. 6 Candle Holders

No. 39—Candelabrum
3 Light, 2 Arms. Assembled With Center Bobache and "A" Prisms
Base 18 In. Special 15½ In. Height 21 In.

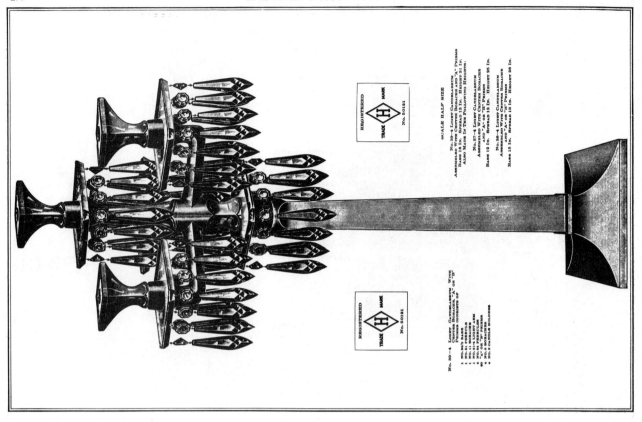

SCALE HALF SIZE

No. 39—4 Light Candelabrum Assembled with Center Bobache and "A" Prisms Base 13 In. Spread 13 In. Height 31 In. Also Made in the Following Heights:

No. 37—4 Light Candelabrum Assembled with Center Bobache and "A" or "B" Prisms Base 13 In. Spread 13 In. Height 25 In.

No. 38—4 Light Candelabrum Assembled with Center Bobache and "A" or "B" Prisms Base 13 In. Spread 13 In. Height 22 In.

No. 39—4 Light Candelabrum with Center Bobache "A" or "B" Prisms Consists of

1   No. 303 Base
1   No. 31 Ferrule
1   No. 11 Bobache
1   No. 312 Light Arm
4   No. 61 Ferrules
80 "A" or "B" Prisms
20 No. 6 Bobaches
4   No. 6 Candle Holders

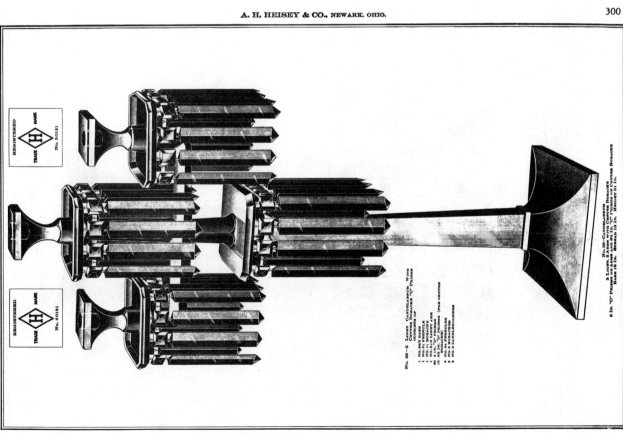

No. 39—3 Light Candelabrum with Center Bobache "C" Prisms Consists of

1   No. 303 Base
1   No. 31 Ferrule
1   No. 11 Bobache
1   No. 312 Light Arm
3   No. 61 Ferrules
60 6 In. "C" Prisms
12 No. 64 Ferrules
3   No. 6 Bobaches
12 6½ In. "C" Prisms (for Center Bobache)
3   No. 6 Candle Holders

No. 30—Candelabrum 3 Light, 3 Arms with Center Bobache 6 In. "C" Prisms on Arms and 6½ In. "C" Prism on Center Bobache Base 13 In. Spread 13 In. Height 21 In.

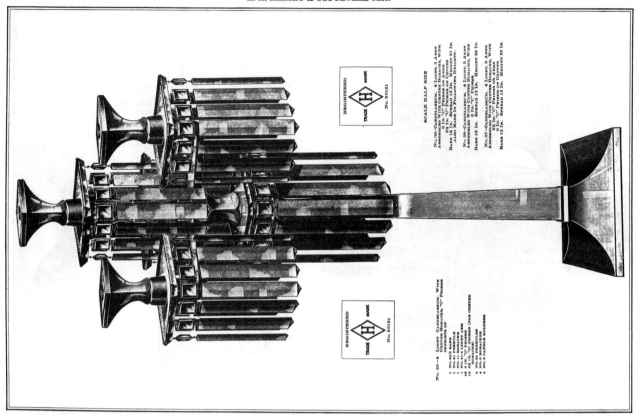

REGISTERED
TRADE **H** MARK
No. 50131

REGISTERED
TRADE **H** MARK
No. 50131

SCALE HALF SIZE

No. 39—4 Light Candelabrum with
Center Bobache, "C" Prisms
consists of

1	No. 39's Base
1	No. 61 Ferrule
1	No. 11 Bobache
1	No. 31-4 Light Arm
48	6 In. "C" Prisms
12	6½ In. "C" Prisms (for Center Bobache)
4	No. 54 Bobaches
4	No. 9 Bobaches
4	No. 6 Candle Holders

No. 39—Candelabrum, 4 Light, 3 Arms
Assembled with Center Bobache, with
6½ In. "C" Prisms on Center
6½ In. "C" Prisms on Arms
Base 18 In. Spread 12 In. Height 21 In.
Also Made in Following Heights:

No. 38—Candelabrum, 4 Light, 3 Arms
Assembled with Center Bobache, with
6 In. "C" Prisms
Base 15 In. Spread 13 In. Height 23 In.

No. 37—Candelabrum, 4 Light, 3 Arms
Assembled with Center Bobache, with
5½ In. "C" Prisms on Arms
6 In. "C" Prisms on Center
Base 12 In. Spread 13 In. Height 25 In.

REGISTERED
TRADE **H** MARK
No. 50131

CANDELABRUM

SCALE HALF SIZE

REGISTERED
TRADE **H** MARK
No. 50131

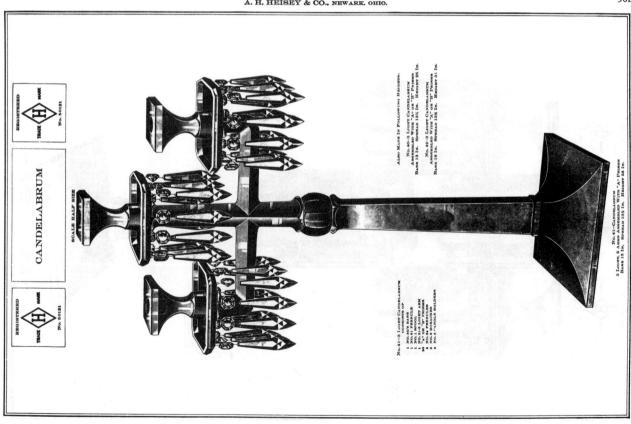

No. 41—3 Light Candelabrum
consists of

1	No. 39's Base
1	No. 61 Ferrule
1	No. 1 Spool
1	No. 31-3 Light Arm
36	"A" or "B" Prisms
3	No. 54 Ferrules
3	No. 9 Bobaches
3	No. 6 Candle Holders

Also Made in Following Heights:

No. 40—3 Light Candelabrum
Assembled with "A" or "B" Prisms
Base 12 In. Spread 13½ In. Height 25 In.

No. 42—3 Light Candelabrum
Assembled with "A" or "B" Prisms
Base 18 In. Spread 13½ In. Height 31 In.

No. 41—Candelabrum
3 Light, 2 Arms Assembled with "A" Prisms
Base 15 In. Spread 13½ In. Height 28 In.

No. 411 PATTERN

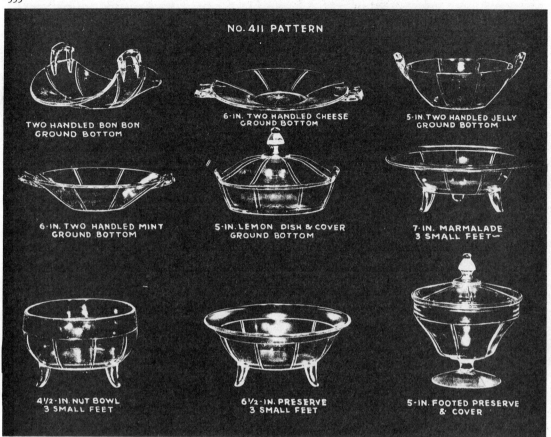

TWO HANDLED BON BON
GROUND BOTTOM

6-IN. TWO HANDLED CHEESE
GROUND BOTTOM

5-IN. TWO HANDLED JELLY
GROUND BOTTOM

6-IN. TWO HANDLED MINT
GROUND BOTTOM

5-IN. LEMON DISH & COVER
GROUND BOTTOM

7-IN. MARMALADE
3 SMALL FEET—

4½-IN. NUT BOWL
3 SMALL FEET

6½-IN. PRESERVE
3 SMALL FEET

5-IN. FOOTED PRESERVE
& COVER

Heisey's ◇H◇ Glassware

No. 411 PATTERN

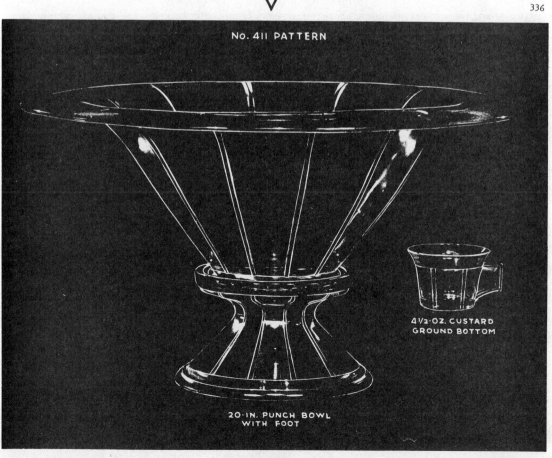

4½-OZ. CUSTARD
GROUND BOTTOM

20-IN. PUNCH BOWL
WITH FOOT

Heisey's ◇H◇ Glassware

No. 411 PATTERN

5-OZ. SHERBET   4-OZ. OYSTER COCKTAIL   FINGER BOWL   5-IN. HI-FOOT JELLY

8-OZ. GOBLET   5½-OZ. SAUCER CHAMPAGNE   3-OZ. WINE   4-OZ. PARFAIT   7-OZ. LUNCHEON GOBLET

Heisey's ◇H◇ Glassware

No. 411 PATTERN

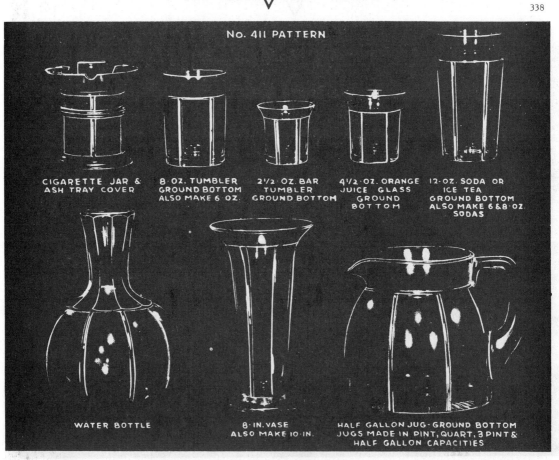

CIGARETTE JAR & ASH TRAY COVER   8-OZ. TUMBLER GROUND BOTTOM ALSO MAKE 6-OZ.   2½-OZ. BAR TUMBLER GROUND BOTTOM   4½-OZ. ORANGE JUICE GLASS GROUND BOTTOM   12-OZ. SODA OR ICE TEA GROUND BOTTOM ALSO MAKE 6 & 8-OZ. SODAS

WATER BOTTLE   8-IN. VASE ALSO MAKE 10-IN.   HALF GALLON JUG-GROUND BOTTOM JUGS MADE IN PINT, QUART, 3 PINT & HALF GALLON CAPACITIES

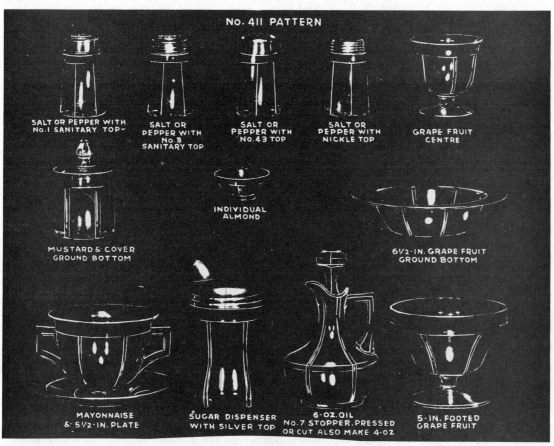

No. 411 PATTERN

SALT OR PEPPER WITH No.1 SANITARY TOP

SALT OR PEPPER WITH No.3 SANITARY TOP

SALT OR PEPPER WITH No.43 TOP

SALT OR PEPPER WITH NICKLE TOP

GRAPE FRUIT CENTRE

MUSTARD & COVER GROUND BOTTOM

INDIVIDUAL ALMOND

6½-IN. GRAPE FRUIT GROUND BOTTOM

MAYONNAISE & 5½-IN. PLATE

SUGAR DISPENSER WITH SILVER TOP

6-OZ. OIL No.7 STOPPER, PRESSED OR CUT ALSO MAKE 4-OZ

5-IN. FOOTED GRAPE FRUIT

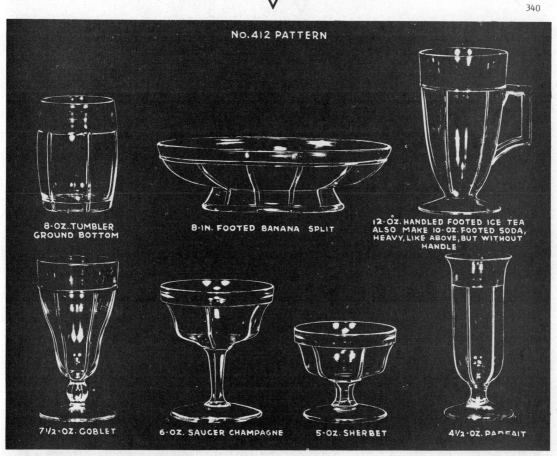

No. 412 PATTERN

8-OZ. TUMBLER GROUND BOTTOM

8-IN. FOOTED BANANA SPLIT

12-OZ. HANDLED FOOTED ICE TEA ALSO MAKE 10-OZ. FOOTED SODA, HEAVY, LIKE ABOVE, BUT WITHOUT HANDLE

7½-OZ. GOBLET

6-OZ. SAUCER CHAMPAGNE

5-OZ. SHERBET

4½-OZ. PARFAIT

No. 412 & 413 PATTERN

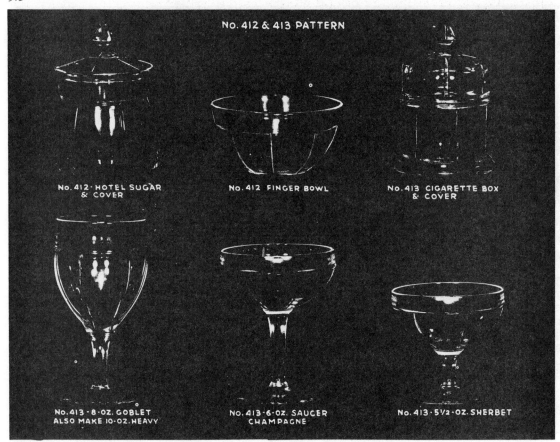

No. 412 - HOTEL SUGAR & COVER

No. 412 FINGER BOWL

No. 413 CIGARETTE BOX & COVER

No. 413 - 8 - OZ. GOBLET ALSO MAKE 10 - OZ. HEAVY

No. 413 - 6 - OZ. SAUCER CHAMPAGNE

No. 413 - 5½ - OZ. SHERBET

Heisey's  Glassware

342

NO. 451 PATTERN

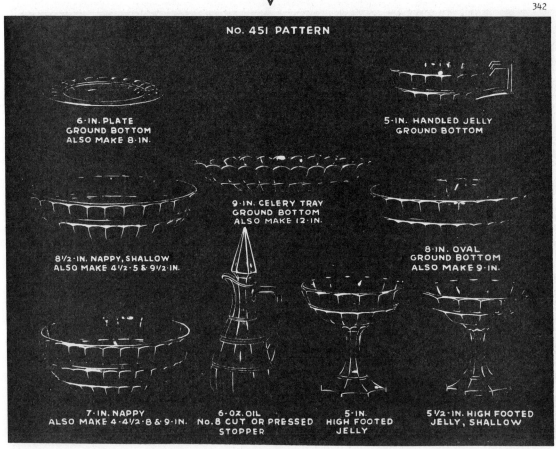

6 - IN. PLATE GROUND BOTTOM ALSO MAKE 8 - IN.

5 - IN. HANDLED JELLY GROUND BOTTOM

9 - IN. CELERY TRAY GROUND BOTTOM ALSO MAKE 12 - IN.

8½ - IN. NAPPY, SHALLOW ALSO MAKE 4½ - 5 & 9½ - IN.

8 - IN. OVAL GROUND BOTTOM ALSO MAKE 9 - IN.

7 - IN. NAPPY ALSO MAKE 4 - 4½ - 8 & 9 - IN.

6 - OZ. OIL No. 8 CUT OR PRESSED STOPPER

5 - IN. HIGH FOOTED JELLY

5½ - IN. HIGH FOOTED JELLY, SHALLOW

No. 451 PATTERN

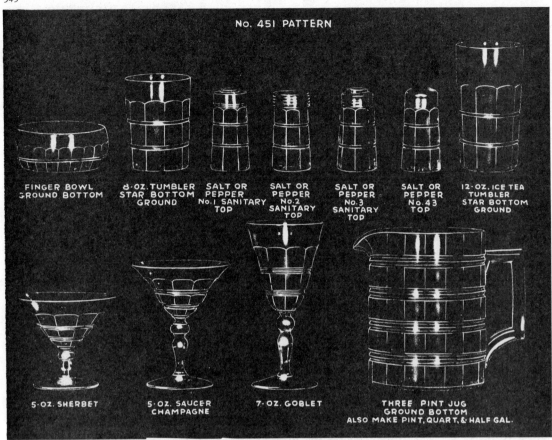

FINGER BOWL
GROUND BOTTOM

8-OZ. TUMBLER
STAR BOTTOM
GROUND

SALT OR
PEPPER
No.1 SANITARY
TOP

SALT OR
PEPPER
No.2
SANITARY
TOP

SALT OR
PEPPER
No.3
SANITARY
TOP

SALT OR
PEPPER
No.43
TOP

12-OZ. ICE TEA
TUMBLER
STAR BOTTOM
GROUND

5-OZ. SHERBET

5-OZ. SAUCER
CHAMPAGNE

7-OZ. GOBLET

THREE PINT JUG
GROUND BOTTOM
ALSO MAKE PINT, QUART, & HALF GAL.

No. 473 PATTERN

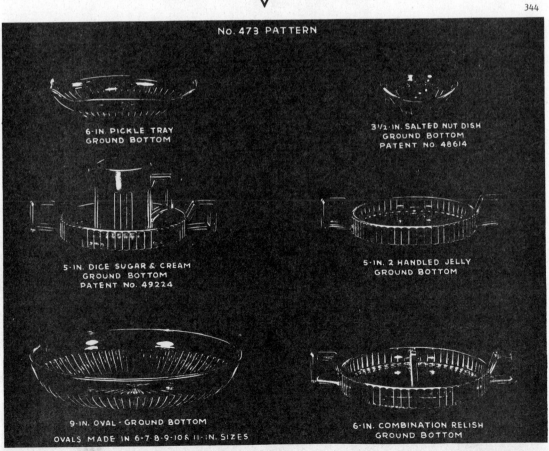

6-IN. PICKLE TRAY
GROUND BOTTOM

3½-IN. SALTED NUT DISH
GROUND BOTTOM
PATENT NO. 48614

5-IN. DICE SUGAR & CREAM
GROUND BOTTOM
PATENT NO. 49224

5-IN. 2 HANDLED JELLY
GROUND BOTTOM

9-IN. OVAL - GROUND BOTTOM
OVALS MADE IN 6-7-8-9-10 & 11-IN. SIZES

6-IN. COMBINATION RELISH
GROUND BOTTOM

No. 1170 PATTERN

4-IN. CHOW CHOW
GROUND BOTTOM

5-IN. BOUILLON CUP &
6³/4-IN. PLATE, GROUND BOTTOM

CUP & SAUCER
GROUND BOTTOM

8-IN. NAPPY-GROUND BOTTOM
ALSO MAKE 4¹/2-IN.

8-IN. PLATE - GROUND BOTTOM
—ALSO MAKE 6-7-10³/4 & 14-IN. SIZES

9-IN. VEGETABLE DISH-GROUND BOTTOM

10¹/2-IN. CHEESE & CRACKER-GROUND BOTTOM

·10-IN. SPICE TRAY-GROUND BOTTOM

12-IN. OVAL PLATTER-GROUND BOTTOM

Heisey's ⟨H⟩ Glassware

346

No. 1170 PATTERN

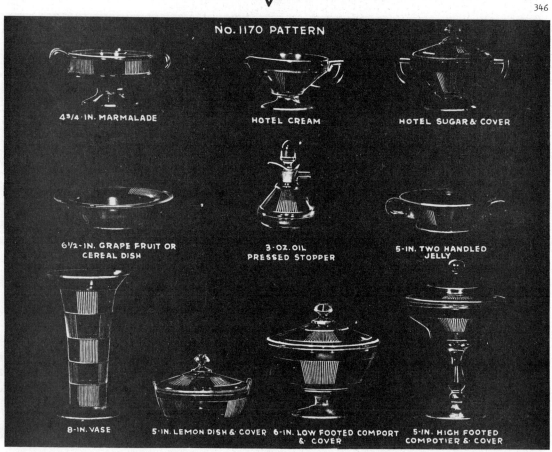

4³/4-IN. MARMALADE

HOTEL CREAM

HOTEL SUGAR & COVER

6¹/2-IN. GRAPE FRUIT OR
CEREAL DISH

3-OZ. OIL
PRESSED STOPPER

5-IN. TWO HANDLED
JELLY

8-IN. VASE

5-IN. LEMON DISH & COVER

6-IN. LOW FOOTED COMPORT
& COVER

5-IN. HIGH FOOTED
COMPOTIER & COVER

No. 1170 PATTERN

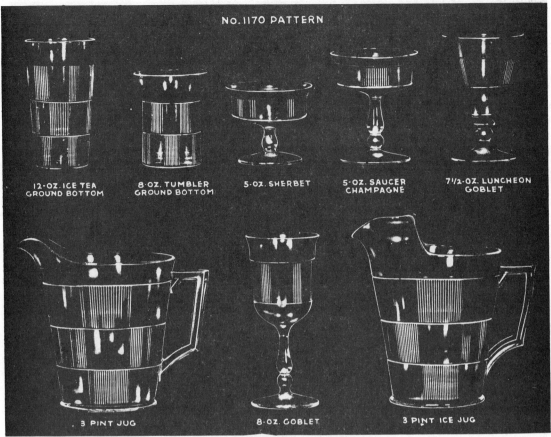

12-OZ. ICE TEA
GROUND BOTTOM

8-OZ. TUMBLER
GROUND BOTTOM

5-OZ. SHERBET

5-OZ. SAUCER
CHAMPAGNE

7½-OZ. LUNCHEON
GOBLET

3 PINT JUG

8-OZ. GOBLET

3 PINT ICE JUG

Heisey's  Glassware

348

No. 1184 PATTERN

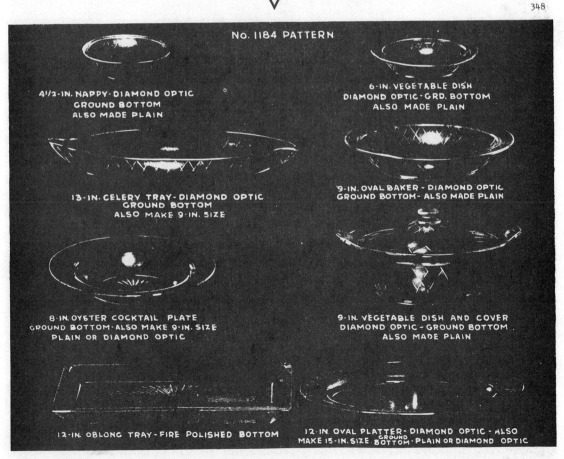

4½-IN. NAPPY-DIAMOND OPTIC
GROUND BOTTOM
ALSO MADE PLAIN

6-IN. VEGETABLE DISH
DIAMOND OPTIC-GRD. BOTTOM
ALSO MADE PLAIN

13-IN. CELERY TRAY-DIAMOND OPTIC
GROUND BOTTOM
ALSO MAKE 9-IN. SIZE

9-IN. OVAL BAKER - DIAMOND OPTIC
GROUND BOTTOM- ALSO MADE PLAIN

8-IN. OYSTER COCKTAIL PLATE
GROUND BOTTOM-ALSO MAKE 9-IN. SIZE
PLAIN OR DIAMOND OPTIC

9-IN. VEGETABLE DISH AND COVER
DIAMOND OPTIC - GROUND BOTTOM
ALSO MADE PLAIN

12-IN. OBLONG TRAY-FIRE POLISHED BOTTOM

12-IN. OVAL PLATTER-DIAMOND OPTIC - ALSO
MAKE 15-IN. SIZE-GROUND BOTTOM- PLAIN OR DIAMOND OPTIC

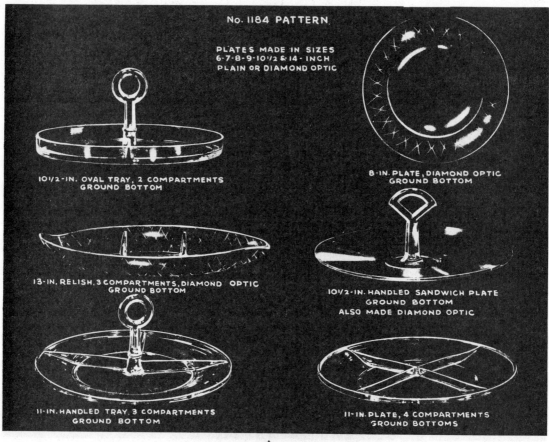

No. 1184 PATTERN

PLATES MADE IN SIZES
6-7-8-9-10½ & 14-INCH
PLAIN OR DIAMOND OPTIC

10½-IN. OVAL TRAY, 2 COMPARTMENTS
GROUND BOTTOM

8-IN. PLATE, DIAMOND OPTIC
GROUND BOTTOM

13-IN. RELISH, 3 COMPARTMENTS, DIAMOND OPTIC
GROUND BOTTOM

10½-IN. HANDLED SANDWICH PLATE
GROUND BOTTOM
ALSO MADE DIAMOND OPTIC

11-IN. HANDLED TRAY, 3 COMPARTMENTS
GROUND BOTTOM

11-IN. PLATE, 4 COMPARTMENTS
GROUND BOTTOMS

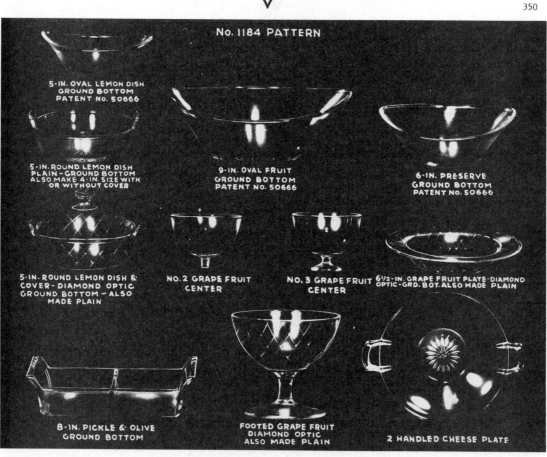

No. 1184 PATTERN

5-IN. OVAL LEMON DISH
GROUND BOTTOM
PATENT No. 50666

5-IN. ROUND LEMON DISH
PLAIN - GROUND BOTTOM
ALSO MAKE 4-IN. SIZE WITH
OR WITHOUT COVER

9-IN. OVAL FRUIT
GROUND BOTTOM
PATENT No. 50666

6-IN. PRESERVE
GROUND BOTTOM
PATENT No. 50666

5-IN. ROUND LEMON DISH &
COVER - DIAMOND OPTIC
GROUND BOTTOM - ALSO
MADE PLAIN

NO. 2 GRAPE FRUIT
CENTER

NO. 3 GRAPE FRUIT
CENTER

6½-IN. GRAPE FRUIT PLATE - DIAMOND
OPTIC - GRD. BOT. ALSO MADE PLAIN

8-IN. PICKLE & OLIVE
GROUND BOTTOM

FOOTED GRAPE FRUIT
DIAMOND OPTIC
ALSO MADE PLAIN

2 HANDLED CHEESE PLATE

NO. 1184 PATTERN

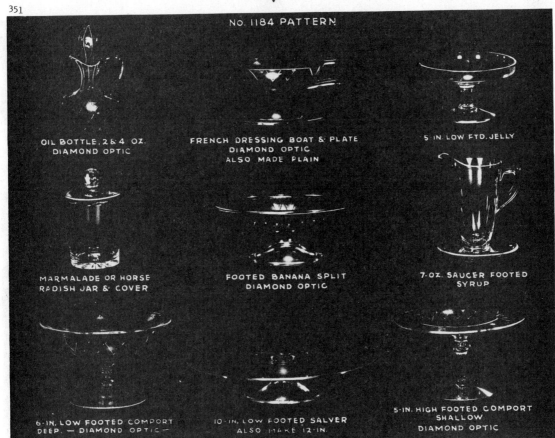

OIL BOTTLE, 2 & 4 OZ.
DIAMOND OPTIC

FRENCH DRESSING BOAT & PLATE
DIAMOND OPTIC
ALSO MADE PLAIN

5-IN. LOW FTD. JELLY

MARMALADE OR HORSE
RADISH JAR & COVER

FOOTED BANANA SPLIT
DIAMOND OPTIC

7-OZ. SAUCER FOOTED
SYRUP

6-IN. LOW FOOTED COMPORT
DEEP. — DIAMOND OPTIC —

10-IN. LOW FOOTED SALVER
ALSO MAKE 12-IN.

5-IN. HIGH FOOTED COMPORT
SHALLOW
DIAMOND OPTIC

NO. 1184 PATTERN

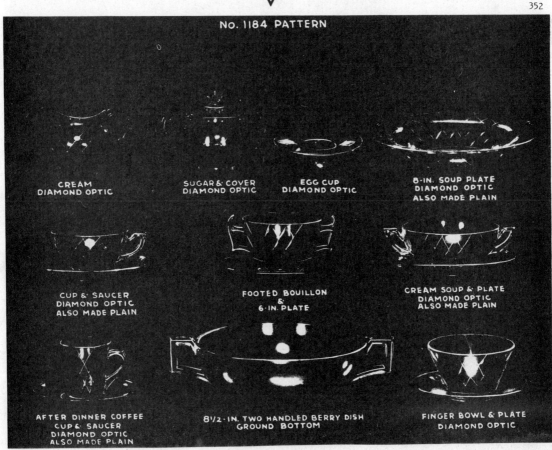

CREAM
DIAMOND OPTIC

SUGAR & COVER
DIAMOND OPTIC

EGG CUP
DIAMOND OPTIC

8-IN. SOUP PLATE
DIAMOND OPTIC
ALSO MADE PLAIN

CUP & SAUCER
DIAMOND OPTIC
ALSO MADE PLAIN

FOOTED BOUILLON
&
6-IN. PLATE

CREAM SOUP & PLATE
DIAMOND OPTIC
ALSO MADE PLAIN

AFTER DINNER COFFEE
CUP & SAUCER
DIAMOND OPTIC
ALSO MADE PLAIN

8½-IN. TWO HANDLED BERRY DISH
GROUND BOTTOM

FINGER BOWL & PLATE
DIAMOND OPTIC

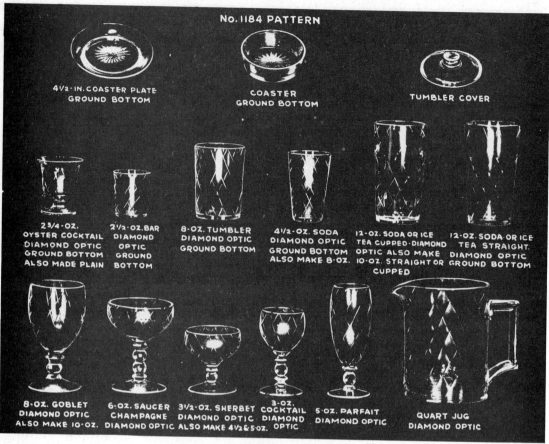

No. 1184 PATTERN

4½-IN. COASTER PLATE
GROUND BOTTOM

COASTER
GROUND BOTTOM

TUMBLER COVER

2¾-OZ.
OYSTER COCKTAIL
DIAMOND OPTIC
GROUND BOTTOM
ALSO MADE PLAIN

2½-OZ. BAR
DIAMOND
OPTIC
GROUND
BOTTOM

8-OZ. TUMBLER
DIAMOND OPTIC
GROUND BOTTOM

4½-OZ. SODA
DIAMOND OPTIC
GROUND BOTTOM
ALSO MAKE 8-OZ.

12-OZ. SODA OR ICE
TEA CUPPED-DIAMOND
OPTIC ALSO MAKE
10-OZ. STRAIGHT OR
CUPPED

12-OZ. SODA OR ICE
TEA STRAIGHT.
DIAMOND OPTIC
GROUND BOTTOM

8-OZ. GOBLET
DIAMOND OPTIC
ALSO MAKE 10-OZ.

6-OZ. SAUCER
CHAMPAGNE
DIAMOND OPTIC

3½-OZ. SHERBET
DIAMOND OPTIC
ALSO MAKE 4½ & 5 OZ.

3-OZ.
COCKTAIL
DIAMOND
OPTIC

5-OZ. PARFAIT
DIAMOND OPTIC

QUART JUG
DIAMOND OPTIC

Heisey's ⟨H⟩ Glassware

354

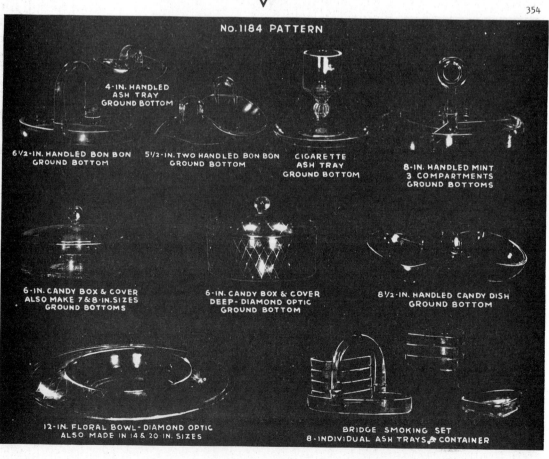

No. 1184 PATTERN

4-IN. HANDLED
ASH TRAY
GROUND BOTTOM

6½-IN. HANDLED BON BON
GROUND BOTTOM

5½-IN. TWO HANDLED BON BON
GROUND BOTTOM

CIGARETTE
ASH TRAY
GROUND BOTTOM

8-IN. HANDLED MINT
3 COMPARTMENTS
GROUND BOTTOMS

6-IN. CANDY BOX & COVER
ALSO MAKE 7 & 8-IN. SIZES
GROUND BOTTOMS

6-IN. CANDY BOX & COVER
DEEP-DIAMOND OPTIC
GROUND BOTTOM

8½-IN. HANDLED CANDY DISH
GROUND BOTTOM

12-IN. FLORAL BOWL-DIAMOND OPTIC
ALSO MADE IN 14 & 20-IN. SIZES

BRIDGE SMOKING SET
8-INDIVIDUAL ASH TRAYS & CONTAINER

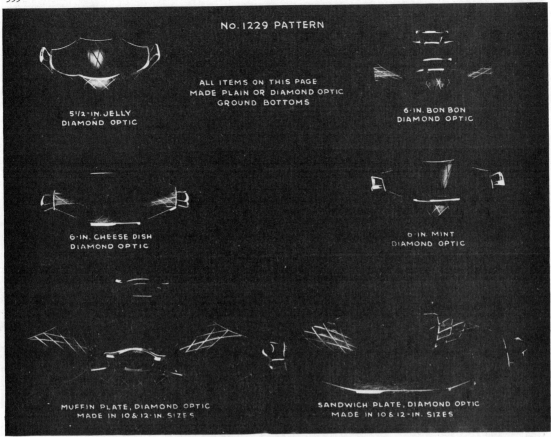

No. 1229 PATTERN

ALL ITEMS ON THIS PAGE
MADE PLAIN OR DIAMOND OPTIC
GROUND BOTTOMS

5½-IN. JELLY
DIAMOND OPTIC

6-IN. BON BON
DIAMOND OPTIC

6-IN. CHEESE DISH
DIAMOND OPTIC

6-IN. MINT
DIAMOND OPTIC

MUFFIN PLATE, DIAMOND OPTIC
MADE IN 10 & 12-IN. SIZES

SANDWICH PLATE, DIAMOND OPTIC
MADE IN 10 & 12-IN. SIZES

Heisey's $\langle H \rangle$ Glassware

356

No. 1229 PATTERN

ALL ITEMS ON THIS PAGE
MADE PLAIN, OR DIAMOND OPTIC

13-IN. HORS' D' OEUVRE
GROUND BOTTOM

5½-IN. FOOTED MAYONNAISE

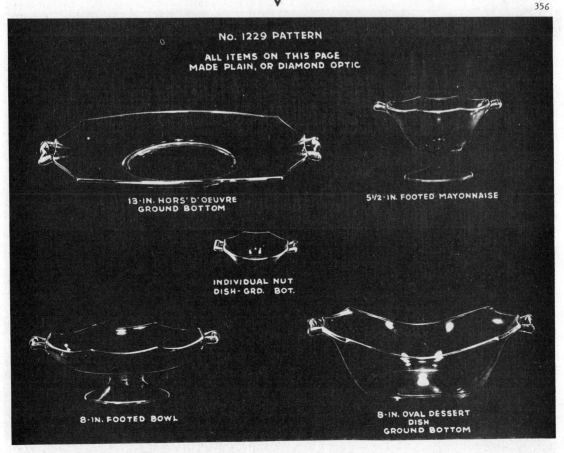

INDIVIDUAL NUT
DISH- GRD. BOT.

8-IN. FOOTED BOWL

8-IN. OVAL DESSERT
DISH
GROUND BOTTOM

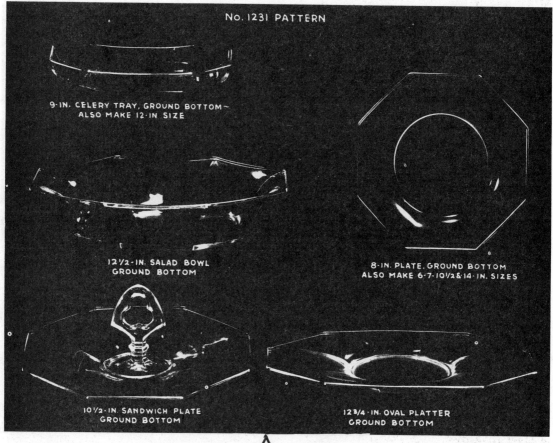

No. 1231 PATTERN

9-IN. CELERY TRAY, GROUND BOTTOM ~
ALSO MAKE 12-IN SIZE

12½-IN. SALAD BOWL
GROUND BOTTOM

8-IN. PLATE, GROUND BOTTOM
ALSO MAKE 6-7-10½ & 14-IN. SIZES

10½-IN. SANDWICH PLATE
GROUND BOTTOM

12¾-IN. OVAL PLATTER
GROUND BOTTOM

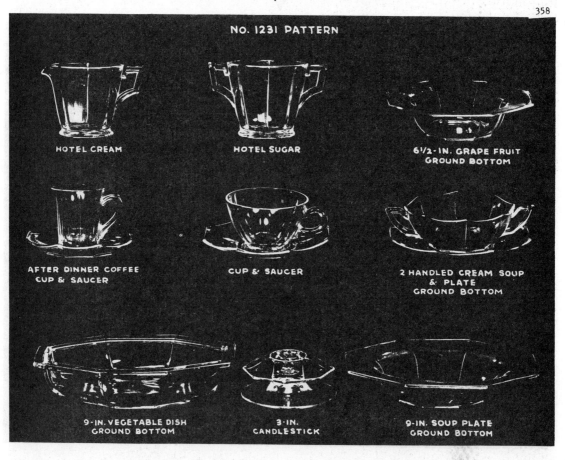

No. 1231 PATTERN

HOTEL CREAM

HOTEL SUGAR

6½-IN. GRAPE FRUIT
GROUND BOTTOM

AFTER DINNER COFFEE
CUP & SAUCER

CUP & SAUCER

2 HANDLED CREAM SOUP
& PLATE
GROUND BOTTOM

9-IN. VEGETABLE DISH
GROUND BOTTOM

3-IN.
CANDLESTICK

9-IN. SOUP PLATE
GROUND BOTTOM

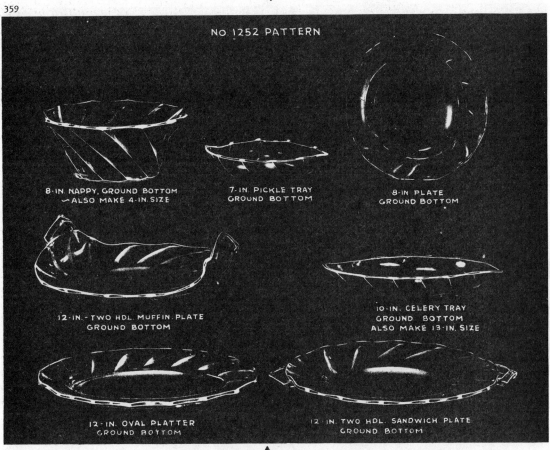

No. 1252 PATTERN

8-IN. NAPPY, GROUND BOTTOM
— ALSO MAKE 4-IN. SIZE

7-IN. PICKLE TRAY
GROUND BOTTOM

8-IN PLATE
GROUND BOTTOM

12-IN.- TWO HDL. MUFFIN PLATE
GROUND BOTTOM

10-IN. CELERY TRAY
GROUND BOTTOM
ALSO MAKE 13-IN. SIZE

12-IN. OVAL PLATTER
GROUND BOTTOM

12-IN. TWO HDL. SANDWICH PLATE
GROUND BOTTOM

No. 1252 PATTERN

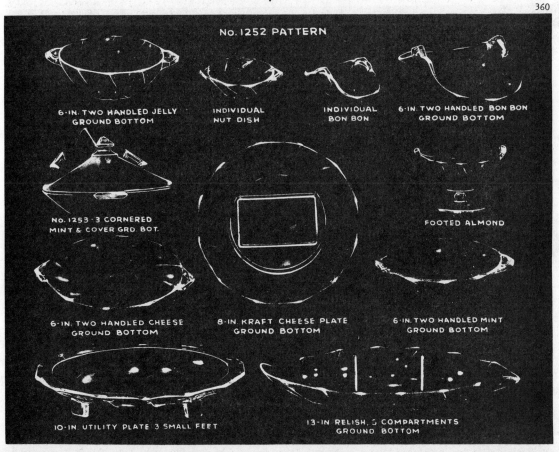

6-IN. TWO HANDLED JELLY
GROUND BOTTOM

INDIVIDUAL
NUT DISH

INDIVIDUAL
BON BON

6-IN. TWO HANDLED BON BON
GROUND BOTTOM

NO. 1253-3 CORNERED
MINT & COVER GRD. BOT.

FOOTED ALMOND

6-IN. TWO HANDLED CHEESE
GROUND BOTTOM

8-IN. KRAFT CHEESE PLATE
GROUND BOTTOM

6-IN. TWO HANDLED MINT
GROUND BOTTOM

10-IN. UTILITY PLATE 3 SMALL FEET

13-IN RELISH, 3 COMPARTMENTS
GROUND BOTTOM

No. 1252 PATTERN

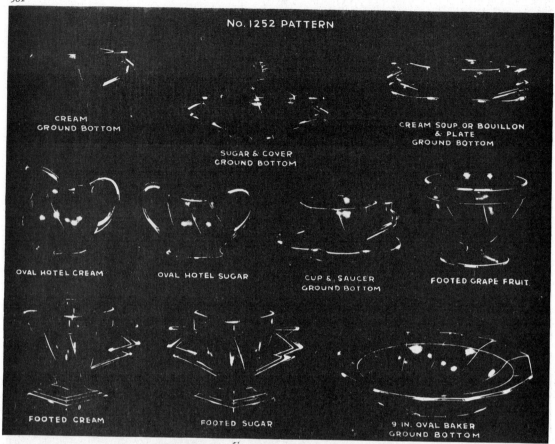

CREAM
GROUND BOTTOM

SUGAR & COVER
GROUND BOTTOM

CREAM SOUP, OR BOUILLON
& PLATE
GROUND BOTTOM

OVAL HOTEL CREAM

OVAL HOTEL SUGAR

CUP & SAUCER
GROUND BOTTOM

FOOTED GRAPE FRUIT

FOOTED CREAM

FOOTED SUGAR

9 IN. OVAL BAKER
GROUND BOTTOM

Heisey's ⟨H⟩ Glassware

No. 1252 PATTERN

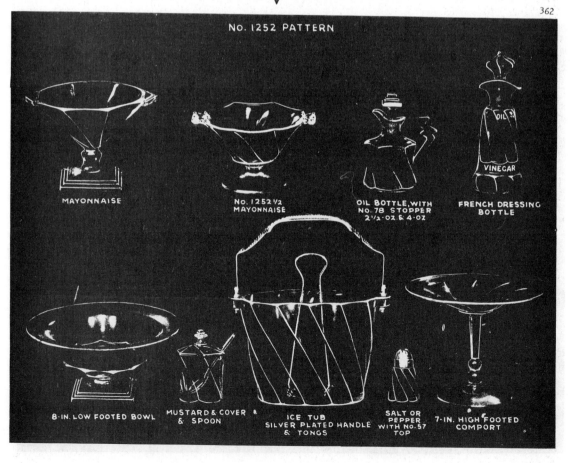

MAYONNAISE

No. 1252½
MAYONNAISE

OIL BOTTLE, WITH
No. 78 STOPPER
2½-OZ. & 4-OZ.

FRENCH DRESSING
BOTTLE

8-IN. LOW FOOTED BOWL

MUSTARD & COVER &
& SPOON

ICE TUB
SILVER PLATED HANDLE
& TONGS

SALT OR
PEPPER
WITH No. 57
TOP

7-IN. HIGH FOOTED
COMPORT

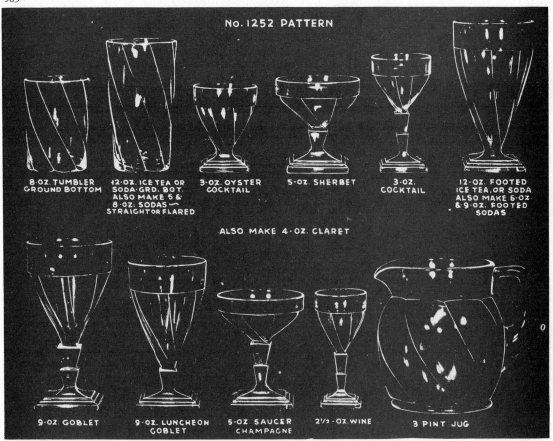

No. 1252 PATTERN

8-OZ. TUMBLER
GROUND BOTTOM

12-OZ. ICE TEA OR
SODA-GRD. BOT.
ALSO MAKE 5 &
8-OZ. SODAS —
STRAIGHT OR FLARED

3-OZ. OYSTER
COCKTAIL

5-OZ. SHERBET

3-OZ.
COCKTAIL

12-OZ. FOOTED
ICE TEA, OR SODA
ALSO MAKE 6-OZ.
& 9-OZ. FOOTED
SODAS

ALSO MAKE 4-OZ. CLARET

9-OZ. GOBLET

9-OZ. LUNCHEON
GOBLET

5-OZ. SAUCER
CHAMPAGNE

2½-OZ. WINE

3 PINT JUG

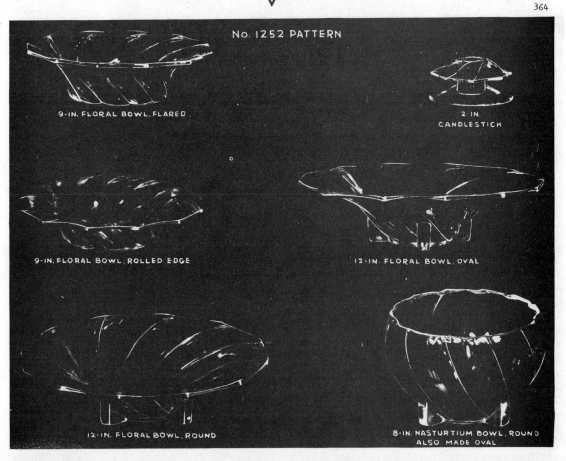

No. 1252 PATTERN

9-IN. FLORAL BOWL, FLARED

2-IN.
CANDLESTICK

9-IN. FLORAL BOWL, ROLLED EDGE

12-IN. FLORAL BOWL, OVAL

12-IN. FLORAL BOWL, ROUND

8-IN. NASTURTIUM BOWL, ROUND
ALSO MADE OVAL

365

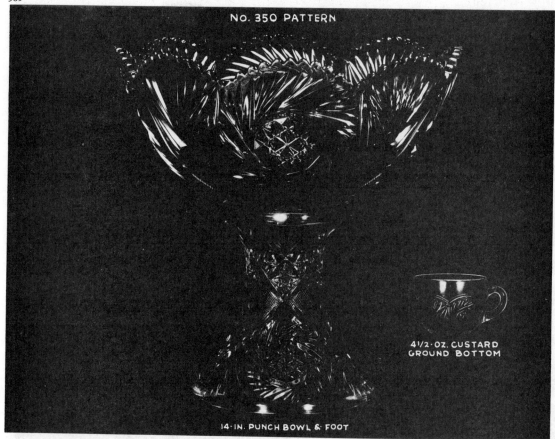

NO. 350 PATTERN

4½-OZ. CUSTARD
GROUND BOTTOM

14-IN. PUNCH BOWL & FOOT

Heisey's ⟨H⟩ Glassware

366

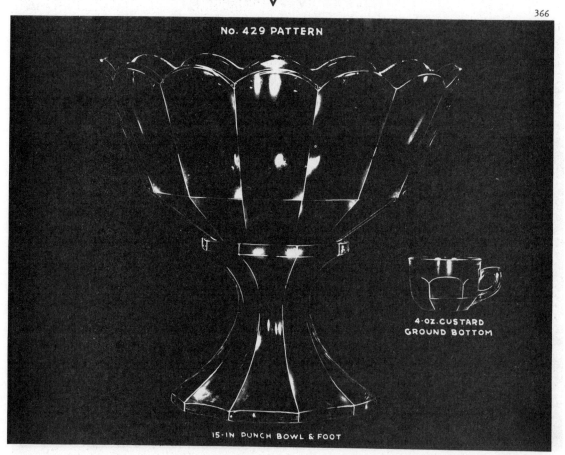

No. 429 PATTERN

4-OZ. CUSTARD
GROUND BOTTOM

15-IN PUNCH BOWL & FOOT

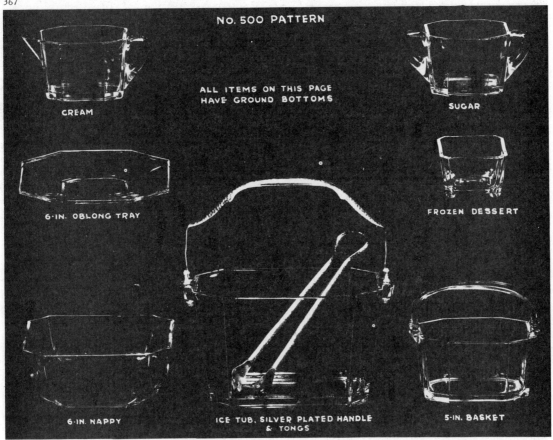

NO. 500 PATTERN

CREAM

ALL ITEMS ON THIS PAGE
HAVE GROUND BOTTOMS

SUGAR

6-IN. OBLONG TRAY

FROZEN DESSERT

6-IN. NAPPY

ICE TUB, SILVER PLATED HANDLE
& TONGS

5-IN. BASKET

Heisey's ⟨H⟩ Glassware

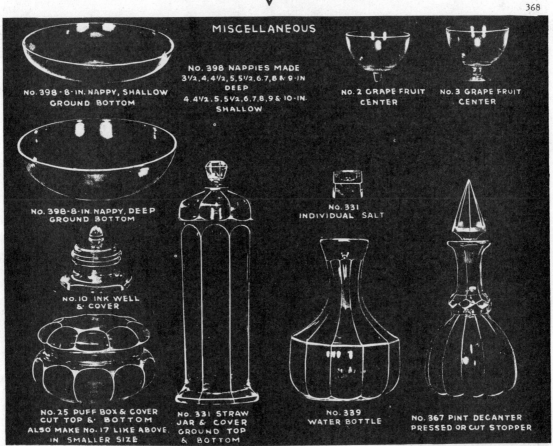

MISCELLANEOUS

NO. 398 - 8-IN. NAPPY, SHALLOW
GROUND BOTTOM

NO. 398 NAPPIES MADE
3½, 4, 4½, 5, 5½, 6, 7, 8 & 9-IN.
DEEP
4, 4½, 5, 5½, 6, 7, 8, 9 & 10-IN.
SHALLOW

NO. 2 GRAPE FRUIT
CENTER

NO. 3 GRAPE FRUIT
CENTER

NO. 398-8-IN. NAPPY, DEEP
GROUND BOTTOM

NO. 331
INDIVIDUAL SALT

NO. 10 INK WELL
& COVER

NO. 25 PUFF BOX & COVER
CUT TOP & BOTTOM
ALSO MAKE NO. 17 LIKE ABOVE.
IN SMALLER SIZE

NO. 331 STRAW
JAR & COVER
GROUND TOP
& BOTTOM

NO. 339
WATER BOTTLE

NO. 367 PINT DECANTER
PRESSED OR CUT STOPPER

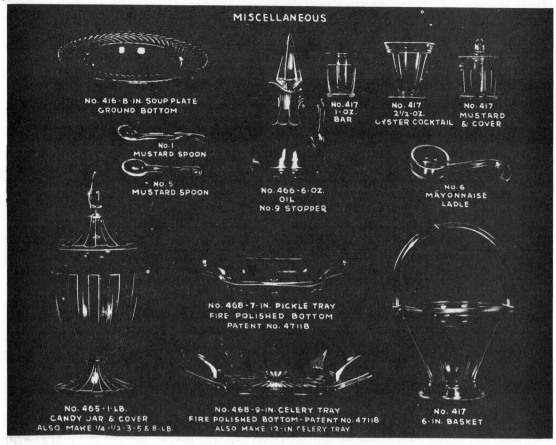

MISCELLANEOUS

NO. 416-8-IN. SOUP PLATE
GROUND BOTTOM

NO. 417
1-OZ.
BAR

NO. 417
2 1/2-OZ.
OYSTER COCKTAIL

NO. 417
MUSTARD
& COVER

No.1
MUSTARD SPOON

No.5
MUSTARD SPOON

NO. 466-6-OZ.
OIL
NO. 9 STOPPER

No. 6
MAYONNAISE
LADLE

NO. 468-7-IN. PICKLE TRAY
FIRE-POLISHED BOTTOM
PATENT NO. 47118

NO. 465-1-LB.
CANDY JAR & COVER
ALSO MAKE 1/4-1/2-3-5 & 8-LB.

No. 468-9-IN- CELERY TRAY
FIRE POLISHED BOTTOM- PATENT No. 47118
ALSO MAKE 12-IN CELERY TRAY

No. 417
6-IN. BASKET

Heisey's $\langle H \rangle$ Glassware

370

MISCELLANEOUS

No. 1180 INDIVIDUAL NUT
GROUND BOTTOM

No. 1189-13-IN. CELERY TRAY- GROUND OR FIRE
POLISHED BOTTOM-PATENT No. 65870
ALSO MAKE 9-IN.
No. 1189-13-IN. PICKLE & OLIVE LIKE CELERY TRAY
WITH TWO COMPARTMENTS

No. 1186 CUP & SAUCER
DIAMOND OPTIC
ALSO MADE PLAIN

NO. 1183-5-OZ.
PARFAIT OPTIC
ALSO MADE PLAIN

No. 1185-12-IN. CELERY TRAY- GROUND BOTTOM
ALSO MADE DIAMOND OPTIC
MADE WITH FIRE POLISHED BOTTOM
PLAIN ONLY

No. 1186-7-IN.
HIGH FOOTED COMPORT
SHALLOW-DIAMOND OPTIC

NO. 1183-6-IN. COMPORT
SWIRL OPTIC

No. 1181 CHEESE & CRACKER
GROUND BOTTOM

No. 1186-6-IN.
HIGH FOOTED COMPORT DEEP
DIAMOND OPTIC-ALSO MADE PLAIN

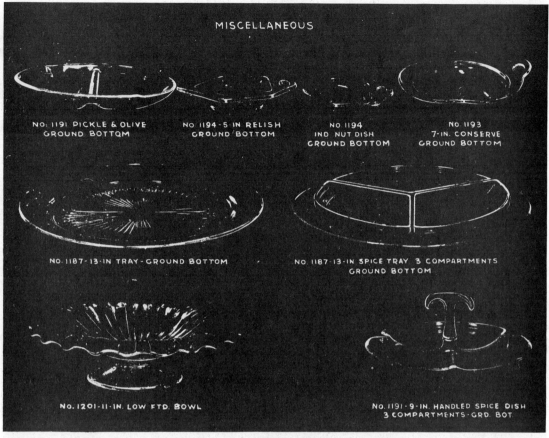

MISCELLANEOUS

No. 1191 PICKLE & OLIVE
GROUND BOTTOM

No. 1194 - 5 IN RELISH
GROUND BOTTOM

No. 1194
IND. NUT DISH
GROUND BOTTOM

No. 1193
7-IN. CONSERVE
GROUND BOTTOM

No. 1187-13-IN TRAY - GROUND BOTTOM

No. 1187-13-IN SPICE TRAY 3 COMPARTMENTS
GROUND BOTTOM

No. 1201-11-IN. LOW FTD. BOWL

No. 1191-9-IN. HANDLED SPICE DISH
3 COMPARTMENTS - GRD. BOT.

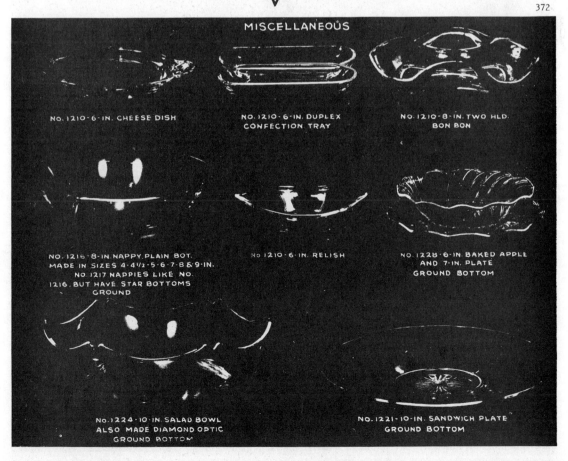

MISCELLANEOUS

No. 1210-6-IN. CHEESE DISH

No. 1210-6-IN. DUPLEX
CONFECTION TRAY

No. 1210-8-IN. TWO HLD.
BON BON

No. 1216-8-IN. NAPPY, PLAIN BOT.
MADE IN SIZES 4-4½-5-6-7-8 & 9-IN.
No. 1217 NAPPIES LIKE No.
1216, BUT HAVE STAR BOTTOMS
GROUND

No. 1210-6-IN. RELISH

No. 1228-6-IN. BAKED APPLE
AND 7-IN. PLATE
GROUND BOTTOM

No. 1224-10-IN. SALAD BOWL
ALSO MADE DIAMOND OPTIC
GROUND BOTTOM

No. 1221-10-IN. SANDWICH PLATE
GROUND BOTTOM

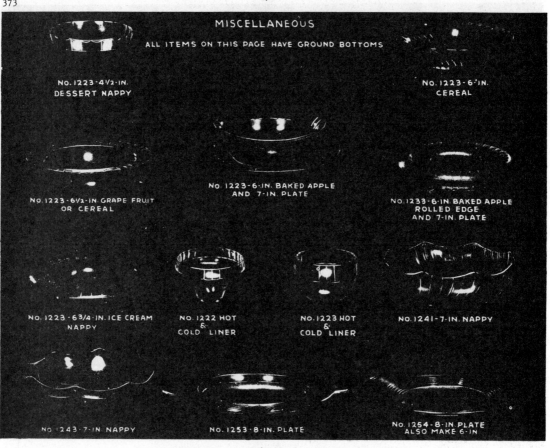

MISCELLANEOUS
ALL ITEMS ON THIS PAGE HAVE GROUND BOTTOMS

NO. 1223-4½-IN.
DESSERT NAPPY

NO. 1223-6-IN.
CEREAL

NO. 1223-6½-IN. GRAPE FRUIT
OR CEREAL

NO. 1223-6-IN. BAKED APPLE
AND 7-IN. PLATE

NO. 1233-6-IN. BAKED APPLE
ROLLED EDGE
AND 7-IN. PLATE

NO. 1223-6¾-IN. ICE CREAM
NAPPY

NO. 1222 HOT
&
COLD LINER

NO. 1223 HOT
&
COLD LINER

NO. 1241-7-IN. NAPPY

NO. 1243-7-IN. NAPPY

NO. 1253-8-IN. PLATE

NO. 1254-8-IN. PLATE
ALSO MAKE 6-IN

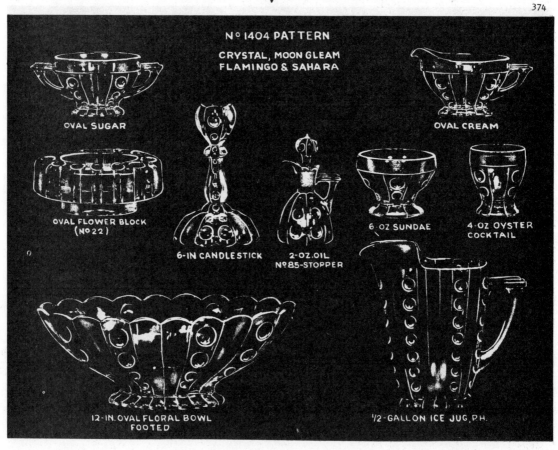

Nº 1404 PATTERN
CRYSTAL, MOON GLEAM
FLAMINGO & SAHARA

OVAL SUGAR

OVAL CREAM

OVAL FLOWER BLOCK
(Nº 22)

6-IN CANDLESTICK

2-OZ. OIL
Nº 85-STOPPER

6-OZ SUNDAE

4-OZ OYSTER
COCKTAIL

12-IN. OVAL FLORAL BOWL
FOOTED

½-GALLON ICE JUG, P.H.

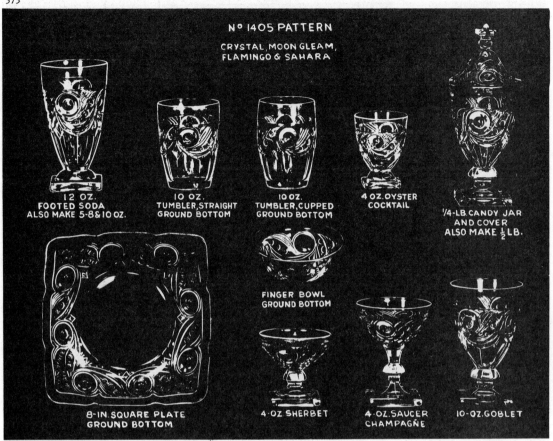

NO 1405 PATTERN

CRYSTAL, MOON GLEAM,
FLAMINGO & SAHARA

12 OZ.
FOOTED SODA
ALSO MAKE 5-8 & 10 OZ.

10 OZ.
TUMBLER, STRAIGHT
GROUND BOTTOM

10 OZ.
TUMBLER, CUPPED
GROUND BOTTOM

4 OZ. OYSTER
COCKTAIL

¼-LB. CANDY JAR
AND COVER
ALSO MAKE ½ LB.

8-IN. SQUARE PLATE
GROUND BOTTOM

FINGER BOWL
GROUND BOTTOM

4-OZ SHERBET

4-OZ. SAUCER
CHAMPAGNE

10-OZ. GOBLET

A. H. HEISEY & CO., NEWARK, OHIO.

REGISTERED
TRADE ◆H◆ MARK
No. 50121

BED ROOM SETS

REGISTERED
TRADE ◆H◆ MARK
No. 50121

SCALE HALF SIZE

No. 150—No. 1 Bed Room Set consists of
1 12-IN. TRAY, GROUND BOTTOM
1 HDL. CANDLESTICK
1 1½ QUART JUG
1 TUMBLER

Colonial Bed Room Set consists of
1 353 10-IN. TRAY, FIRE POLISHED BOTTOM
1 341 1 QT. TANKARD AND COVER
1 150 MATCH STAND
1 341½ TUMBLER
1 22 5-IN. HDL. CANDLESTICK

No. 352 Bed Room Set

No. 352—Bed Room Set consists of
1 352 12-IN. TRAY, FIRE POLISHED BOTTOM
1 300 1 PT. DECANTER (NO STOPPER)
1 150 MATCH BOX
1 300 8 OZ. TUMBLER
1 22 5-IN. HDL. CANDLESTICK

No. 150—No. 1 Bed Room Set

Colonial Bed Room Set

BASKETS

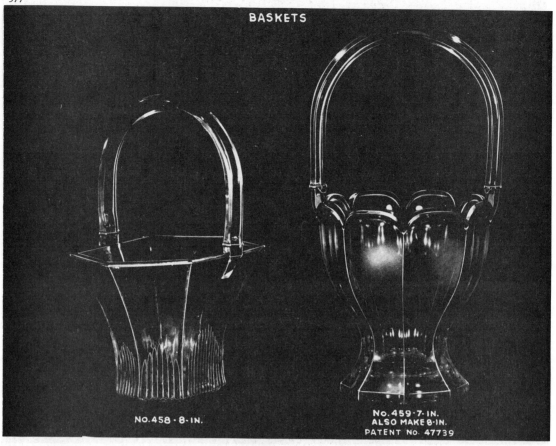

NO. 458 - 8-IN.

No. 459 - 7-IN.
ALSO MAKE 8-IN.
PATENT No. 47739

BASKETS

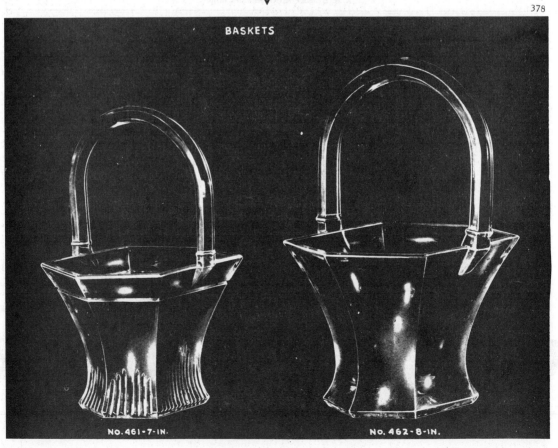

No. 461 - 7-IN.

No. 462 - 8-IN.

379

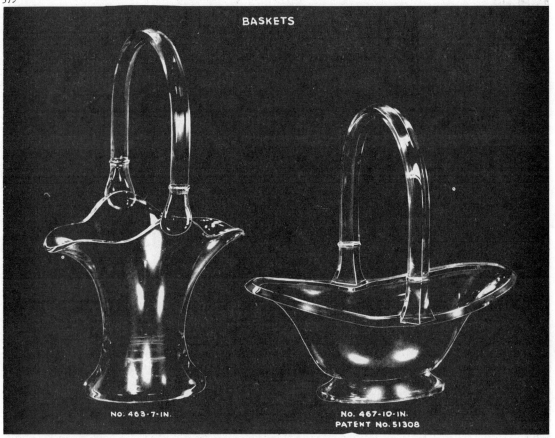

BASKETS

NO. 463-7-IN.

No. 467-10-IN.
PATENT No. 51308

380

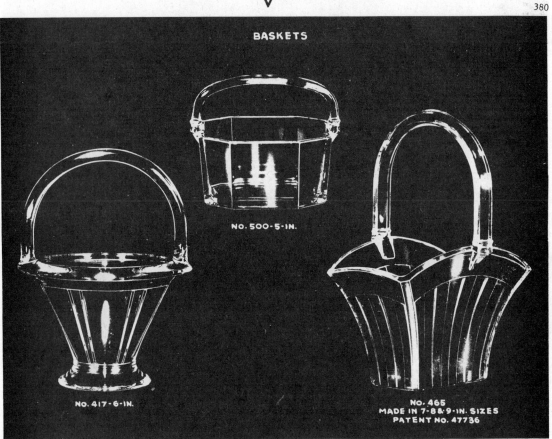

BASKETS

NO. 500-5-IN.

NO. 417-6-IN.

NO. 465
MADE IN 7-8 & 9-IN. SIZES
PATENT NO. 47736

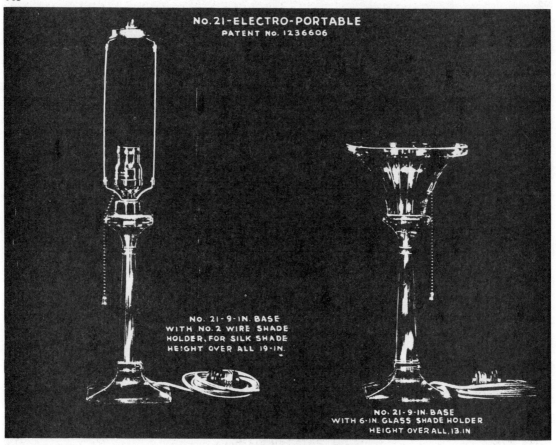

No. 21-ELECTRO-PORTABLE
PATENT No. 1236606

No. 21-9-IN. BASE
WITH No. 2 WIRE SHADE
HOLDER, FOR SILK SHADE
HEIGHT OVER ALL 19-IN.

No. 21-9-IN. BASE
WITH 6-IN. GLASS SHADE HOLDER
HEIGHT OVER ALL, 13-IN.

Heisey's ⬦H⬦ Glassware

No. 21-ELECTRO-PORTABLE
PATENT No. 1236606

7½-IN. SATIN FINISH SHADE
WITH No. 1 CUTTING

8-IN. SATIN FINISH SHADE WITH No. 2
CUTTING - ALSO FURNISHED PLAIN

No. 21-9-IN. ELECTRO-PORTABLE, 5-IN. GLASS SHADE HOLDER: 7½ S/F
SHADE 4½-IN. C PRISMS. ALSO FITTED WITH 6-IN. METAL SHADE HOLDER

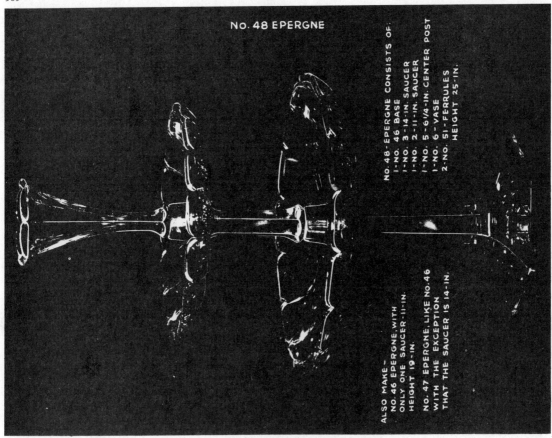

NO. 48 EPERGNE

NO. 48 EPERGNE CONSISTS OF:
1-NO. 46 BASE
1-NO. 3-14-IN. SAUCER
1-NO. 2-11-IN. SAUCER
1-NO. 5-6¼-IN. CENTER POST
1-NO. 6-VASE
2-NO. 51-FERRULES
HEIGHT 25-IN.

ALSO MAKE—
NO. 46 EPERGNE-WITH
ONLY ONE SAUCER-11-IN.
HEIGHT 19-IN.

NO. 47 EPERGNE-LIKE NO.46
WITH THE EXCEPTION
THAT THE SAUCER IS 14-IN.

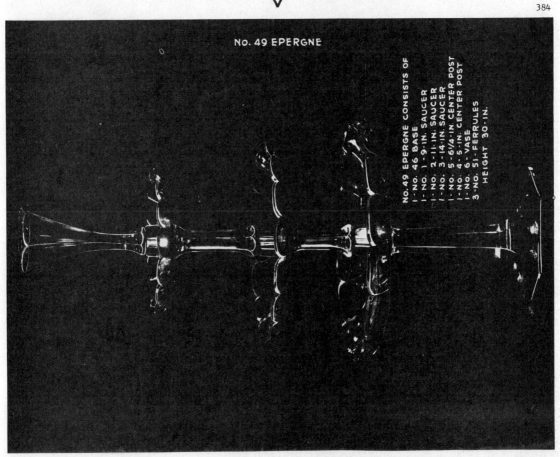

NO. 49 EPERGNE

NO. 49 EPERGNE CONSISTS OF
1-NO. 46 BASE
1-NO. 1-9-IN. SAUCER
1-NO. 2-11-IN. SAUCER
1-NO. 3-14-IN. SAUCER
1-NO. 5-6¼-IN. CENTER POST
1-NO. 4-5-IN. CENTER POST
1-NO. 6-VASE
3-NO. 51-FERRULES
HEIGHT 30-IN.

REGISTERED
TRADE H MARK
No. 50121

No. 150
BED ROOM SETS

REGISTERED
TRADE H MARK
No. 50121

SCALE HALF SIZE

No. 150—No. 2 Bed Room Set consists of
1 10-IN. TRAY, FIRE POLISHED BOTTOM
1 PINT TANKARD AND COVER
1 TUMBLER
1 MATCH BOX AND COVER
1 SAUCER FOOT CANDLESTICK

No. 150—No. 4 Bed Room Set
LIKE NO. 2, TRAY GROUND BOTTOM

No. 150—No. 3 Bed Room Set consists of
1 10-IN. TRAY, FIRE POLISHED BOTTOM
1 PINT TANKARD AND COVER
1 TUMBLER
1 MATCH STAND
1 SAUCER FOOT CANDLESTICK

No. 150—No. 5 Bed Room Set
LIKE NO. 3, TRAY GROUND BOTTOM

No. 150—No. 2 Bed Room Set

No. 150—No. 3 Bed Room Set

Heisey's H Glassware

NO. 1401 PATTERN

NO. 1401 1/2 CUP & SAUCER

AFTER DINNER COFFEE
CUP & SAUCER

CUP & SAUCER

BOUILLON & PLATE

13-IN. CELERY TRAY, GROUND BOTTOM
ALSO MAKE 10-IN.

14-IN. OVAL PLATTER, GROUND BOTTOM

CREAM SOUP & PLATE

NO. 1401 PATTERN

INDIVIDUAL
NUT DISH

6-IN. FOOTED JELLY
2 HANDLES

5½-IN. FOOTED
MAYONNAISE

6-IN. FOOTED MINT

6-IN. BON BON
GROUND BOTTOM

SALT OR
PEPPER
NO. 57 TOP

5-IN. PRESERVE · 2 HDLS.

MUSTARD
& COVER

6-IN. CANDLESTICK

13-IN. PICKLE & OLIVE · 2 COMPARTMENTS
GROUND BOTTOM

4-OZ. OIL
NO. 83 STOPPER

TABLE AND HOTEL TUMBLERS

388

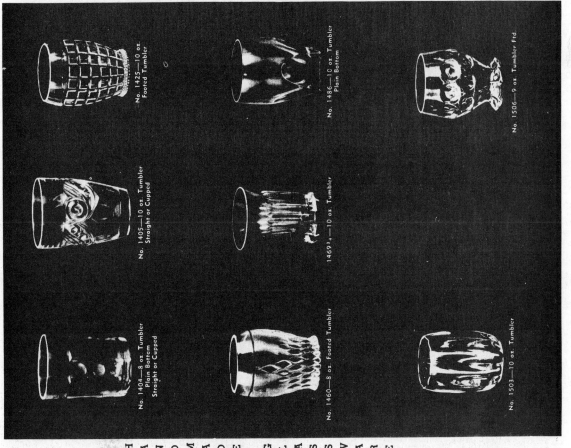

No. 1425—10 oz.
Footed Tumbler

No. 1486—10 oz. Tumbler
Plain Bottom

No. 1506—9 oz. Tumbler Ftd.

No. 1405—10 oz. Tumbler
Straight or Cupped

1469³¼—10 oz. Tumbler

No. 1404—8 oz. Tumbler
Plain Bottom
Straight or Cupped

No. 1460—8 oz. Footed Tumbler

No. 1503—10 oz. Tumbler

A. H. HEISEY & CO., ◇H◇ NEWARK, OHIO

HANDMADE GLASSWARE

H A N D M A D E   G L A S S W A R E

BAR TUMBLERS
GROUND BOTTOMS
TODDY & OLD FASHIONS & COASTERS

1469—2½ oz.
Not Ground

No. 1425—2 oz.
Not Ground

No. 1184—2½ oz.
Bar (236)
Ground Bottom
Diamond Optic
Straight or Flared

No. 248—2½ oz.
Plain Bottom
Straight or Flared

No. 236—2½ oz.
Bar (1184)
Plain Bottom
Also made
Diamond Optic
Straight or Flared

No. 1425—8 oz.
Old Fashion Cocktail

No. 1404—6½ oz.
Toddy

No. 299—6 oz.
Toddy Optic

No. 1486—2 oz. Bar

No. 1486—7 oz. Old Fashion

No. 1469—8 oz. Old Fashion

No. 10 Coaster
Figured Bottom

No. 1506—4'' Coaster

No. 1503—4'' Coaster

No. 1468—4 in. Coaster

No. 1467—3½ in. Coaster

A. H. HEISEY & CO.   NEWARK, OHIO

A. H. HEISEY & CO.   NEWARK, OHIO

SODAS
GROUND BOTTOMS

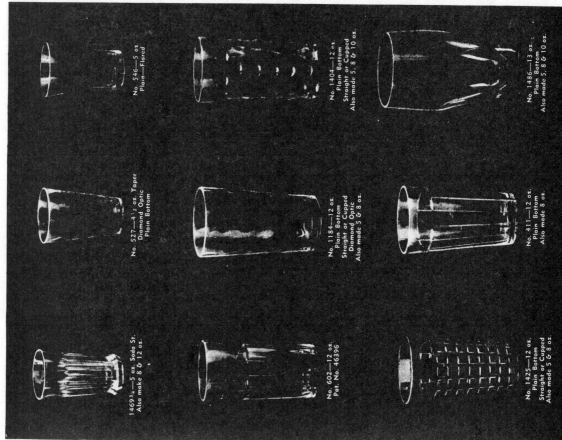

No. 546—5 oz.
Plain—Flared

No. 1404—12 oz.
Plain Bottom
Straight or Cupped
Also made 5, 8 & 10 oz.

No. 1486—13 oz.
Plain Bottom
Also made 5, 8 & 10 oz.

No. 527—4½ oz. Taper
Diamond Optic
Plain Bottom

No. 1184—12 oz.
Plain Bottom
Straight or Cupped
Diamond Optic
Also made 5 & 8 oz.

No. 41—12 oz.
Plain Bottom
Also made 8 oz.

1469½—5 oz. Soda St.
Also make 8 & 12 oz.

No. 602—12 oz.
Pat. No. 46396

No. 1425—12 oz.
Plain Bottom
Straight or Cupped
Also made 5 & 8 oz.

H A N D M A D E   G L A S S W A R E

391

ICE TEA TUMBLERS
GROUND BOTTOMS

No. 1404—12 oz.
Plain Bottom
Straight or Cupped

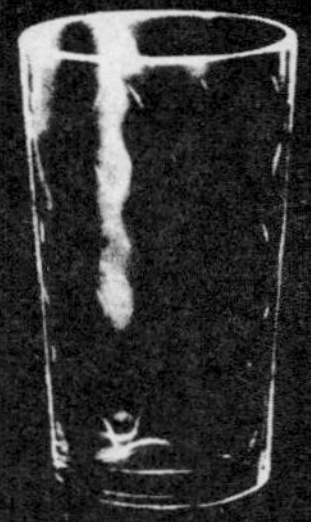

No. 1184—12 oz.
Plain Bottom
Diamond Optic
Straight or Cupped

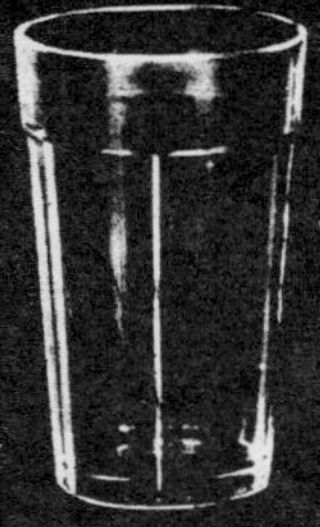

No. 411—12 oz.
Plain Bottom
Straight

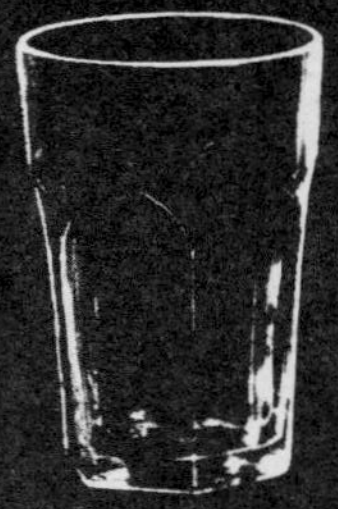

No. 120—12 oz.
Plain Bottom
Colonial—Straight
Also made Flared

FOOTED AND HANDLED ICE TEAS OR SODAS

No. 1404—12 oz.
Footed Soda or Ice Tea

No. 1469—12 oz.

No. 1425—12 oz.

No. 1405—12 oz.

No. 412—12 oz.
Footed & Handled Ice Tea
Also made Sham

A. H. HEISEY & CO.,   NEWARK, OHIO

No. 300 COLONIAL PATTERN

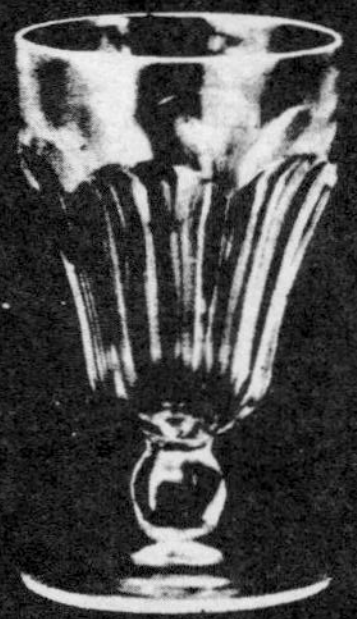

7 oz. Low Footed
Goblet or Tumbler

4½ oz. Low Footed Sherbet
Shallow

Individual Sugar

Individual Cream

7 oz.
Goblet

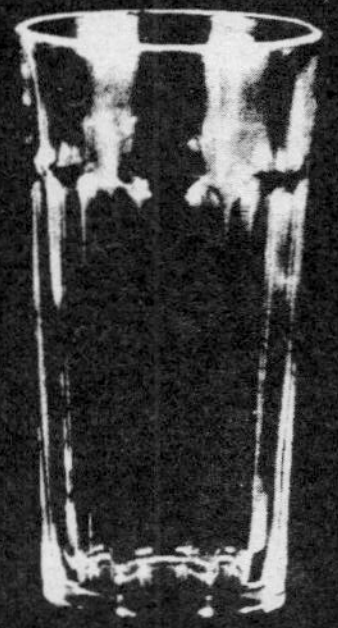

12 oz.
Schoppen Straight
Ground Bottom
Also made 5 & 9 oz.

A. H. HEISEY & CO.,   NEWARK, OHIO

NO. 341 "OLD WILLIAMSBURG" COLONIAL PATTERN

HANDMADE GLASSWARE

4½ oz. Saucer Champagne (No. 373)

5 oz. Sherbet (No. 373)

9 oz. Goblet (No. 373)

2 oz. Wine (No. 373)

3 oz. Cocktail (No. 373)

4½ oz. Claret (No. 373)

Finger Bowl (No. 352)

12 oz. Schoppen Straight (No. 300) Ground Bottom Also made 5 & 9 oz.

1 oz. Cordial (No. 373)

A. H. HEISEY & CO.   NEWARK, OHIO

No. 341 OLD WILLIAMSBURG COLONIAL PATTERN

HANDMADE GLASSWARE

8 oz. Tumbler (341½) Ground Bottom

Finger Bowl (No. 341½) Small Straight Also made Flared

1 pt.—Decanter made with No. 48 P S & C S

2 oz. Oil & No. 2 P S Ground In. Also made 4 & 6 oz.

No. 1150—6 in. Colonial Plate Star Bottom Ground Also made 4½, 5, 5½, 6½, 7, 8

Water Bottle (No. 339)

A. H. HEISEY & CO.   NEWARK, OHIO

No. 341 OLD WILLIAMSBURG COLONIAL PATTERN

4½ oz. Custard
Ground Bottom

13 in. High Footed Punch Bowl.—Straight
Also made in 14 in. Flared
Also made 13 & 14 in. without Foot

A. H. HEISEY & CO.,   NEWARK, OHIO

No. 393 PATTERN

8 oz. Tumbler
Ground Bottom
Also made 9 oz.

4½ oz. Low Footed Sherbet
Straight
Also made Cupped & Flared
(No. 393½)

Individual Sugar
Ground Bottom

Individual Cream
Ground Bottom

4½ oz.
Parfait

9 in. Celery Tray
Ground Bottom
Also made 12 in.

4½ oz. Custard
Ground Bottom

No. 3 Salt or Pepper
No. 1 San. Top

No. 3 Salt or Pepper
No. 643 Top

Round Cream

Round Sugar & Cover

3 pt. Jug
Stuck Handle
Also made 12 oz., 1 pt., 1 qt. & ½ gal.

8 in. Nappy
Ground Bottom
Also made 4, 4½, 7 & 9 in.
(No. 393½)

A. H. HEISEY & CO.,   NEWARK, OHIO

NO. 398 - 406 NAPPIES
Star Ground Bottom

HANDMADE GLASSWARE

No. 406—4½ in. Nappy
Also made 4, 5, 6, 7, 8 & 9 in.

No. 398—4 in. Nappy
Also made 4½, 5, 6, 7 & 8 in.

NO. 411 - PATTERN - PATENT NO. 63947

5 in. Nappy
Ground Bottom

6 oz. Sham Soda
Ground Bottom
Also made 6, 8 & 12 oz. Reg.

No. 3 Salt or Pepper
No. 1 San. Top

No. 3 Salt or Pepper
No. 643 Salt Proof Top

8 oz. Tumbler
Ground Bottom

Sugar Dispenser with Silver Top

1 qt. Jug and Cover

GLASSWARE

A. H. HEISEY & CO.,   NEWARK, OHIO

No. 412 PATTERN

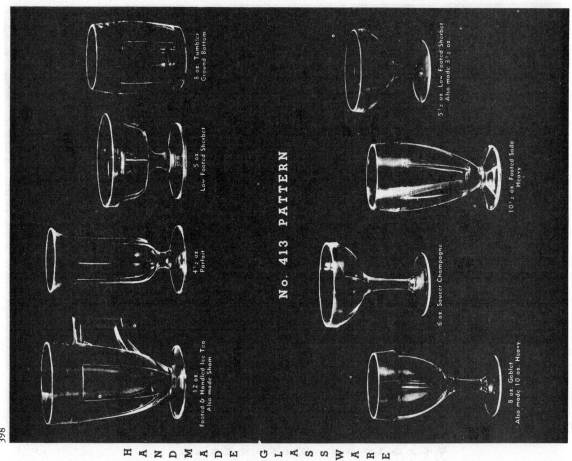

HANDMADE GLASSWARE

8 oz. Tumbler
Ground Bottom

5 oz.
Low Footed Sherbet

4½ oz.
Parfait

12 oz.
Footed & Handled Ice Tea
Also made Sham

No. 413 PATTERN

5½ oz. Low Footed Sherbet
Also made 3½ oz.

10½ oz. Footed Soda
Heavy

6 oz. Saucer Champagne

8 oz. Goblet
Also made 10 oz. Heavy

GLASSWARE

A. H. HEISEY & CO.,   NEWARK, OHIO

No. 433 PATTERN – Patent No. 41533

HANDMADE GLASSWARE

4½ oz.
Custard
Ground Bottom

15 in.
Punch Bowl & Foot
9½ qts.

21 in. Buffet Plate

No. 1184 PATTERN

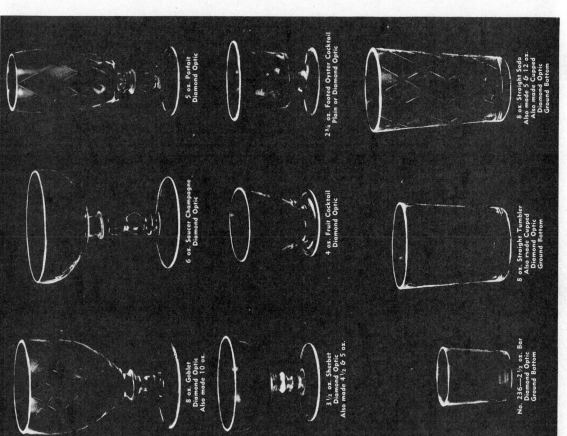

8 oz. Goblet
Diamond Optic
Also made 10 oz.

6 oz. Saucer Champagne
Diamond Optic

5 oz. Parfait
Diamond Optic

3½ oz. Sherbet
Diamond Optic
Also made 4½ & 5 oz.

4 oz. Fruit Cocktail
Diamond Optic

2¾ oz. Footed Oyster Cocktail
Plain or Diamond Optic

No. 236—2½ oz. Bar
Diamond Optic
Ground Bottom

8 oz. Straight Tumbler
Also made Cupped
Diamond Optic
Ground Bottom

8 oz. Straight Soda
Also made 5 & 12 oz.
Diamond Optic
Ground Bottom

HANDMADE GLASSWARE

No. 1184 PATTERN

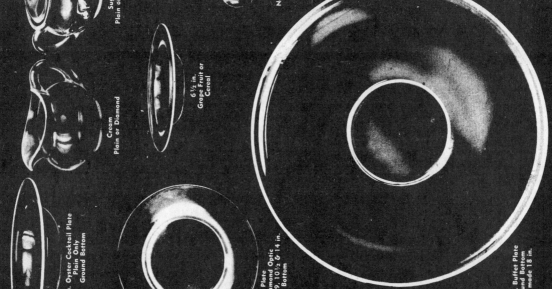

Sugar & Cover
Plain or Diamond Optic

Cream
Plain or Diamond

6½ in.
Grape Fruit or
Cereal

2 oz. Oil &
No. 1 P/S Ground in
Diamond Optic
Also made 4 oz.

8 in. Oyster Cocktail Plate
Plain Only
Ground Bottom

8 in. Plate
Plain or Diamond Optic
Also made 6, 7, 9, 10½ & 14 in.
Ground Bottom

16 in. Buffet Plate
Ground Bottom
Also made 18 in.

A. H. HEISEY & CO., NEWARK, OHIO

No. 1404 OLD SANDWICH PATTERN

2½ oz. Wine

4 oz. Sherbet

10 oz. Low Footed Tumbler

4½ oz. Parfait

6 oz. Sundae

8 oz. Soda or Ice Tea
Ground Bottom
Straight or Cupped
Also made 5, 10 & 12 oz.

3 oz. Cocktail

5 oz. Saucer Champagne

8 oz. Tumbler
Ground Bottom
Straight or Cupped

10 oz. Low Footed Goblet

12 oz.
Footed Soda or Ice Tea

4 oz. Oyster Cocktail

A. H. HEISEY & CO., NEWARK, OHIO

No. 1404 OLD SANDWICH PATTERN

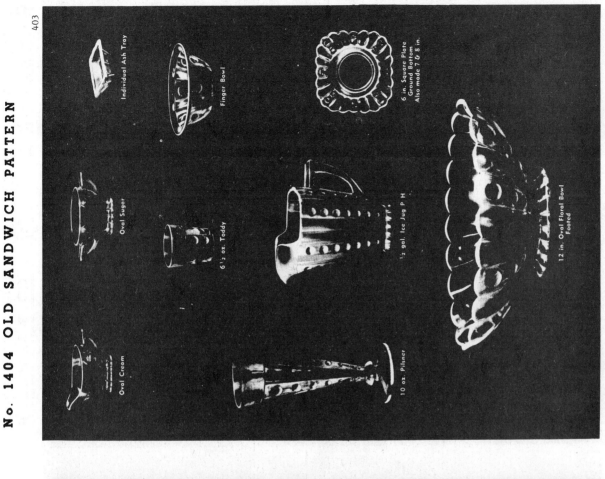

Individual Ash Tray

Finger Bowl

6 in. Square Plate
Ground Bottom
Also made 7 & 8 in.

Oval Sugar

6½ oz. Toddy

½ gal. Ice Jug P H

12 in. Oval Floral Bowl
Footed

Oval Cream

10 oz. Pilsner

A. H. HEISEY & CO.   NEWARK, OHIO

No. 1405 IPSWICH PATTERN

4 oz. Sherbet

4 oz. Oyster Cocktail

7 in. Square Plate
Ground Bottom
Also made 8 in.

Finger Bowl & 6 in. Plate

11 in. Floral Bowl

4 oz. Saucer Champagne

10 oz. Footed Soda
Also made 5 & 12 oz.

10 oz. Goblet

10 oz. Tumbler
Ground Bottom
Straight or Cupped

Footed Center Piece
with Vase and "A" Prisms

A. H. HEISEY & CO.   NEWARK, OHIO

No. 1425 VICTORIAN PATTERN

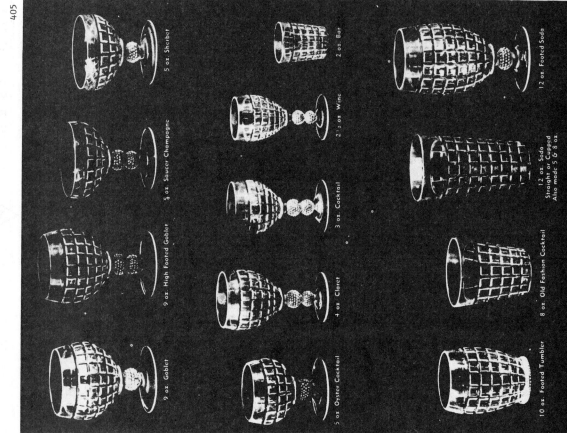

HANDMADE GLASSWARE

5 oz Sherbet

2 oz. Bar

12 oz. Footed Soda

5 oz. Saucer Champagne

2½ oz. Wine

12 oz. Soda
Straight or Cupped
Also made 5 & 8 oz.

9 oz. High Footed Goblet

3 oz. Cocktail

8 oz. Old Fashion Cocktail

9 oz. Goblet

4 oz. Claret

5 oz. Oyster Cocktail

10 oz. Footed Tumbler

A. H. HEISEY & CO.,　　NEWARK, OHIO

No. 1425 VICTORIAN PATTERN

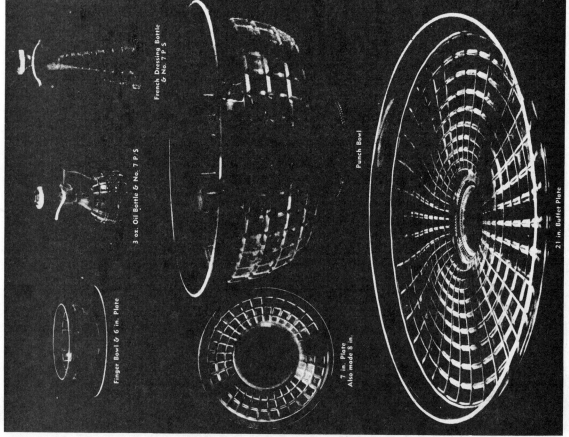

HANDMADE GLASSWARE

Finger Bowl & 6 in. Plate

3 oz. Oil Bottle & No. 7 P.S

French Dressing Bottle
& No. 7 P.S

Punch Bowl

7 in. Plate
Also made 8 in.

21 in. Buffet Plate

A. H. HEISEY & CO.,　　NEWARK, OHIO

No. 1425 VICTORIAN PATTERN

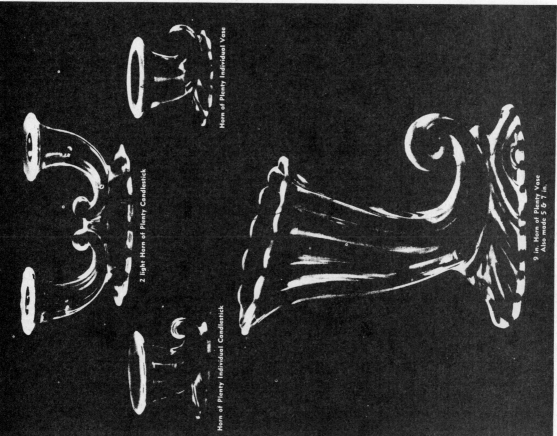

5 oz. Custard

4 in. Vase

5½ in. Vase

6 in. Footed Vase

Individual Cigarette Holder & Ash Tray

¼ lb. Butter Dish & Cover

Salt or Pepper & No. 1 Sanitary Top

Cream

Salt or Pepper & No. 643 Metal Top

Salt or Pepper & No. 2 Sanitary Top

Sugar

27 oz. Rye Bottle & No. 99 P/S

A. H. HEISEY & CO., NEWARK, OHIO

No. 1428 WARWICK PATTERN

Horn of Plenty Individual Vase

2 light Horn of Plenty Candlestick

Horn of Plenty Individual Candlestick

9 in. Horn of Plenty Vase
Also made 5 & 7 in.

A. H. HEISEY & CO., NEWARK, OHIO

No. 1469 RIDGELEIGH PATTERN

HANDMADE GLASSWARE

4½ oz. Sherbet

4 oz. Claret

2½ oz. Bar

8 oz. Old Fashion

9 oz. Goblet

3½ oz. Cocktail

12 oz. Soda Ftd.
Also make 5 oz.

5 oz. Saucer Champagne

4 oz. Oyster Cocktail

2½ oz. Wine

No. 1469 RIDGELEIGH PATTERN

HANDMADE GLASSWARE

13½ in. Sandwich Plate
Also make 11½ in.

12 in. Oval Floral Bowl

9 in. Salad Bowl

8½ in. Berry Bowl Cupped

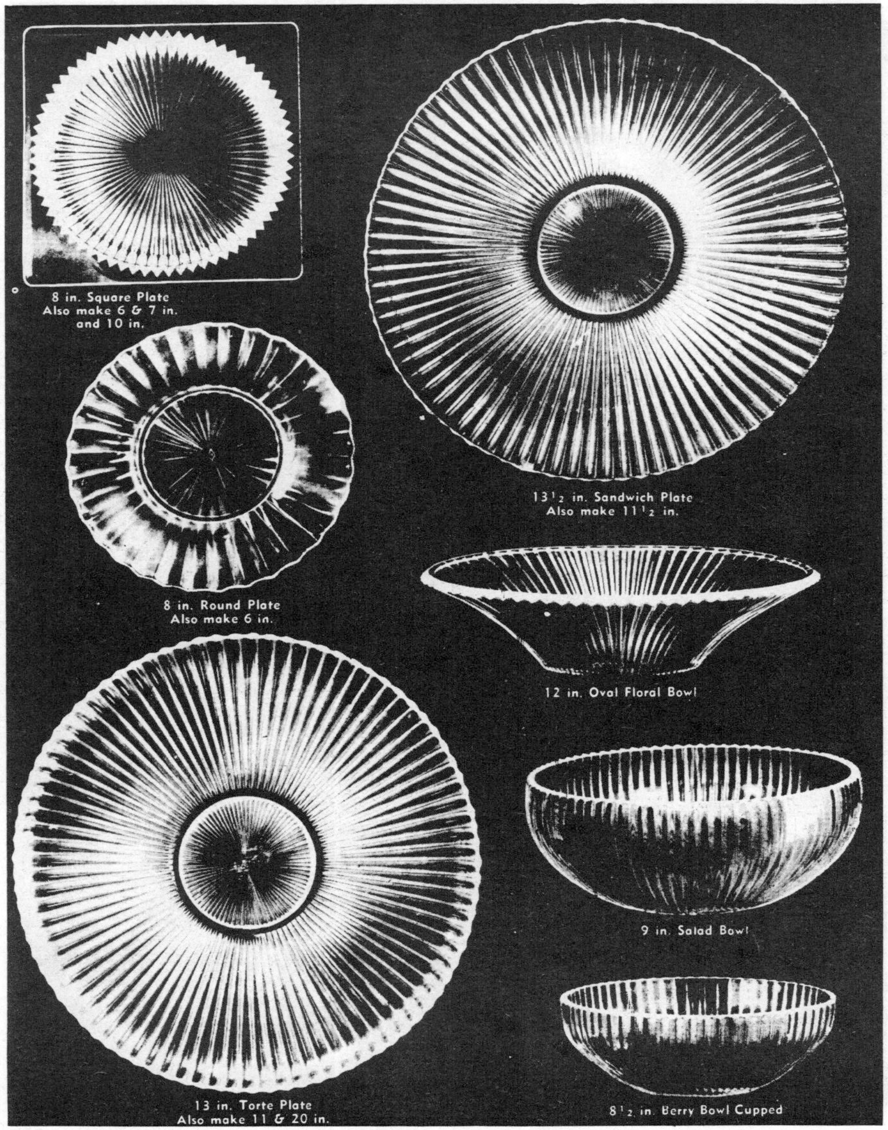

8 in. Square Plate
Also make 6 & 7 in.
and 10 in.

8 in. Round Plate
Also make 6 in.

13 in. Torte Plate
Also make 11 & 20 in.

No. 1469 RIDGELEIGH PATTERN

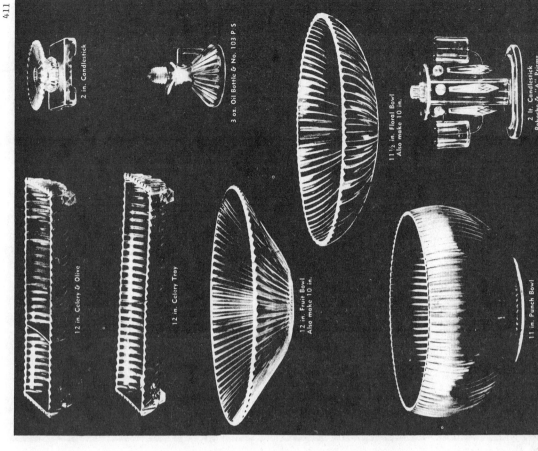

2 in. Candlestick

3 oz. Oil Bottle & No. 103 P S

11½ in. Floral Bowl
Also make 10 in.

12 in. Celery & Olive

12 in. Celery Tray

12 in. Fruit Bowl
Also make 10 in.

11 in. Punch Bowl

2 lt. Candlestick
Bobeche & "A" Prisms
Consists of:
1——1469—2 lt. Candlestick
1——1469 2. Bobeche
6——"A" Prisms

A. H. HEISEY & CO.,   NEWARK, OHIO

No. 1469 RIDGELEIGH PATTERN

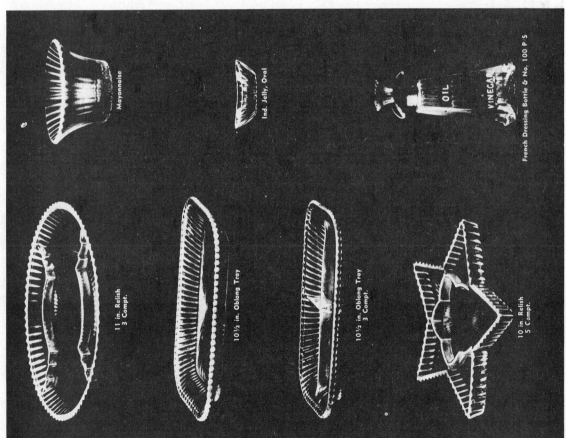

Mayonnaise

Ind. Jelly, Oval

French Dressing Bottle & No. 100 P S
OIL
VINEGAR

11 in. Relish
3 Compt.

10½ in. Oblong Tray

10½ in. Oblong Tray
3 Compt.

10 in. Relish
5 Compt.

A. H. HEISEY & CO.,   NEWARK, OHIO

No. 1469 RIDGELEIGH PATTERN

HANDMADE GLASSWARE

Ind. Cream & Sugar Tray

Sugar

Ind. Sugar, Oval

Ind. Cream, Oval

Cream

Ind. Vase No. 1

Ind. Vase No. 2

Ind. Vase No. 3

Ind. Vase No. 4

Ind. Vase No. 5

3½ in. Vase

6 in. Vase
Also made flared

6 in. Candle Vase

7 in. Ball Vase
Also made Saturne Optic

A. H. HEISEY & CO.   NEWARK, OHIO

No. 1469 RIDGELEIGH PATTERN

HANDMADE GLASSWARE

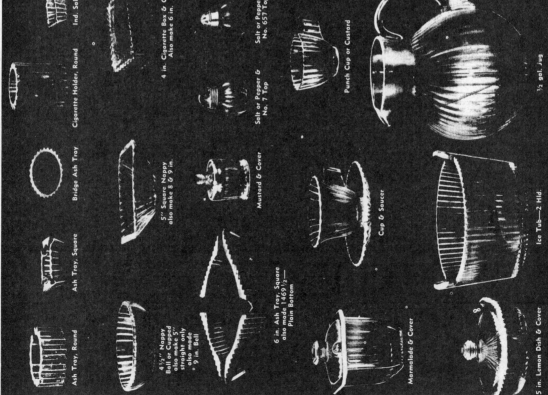

Ash Tray, Round

Ash Tray, Square

Bridge Ash Tray

Cigarette Holder Round

Ind. Salt

4½" Nappy
Ball or Cupped
also make 5"
straight only
also made
9 in. Bell

5" Square Nappy
also make 8 & 9 in.

4 in. Cigarette Box & Cover
Also make 6 in.

6 in. Ash Tray, Square
also made 1469½—
Plain Bottom

Mustard & Cover

Salt or Pepper &
No. 7 Top

Salt or Pepper &
No. 657 Top

Marmalade & Cover

Cup & Saucer

Punch Cup or Custard

5 in. Lemon Dish & Cover

Ice Tub—2 Hld.

½ gal. Jug

A. H. HEISEY & CO.   NEWARK, OHIO

No. 1469½ and 1469¾ RIDGELEIGH PATTERN

HANDMADE GLASSWARE

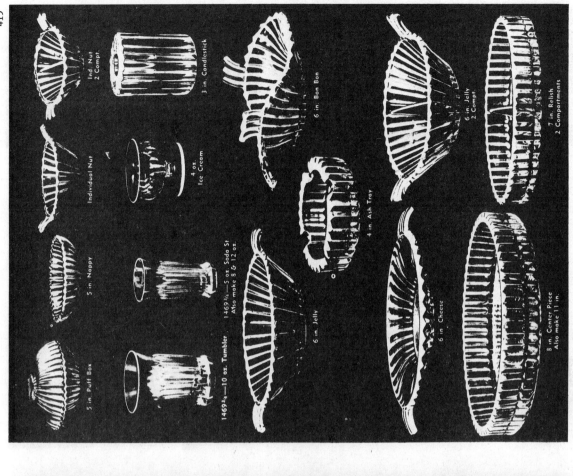

Ind. Nut 2 Compt.

Individual Nut

5-in. Nappy

5-in. Puff Box

3-in. Candlestick

4 oz. Ice Cream

1469¾—10 oz. Tumbler

1469¾—5 oz. Soda St. Also make 8 & 12 oz.

6-in. Bon Bon

4-in. Ash Tray

6-in. Jelly

6-in. Jelly 2 Compt.

6-in. Cheese

7-in. Relish 2 Compartments

8-in. Center Piece Also make 11-in.

A. H. HEISEY & CO., NEWARK, OHIO

No. 1488 "COLEPORT" PATTERN

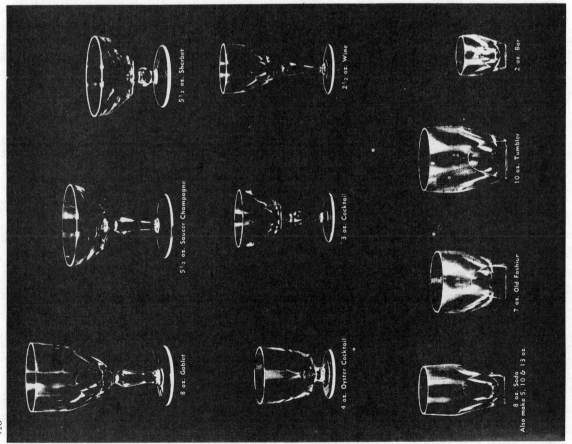

5½ oz. Sherbet

2½ oz. Wine

2 oz. Bar

5½ oz. Saucer Champagne

3 oz. Cocktail

10 oz. Tumbler

8 oz. Goblet

4 oz. Oyster Cocktail

7 oz. Old Fashion

8 oz. Soda Also make 5, 10 & 13 oz.

HANDMADE GLASSWARE

A. H. HEISEY & CO., NEWARK, OHIO

417

No. 1486 "COLEPORT" PATTERN

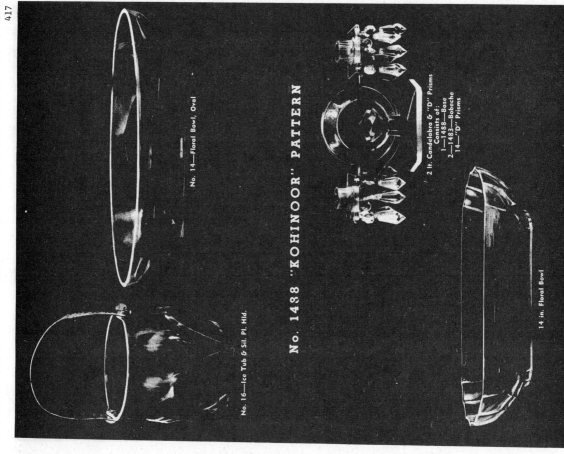

No. 14—Floral Bowl, Oval

No. 16—Ice Tub & Sil. Pl. Hld.

No. 1488 "KOHINOOR" PATTERN

2 lt. Candelabra & "D" Prisms
Consists of:
1—1488—Base
2—1483—Bobeche
14—"D" Prisms

14 in. Floral Bowl

A. H. HEISEY & CO., NEWARK, OHIO

No. 1495 FERN PATTERN

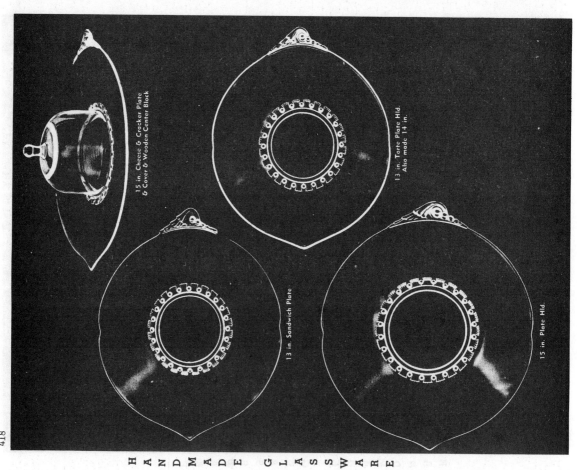

15 in. Cheese & Cracker Plate
& Cover & Wooden Center Block

13 in. Torte Plate Hld.
Also made 14 in.

13 in. Sandwich Plate

15 in. Plate Hld.

418

A. H. HEISEY & CO., NEWARK, OHIO

419

No. 1495 FERN PATTERN

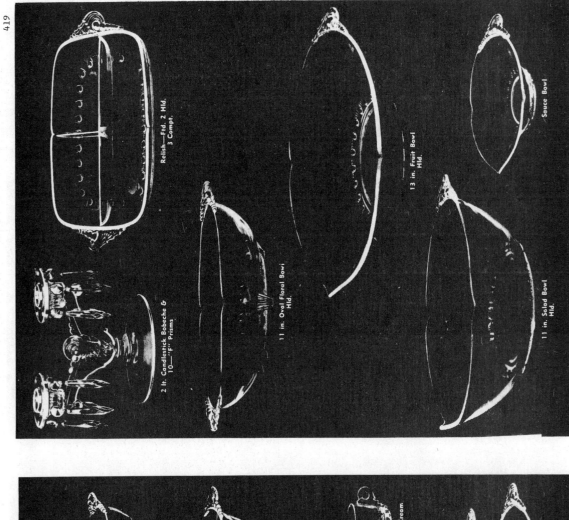

Relish—Frd. 2 Hld. 3 Compt.

2 lt. Candlestick, Bobeche & 10—"F" Prisms

11 in. Oval Floral Bowl, Hld.

13 in. Fruit Bowl Hld.

Sauce Bowl

11 in. Salad Bowl Hld.

A. H. HEISEY & CO.   NEWARK, OHIO

No. 1495 FERN PATTERN

6 in. Bon Bon Hld.

6 in. Cheese Hld.

4½ in. Nappy

6 in. Tid Bit Hld.

6 in. Mint Hld.

Twin Mayonnaise Hld.

6 in. Jelly Hld.

Ind. Cream

Ind. Sugar

Cream

Sugar

Whipped Cream or Mayonnaise Hld. & 8 in. Plate

Jello Dish 2 Hld. & Frd.

420

A. H. HEISEY & CO.   NEWARK, OHIO

No. 1503 CRYSTOLITE PATTERN

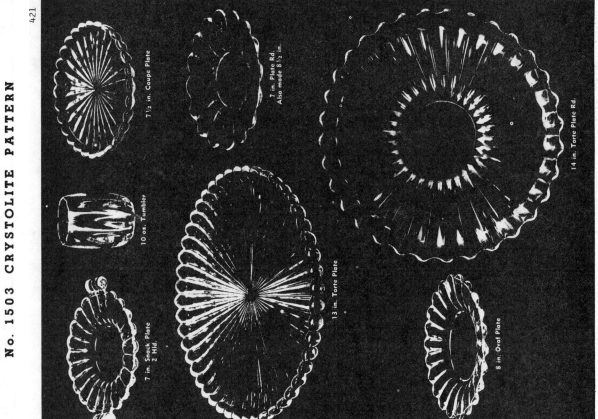

HANDMADE GLASSWARE

7½ in. Coupe Plate

7 in. Plate Rd.
Also made 8½ in.

14 in. Torte Plate Rd.

10 oz. Tumbler

7 in. Snack Plate
2 Hld.

13 in. Torte Plate

8 in. Oval Plate

A. H. HEISEY & CO.,   NEWARK, OHIO

No. 1503 CRYSTOLITE PATTERN

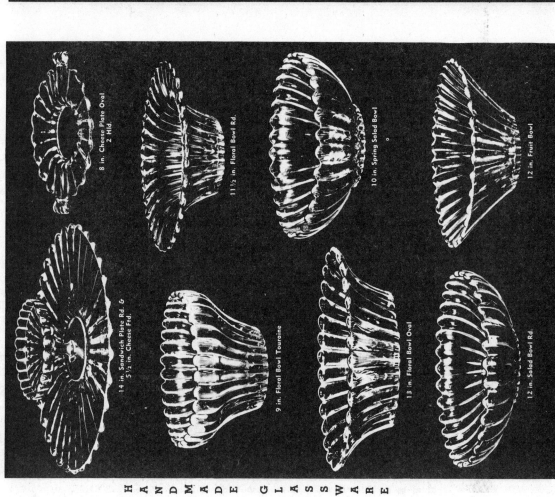

HANDMADE GLASSWARE

8 in. Cheese Plate Oval
2 Hld.

11½ in. Floral Bowl Rd.

10 in. Spring Salad Bowl

12 in. Fruit Bowl

14 in. Sandwich Plate Rd. &
5½ in. Cheese Ftd.

9 in. Floral Bowl Touraine

13 in. Floral Bowl Oval

12 in. Salad Bowl Rd.

A. H. HEISEY & CO.,   NEWARK, OHIO

423

No. 1503 CRYSTOLITE PATTERN

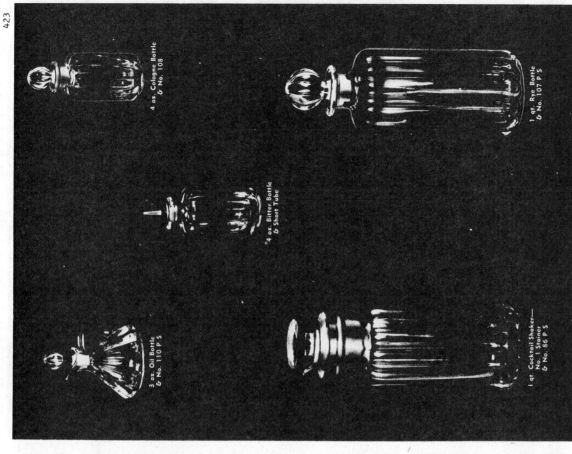

4 oz. Cologne Bottle
& No. 108

1 qt. Rye Bottle
& No. 107 P/S

°4 oz. Bitter Bottle
& Short Tube

3 oz. Oil Bottle
& No. 110 P/S

1 qt. Cocktail Shaker—
No. 1 Strainer
& No. 86 P/S

A. H. HEISEY & CO.   NEWARK, OHIO

No. 1503 CRYSTOLITE PATTERN

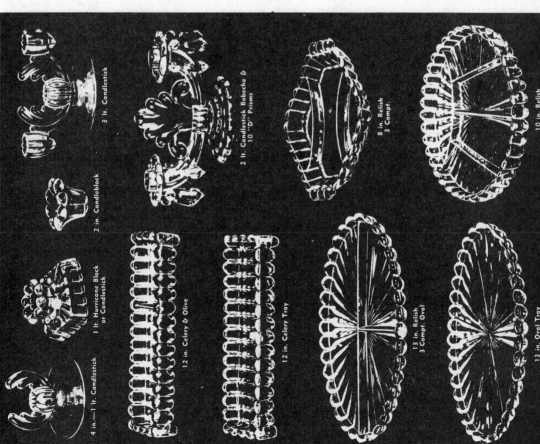

3 lt. Candlestick

2 in. Candleblock

1 lt. Hurricane Block
or Candlestick

2 lt. Candlestick Bobeche &
10 "D" Prisms

8 in. Relish
3 Compt.

10 in. Relish
5 Compt.

4 in.—1 lt. Candlestick

12 in. Celery & Olive

12 in. Celery Tray

13 in. Relish
3 Compt. Oval

13 in. Oval Tray

A. H. HEISEY & CO.   NEWARK, OHIO

424

No. 1503 CRYSTOLITE PATTERN

HANDMADE GLASSWARE

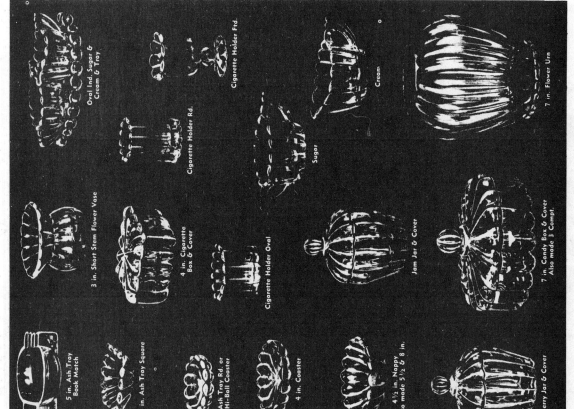

7 in. Bon Bon 2 Hld.

6 in. Jelly 2 Hld.

6 in. Preserve 2 Hld. & Cover

Hollandaise Sauce Bowl & 8 in. Oval Plate

5 in.—1000 Island Dressing Bowl Round & 7 in. Plate

6 in. Jelly 2 Hld. 2 Compt.

6 in. Pickle Oval

Oval Mayonnaise Hld. & 8 in. Oval Plate & No. 7 Ladle

5 in. 1000 Island Dressing Bowl Crimped

A. H. HEISEY & CO., NEWARK, OHIO

No. 1503 "CRYSTOLITE" PATTERN

HANDMADE GLASSWARE

Oval Ind. Sugar & Cream & Tray.

Cigarette Holder Rd.

Cigarette Holder Ftd.

Sugar

Cream

7 in. Flower Urn

5 in. Ash Tray Book Match

3½ in. Ash Tray Square

Ash Tray Rd. or Hi-Ball Coaster

4 in. Coaster

4½ in. Nappy Also made 5½ & 8 in.

3 in. Short Stem Flower Vase

4 in. Cigarette Box & Cover

Cigarette Holder Oval

Jam Jar & Cover

7 in. Candy Box & Cover Also made 3 Compt.

Cherry Jar & Cover

A. H. HEISEY & CO., NEWARK, OHIO

No. 1503 "CRYSTOLITE" PATTERN

HANDMADE GLASSWARE

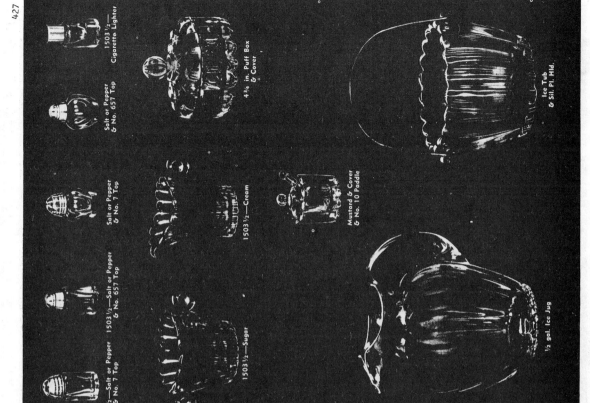

1503½—Cigarette Lighter

Salt or Pepper & No. 657 Top

Salt or Pepper & No. 7 Top

1503½—Salt or Pepper & No. 657 Top

1503½—Salt or Pepper & No. 7 Top

1503½—Salt or Pepper & No. 7 Top

4¾ in. Puff Box & Cover

1503½—Cream

1503½—Sugar

Mustard & Cover & No. 10 Paddle

Ice Tub & Sil. Pl. Hld.

½ gal. Ice Jug

A. H. HEISEY & CO., NEWARK, OHIO

No. 1506 "WHIRLPOOL" PATTERN

16—8 in. Frd. Cheese Plate

13—7 in. Snack Plate

4—2½ oz. Wine

5—Oyster Cocktail

3—3½ oz. Cocktail

7—9 oz. Tumbler

2—5 oz. Saucer Champagne

6—5 oz. Frd. Soda (Fruit Juice)

1—10 oz. Goblet

8—12 oz. Frd. Soda (Ice Tea)

17—13 in. Torte Plate
18—14 in. Sandwich Plate

14—7 in. Round Plate
15—8 in. Round Plate

19—18 in. Torte Plate

HANDMADE GLASSWARE

A. H. HEISEY & CO., NEWARK, OHIO

No. 1506 "WHIRLPOOL" PATTERN

HAND MADE GLASSWARE

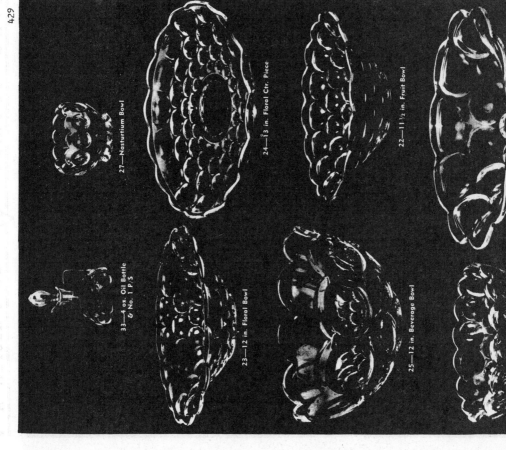

27—Nasturtium Bowl

24—13 in. Floral Ctr. Piece

22—11½ in. Fruit Bowl

26—15 in. Orange Bowl

33—4 oz. Oil Bottle & No. 1 P/S

23—12 in. Floral Bowl

25—12 in. Beverage Bowl

21—9 in. Salad Bowl

A. H. HEISEY & CO., NEWARK, OHIO

No. 1506 "WHIRLPOOL" PATTERN

58—7 in. Mayonnaise Plate Ftd.

56—1000 Isl. Dressing Bowl

57—Ftd. Mayonnaise Bowl
60—6½" Mayonnaise Plate Rd.

42—3 lt. Candle Stick

41—3 in. Candle Block

51—5 in. Jelly—2 Hld.

53—7 in. Bon Bon. 2 Hld.

52—5 in. Jelly, 2 Hld., 2 Compt.

46—13 in. Celery Tray

47—10 in. 4 Compt. Relish

HAND MADE GLASSWARE

A. H. HEISEY & CO., NEWARK, OHIO

H A N D M A D E   G L A S S W A R E

No. 1506   "WHIRLPOOL" PATTERN

79—Custard Cup

63—3½ in. Violet Vase

71—Ind. Sugar   72—Ind. Cream
73—Ind. Sugar & Cream Tray

85—4⅛ in. Nappy
86—5½ in. Nappy

96—4 in. Ash Tray, Square

107—4 in. Coaster

65—6 in. Sweet Pea Vase

74—Cream. Ftd.

88—5½ in. Nappy
Stuck Handle, 3 Cornered

95—4 in. Cig. Box & Cover

92—Cigarette Lighter

64—4 in. Pansy Vase

75—Sugar, Ftd.

87—5½ in. Nappy
Stuck Handle, Round

103—Butter Dish & Cover

105—Salt or Pepper
No. 657 Top

106—Salt or Pepper
No. 7 Top

A. H. HEISEY & CO.,   NEWARK, OHIO

No. 1509   QUEEN ANN PATTERN

16 in. Snack Plate
& Center Ftd.

6 in. Plate Square
Also make 7 & 8 in.

12 in. Sandwich Plate
2 Hld Round

4½ in. Plate Rd.
Also make 6, 7, 8 & 10½ in.

12 in. Sandwich Plate
2 Hld Square

15 in. Social Hour Tray
, Torte Plate.

H A N D M A D E   G L A S S W A R E

A. H. HEISEY & CO.,   NEWARK, OHIO

433

No. 1509   QUEEN ANN PATTERN

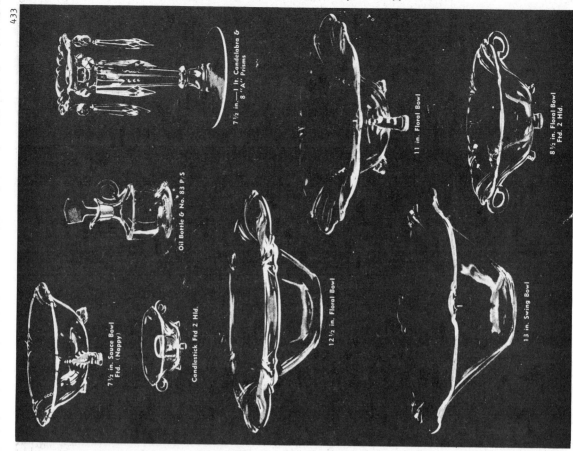

7½ in.–1 lt. Candelabra & 8 "A" Prisms

Oil Bottle & No. 83 P.S

11 in. Floral Bowl

8½ in. Floral Bowl Ftd. 2 Hld.

7½ in. Sauce Bowl Ftd. (Nappy)

Candlestick Ftd 2 Hld.

12½ in. Floral Bowl

13 in. Swing Bowl

No. 1509   QUEEN ANN PATTERN

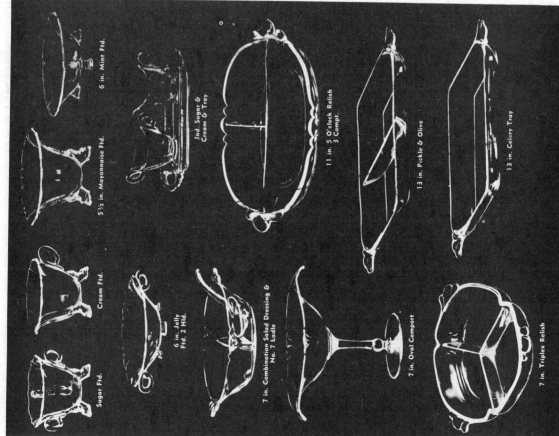

6 in. Mint Ftd.

5½ in. Mayonnaise Ftd.

Ind. Sugar & Cream & Tray

11 in. 5 O'clock Relish 3 Compt.

13 in. Pickle & Olive

13 in. Celery Tray

Cream Ftd.

Sugar Ftd.

6 in. Jelly Ftd. 2 Hld.

7 in. Combination Salad Dressing & No. 7 Ladle

7 in. Oval Comport

7 in. Triplex Relish

434

No. 1509   QUEEN ANN PATTERN

HANDMADE GLASSWARE

Mustard & Cover & No. 10 Paddle

Ind. Nut Dish

6½ in. Lemon & Cover

3 pt. Jug Ftd. Stock Hld.

Ftd. Salt or Pepper & No. 657 Top

6 in. Grape Fruit

Cream Soup & 7 in. Plate

Marmalade & Cover & No. 4 Spoon

Ftd. Salt or Pepper & No. 7 Top

4½ in. Nappy Also make 8 in.

Cup & Saucer

Ice Cube Bucket & Sil. Pl. Hld.

A. H. HEISEY & CO.,   NEWARK, OHIO

No. 1511   TOURJOURS PATTERN

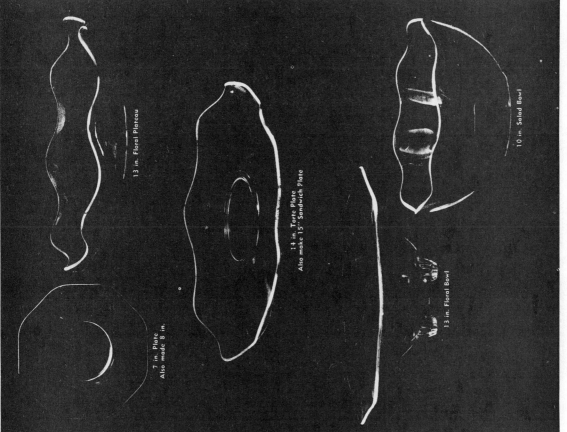

13 in. Floral Plateau

7 in. Plate Also made 8 in.

14 in. Torte Plate Also make 15" Sandwich Plate

13 in. Floral Bowl

10 in. Salad Bowl

HANDMADE GLASSWARE

A. H. HEISEY & CO.,   NEWARK, OHIO

No. 1511 TOURJOURS PATTERN

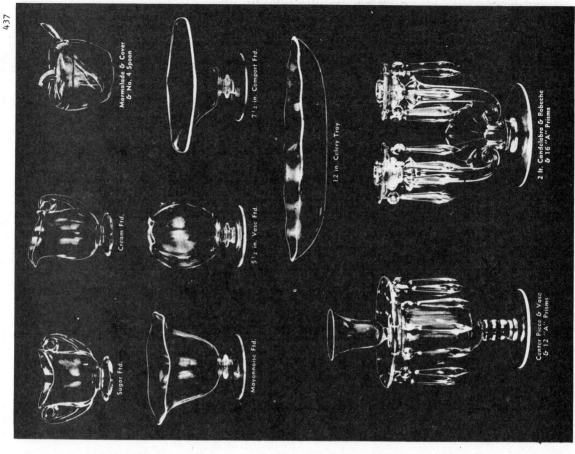

Marmalade & Cover & No. 4 Spoon

Cream Ftd.

Sugar Ftd.

7½ in. Comport Ftd.

5½ in. Vase Ftd.

Mayonnaise Ftd.

12 in. Celery Tray

2 lt. Candelabra & Bobeche & 16 "A" Prisms

Center Piece & Vase & 12 "A" Prisms

A. H. HEISEY & CO., NEWARK, OHIO

No. 4044 "NEW ARA" PATTERN

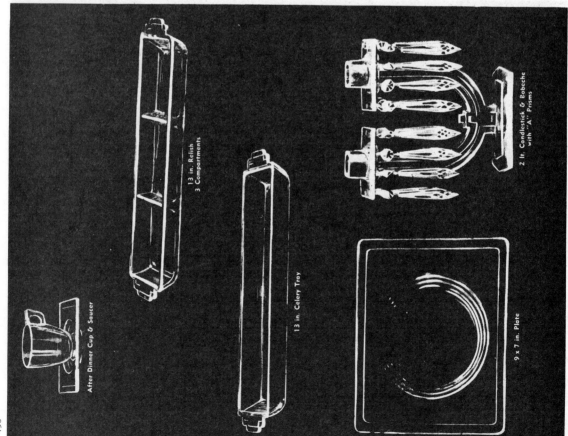

After Dinner Cup & Saucer

13 in. Relish 3 Compartments

13 in. Celery Tray

2 lt. Candlestick & Bobeche with "A" Prisms

9 x 7 in. Plate

A. H. HEISEY & CO., NEWARK, OHIO

MISCELLANEOUS ITEMS

HANDMADE GLASSWARE

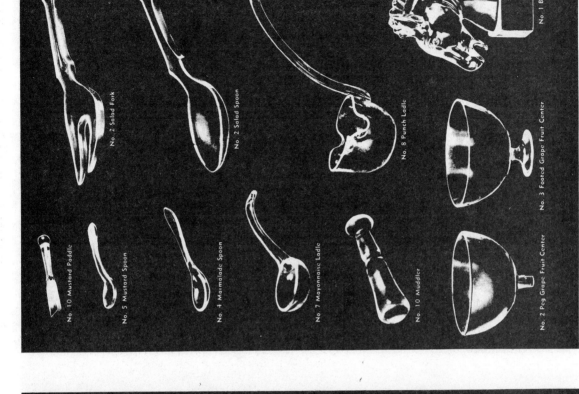

No. 2 Salad Fork

No. 2 Salad Spoon

No. 8 Punch Ladle

No. 1 Book End (Horse)

No. 10 Mustard Paddle

No. 5 Mustard Spoon

No. 4 Marmalade Spoon

No. 7 Mayonnaise Ladle

No. 10 Muddler

No. 2 Peg Grape Fruit Center

No. 3 Footed Grape Fruit Center

MISCELLANEOUS ITEMS

HANDMADE GLASSWARE

No. 339—Water Bottle Ground Bottom

No. 1101—5 oz. Custard Plain or Diamond Optic

No. 473 3½ in. Salad Nut Dish

No. 820 10 oz. Goblet

No. 1212—4 oz. Custard

No. 500—12 in. Oblong Variety Tray 4 Compartments

No. 300½—No. 1 Water Bottle

No. 407—7" Plate Star Ground Bottom

MISCELLANEOUS ITEMS

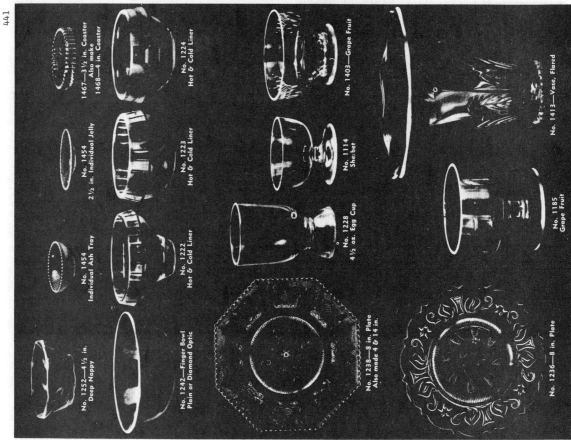

HANDMADE GLASSWARE

No. 1467—3½ in. Coaster
Also make
1468—4 in. Coaster

No. 1454
2½ in. Individual Jelly

No. 1454
Individual Ash Tray

No. 1252—4½ in.
Deep Nappy

No. 1224
Hot & Cold Liner

No. 1223
Hot & Cold Liner

No. 1222
Hot & Cold Liner

No. 1242—Finger Bowl
Plain or Diamond Optic

No. 1403—Grape Fruit

No. 1114
Sherbet

No. 1228
4½ oz. Egg Cup

No. 1238—8 in. Plate
Also made 4 & 14 in.

No. 1413—Vase, Flared

No. 1185
Grape Fruit

No. 1236—8 in. Plate

A. H. HEISEY & CO. ◇ NEWARK, OHIO

MISCELLANEOUS ITEMS

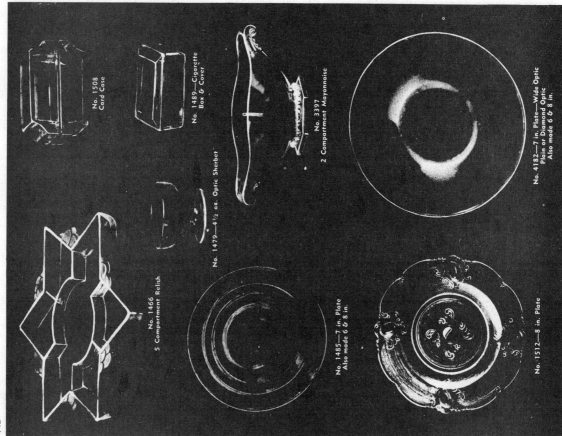

HANDMADE GLASSWARE

No. 1508
Card Case

No. 1489—Cigarette
Box & Cover

No. 3397
2 Compartment Mayonnaise

No. 1466
5 Compartment Relish

No. 1479—4½ oz. Optic Sherbet

No. 4182—7 in. Plate—Wide Optic
Plain or Diamond Optic
Also made 6 & 8 in.

No. 1485—7 in. Plate
Also made 6 & 8 in.

No. 1512—8 in. Plate

A. H. HEISEY & CO., ◇ NEWARK, OHIO

MISCELLANEOUS SALTS AND PEPPERS

HANDMADE GLASSWARE

No. 1469—Salt or Pepper
& No. 657 Top

No. 1469—Salt or Pepper
& No. 7 Top

No. 1503—Salt or Pepper
& No. 657 Top

No. 1503—Salt or Pepper
& No. 7 Top

No. 1506—Salt or Pepper
& No. 657 Top

No. 1506—Salt or Pepper
& No. 7 Top

No. 1425—Salt or Pepper
& No. 643 Metal Top

No. 1425 Salt or Pepper
& No. 2 San. Top

Salt or Pepper
& No. 1 Sanitary Top

No. 393—No. 3
Salt or Pepper
No. 643 Top

No. 393—No. 3
Salt or Pepper
No. 1 San. Top

No. 1509—Salt or Pepper
No. 7 Glass Top

No. 1509—Salt or Pepper
No. 657 Salt Proof Top

A. H. HEISEY & CO.   NEWARK, OHIO

MISCELLANEOUS ASH TRAYS

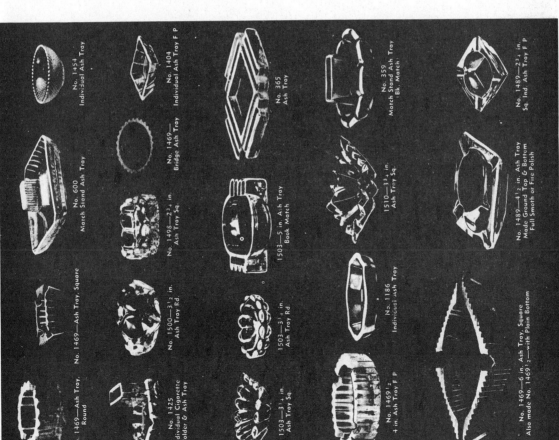

No. 1469—Ash Tray,
Round

No. 1469—Ash Tray, Square

No. 600
Match Stand Ash Tray

No. 1454
Individual Ash Tray

No. 425
Individual Cigarette
Holder & Ash Tray

No. 1500—3½ in.
Ash Tray Rd.

No. 1498—2¾ in.
Ash Tray Sq.

No. 1469—
Bridge Ash Tray

No. 1404
Individual Ash Tray F P

1503—3½ in.
Ash Tray Sq.

1503—3½ in.
Ash Tray Rd

1503—5 in Ash Tray
Book Match

No. 365
Ash Tray

No. 1469½
4 in. Ash Tray F P

No. 1186
Individual Ash Tray

1510—3¾ in.
Ash Tray Sq.

No. 359
Match Stand Ash Tray
Bk. Match

No. 1469—6 in. Ash Tray, Square
Also made No. 1469½—with Plain Bottom

No. 1489—4½ in. Ash Tray
Made Ground Top & Bottom
Full Smooth or Fire Polish

No. 1489—2¾ in.
Sq. Ind. Ash Tray F P

HANDMADE GLASSWARE

A. H. HEISEY & CO.   NEWARK, OHIO

CANDLESTICKS

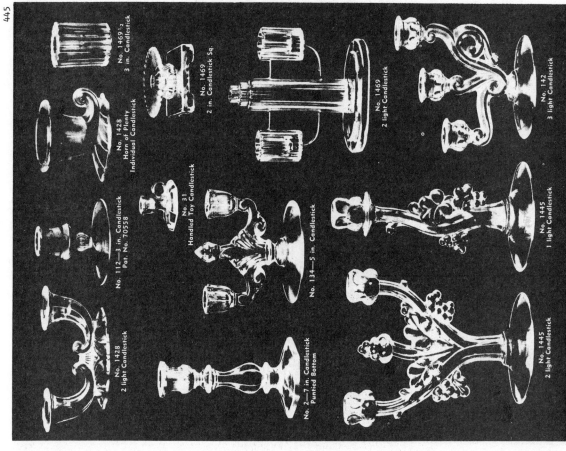

No. 1469½
3 in. Candlestick

No. 1428
Horn of Plenty
Individual Candlestick

No. 1469
2 in. Candlestick Sq.

No. 1469
2 light Candlestick

No. 142
3 light Candlestick

No. 112—3 in. Candlestick
Pat. No. 70558

No. 31
Handled Toy Candlestick

No. 1445
1 light Candlestick

No. 1428
2 light Candlestick

No. 134—5 in. Candlestick

No. 2—7 in. Candlestick
Punted Bottom

No. 1445
2 light Candlestick

CANDLESTICKS

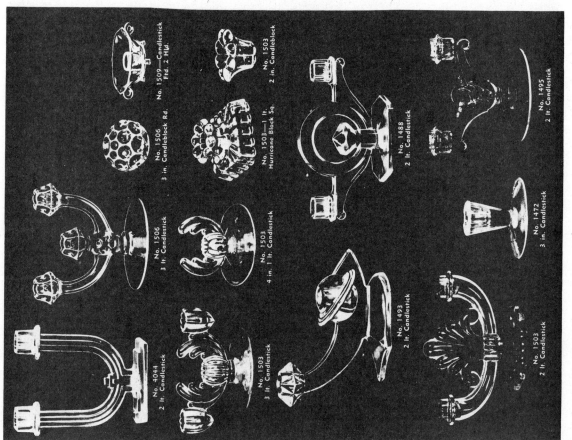

No. 1509—Candlestick
Ftd. 2 Hld.

No. 1503
2 in. Candleblock

No. 1506
3 in. Candleblock Rd.

No. 1503—1 lt.
Hurricane Block Sq.

No. 1495
2 lt. Candlestick

No. 1506
3 lt. Candlestick

No. 1503
4 in. 1 lt. Candlestick

No. 1488
2 lt. Candlestick

No. 1472
3 in. Candlestick

No. 4044
2 lt. Candlestick

No. 1503
3 lt. Candlestick

No. 1493
2 lt. Candlestick

No. 1503
2 lt. Candlestick

FLORAL BOWLS

No. 1472
12 in. Floral Bowl
Also made 9 in.

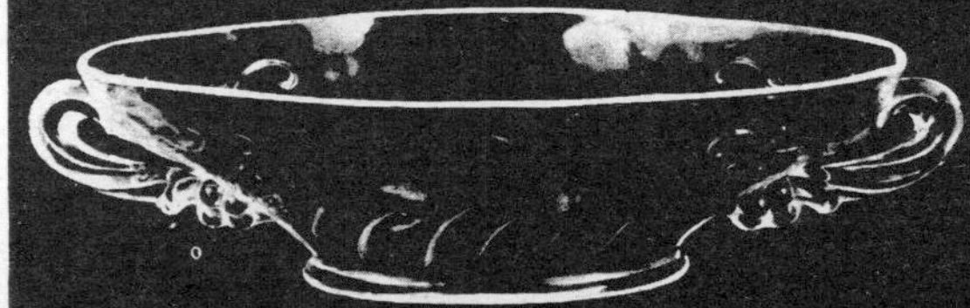

No. 1405
11 in. Footed Floral Bowl

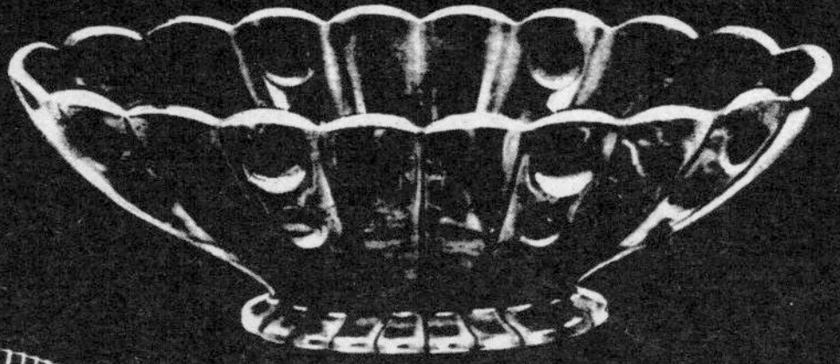

No. 1404
12 in. Oval Footed Floral Bowl

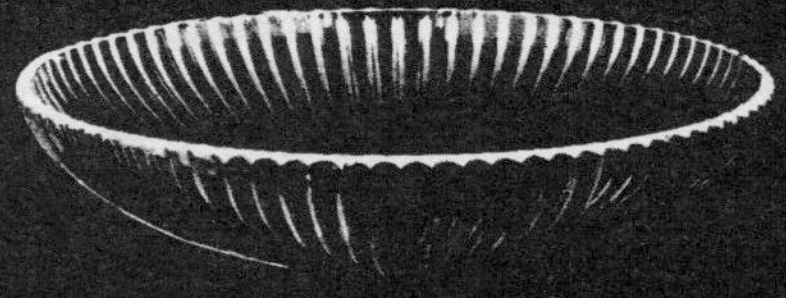

No. 1445
Oval Floral Bowl

No. 1469—12 in. Oval Floral Bowl

No. 1469—11½ in. Floral Bowl
Also make 10 in.

A. H. HEISEY & CO.,   NEWARK, OHIO

FLORAL BOWLS

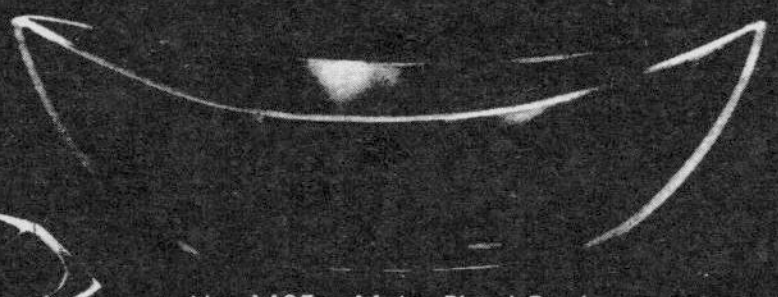

No. 1497—11 in. Floral Bowl
Also made 8 & 13 in.

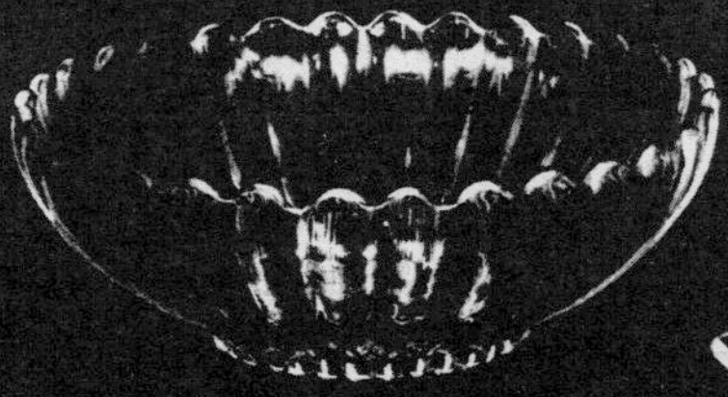

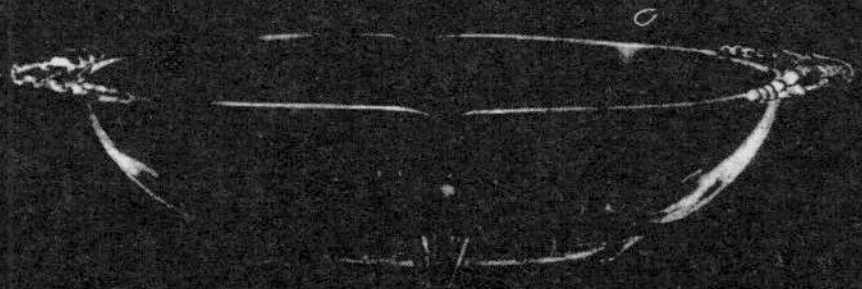

No. 1495—11 in. Floral Bowl
Oval Hld.

No. 1503—13 in. Floral Bowl
Oval

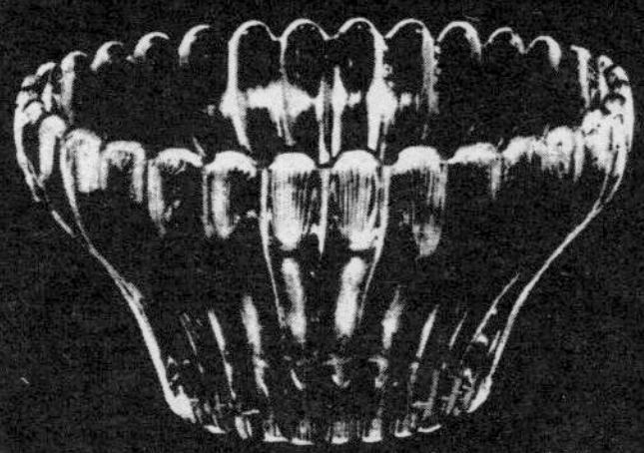

No. 1488—14 in. Floral Bowl Oblong

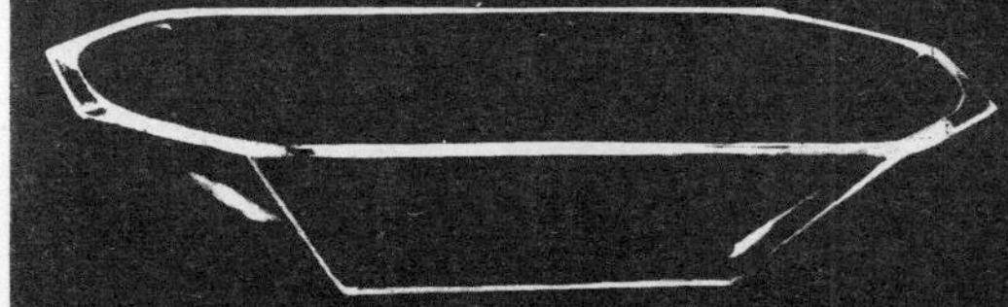

No. 1489—14 in. Floral Bowl Oblong

No. 1503—11½ in. Floral Bowl
Round

No. 1503—9 in. Floral Bowl
Touraine

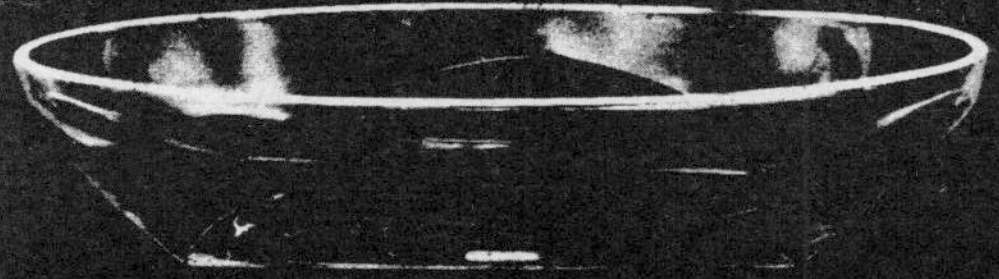

No. 1486—Oval Floral Bowl

A. H. HEISEY & CO.,   NEWARK, OHIO

No. 300 PATTERN CANDELABRA

H A N D M A D E G L A S S W A R E

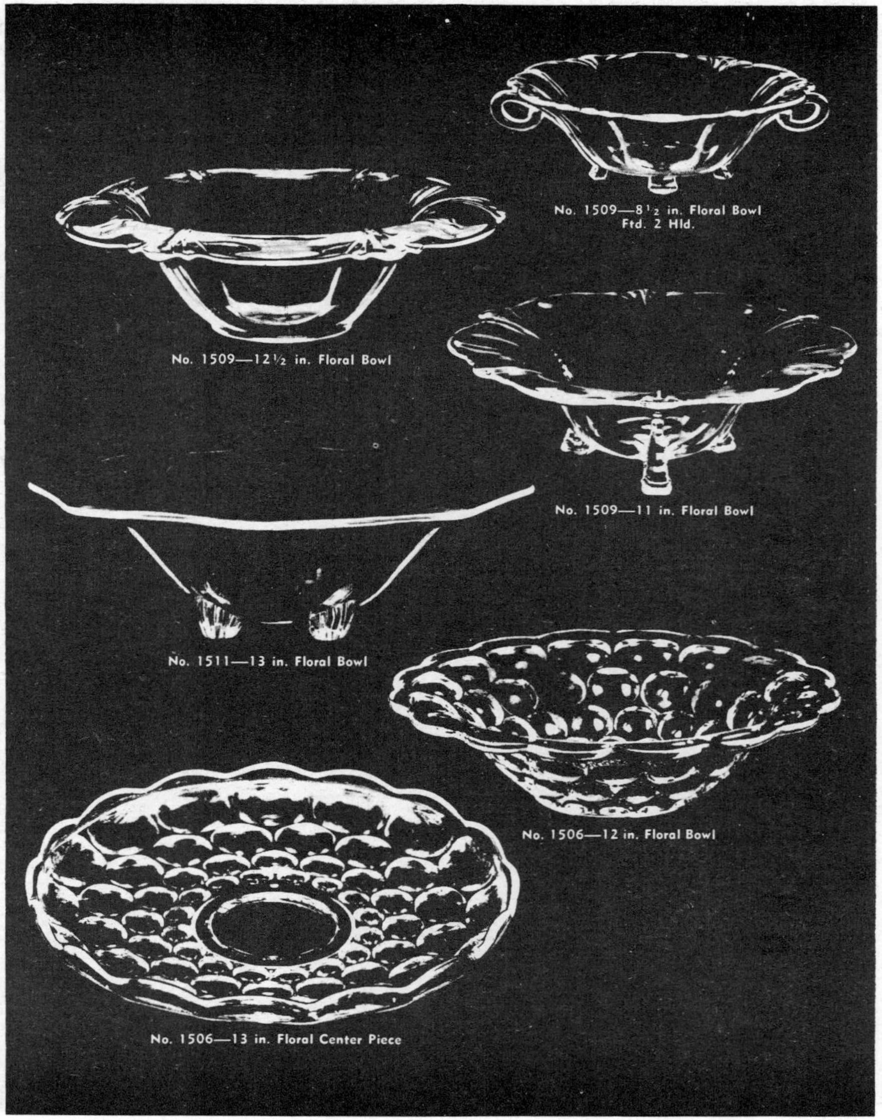

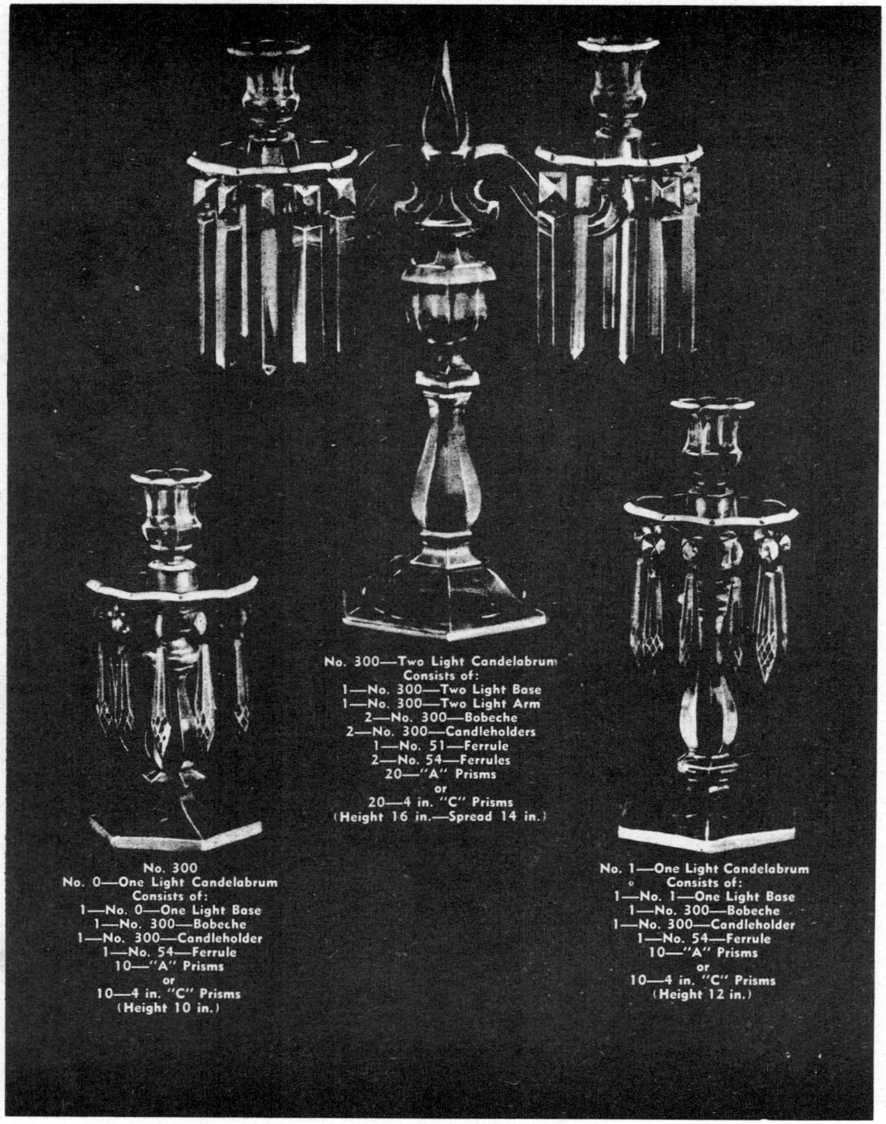

No. 300—Two Light Candelabrum
Consists of:
1—No. 300—Two Light Base
1—No. 300—Two Light Arm
2—No. 300—Bobeche
2—No. 300—Candleholders
1—No. 51—Ferrule
2—No. 54—Ferrules
20—"A" Prisms
or
20—4 in. "C" Prisms
(Height 16 in.—Spread 14 in.)

No. 300
No. 0—One Light Candelabrum
Consists of:
1—No. 0—One Light Base
1—No. 300—Bobeche
1—No. 300—Candleholder
1—No. 54—Ferrule
10—"A" Prisms
or
10—4 in. "C" Prisms
(Height 10 in.)

No. 1—One Light Candelabrum
Consists of:
1—No. 1—One Light Base
1—No. 300—Bobeche
1—No. 300—Candleholder
1—No. 54—Ferrule
10—"A" Prisms
or
10—4 in. "C" Prisms
(Height 12 in.)

FLORAL BOWLS

H A N D M A D E G L A S S W A R E

No. 1509—8½ in. Floral Bowl
Ftd. 2 Hld.

No. 1509—12½ in. Floral Bowl

No. 1509—11 in. Floral Bowl

No. 1511—13 in. Floral Bowl

No. 1506—12 in. Floral Bowl

No. 1506—13 in. Floral Center Piece

No. 300 PATTERN CANDELABRA

451

No. 300—Four Light Candelabrum
Consists of:
1—No. 300—Four Light Base
1—No. 300—Four Light Arm
4—No. 300—Bobeche
4—No. 300—Candleholders
1—No. 51—Ferrule
4—No. 54—Ferrules
40—"A" Prisms
or
40—4 in. "C" Prisms
(Height 21 in.—Spread 14 in.)

No. 300—Three Light Candelabrum
Consists of:
1—No. 300—Three Light Base
1—No. 300—Three Light Arm
3—No. 300—Bobeche
3—No. 300—Candleholders
1—No. 51—Ferrule
3—No. 54—Ferrules
30—"A" Prisms
or
30—4 in. "C" Prisms
(Height 20½ in.—Spread 14 in.)

A. H. HEISEY & CO.,   NEWARK, OHIO

No. 300½ PATTERN CANDELABRA

452

No. 300½—Three Light Candelabrum
Consists of:
1—No. 300—Three Light Base
1—No. 300—Three Light Arm
3—No. 300—Bobeche
1—No. 6—Bobeche
3—No. 300—Candleholders
1—No. 51—Ferrule
3—No. 54—Ferrules
42—"A" Prisms
or
30—"A" Prisms & 12—5½ in. "C" Prisms
(Height 20½ in.—Spread 14 in.)

No. 300—Five Light Candelabrum
Consists of:
1—No. 300—Five Light Base
4—No. 300—Single Light Arms
5—No. 300—Bobeche
5—No. 300—Candleholders
1—Center Post
1—Upper Hemisphere
1—Lower Hemisphere
5—No. 54—Ferrules
1—Metal Five Light Socket
50—"A" Prisms
(Height 25 in.—Spread 18 in.)

A. H. HEISEY & CO.,   NEWARK, OHIO

No. 300½ PATTERN CANDELABRA
No. 300¾

No. 300½—Four Light Candelabrum
Consists of:
1—No. 300—Four Light Base
1—No. 300—Four Light Arm
4—No. 300—Candleholder
1—No. 6—Bobeche
1—No. 51—Ferrule
52—No. 54—Ferrules
52—No. "A" Prisms or
40—No. "C" 5½ in. Prisms
Height 21 in.—Spread 14 in.

No. 300¾—Four Light Candelabrum
Consists of:
1—No. 300—Four Light Base
1—No. 300—Four Light Arm
4—No. 5—Bobeche
1—No. 6—Bobeche
4—No. 5—Candleholders
1—No. 51—Ferrule
4—No. 54—Ferrules
60—5 in. "C" Prisms
(Height 21 in.—Spread 14 in.)

No. 301 PATTERN CANDELABRA

No. 301—Two Light Candelabrum
Consists of:
1—No. 301—Two Light Base
1—No. 300—Two Light Arm
2—No. 300—Bobeche
2—No. 300—Candleholders
2—No. 51—Ferrule
2—No. 54—Ferrules
20—4 in. "A" Prisms
or
20—4 in. "C" Prisms
(Height 10½ in.)

No. 301—Three Light Candelabrum
Consists of:
1—No. 301—Three Light Base
1—No. 300—Three Light Arm
3—No. 300—Bobeche
3—No. 300—Candleholders
3—No. 51—Ferrule
3—No. 54—Ferrules
30—4 in. "C" Prisms
or
30—4 in. "A" Prisms
(Height 10½ in.—Spread 13 in.)

No. 301 PATTERN CANDELABRA

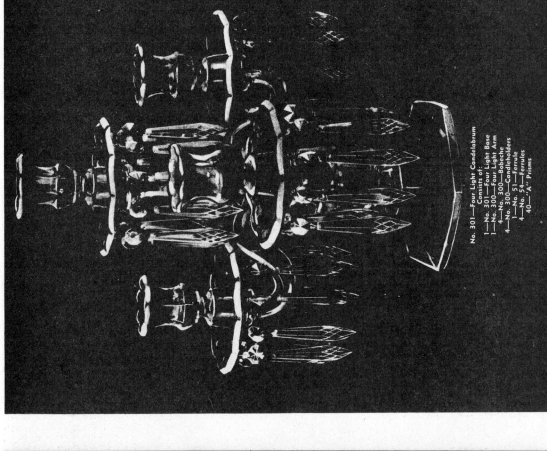

No. 301—Four Light Candelabrum
Consists of:
1—No. 301—Four Light Base
1—No. 300—Four Light Arm
4—No. 300—Bobeche
4—No. 300—Candleholders
4—No. 51—Ferrule
4—No. 54—Ferrules
40—"A" Prisms

A. H. HEISEY & CO., NEWARK, OHIO

No. 400, AND 401 PATTERN CANDELABRA

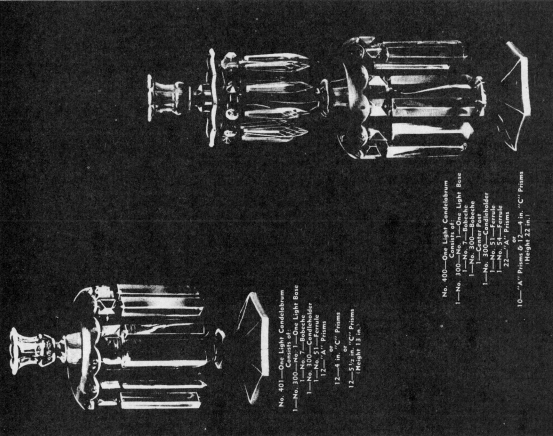

No. 401—One Light Candelabrum
Consists of:
1—No. 300—One Light Base
1—No. 7—Bobeche
1—No. 300—Candleholder
1—No. 51—Ferrule
12—"A" Prisms
or
12—4 in. "C" Prisms
12—5½ in. "C" Prisms
(Height 13 in.)

No. 400—One Light Candelabrum
Consists of:
1—No. 300—One Light Base
1—No. 7—Bobeche
1—No. 300—Bobeche
1—Center Post
1—No. 300—Candleholder
1—No. 51—Ferrule
1—No. 54—Ferrule
22—"A" Prisms
or
10—"A" Prisms & 12—4 in. "C" Prisms
(Height 22 in.)

A. H. HEISEY & CO., NEWARK, OHIO

MISCELLANEOUS CANDELABRA

H A N D M A D E   G L A S S W A R E

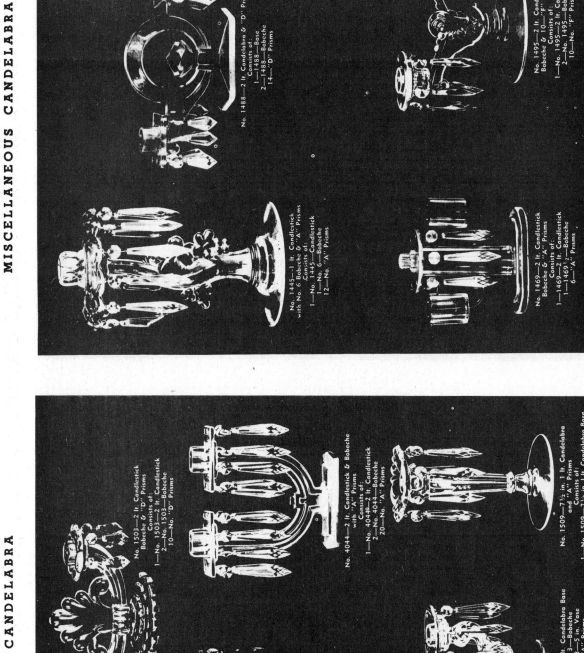

No. 1488—2 lt. Candelabra & "D" Prisms
Consists of:
1—1488—Base
2—1488—Bobeche
14—"D" Prisms

No. 1445—1 lt. Candlestick
with No. 6 Bobeche & "A" Prisms
Consists of:
1—No. 1445—Candlestick
1—No. 6—Bobeche
12—No. "A" Prisms

No. 1495—2 lt. Candlestick
Bobeche & 10—"F" Prisms
Consists of:
1—No. 1495—2 lt. Candlestick
2—No. 1495—Bobeche
10—No. "F" Prisms

No. 1469—2 lt. Candlestick
Bobeche & "A" Prisms
Consists of:
1—1469—2 lt. Candlestick
1—1469 ?—Bobeche
6—No. "A" Prisms

A. H. HEISEY & CO., NEWARK, OHIO

MISCELLANEOUS CANDELABRA

H A N D M A D E   G L A S S W A R E

No. 1503—2 lt. Candlestick
Bobeche & "D" Prisms
Consists of:
1—No. 1503—2 lt. Candlestick
2—No. 1503—Bobeche
10—No. "D" Prisms

No. 4044—2 lt. Candlestick & Bobeche
with "A" Prisms
Consists of:
1—No. 4044—2 lt. Candlestick
2—No. 4044—Bobeche
20—No. "A" Prisms

No. 1509—7½ in. 1 lt. Candelabra
and "A" Prisms
Consists of:
1—No. 1509—7½ in. 1 lt. Candelabra Base
8—No. "A" Prisms

No. 1511—2 lt. Candelabra
Bobeche & 16 "A" Prisms
Consists of:
1—No. 1511—2 lt. Candelabra Base
2—No. 1511—Bobeche
16—No. "A" Prisms

No. 1513—3 lt. Candelabra,
Vase, Bobeche & "A" Prisms
Consists of:
1—1513—3 lt. Candelabra Base
2—1513—Bobeche
1—5013—5 in. Vase
No. "A" Prisms

A. H. HEISEY & CO., NEWARK, OHIO

No. 301 GIRONDOLES

No. 30—3 lt. Girondole
with "A" Prisms and
Four Shades of Buttons
Consists of:
1—No. 301—3 lt. Base
1—No. 310—3 lt. Arm
3—No. 310—Bobeche
3—No. 300—Candleholder
1—No. 5—Ferrule
3—No. 5—Ferrule
24—No. "A," 4 in. Prisms or
24—No. "A," 4 in. Prisms
4—16—Button Strands
2—2—Way Buttons
(Height 10½ in.—spread 13 in.)

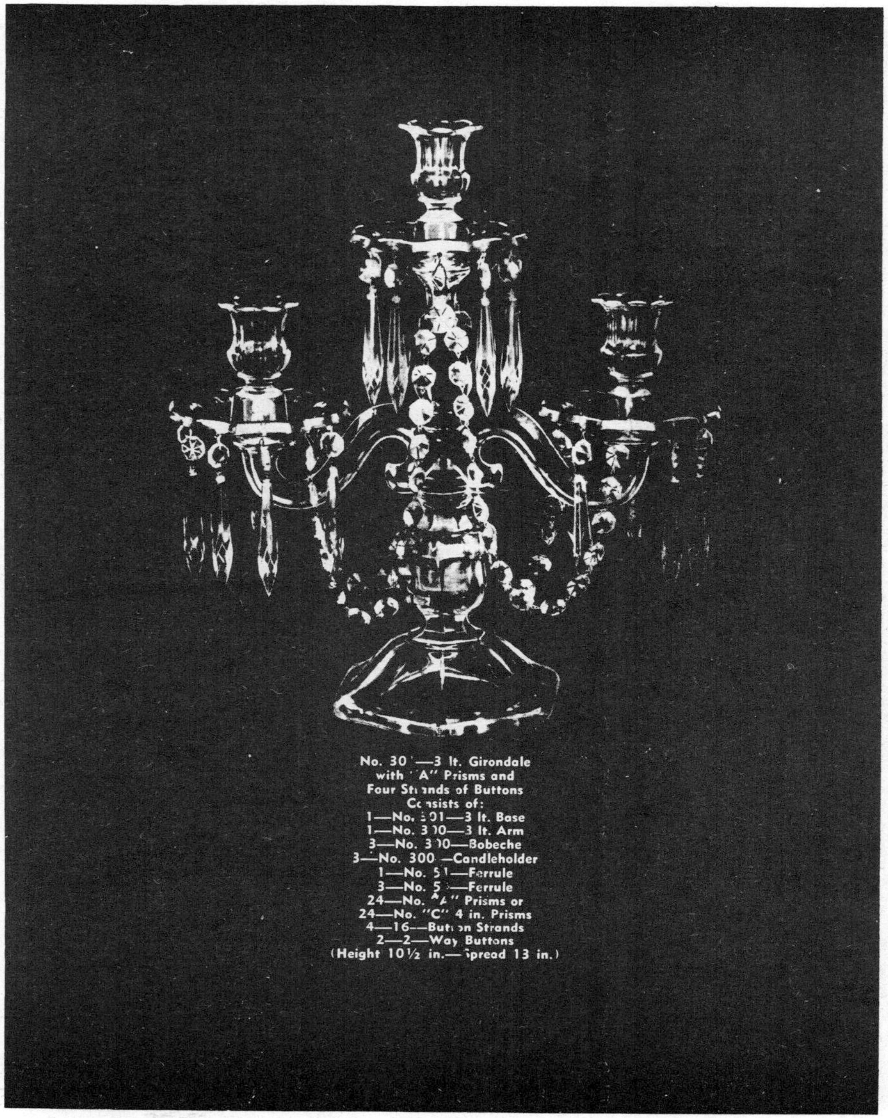

A. H. HEISEY & CO., NEWARK, OHIO

No. 201 PATTERN ELECTRIC LAMP

No. 201—Candlelamp Complete
Consists of:
1—No. 201—9 in. Base
1—No. 6—Bobeche
1—10 ft. Cord
1—Switch
1—Socket
1—Socket Cover
1—Candle Bulb
1—No. 4060—6 in. Shade
Plain or Decorated
12—No. "A" Prisms or
12—No. "C" 6½ Prisms
(Height, 15 in.)

A. H. HEISEY & CO., NEWARK, OHIO

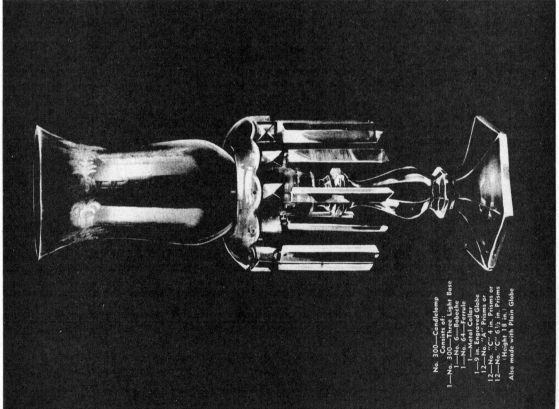

No. 301 and No. 1503 ELECTRIC LAMPS

HANDMADE GLASSWARE

301—1-Lite
Electric Lamp

1503—1-Lite
Electric Lamp

A. H. HEISEY & CO., NEWARK, OHIO

No. 300 PATTERN CANDLELAMP

No. 300—Candlelamp
Consists of:
1—No. 300—Three Light Base
1—No. 6—Bobeche
1—No. 64—Ferrule
1—Metal Collar
1—9 in. Engraved Globe
12—No. "A" 4 in. Prisms or
12—No. "C" 4 in. Prisms or
12—No. "C" 6½ in. Prisms
(Height 18 in.)
Also made with Plain Globe

HANDMADE GLASSWARE

A. H. HEISEY & CO., NEWARK, OHIO

No. 301 1 LT HURRICANE LAMP

No. 301—1 lt. Hurricane Lamp
with No. 300—9 in. Plain Globe
Consists of:
1—No. 301—2 lt. Base
1—No. 64—Ferrule
1—No. 300—Collar for Globe
1—No. 300—9 in. Globe Plain or
Etched. No. 450 or Engraved or
Cut No. 918 or
1—No. 300—12 in. Globe Plain or
Etched No. 450 or Cut No. 917 or
Cut No. 918

No. 301 2 LT HURRICANE LAMP

No. 301—2 lt. Hurricane Lamp
with No. 300—9 in. Plain Globe
Consists of:
1—No. 301—2 lt. Base
1—No. 5—Ferrule
1—No. 5—2 lt. Arm
2—No. 5—Ferrules
2—No. 300—Metal Rings
2—No. 402—Bobeche
2—No. 300—Candleholders
20—No. 2—A Prisms
2—No. 300—9 in. Plain Globes or
Engraved or Cut No. 918 or
Etched No. 450 or
2—No. 300—12 in. Plain Globes or
Cut No. 917 or Cut No. 918 or
Etched No. 450

No. 1503 1 Lt Hurricane Lamp

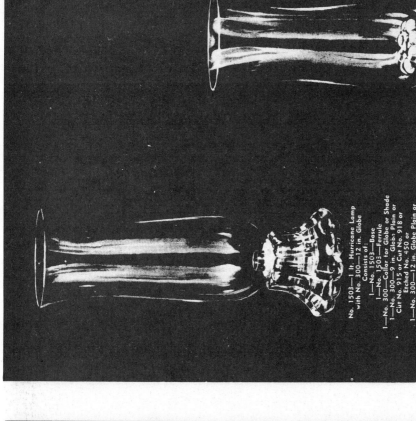

No. 1503—1 lt. Hurricane Lamp
with No. 300—12 in. Globe
Consists of:
1—No. 1503—Base
1—No. 1503—Ferrule
1—No. 300—Collar for Globe or Shade
1—No. 300—9 in. Globe Plain or
Cut No. 915 or Cut No. 918 or
Etched No. 450 or
1—No. 300—12 in. Globe Plain or
Cut No. 917 or Cut No. 918 or
Etched No. 450 or
1—No. 4062—6 in. w/o Shade or
Cut No. 915

No. 1503—1 lt. Hurricane Block
or Candlestick with
No. 4061—10 in. Plain Shade

A. H. HEISEY & CO., NEWARK, OHIO

BARS, TUMBLERS, & SODAS

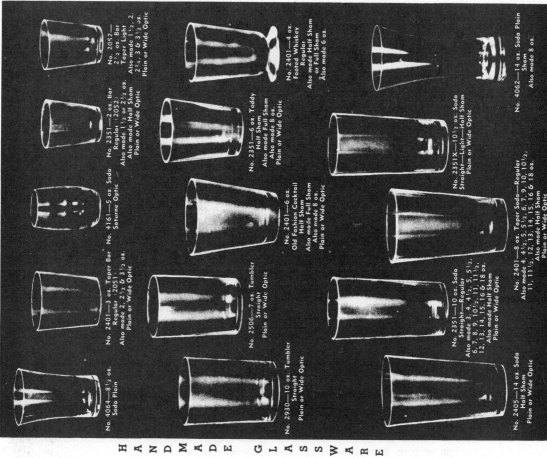

No. 4064—8½ oz.
Soda Plain

No. 2401—3 oz. Taper Bar
Regular (2051)
Also made 2, 2½ & 3½ oz.
Plain or Wide Optic

No. 4161—5 oz. Soda
Saturne Optic

No. 2506—7 oz. Tumbler
Straight
Plain or Wide Optic

No. 2930—10 oz. Tumbler
Straight
Plain or Wide Optic

No. 2052—
2½ oz. Bar
Taper Light
Also made 1½, 2,
2¾, 3 & 3½ oz.
Plain or Wide Optic

No. 2351—2 oz. Bar
Regular (2052)
Also made 1½ or 2½ oz.
Also made Half Sham
Plain or Wide Optic

No. 2351—6 oz. Toddy
Half Sham
Also made Full Sham
Also made 8 oz.
Plain or Wide Optic

No. 2401—6 oz.
Old Fashion Cocktail
Half Sham
Also made Full Sham
Also made 8 oz.
Plain or Wide Optic

No. 2351—10 oz. Soda
Straight—Regular
Also made 3, 4, 4½, 5, 5½;
6, 7, 8, 9, 10, 10½, 11½;
12, 13, 14, 15, 16 & 18 oz.
Also made Half Sham
Plain or Wide Optic

No. 2405—14 oz. Soda
Half Sham
Plain or Wide Optic

No. 2401—4 oz.
Footed Whiskey
Regular
Also made Half Sham
or Full Sham
Also made 6 oz.

No. 2351X—10½ oz. Soda
Straight—Light—Half Sham
Plain or Wide Optic

No. 2401—8 oz. Taper Soda—Regular
Also made 4, 4½, 5, 5½, 6, 7, 9, 10, 10½;
11, 11½, 12, 13, 14, 15, 16 & 18 oz.
Also made Half Sham
Plain or Wide Optic

No. 4062—14 oz. Soda Plain
Sham
Also made 8 oz.

A. H. HEISEY & CO., NEWARK, OHIO

NO. 3304 UNIVERSAL PATTERN PULL STEM

PLAIN ONLY

HANDMADE GLASSWARE

2½ oz. Wine — 1 oz. Pousse Cafe — 1 oz. Cordial — 1¼ oz. Pony Brandy — 2 oz. Sherry — 2½ oz. Creme de Menthe — Finger Bowl (4075) — 4 oz. Oyster Cocktail (3389) — 3½ oz. Cocktail Also made 3 oz. — 3 oz. Burgundy — 5½ oz. Saucer Champagne — 5 oz. Parfait — 6½ oz. Champagne — 4½ oz. Claret — 5½ oz. Sherbet — Cocktail Icer & Liner — 6 oz. Rhine Wine Also made 4 oz. — 6 oz. Champagne Hollow Stem — 10 oz. Pilsner — 10 oz. Goblet

A. H. HEISEY & CO., NEWARK, OHIO

No. 3333 OLD GLORY PATTERN

PLAIN ONLY

HANDMADE GLASSWARE

Oyster Cocktail (3542) — 4½ oz. Parfait — 5½ oz. Sundae or Sherbet — 5½ oz. Saucer Champagne — Finger Bowl (3309) — ¾ oz. Pousse Cafe — 2 oz. Sherry — 4½ oz. Claret — 2 oz. Wine — 1 oz. Cordial — 3 oz. Cocktail — 6 oz. Grape Juice — 3 oz. Burgundy — 9 oz. Goblet

A. H. HEISEY & CO., NEWARK, OHIO

No. 3350 WABASH PATTERN Pat. No. 64040
WIDE OPTIC ONLY

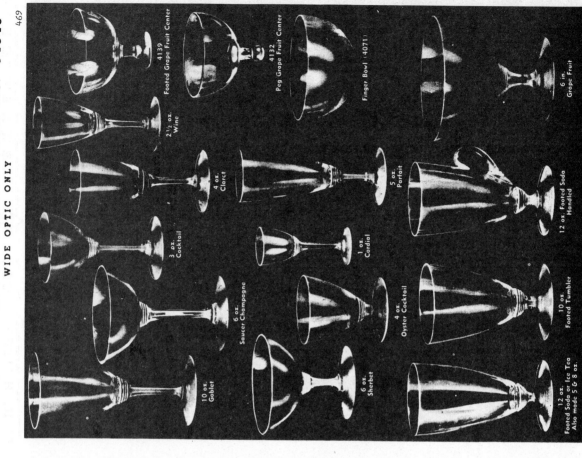

HANDMADE GLASSWARE

Footed Grape Fruit Center 4139

Peg Grape Fruit Center 4132

Finger Bowl 4071

6 in. Grape Fruit

2½ oz. Wine

4 oz. Claret

5 oz. Parfait

12 oz. Footed Soda Handled

3 oz. Cocktail

1 oz. Cordial

4 oz. Oyster Cocktail

10 oz. Footed Tumbler

6 oz. Saucer Champagne

6 oz. Sherbet

12 oz. Footed Soda or Ice Tea Also made 5 & 8 oz.

10 oz. Goblet

A. H. HEISEY & CO., NEWARK, OHIO

No. 3368 ALBEMARLE PATTERN
DIAMOND OPTIC ONLY

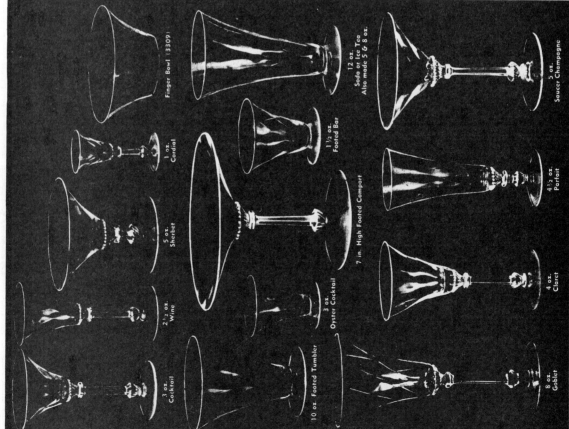

HANDMADE GLASSWARE

Finger Bowl (3309)

1 oz. Cordial

1½ oz. Footed Bar

12 oz. Soda or Ice Tea Also made 5 & 8 oz.

5 oz. Saucer Champagne

2½ oz. Wine

5 oz. Sherbet

7 in. High Footed Comport

4½ oz. Parfait

3 oz. Cocktail

3 oz. Oyster Cocktail

10 oz. Footed Tumbler

4 oz. Claret

8 oz. Goblet

A. H. HEISEY & CO., NEWARK, OHIO

HANDMADE GLASSWARE

No. 3389 DUQUESENE PATTERN
PLAIN ONLY

1 oz.
Cordial

2½ oz.
Wine

5 oz.
Parfait

3 oz.
Cocktail

Finger Bowl 4071

4 oz.
Oyster Cocktail

10 oz.
Footed Tumbler

5 oz.
Sherbet

5 oz.
Saucer Champagne

12 oz.
Footed Soda
Also made 5 & 8 oz.

4 oz.
Claret

9 oz.
Goblet

A. H. HEISEY & CO., NEWARK, OHIO

No. 3390 CARCASSONNE PATTERN
PLAIN OR WIDE OPTIC

HANDMADE GLASSWARE

6 oz.
Sherbet

2 oz.
Footed Bar

2½ oz.
Wine

3 oz.
Oyster Cocktail

3 oz.
Cocktail

4 oz.
Claret

6 oz.
Saucer Champagne

11 oz. Goblet
Short Stem

12 oz.
Footed Soda or Ice Tea
Also made 5 & 8 oz.

12 oz.
Flagon

10½ oz.
Morning After

11 oz. Goblet
Tall Stem

A. H. HEISEY & CO., NEWARK, OHIO

No. 3390 CARCASSONNE PATTERN
WIDE OPTIC ONLY

HANDMADE GLASSWARE

Footed Finger Bowl

8 in. Footed Vase

Cigarette Holder

1 pt. Footed Decanter & No. 84 P/S

A. H. HEISEY & CO., NEWARK, OHIO

No. 3404 SPANISH PATTERN
WIDE OPTIC ONLY

HANDMADE GLASSWARE

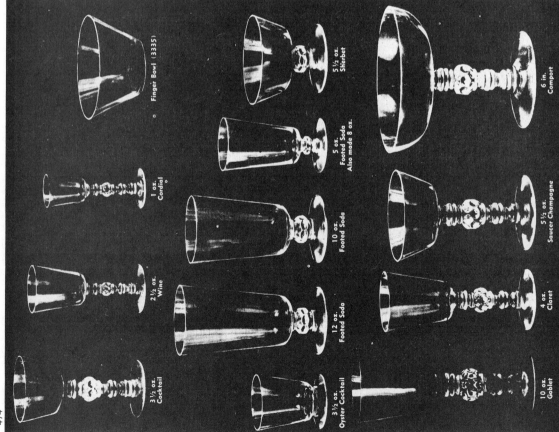

Finger Bowl (3335)

5½ oz. Sherbet

6 in. Comport

1 oz. Cordial

5 oz. Footed Soda Also made 8 oz.

2½ oz. Wine

10 oz. Footed Soda

5½ oz. Saucer Champagne

3½ oz. Cocktail

12 oz. Footed Soda

4 oz. Claret

3½ oz. Oyster Cocktail

10 oz. Goblet

A. H. HEISEY & CO., NEWARK, OHIO

No. 3408 JAMESTOWN PATTERN
WIDE OPTIC ONLY

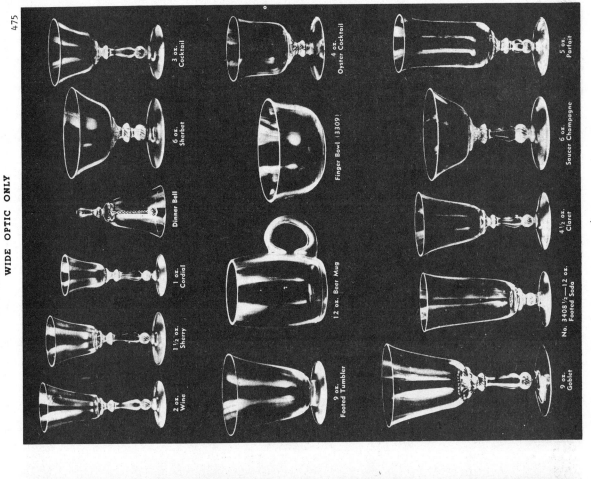

HANDMADE GLASSWARE

3 oz. Cocktail

4 oz. Oyster Cocktail

5 oz. Parfait

6 oz. Sherbet

Finger Bowl (3309)

6 oz. Saucer Champagne

Dinner Bell

4½ oz. Claret

1 oz. Cordial

12 oz. Beer Mug

No. 3408½—12 oz. Footed Soda

1½ oz. Sherry

2 oz. Wine

9 oz. Footed Tumbler

9 oz. Goblet

A. H. HEISEY & CO., NEWARK, OHIO

NEWARK, OHIO

No. 3411 MONTE CRISTO PATTERN
WIDE OPTIC ONLY

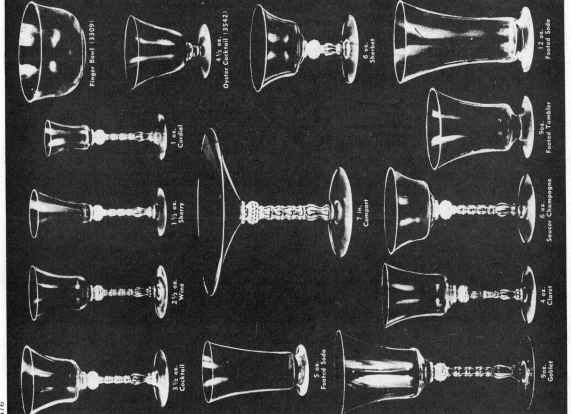

Finger Bowl (3309)

4½ oz. Oyster Cocktail (3542)

6 oz. Sherbet

12 oz. Footed Soda

1 oz. Cordial

9 oz. Footed Tumbler

1½ oz. Sherry

7 in. Comport

2½ oz. Wine

6 oz. Saucer Champagne

4 oz. Claret

3½ oz. Cocktail

5 oz. Footed Soda

9 oz. Goblet

HANDMADE GLASSWARE

A. H. HEISEY & CO.,

NO. 4004 - "JACOBEAN" - PATTERN

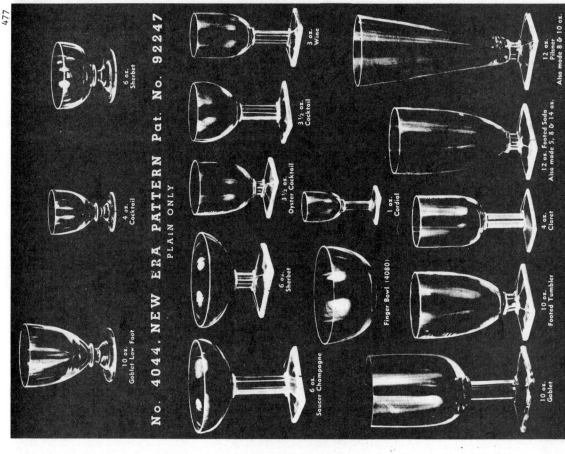

6 oz. Sherbet

4 oz. Cocktail

10 oz. Goblet Low Foot

No. 4044. NEW ERA PATTERN Pat. No. 92247
PLAIN ONLY

HANDMADE GLASSWARE

3 oz. Wine

3½ oz. Cocktail

3½ oz. Oyster Cocktail

6 oz. Sherbet

6 oz. Saucer Champagne

1 oz. Cordial

Finger Bowl (4080)

10 oz. Goblet

12 oz. Pilsner Also made 8 & 10 oz.

12 oz. Footed Soda Also made 5, 8 & 14 oz.

4 oz. Claret

10 oz. Footed Tumbler

A. H. HEISEY & CO., NEWARK, OHIO

No. 4054 CORONATION PATTERN
PLAIN ONLY

HANDMADE GLASSWARE

11 oz. Hot Toddy Half Sham

8 oz. Old Fashion Half Sham

4 oz. Cocktail Ftd.

3 oz. Cocktail Half Sham

2½ oz. Bar Half Sham Also made 1 oz.

8 oz. Soda Half Sham Also made 5, 10 & 13 oz.

14 oz. Slim Jim Half Sham Also made 12 oz.

30 oz. Martini Mixer

28 oz. Cocktail Shaker, No. 1 Strainer & No. 86 P/S

½ gal. Jug

½ gal. Ice Tankard

A. H. HEISEY & CO., NEWARK, OHIO

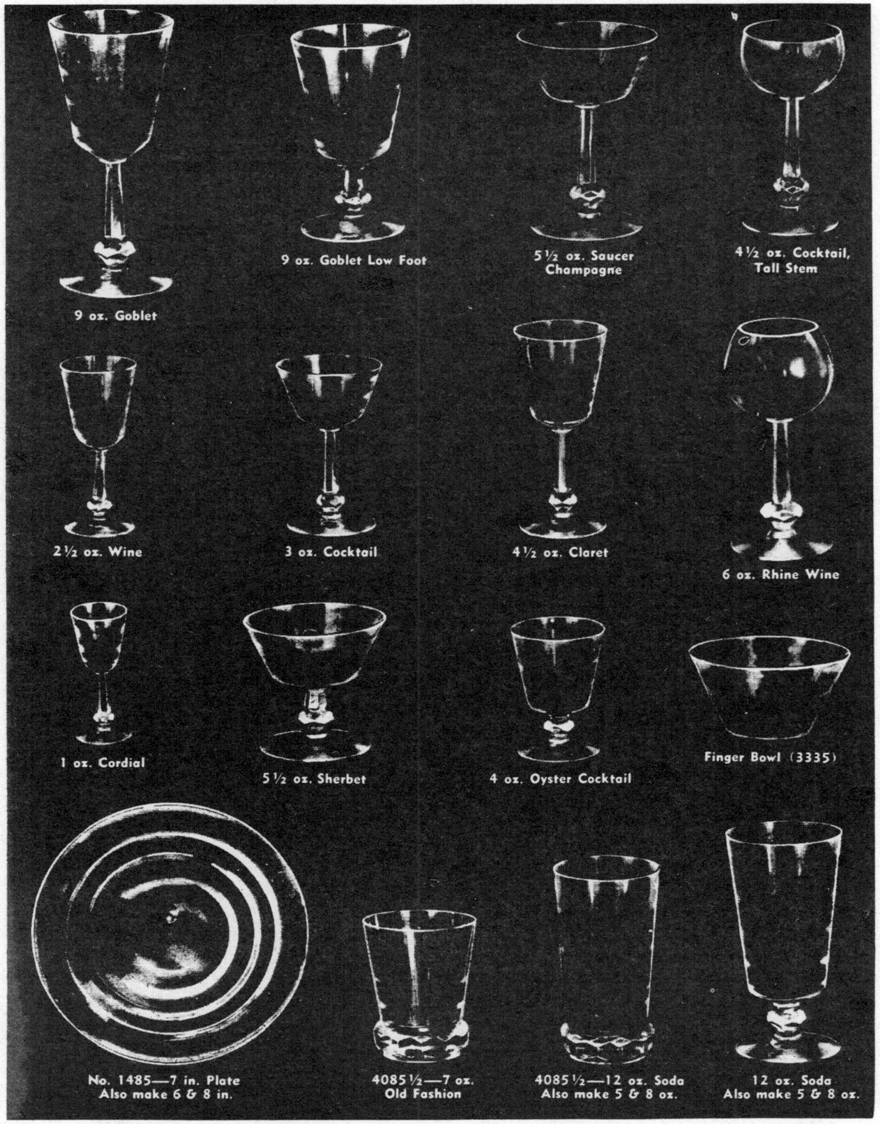

No. 4055 PARK LANE PATTERN

PLAIN ONLY

HANDMADE GLASSWARE

3 oz. Cocktail

1 oz. Cordial

2½ oz. Wine

1½ oz. Sherry

6 oz. Saucer Champagne

6 oz. Sherbet

Finger Bowl (4080)

3 oz. Oyster Cocktail

5 oz. Footed Soda
Also made 9 oz.

13 oz. Footed Soda

4 oz. Claret

10 oz. Goblet

A. H. HEISEY & CO., NEWARK, OHIO

No. 4085 "KOHINOOR" PATTERN

SATURNE OPTIC ONLY

4½ oz. Cocktail, Tall Stem

6 oz. Rhine Wine

Finger Bowl (3335)

12 oz. Soda
Also make 5 & 8 oz.

5½ oz. Saucer Champagne

4½ oz. Claret

4 oz. Oyster Cocktail

4085½—12 oz. Soda
Also make 5 & 8 oz.

9 oz. Goblet Low Foot

3 oz. Cocktail

5½ oz. Sherbet

4085½—7 oz. Old Fashion

9 oz. Goblet

2½ oz. Wine

1 oz. Cordial

No. 1485—7 in. Plate
Also make 6 & 8 in.

HANDMADE GLASSWARE

A. H. HEISEY & CO., NEWARK, OHIO

NO. 4090 · COVENTRY PATTERN
PLAIN ONLY

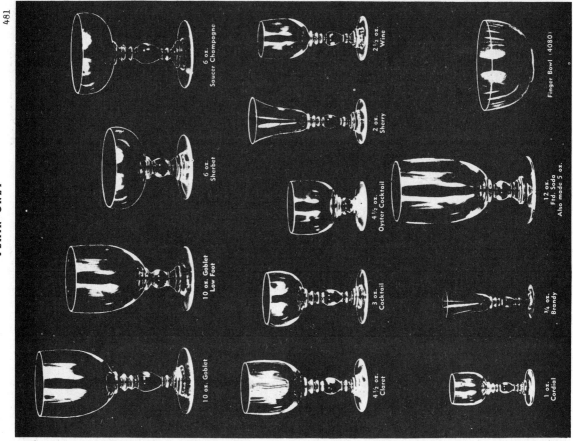

6 oz. Saucer Champagne

6 oz. Sherbet

10 oz. Goblet Low Foot

10 oz. Goblet

2½ oz. Wine

2 oz. Sherry

4½ oz. Oyster Cocktail

3 oz. Cocktail

4½ oz. Claret

Finger Bowl (4080)

12 oz. Ftd. Soda Also made 5 oz.

¾ oz. Brandy

1 oz. Cordial

A. H. HEISEY & CO., NEWARK, OHIO

No. 4091 · KIMBERLY PATTERN
PLAIN ONLY

5½ oz. Saucer Champagne

10 oz. Goblet Low Foot

10 oz. Goblet

1 oz. Cordial

2 oz. Wine

3 oz. Cocktail

4½ oz. Claret

4091½ oz.–12 oz. Ftd. Soda Also made 5 oz.

Finger Bowl (3335)

5½ oz. Sherbet

Oyster Cocktail (3542)

A. H. HEISEY & CO., NEWARK, OHIO

No. 4092 KENILWORTH PATTERN
WIDE OPTIC ONLY

H A N D M A D E   G L A S S W A R E

3 oz.
Oyster Cocktail

2 oz. Wine

Finger Bowl 3335

4½ oz.
Claret

1½ oz. Sherry
Tall Stem

3 oz.
Cocktail

3 oz. Brandy
Tall Stem

5½ oz.
Sherbet

5½ oz.
Saucer Champagne

1 oz. Cordial
Tall Stem

4092½ — 5 oz.
Ftd. Soda
Also made 12 oz.

10 oz.
Goblet

6 oz.
Rhine Wine

Brandy Sniffer

5½ in.
Comport

A. H. HEISEY & CO.,   NEWARK, OHIO

NO. 5003 - CRYSTOLITE - PATTERN

5 in.
Comport

Finger Bowl (4080)

3½ oz.
Cocktail

3½ oz.
Oyster Cocktail

5 oz.
Ftd. Soda
Also made 12 oz.

6 oz.
Sherbet

12 oz.
Soda Regular
Also made 5 oz.

3½ oz.
Claret

10 oz.
Goblet Low Foot

10 oz.
Tumbler Regular

H A N D M A D E   G L A S S W A R E

A. H. HEISEY & CO.,   NEWARK, OHIO

HANDMADE GLASSWARE

No. 5009   QUEEN ANN PATTERN
WIDE OPTIC ONLY

3½ oz. Cocktail

5 oz. Saucer Champagne

10 oz. Goblet

Finger Bowl 3309

4 oz. Oyster Cocktail

2½ oz. Wine

4 oz. Claret

12 oz. Ftd. Soda
Also made 5 oz.

A. H. HEISEY & CO.,   NEWARK, OHIO

No. 5010 "SYMPHONE" PATTERN
MEDIUM OPTIC ONLY

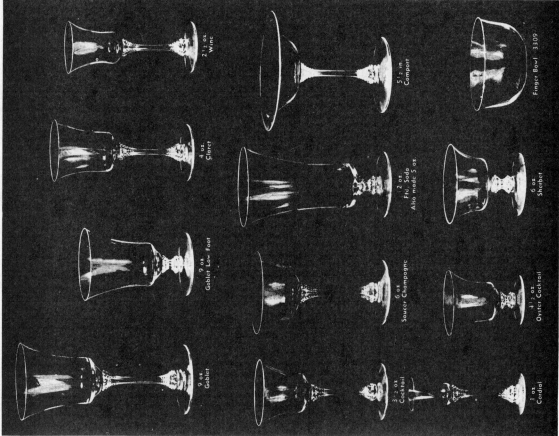

2½ oz. Wine

4 oz. Claret

9 oz. Goblet Low Foot

9 oz. Goblet

5½ in. Comport

2 oz. Ftd. Soda
Also made 5 oz.

6 oz. Sherbet

Finger Bowl 3309

6 oz. Saucer Champagne

4½ oz. Oyster Cocktail

3½ oz. Cocktail

1 oz. Cordial

HANDMADE GLASSWARE

A. H. HEISEY & CO.,   NEWARK, OHIO

HANDMADE GLASSWARE

No. 5011 "YORKTOWN" PATTERN

PLAIN ONLY

DOUBLE SHAM

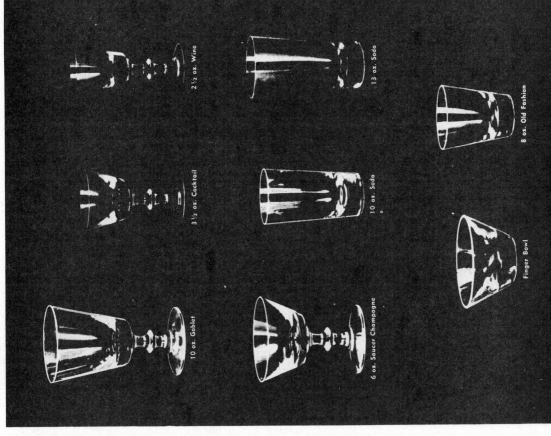

- 2½ oz. Wine
- 13 oz. Soda
- 3½ oz. Cocktail
- 10 oz. Soda
- 8 oz. Old Fashion
- 10 oz. Goblet
- 6 oz. Saucer Champagne
- Finger Bowl

A. H. HEISEY & CO., NEWARK, OHIO

No. 5013 "SHASTA" PATTERN

WIDE OPTIC ONLY

- 3½ oz. Cocktail
- 6 oz. Sherbet
- 2½ oz. Wine
- 4 oz. Claret
- 1 oz. Cordial
- 6 oz. Saucer Champagne
- 12 oz. Ftd. Soda Also made 5 oz.
- 4 oz. Oyster Cocktail
- 10 oz. Goblet
- 5 in. Comport
- Finger Bowl 4080

HANDMADE GLASSWARE

A. H. HEISEY & CO., NEWARK, OHIO

MISCELLANEOUS STEMWARE

HANDMADE GLASSWARE

No. 3428—2 oz.
Sherry
Plain Only

No. 3311—1½ oz.
Sherry—Plain
Also made 2½ oz.

No. 3542—4½ oz.
Oyster Cocktail
Plain or Wide Optic

No. 3405—3 oz.
Cocktail
Plain or Wide Optic

No. 4049—4½ oz.
Hot Whiskey
Plain Only

No. 3428—3½ oz.
Cocktail
Plain Only

No. 4002—4 oz.
Agua Caliente Coffee or Cocktail
Plain Only

No. 3419—22 oz.
Brandy Sniffer
Plain Only

No. 3404—6 in. Comport
Wide Optic Only

No. 3411—7 in. Comport
Wide Optic Only

No. 3368—7 in. Comport
Diamond Optic Only

A. H. HEISEY & CO., NEWARK, OHIO

MISCELLANEOUS STEMWARE

HANDMADE GLASSWARE

No. 4052
Sherbet 4051
Plain Only

No. 4052—10 oz. Goblet
Low Footed

No. 3801—Grape Fruit
Low Footed
Plain or Wide Optic

No. 4139—Grape Fruit Center
Footed
Plain Only

No. 4132
Peg Grape Fruit Center
Plain Only

No. 4052—14 oz. Soda
Also made 5 oz.

No. 4052—10 oz.
Tumbler

No. 4052
Parfait or Whiskey

A. H. HEISEY & CO., NEWARK, OHIO

MISCELLANEOUS ITEMS

HANDMADE GLASSWARE

No. 4266—5 oz.
Custard
Plain Only

No. 4058—5 oz.
Custard
Wide Optic Only

No. 4058
Punch Bowl & Cover
Wide Optic Only

No. 4056—11 in. Salad Bowl
Plain and Saturne Optic
Also made 9 in.

No. 3420—12 oz. Pilsner
Also made 8 & 10 oz.

No. 3806—4½ in.
Mushroom Cover
Plain Only

A. H. HEISEY & CO.,   NEWARK, OHIO

MISCELLANEOUS ITEMS

HANDMADE GLASSWARE

No. 4121
Marmalade & Cover
Plain or Diamond Optic

No. 4225—1 qt.
Rock & Rye Bottle
& No. 86 P/S
Plain Only

No. 4057—Ice Tub
Saturne Optic Only

No. 4059—42 oz.
Water Bottle
Plain or Diamond Optic

No. 4225—1 qt.   No. 86 P/S
Cocktail Shaker   Plain Only   Also made 2 qt.

No. 1 Strainer

A. H. HEISEY & CO.,   NEWARK, OHIO

HANDMADE GLASSWARE

MISCELLANEOUS VASES

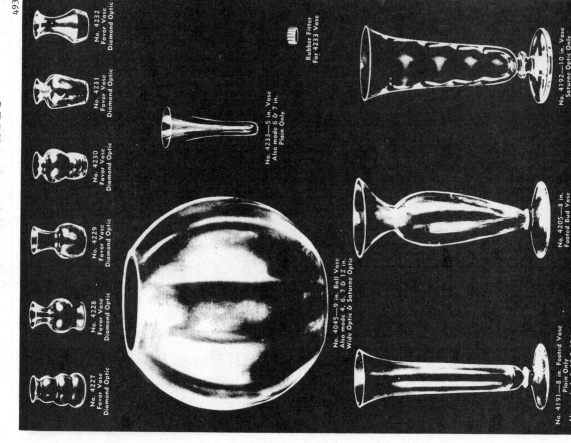

No. 4232
Favor Vase
Diamond Optic

No. 4231
Favor Vase
Diamond Optic

No. 4230
Favor Vase
Diamond Optic

No. 4229
Favor Vase
Diamond Optic

No. 4228
Favor Vase
Diamond Optic

No. 4227
Favor Vase
Diamond Optic

Rubber Fitter
For 4233 Vase

No. 4233—5 in. Vase
Also made 6 & 7 in.
Plain Only

No. 4192—10 in. Vase
Saturne Optic Only

No. 4045—9 in. Ball Vase
Also made 4, 6, 7 & 12 in.
Wide Optic & Saturne Optic

No. 4205—8 in.
Footed Bud Vase
Diamond Optic Only

No. 4191—8 in. Footed Vase
Plain Only
Also made 4, 6, 10 & 12 in.

A. H. HEISEY & CO.,   NEWARK, OHIO

A. H. HEISEY & CO.,   NEWARK, OHIO

MISCELLANEOUS VASES

No. 5012—7 in. Vase
Plain Only

No. 4196—12 in. Vase Sham
Also made 8 in.
Saturne Optic Only

No. 4057—10½ in. Vase
Also made 5, 7 & 9 in.
Saturne Optic Only

No. 5015—9 in. Vase Ftd.

JUGS

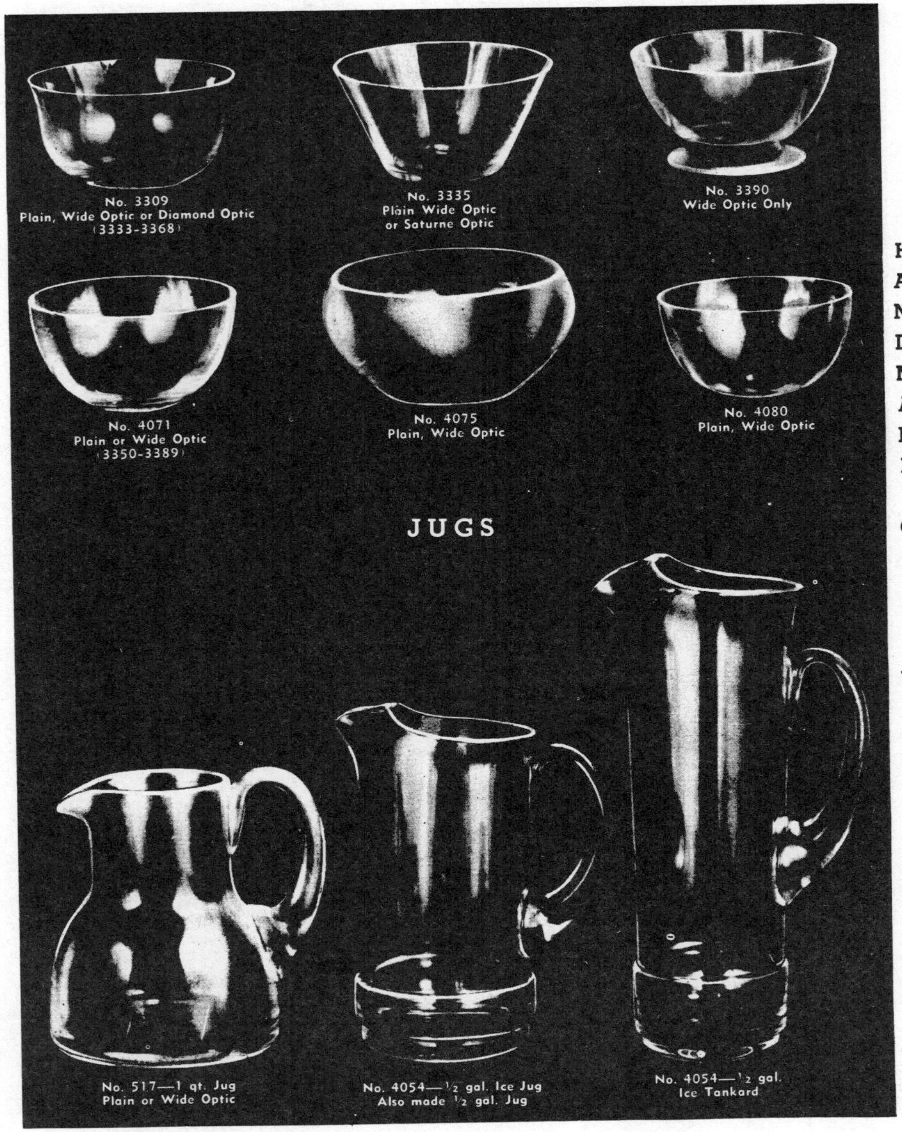

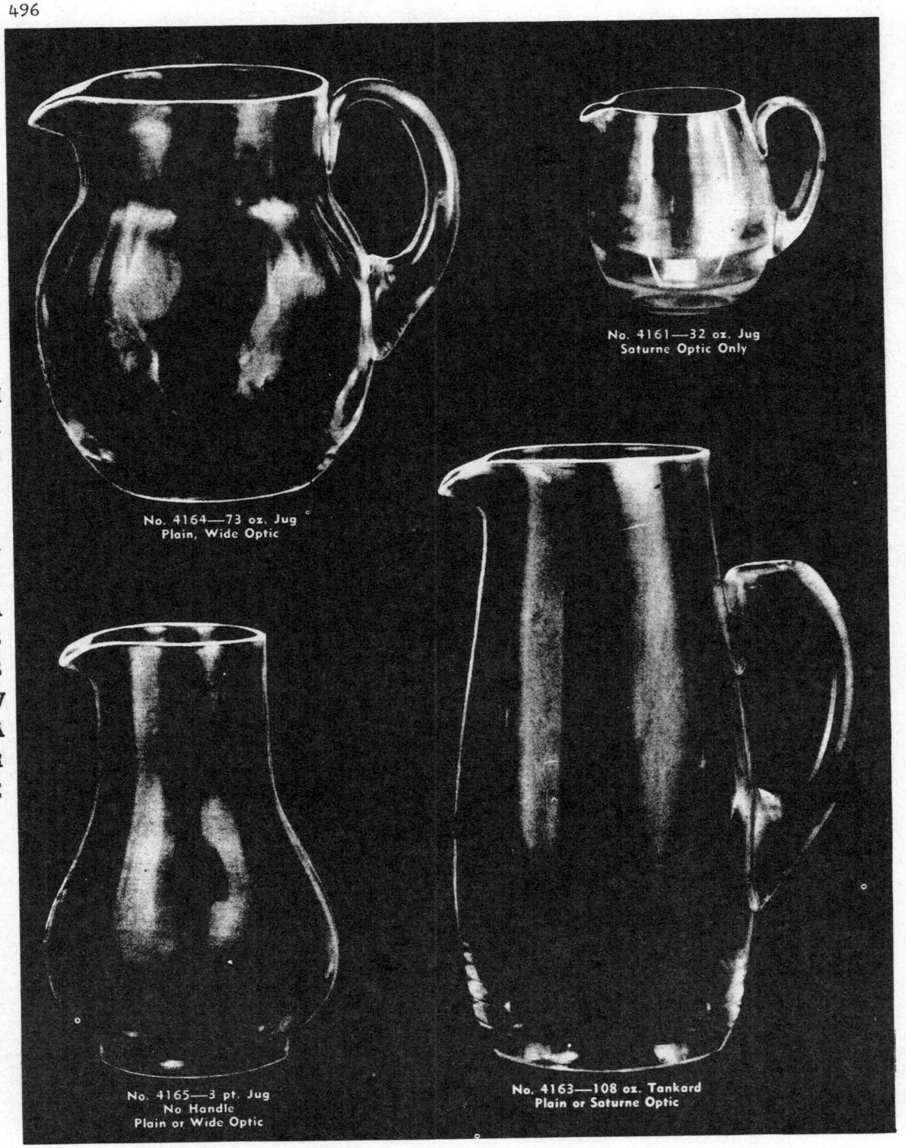

No. 4164—73 oz. Jug
Plain, Wide Optic

No. 4161—32 oz. Jug
Saturne Optic Only

No. 4165—3 pt. Jug
No Handle
Plain or Wide Optic

No. 4163—108 oz. Tankard
Plain or Saturne Optic

HANDMADE GLASSWARE

FINGER BOWLS

No. 3309
Plain, Wide Optic or Diamond Optic
(3333-3368)

No. 3335
Plain Wide Optic
or Saturne Optic

No. 3390
Wide Optic Only

No. 4071
Plain or Wide Optic
(3350-3389)

No. 4075
Plain, Wide Optic

No. 4080
Plain, Wide Optic

JUGS

No. 517—1 qt. Jug
Plain or Wide Optic

No. 4054—½ gal. Ice Jug
Also made ½ gal. Jug

No. 4054—½ gal.
Ice Tankard

HANDMADE GLASSWARE

DECANTERS

H A N D M A D E   G L A S S W A R E

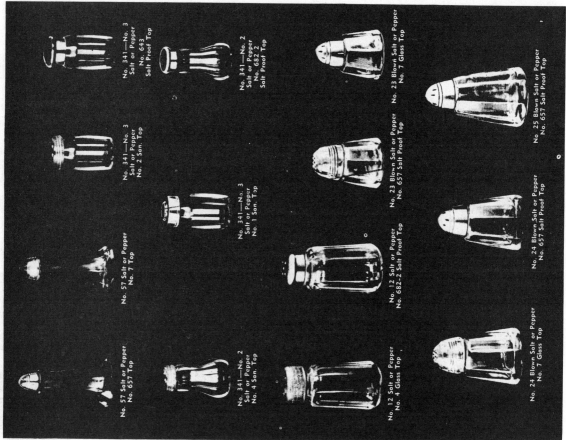

No. 4027—32 oz. Decanter & No. 48 C/S
Plain or Diamond Optic

No. 3390—1 pt. Decanter & No. 84 P/S
Wide Optic Only

No. 4035—32 oz. Decanter & No. 48 C/S
Plain Only

No. 4036—1 pt. Decanter & No. 101 P/S
Plain Only

A. H. HEISEY & CO.,   NEWARK, OHIO

MISCELLANEOUS SALTS AND PEPPERS

No. 57 Salt or Pepper
No. 657 Top

No. 57 Salt or Pepper
No. 7 Top

No. 341—No. 3
Salt or Pepper
No. 643 Salt Proof Top

No. 341—No. 2
Salt or Pepper
No. 682-2 Salt Proof Top

No. 23 Blown Salt or Pepper
No. 7 Glass Top

No. 25 Blown Salt or Pepper
No. 657 Salt Proof Top

No. 341—No. 2
Salt or Pepper
No. 4 San. Top

No. 341—No. 3
Salt or Pepper
No. 2 San. Top

No. 341—No. 3
Salt or Pepper
No. 1 San. Top

No. 23 Blown Salt or Pepper
No. 657 Salt Proof Top

No. 24 Blown Salt or Pepper
No. 657 Salt Proof Top

No. 12 Salt or Pepper
No. 4 Glass Top

No. 12 Salt or Pepper
No. 682-2 Salt Proof Top

No. 24 Blown Salt or Pepper
No. 7 Glass Top

H A N D M A D E   G L A S S W A R E

A. H. HEISEY & CO.,   NEWARK, OHIO

PRICING INFORMATION

The prices for the Heisey pieces in this volume have been determined by a number of methods. Auction results, show dealer prices and opinions from many Heisey experts were used to establish our final price on each item.

Prices will vary in separate regions of the country, as well as in various antique and collectible shows throughout. The listed prices in this book are what we feel to be appropriate average values.

However, this is only a guide and L-W Books cannot be held responsible for gains or losses while using this book.

ANIMAL AND FIGURE PRICE GUIDE
(* illustrated)

*Airedale - 5 3/4" high $550
*Asiatic Pheasant - 10 1/2" high $325
Bull - 4" high $1,500
Bunnies (head up) (down) 2 3/8" high $150
*Cherub Candlestick - Frosted $900
Chick - 1" high $75
*Clydesdale - 7 1/4" high $525
Cygnet - 2 1/8" high $300
*Donkey - 6 1/2" high $75
*Ducklings - sitting or floating $150
Duck Stopper - $50
*Elephant - 4" high $250
Elephant - 4 1/2" high $275
Elephant - 5 7/8" high $350
*Fighting Rooster - 8" high $150
*Filly Horse - head forward or backward $2,300
*Fish Bookend -6 5/8" high $130
*Fish Bowl - 9" high $600
Fish Candlestick - 5" high $260
Fish Match Holder - 3" high $150
*Flying Mare - 8 7/8" high $3,000
Gazelle - 11" high $1,600
*Giraffe - 11" high either pose $200
*Girl Figurine - 4 1/4" high $1,200
*Goose (wings half way) - 4 1/4" high $175
Goose (wings down) - 2 3/4" high $325
Goose (wings up) - 6 1/2" high $175
*Horse Head Bookend -6 7/8" high $160
*Rearing Horse Bookend - 7 7/8" high $450

*Show Horse - 7 3/8" high $650
Plug Horse - 4" high $125
*Horse Head Stopper - large $150
*Horse Head Stopper - small $100
*Mallard (wings down) - 4 1/2" high $250
*Mallard (wings up) - 6 3/4" high $200
*Mallard (wings half way) - 5" high $200
*Madonna - frosted $175
*Ringneck Pheasant - 4 3/4" high $160
Pig - 3 1/8" high $675
*Piglets - standing or sitting $80
Ponies - rearing $200, kicking $160, standing $160
*Pouter Pigeon - 6 1/4" high $650
*Rabbithead Bookend - 6 1/4" $1,600
Rabbit - 4 5/8" high $650
*Rabbit Paperweight - 2 3/4" high $200
*Ram's Head Decanter Stopper - $425
Rooster - 5 5/8" high $400
*Rooster Stopper - $60
*Rooster Vase - 6 1/2" high $125
*Scottie - 3 1/2" high $150
*Sparrow - 2 1/4" high $100
Swan - 7" high $1,100
Tiger Paperweight - 2 3/8" high $1,200
*Tropical Fish Piece - 12" high $1,500
*Victorian Belle - Frosted $140
Wood Duck - 4 1/2" high $700

PRICE GUIDE

Plate 1
#150-$25,#152-$30,others $10-20

Plate 2
#171-$35, others $10-20

Plate 3
#181 & #350-$35, others $10-20

Plate 4
#s 379 1/2, 385 ,433, 439-$30-40
others $10-20

Plate 5
$10-20 each

Plate 6
#379 1/2-$25, others $10-20

Plate 7
$5-15 each

Plate 8
#150-$25,#433-$40,others $10-20

Plate 9
$10-20 each

Plate 10
$10-20 each

Plate 11
$15-25 each

Plate 12
$15-25 each

Plate 13
$10-20 each

Plate 14
$10-20 each

Plate 15
All #392-$15-25, All #433-$25-35

Plate 16
#504-$20, others $5-15

Plate 17
$10-20 each

Plate 18
$10-20 each

Plate 19
$10-20 each

Plate 20
$10-20 each

Plate 21
$10-20 each

Plate 22
#433 5oz. straight-$40, others $10-20

Plate 23
$10-20 each

Plate 24
$10-20 each

Plate 25
$10-20 each

Plate 26
$10-20 each

Plate 27
$10-20 each

Plate 28
$20-30 each

Plate 29
#433- $30-40, others $10-20

Plate 30
$15-25 each

Plate 31
$15-25 each

Plate 32
$15-25 each

Plate 33
$15-25 each

Plate 34
#433-$50, others $15-25

Plate 35
#433-$45, others $15-25

Plate 36
$15-25 each

Plate 37
#433-$50, others $20-25

Plate 38
#433-$50, others $20-30

Plate 39
$20-30 each

Plate 40
$20-30 each

Plate 41
$20-40 each

Plate 42
$20-40 each

Plate 43
$15-25 each

Plate 44
$15-25 each

Plate 45
$10-20 each

Plate 46
$15-25 each

Plate 47
$10-20 each

Plate 48
$10-20 each

Plate 49
$10-20 each

Plate 50
$10-20 each

Plate 51
$10-20 each

Plate 52
$10-20 each

Plate 53
$15-25 each

Plate 54
$15-30 each

Plate 55
$10-20 each

Plate 56
3 1/2 oz. Burg., 2 oz. Wine, Cordial,
2 oz. Sherry - $85+, others $25-35

Plate 57
$10-20 each

Plate 58
$15-25 each

Plate 59
$10-20 each

Plate 60
#433-$50, others $10-20

Plate 61
$10-20 each

Plate 62
$10-20 each

Plate 63
#433-$60, others $20-30

Plate 64
#433-$45, others $10-20

Plate 65
$10-20 each

Plate 66
$10-20 each

Plate 67
#433-$40, others $10-20

Plate 68
$15-30 each

Plate 69
#433-$40, others $20-30

PRICE GUIDE

Plate 70
$10-20 each

Plate 71
$10-20 each

Plate 72
$15-25 each

Plate 73
#433-$35, others $10-20

Plate 74
$25-40 each

Plate 75
$35-50 each

Plate 76
$10-20 each

Plate 77
$10-15 each

Plate 78
$10-15 each, with plates $15-30

Plate 79
$10-15 each

Plate 80
$10-20 each

Plate 81
$10-20 each

Plate 82
$10-15 each

Plate 83
$10-15 each

Plate 84
$10-15 each

Plate 85
$10-20 each

Plate 86
$100-150 each

Plate 87
$100-150 each

Plate 88
$100-150 each

Plate 89
$125-160 each

Plate 90
$75-110 each

Plate 91
Punch Bowl-$150, others $10-15

Plate 92
Punch Bowl-$125, others $10-15

Plate 93
Punch Bowl-$125, others $10-15

Plate 94
Punch Bowl-$125, others $10-15

Plate 95
Punch Bowl-$125, others $10-15

Plate 96
Punch Bowl-$175, Custard-$25

Plate 97
Punch Bowl-$260, Custard-$25

Plate 98
15" Bowl-$155, Custard-$20

Plate 99
Punch Bowl-$150, others $10-15

Plate 100
Punch Bowl-$150, others $10-20

Plate 101
Punch Bowl-$300, others $20-30

Plate 102
#433-$40, others $20-30

Plate 103
$20-40 each

Plate 104
#350-$35, others $20-30

Plate 105
$15-25 each

Plate 106
#433-$35, others $10-20

Plate 107
$50-75 each

Plate 108
#433-$80, others $40-50

Plate109
$75-125 each

Plate 110
$75-125 each

Plate 111
#433-$35, others $10-15

Plate 112
#433-$35, others $10-15

Plate 113
#433-$35, others $10-15

Plate 114
$10-15 each

Plate 115
$50-75 each

Plate 116
$40-60 each

Plate 117
#433-$70, others $35-50

Plate 118
Oils-$40-55, Stoppers $5-10

Plate 119
$50-70 each

Plate 120
Bottom row first 3-$75-100
others $40-60

Plate 121
#433-$60, #150-45, others $25-35

Plate 122
#433-$70, others $35-55

Plate 123
$25-45 each

Plate 124
#341-$70, #352-$100, #353-$65
#354-$80

Plate 125
#429-$100, others $80

Plate 126
5lb-$110, others $60-85

Plate 127
#352, 1/2lb-$65,1lb-$65,2lb-$80,
4lb-$125   #433, 1/2lb-$100
1lb-$100, 2lb-$200, 4lb-$200

Plate 128
#360-$80, #359-$75, #1183-$15
others $35-45

Plate 129
Butter& Cover-$85, Sugar& Cover-$40
Spoon-$35, Cream-$35, Nappy-$10-25

Plate 130
10"-$35, 10 1/2"-$35, 12"-$40
others $10-30

Plate 131
$20-35 each

Plate 132
Punch Bowl-$175, others $10-15

Plate 133
Pint-$45, 1 1/4 Pt-$45, Quart-$50
1 1/4 qt-$70, 3 pt-$80, 1/2 gal-$100
3 qt-$100

Plate 134
Water Bottle-$70, 9" Foot Bowl-$85
Squat Water Bottle-$75, others $15

Plate 135
$15-30 each

PRICE GUIDE

Plate 136
Pint Tankard-$90, 14 oz. footed-$50
Pint Tankard w/cover -$110
others $15-30

Plate 137
Oyster Cocktail-$45, 3 pc Oyster-$70
Horseradish-$70, Toothpick-$45
Salts-$25-30,Sugars-$40 ea.
Mustard Spoon-$15, Oils-$60-70
Syrup-$80, Pickle Jar-$80,
Hotel Cream-$30, Hotel Sugar-$30

Plate 138
Pint Tankard-$85, Water Set-$140
Qt. Jug-$80, 13" Water Set-$200
10" Water Set-$150

Plate 139
Bedroom Sets-$150-200,
others $45-60

Plate 140
Top two rows-$10-20
Bottom two rows-$40-60

Plate 141
$60-80 each

Plate 142
Punch Bowl-$175, others $15

Plate 143
Tumblers-$15-25, Qt. Jug-$50
3 Pt. Jug-$70, 1/2 Gal. Jug-$75
3 Qt. Jug-$100

Plate 144
$15-25 each

Plate 145
Water Bottle-$65, others $15-25

Plate 146
All Salts-$20-25, others $45-65

Plate 147
Bitter Bottle-$70, Pint Dec.-$70
Qt. Dec.-$85, others $15-30

Plate 148
Plates-$10,Jelly-$35,Sugar-$35
Cream-$35,Bar-$15, Flared Bar-$20
Tumblers-$15,Water Bottles-$50 each
Jug-$100

Plate 149
Caddies & Jars-$55 each,
others $10 each

Plate 150
4"-$15, 4 1/2"-15, others $35-40 each

Plate 151
4 1/2"-$15,5"-$15,7"$35,9"-$35
10"-$35,11"-$40,Pint Jug-$40
Qt. Jug-$40,3 Pint Jug-$65
1/2 Gal. Jug-$80

Plate 152
Finger Bowl & Salts-$15 each
Custard & Tumbler-$10 each
Oyster-$35, Mustard-$40,
Toothpick-$80, Water Bottle-$50
Oils-$50, Pickle Jar-$65,Syrup-$50
Straw Jar-$100

Plate 153
18 oz. Dec.-$90, Worc. Sauce-$65
Wine Set-$275, Ind. Dec.-$50
20 oz. Dec.-$95

Plate 154
Tumblers-$30 each, Finger Bowls &
Salts-$15-20 each, Oyster-$40
Syrup-$60, Water Bottle-$70
Oils-$50-65 each

Plate 155
4" to 6"-$15 each, 7"-$25, 8"-$35
9"-$40, 10"-$50

Plate 156
1st Row-$15-20
2nd Row-$25-45
3rd Row-$55-70

Plate 157
14"-$55, 15"-$55, #1 6"- $45
others $15-30

Plate 158
Middle Column-$50-60 each
others-$15-30 each

Plate 159
Finger Bowls-$15 each, Mayo-$40
2 pc. Oyster-$40, 3 pc. Oyster-$50
Celery Trays-$40-50, Cheese-$150
Pickle & Spoon-$25 each

Plate 160
$25-40 each

Plate 161
$35-50 each

Plate 162
7 1/2"-$45, 8 1/2"-$45, 11"-$60
7" & 8" covered-$80 each

Plate 163
Punch Bowl-$175, others $15 each

Plate 164
Punch Bowl- $175, others $15 each

Plate 165
Tumblers-$15, Water Bottle-$65
Tankards-$70-90, Rock & Rye-$100
24oz. Dec.-$100

Plate 166
Tumbler-$15, Ice Tub-$60
Pt. Tankard-$75, Qt. Tankard-$80
3 Pt. Tankard-$100, 1/2 Gal.-$130

Plate 167
$25-35 each

Plate 168
Salts-$15-20, Toothpick-$90
Oils-$45-60

Plate 169
Cream & Sugar-$30-35 each
others $50-70

Plate 170
1 lb.-$50, 2 lb.-$55, 3 lb.-$60
5 lb.-$80

Plate 171
Water Sets - $200 each, others $15-20

Plate 172
Sugar-$50, Butter-$80, 9" Nappy-$50
others $20-35

Plate 173
Plates-$20 each
4 1/2" to 8 1/2" Nappys - $20-40
9" to 11" Nappys - $60-75

Plate 174
Finger Bowls-$15-30, Custard-$15
Oyster-$30, Cheese-$135
Punch Bowl-$200

Plate 175
1 Pt.-$60, 1 Qt.-$65, 3 Pt.-$80
1/2 Gal.-$85, 3 Qt.-$100,Tumbler-$15

Plate 176
8" Nappy-$65, 3 Pt. Jug-$150
Punch Bowl-$275, others $20-35

Plate 177
Cream & Sugar w/plate $55 each
Mayo-$65, celery trays-$35-45
others-$15-35

Plate 178
6" Jelly-$50, 10" Bowl-$65,Oyster-$40
Sweet Meat-$60, others $15-30

Plate 179
Tumblers-$15-20
Water Bottles-$50-60, Pt. Jug-$45
Qt. Jug-$60, 3 Pt. Jug-$70
1/2 Gal.Jug-$85

Plate 180
$30-40 each

Plate 181
$25-30 each

Plate 182
Toothpick-$50, Mustard-$50
Pt. Dec.-$55, Qt. Dec.-$60
Oils-$35-50, others $15-30

Plate 183
Wine Set-$160, Whiskey Set-$220
others $20-25

Plate 184
2 Pc. Cheese-$60, Strawberry-$50
others $20-40

PRICE GUIDE

Plate 185
14" Tray-$50, others $20-30

Plate 186
Finger Bowl, Tumb., Sher.,-$10-15 ea.
Oyster-$20, Sugars-$35-40 each
Toothpick-$55, Oils-$40-55, Jug-$100
Must.,Horse.,Pickle,Celery-$45-55 ea.

Plate 187
Straw-$70, Small Spoon-$50
Candy Tray-$45,Cone Holder-$35
Large Spoon-$65, 1 lb. Candy -$60
2 lb. Candy-$75, 4 lb. Candy-$80
1 Qt. Fruit-$165, 2 Qt. Fruit-$190

Plate 188
Cigar Jar-$200, Cologne-$60
Knife Rest-$30, Match Stand-$40
Bedroom Set-$160, Ash Tray-$20
1 1/2 oz. to 5 oz. - $30-50
10 oz. to 24 oz. - $50-70

Plate 189
Perf. Cover-$15, Violet Vase-$20
2 pc. Vase-$40, #4-$50, #1-$70
#5-$60

Plate 190
$50-70 each

Plate 191
$20-40 each

Plate 192
Straw Jars-$40-50, San. Straw-$75
Straw Jar w/cover-$65, Fruit-$100
Candy Trays-$40 each

Plate 193
$35-65 each

Plate 194
Top Row - $15-20
Water Bottle-$70, Qt. Jug-$45
3 Pt. Jug-$60, 1/2 Gal. Jug-$75

Plate 195
Sugars & Creams-$20-30
Oils- $45-75

Plate 196
Syrups-$30-50, with plates-$50-70
Ind. Celery-$20, Tall Celery-$35
Mayo-$50, Marmalade-$60
Almonds-$20 each

Plate 197
Cheese-$60, 10" Tray-$45
Grapefruit w/plate-$40, others $15-20

Plate 198
Mushrooms w/plate- $60-85
others $15-30

Plate 199
Tobacco-$115, Soap Dish-$45
Toothbrush-$40,Mug-$35,Colog.- $80
Match-$70, 2oz. to 8 oz. Jars-$25-40
12 oz. to 30 oz. Jars - $50 - 90

Plate 200
8"-$65, 10"-$80, 12"-$85
15"-$100, 18"-$125

Plate 201
$35-65 each

Plate 202
#1 Fern-$45, #2 Fern-$55
#3 Fern-$75, 8" Nappy-$15
16 oz. Jar-$60, 27 oz. Jar-$80
others $35-50

Plate 203
Straw Jar-$100, 1 Qt. Fruit-$70
Indiv. Sugar, Cream, Butter-$10-25
others $40-50

Plate 204
Finger Bowl-$10, Grapefruit-$20
Match Stand-$40, others $45-75

Plate 205
Butter-$10, 4 & 4 1/2" Nappy-$10-15
7" to 9" Nappy - $25-35

Plate 206
Creams & Sugars - $35 each
others $60-70

Plate 207
$15-35 each

Plate 208
$15-35 each

Plate 209
Tumblers - $15-25, Jugs - $75-90

Plate 210
$15-30 each

Plate 211
$15-30 each

Plate 212
$15-30 each

Plate 213
Sugar-$50, Cream-$35, Spoon-$35
Butter-$90, others $15-20

Plate 214
9" and larger - $50-60, others $15-20

Plate 215
Bottom Row - $25-40, others $15-20

Plate 216
Finger Bowls - $15 each, Plate-$10
Grapefruit-$15, others $30-50

Plate 217
Punch Bowl- $150, others $20 each

Plate 218
Tankard-$85, 1/2 Gal. Jug-$85
others $35-50

Plate 219
1 Pt. Jug-$35, others $50-80

Plate 220
$15-20 each

Plate 221
$10-20 each

Plate 222
Butter-$10, Salts-$15 each
Oils-$50-60, Mustard-$50, Bitters-$55
Pickle Jar-$70

Plate 223
French Dressing w/plate-$55
Tray & Sherbet - $45, Ice Tub-$40
Banana Split-$40, others $25-35

Plate 224
Sugar-$40, Spoon-$40, Cream-$35
Butter-$80, 9" Nappy-$45, 8 1/2"-$40
others $15-20

Plate 225
Water Bottle-$70, Egg Cup-$20
Tumbler-$15, Wine-$35, Goblet-$20
Qt. Jug-$40, 3 Pt. Jug - $50
1/2 Gal. Jug - $60, 3 Qt. jug - $75

Plate 226
Oil-$50, Jelly-$35, Toothpick - $125
Salt/Pepper - $15 each, Syrup-$60
2 Handled Jelly-$40, Salver-$70
Sugar/Cream-$20 each, Celery-$60

Plate 227
Punch Bowl-$165, others $15 each

Plate 228
12" Celery - $50, others $15-30

Plate 229
Qt. Jug-$45, 3 Pt. Jug-$55
1/2 Gal. Jug-$80, Sugar-$35
Cream-$30, Pt. Jug-$30
others $15-20

Plate 230
1 Qt. Fruit-$80, 2 Qt. Fruit-$100
Oil-$60, others $15-20

Plate 231
4" to 7" Nappy - $25-40
8" to 11" Nappy - $60-80
Cream-$45, Spoon-$55, Sugar-$70
Butter-$200

Plate 232
Almond-$35, Nappy-$30, 4 1/2"-$30
8"-$60, Almond w/cover-$65
Ind. Almond-$30, Hotel Ice-$110
Large Ice-$85, Small Ice-$75
Ice Tub w/cover-$200

Plate 233
Butter-$20, 4" to 6 1/2"-$20-35
7" to 10" - $40-60, 13"-$85
15"-$120

PRICE GUIDE

Plate 234
Sm. Cherry-$100, Lg. Cherry-$120
#1 Puff-$80, #3 Puff-$100, Pickle-$80
Celery-$80, 9" Tray-$60, Hair R.-$120
Cheese-$100, Roll Tray - $75

Plate 235
#1 Jelly w/cover-$110
2 Handled Jelly w/cover-$130
5 1/2" Jelly w/cover-$90
5" Jelly w/cover-$85
others $55-70

Plate 236
10"-$110, 9" Shallow-$120
8" Shallow-$90, 7"-$80, 8"-$95
9"-$115

Plate 237
Punch Bowl - $275, others $20

Plate 238
Plate-$100, Bowls-$115-140

Plate 239
Bars & Tumblers-$40-50, Pt. Jug-$95
Water Bottle-$115, Qt. Jug-$110
3 Pt. Jug-$115, 1/2 Gal. Jug-$170

Plate 240
Goblets & Tumblers-$45-55
Pt. Tankard-$110, Qt. Tankard-$155
3 Pt. Tankard-$175, 1/2 Gal. - $200

Plate 241
Sherbets-$20-35, Egg-$40
Tumblers & Goblets-$55-70
Claret-$50, Burgundy-$50, Wine-$60
Cordial-$90, Sherry-$85
Cocktail-$55, Champagne-$60

Plate 242
$60-70 each

Plate 243
Toothpick-$175, Salt/Pepper-$45 each
Oils-$75-100, Finger Bowl-$30
Butter-$115, Sugars/ Creams-$40-50

Plate 244
Spoon-$80, Banana Split-$55
Banana Split Footed-$65
Small Spoon-$55

Plate 245
4" to 6 1/2" Nappy - $30-40
7" to 9" Nappy-$50-70
2 oz. Oil-$75, 4 oz. Oil-$100
6 oz. Oil-$150

Plate 246
#4 Puff-$100, Tumbler-$50
Pint Jug-$110, Qt. Jug-$110
3 Pt. Jug-$120, 1/2 Gal. Jug-$150

Plate 247
Sugar/Cream-$30 each
4" to 7" Nappy-$15-25
8" to 9" Nappy-$40-50

Plate 248
Celery-$40, Oil-$70, Pt. Jug-$45
Qt. Jug-$50, 3 Pt. Jug-$70
1/2 Gal. Jug-$95

Plate 249
Condiment Set-$85, others $10-20

Plate 250
Cond. Sets-$95 each, Oysters-$45 ea.
Butter-$15, others $20-35

Plate 251
Horseradish-$40, Salad Sets-$45 each
others $15-25

Plate 252
$15-30 each

Plate 253
Mustard-$40, Ash Tray-$40
Match Stand-$50, Sherbet-$15
8" Nappy-$25, 3 Pt. Jug-$60
Sandwich Plate-$30, 9" Plate-$20
#447 8" Nappy-$40

Plate 254
Hair Rec.-$75, Puff Boxes-$60-75
Comb. Set-$35, Ind. Sugar-$10
Sugar & Butter-$15, Ind. Cream-$25
Cream/Butter-$40, Spoons-$10-15 ea.
1/2 Gal. Tankard-$85, Tumbler-$20
8" Bowl-$60

Plate 255
$15-20 each

Plate 256
Top Row- $45-55, Rosebowls-$65-75
French Vase-$100

Plate 257
Top Row-$40-50, Bottom Row-$50-70

Plate 258
#351 Flared-$50, #351 Scalloped-$50
#352 #4-$70, #352 #5-$95
#354-$55, #355-$60

Plate 259
Low Vase-$45, Perf. Cover-$15
Bottom Row - $65-75

Plate 260
Ind. Bouquet-$20, 8"-$35, 10"-$35
12"-$50, 15"-$55, 18"-$65

Plate 261
6" to 8" - $40-60, 10" to 12" - $80-85

Plate 262
$50-60 each

Plate 263
$55-70 each

Plate 264
$60-65 each

Plate 265
$50-70 each

Plate 266
#11 Spiral-$70, others $45-55

Plate 267
$55-65 each

Plate 268
$55-65 each

Plate 269
#442-$35, others $60-80

Plate 270
$65-75 each

Plate 271
#444-$125, Carnation-$60
Flower-$60

Plate 272
$45-55 each

Plate 273
$35-45 each

Plate 274
$45-55 each

Plate 275
$60-70 each

Plate 276
$55-65 each

Plate 277
$45-55 each

Plate 278
$45-55 each

Plate 279
Top Row - $30-45 each
Bottom Row - $50-60 each

Plate 280
1 Light - $200, 2 Light - $300

Plate 281
2 Arms - $300, 3 Arms - $350

Plate 282
Left-$90, Middle-$310, Right-$150

Plate 283
#18-$100, #18 w/prisms-$165

Plate 284
$325

Plate 285
$340

Plate 286
#19-$80, #19 w/prisms-$200

Plate 287
$375

PRICE GUIDE

Plate 288
$160

Plate 289
$380

Plate 290
$325

Plate 291
$350

Plate 292
$375

Plate 293
$375

Plate 294
$400

Plate 295
$375

Plate 296
$325

Plate 297
$375

Plate 298
$350

Plate 299
$400

Plate 300
$400

Plate 301
$400

Plate 302
$375

Plate 303
$350

Plate 304
Left-$250, Right-$275

Plate 305
$375

Plate 306
$20-30 each

Plate 307
$20-30 each

Plate 308
$20-30 each

Plate 309
Glasses-$25-35, Coasters-$15-20

Plate 310
$10-20 each

Plate 311
$10-20 each

Plate 312
$10-20

Plate 313
Goblets-$15-25, others $10-20

Plate 314
$10-20 each

Plate 315
Goblets-$15-25, others $10-20

Plate 316
$35-45 each

Plate 317
$30-40 each

Plate 318
$15-20 each

Plate 319
$15-20 each

Plate 320
$15-20 each

Plate 321
$15-20 each

Plate 322
$20-35 each

Plate 323
#1246-$40, others $15-20 each

Plate 324
$10-15 each

Plate 325
$10-15 each

Plate 326
$10-15 each

Plate 327
Bottom Row-$60-70, others $20 each

Plate 328
#63-$10, #64-$10, #69-$10, #76-$10
#77-$40, #4034-$40, others $60-75

Plate 329
Egg Cup-$20, Domino Sugar-$30
Mustard & Cover-$60, Preserve-$30
Cracker/Cheese-$70, Cottage-$20
Dish & Cover-$45, Soda-$15
Celery-$30, Pickle Jar-$70

Plate 330
Mustard-$50, Plate-$20, Preserve-$20
Jelly-$35, Pickle-$30, Custard-$15
Lemon-$65, Celery-$40, 4" Nappy-$15
9" Nappy-$45

Plate 331
4" to 6 1/2"-$15, 7"-$20, 8"-$30

Plate 332
Top Row-$20 each, Oil-$60
others $20-30

Plate 333
Top Row-$15 each, Tankard-$70
Goblet-$35, Jug-$95

Plate 334
Plate-$20, others $30-40

Plate 335
Bon Bon-$35, Cheese-$35, Jelly-$25
Mint-$25, Lemon-$65, Marmalade-$40
Nut Bowl-$40, Preserve-$40
Footed Preserve-$60

Plate 336
Punch Bowl-$200, Custard-$15

Plate 337
High Foot Jelly-$40, Goblet-$30
others $15-20

Plate 338
Cig. Jar-$55, Water Bottle-$60
Vase-$45, Jug-$80
others $20 each

Plate 339
Mustard-$45, Mayo-$45, Sugar-$60
Oil-$60, others $10-20

Plate 340
Banana Split-$40, Ice Tea-$35
others $15-25

Plate 341
Hotel Sugar-$50, Cig. Box-$60
others $15-25

Plate 342
Oil-$65, High Footed Jellies-$30-40 ea
others $15-25

Plate 343
Jug-$95, others $15-20

Plate 344
Pickle-$20, Nut Dish-$15
Sugar & Cream-$40, Jelly-$30
Oval-$25, Relish-$40

Plate 345
Cheese/Cracker-$40, Spice Tray-$35
others $15-25

Plate 346
Oil-$45, Low Comport-$35, High-$50
others $15-25

Plate 347
3 Pt. Jug-$50, 3 Pt. Ice Jug-$65
others $10-20

Plate 348
Vegetable Dish w/cover-$30
others $10-20

PRICE GUIDE

Plate 349
Oval Tray-$30, others $15-20

Plate 350
Lemon Dish w/cover-$25
others $10-15

Plate 351
Oil-$50, French-$35, Comports-$30 ea
others $15-25

Plate 352
$10-15 each

Plate 353
Qt. Jug-$65, others $10-15

Plate 354
Bridge Smoking-$35, others $15-25

Plate 355
$20-30 each

Plate 356
Hors d'Oeuvre-$30, Dessert-$30
others $15-20

Plate 357
Plate-$10, others $15-20

Plate 358
Grapefruit-$10, others $15-25

Plate 359
$10-20 each

Plate 360
Mint w/cover-$30, others $15-20

Plate 361
$10-20 each

Plate 362
Oil-$50, French-$40, Ice Tub-$80
High Comport-$40, others $10-20

Plate 353
3 Pt. Jug-$60, others $10-20

Plate 364
$20-35 each

Plate 365
Punch Bowl-$300, Custard-$15

Plate 367
Nappy-$25, Ice Tub-$70, Basket-$50
others $10-15

Plate 368
Ink-$45, Puff-$50, Straw-$85
Water Bottle-$60, Decanter-$70
others $10-15

Plate 369
Oil Stopper-$50, Candy Jar-$60
Basket-$65, Mustard-$25
others $10-20

Plate 370
Bottom Row-$25 each
others $10-20

Plate 371
Low Bowl-$25, others $10-20

Plate 372
$10-20 each

Plate 373
$10-15 each

Plate 374
Sugar-$25, Cream-$25, Flower-$15
Candlestick-$35, Oil-$45, Sundae-$15
Oyster-$10, Bowl-$65, Ice Jug-$80

Plate 375
Candy Jar-$55, Champagne-$30
others $10-20

Plate 376
#1 Bedroom-$90, #352 Bedroom-$125
Colonial Bedroom-$175

Plate 377
Left-$65, Right-$110

Plate 378
Left-$60, Right-$55

Plate 379
Left-$45, Right-$70

Plate 380
#417-$90, #500-$65, #465-$65

Plate 381
Left-$200, Right-$225

Plate 382
Shades-$150-$200, Lamp-$525

Plate 383
$375

Plate 384
$400

Plate 385
$150-$160 each

Plate 386
$20-25 each

Plate 387
Candlestick-$60, Oil-$60
others $15-30

Plate 388
#1460-$40, others $15-20

Plate 389
Top Row-$40 each, #1486-$40
others $10-20

Plate 390
$20-25 each

Plate 391
Top Row-$20 each, others $35-40

Plate 392
Cream/Sugar Set-$55
others $20-25

Plate 393
1 oz. Cordial-$35, Finger Bowl-$15
others $20-25

Plate 394
Tumbler-$15, Decanter-$70, Oil-$60
Finger Bowl-$10, Water Bottle-$60
Plate-$20

Plate 395
Punch Bowl-$160, Custard-$15

Plate 396
Jug-$75, Round Sugar/Cream-$30
Ind. Sugar/Cream-$25, celery-$25
others $10-20

Plate 397
Jug-$50, Sugar Disp.-$35
others $10-20

Plate 398
$10-15 each

Plate 399
Punch Bowl-$275, Custard-$20
Plate-$85

Plate 400
$10-15 each

Plate 401
$10-15 each

Plate 402
Cream/Sugar-$30, Oil-$30
others $10-20

Plate 403
Cream /Sugar-$45, Pilsner-$35
Ice Jug-$75, Bowl-$45, others $10-15

Plate 404
Goblet-$25, Center Piece-$110
Bowl-$65, others $15-20

Plate 405
2 1/2 oz. Wine-$30, others $15-25 ea.

Plate 406
Finger Bowl-$20, Oil-$60, French-$60
Plate-$15, Punch Bowl-$125
Buffet-$70

Plate 407
Vases-$25-30, Custard-$15
Butter Dish-$60, Cig. Holder-$25
Salt & Peppers-$25-30 each
Rye-$70, Sugar/Cream-$60

Plate 408
2 Light-$50, Ind. Candlestick-$40
Ind. Vase-$25, 9" Vase-$40

PRICE GUIDE

Plate 409
2 1/2 oz. Wine-$50, others $15-25

Plate 410
8" Sq. Plate-$15, Sandwich Plate-$35
8" Round Plate-$15, Oval Floral-$20
Torte Plate-$35, Salad Bowl-$35
Berry Bowl-$35

Plate 411
Celery & Olive-$35, Candlestick-$20
Celery-$30, Oil-$50, Fruit-$50
Floral-$45, Punch Bowl-$90
2 Light Candlestick-$150

Plate 412
11" Relish-$35, Mayo-$25, Oblong-$25
Jelly-$15, 3 Comp. Oblong-$25
10" Relish-$45, French-$65

Plate 413
Ball Vase-$50, others $30-35

Plate 414
Cig. Box-$35, Mustard-$40
Salt/Pepper-$30 pr., Marmalade-$45
Lemon-$35, Ice Tub-$50, Jug-$80
others $10-20

Plate 415
Puff Box-$40, Candlestick-$40
2 Comp. Jelly-$30, Center Piece-$40
2 Comp. Relish-$40, others $15-20

Plate 416
$10-20 each

Plate 417
Ice Tub-$60, Candelabra-$65
Bowls-$35-45

Plate 418
Cheese/Cracker Plate-$70
others $25-30

Plate 419
Bobeche-$70, Sauce Bowl-$20
others $35-40

Plate 420
Twin Mayo-$40, Sugar/Cream set-$60
Ind. Sugar/Cream set-$45, Jello-$35
Whipped Cream-$40, others $15-20

Plate 421
Torte Plates-$35-40, others $10-20

Plate 422
14" Sandwich Plate-$55, Cheese-$15
others $25-35

Plate 423
Oil-$45, Cologne-$60, Bitter-$75
Cocktail-$130, Rye-$140

Plate 424
Top Row-$15-25, Bobeche-$50
others $35-40

Plate 425
6" Preserve-$40, Mayo-$50
Hollandaise-$45, 1,000 Is. Comb.-$50
others $20-30

Plate 426
Jam Jar-$40, Cherry Jar-$40
Candy Box-$70, Flower Urn-$40
Ftd. Cig. Holder-$35, 5" Ash Tray-$30
3 1/2" Ash Tray-$40, others $10-20

Plate 427
Salt/Peppers-$15 each, Cig. Ltr.-$30
Sugar/Cream-$45, Puff Box-$60
Mustard-$35, Ice Jug-$70, Ice Tub-$90

Plate 428
Torte Plates-$35-45, others $15-20 ea.

Plate 429
Oil-$60, Nost. Bowl,-$20
others-$30-40

Plate 430
#41-$15, #51-$15, #58-$35, #52-$30
#53-$25, #56-$25, #46-$40, #57-$40
#47-$40, #42-$45

Plate 431
#64-$35, #56-$35, #63-$35, #103-$40
#95-$40, #92-$40, others $10-15

Plate 432
16" Sand. Plate-$55, 6" Square-$15
12" Sand. Plates-$30-35 each
Social Hour-$40, 4 1/2" Plate-$15

Plate 433
Sauce Bowl-$30, Candlestick-$30
Oil-$50, Candelabra-$60,
12 1/2" Bowl-$50, 11" Bowl-$55
13" Bowl-$45, 8 1/2" Bowl-$30

Plate 434
Sugar/Cream-$50, Mayo-$40, Mint-$30
Jelly-$30, Sugar/Cream/Tray-$60
Salad/Dressing/Ladle-$40
5 O'Clock-$35, Oval Comport-$60
Pickle/Olive-$30, Triplex/Relish-$30
Celery-$25

Plate 435
Mustard-$45, Lemon-$45, Nut-$30
Cream Soup-$40, Ice Cube-$60
Marmalade-$55, Jug-$100

Plate 436
$10-20 each

Plate 437
Sugar/Cream-$45, Marmalade-$40
Mayo-$15, 5 1/2" Vase-$35
Comport-$25, Celery-$15
Center Piece-$150, Candelabra-$160

Plate 438
Bobeche-$100, others $30-40

Plate 439
Book End-$35, others $10-20

Plate 440
Water Bottles-$75, Tray-$40
others $10-20

Plate 441
Grapefruit-$30, Vase-$70
others $10-20

Plate 442
#1466-$70, #1508-$40, #1479-$10
#1489-$35, #1485-$15, #3397-$50
#1512-$20, #4182-$15

Plate 443
$15-20 each

Plate 444
Cig. Holder-$30, others $10-20

Plate 445
#2-$50, #134-$50, #1469 1 light-$60
#1469 2 light-$80, #1445 1 light-$60
#1445 2 light-$80, #142-$85
others $25-35

Plate 446
#4044-$60, #1506 3 light-$75
#1493 2 light-$80, #1488 2 light-$70
#1503 2 light-$60, #1495 2 light-$65
others $20-35

Plate 447
#1472-$45, #1445-$60, #1469-$40
#1405-$60, #1469-$40, #1404-$60

Plate 448
$30-40 each

Plate 449
$30-45 each

Plate 450
Top-$300, Left-$75, Right-$90

Plate 451
Top-$325, Bottom-$225

Plate 452
Top-$190, Bottom-$380

Plate 453
Top-$300, Bottom-$400

Plate 454
Top-$125, Bottom-$175

Plate 455
$250

Plate 456
Top-$95, Bottom-$115

Plate 457
Top Left-$135, Top Right-$110
Bottom Left-$75, Bottom Right-$110

PRICE GUIDE

Plate 458
#1503-$95, #1511-$120, #4044-$120
#1513-$175, #1509-$85

Plate 459
$550

Plate 460
$275

Plate 461
$175-200

Plate 462
$275

Plate 463
$110

Plate 464
$310

Plate 465
$110 each

Plate 466
$15-20 each

Plate 467
$25-30 each

Plate 468
$25-30 each

Plate 469
$25-30 each

Plate 470
1 oz. Cordial-$35, 7" Comport-$45
others $15-25

Plate 471
2 1/2 oz. Wine-$30, 1 oz. Cordial-$35
others $15-20

Plate 472
$25-30 each

Plate 473
Cig. Holder-$35, Finger Bowl-$10
Decanter-$95, Vase-$40

Plate 474
Finger Bowl-$10, Oyster-$15
Sherbet-$15, Comport-$60
others $25-40

Plate 475
Wine-$40, Sherry-$35, Cordial-$50
Dinner Bell-$40, Sherbet-$15
3 oz. Cocktail-$35, Tumbler-$20
Beer Mug-$40, Finger Bowl-$10
4 oz. Cocktail-$15, Goblet-$20
Soda-$20,Claret-$20, Champagne-$20
Parfait-$35

Plate 476
1 oz. Cordial-$40, 7" Comport-$60
Others $15-25

Plate 477
1 oz. Cordial-$40, 12 oz. Pilsner-$35
others $15-25

Plate 478
Martini-$50, Cocktail Shaker-$95
Jug-$70, Tankard-$80
others $15-25

Plate 479
Finger Bowl-$10, 1 oz. Cordial-$30
13 Oz. Soda-$30, others $15-25

Plate 480
Finger Bowl-$10, others $15-25

Plate 481
Finger Bowl-$10, others $20-30

Plate 482
$25-30 each

Plate 483
1 oz. Cordial-$40, 3/4 oz. Brandy, $40
1 1/2 oz. Sherry-$40, 2 oz. Wine-$40
5" Comport-$40, Finger Bowl-$15
others $20-30

Plate 484
5 oz. Comport-$45, others $15-25

Plate 485
2 1/2 oz. Wine-$40, others $15-25

Plate 486
5 1/2" Comport-$40,1 oz. Cordial-$40
others $15-25

Plate 487
2 1/2 oz. Wine $35, others $15-25

Plate 488
5" Comport-$40, others $15-25

Plate 489
#331-$40, #3428-$40, #3419-$50
#3368-$50, #3411-$60, #3404-$70
others $15-20

Plate 490
$15-20 each

Plate 491
#3420-$40, #3806-$40, #4058-$70
#4056-$40, #4266-$20, #4058-$15

Plate 492
#4057-$40, #4121-$45, #4059-$55
Cocktail-$80, Rock & Rye-$70

Plate 493
$30-40 each

Plate 494
$40-50 each

Plate 495
Finger Bowls-$15 ea.,others $45-50 ea

Plate 496
Top Left-$50, Top Right-$45
Bottom Left-$45, Bottom Left-$70

Plate 497
$85-100 each

Plate 498
$15-20 each